THE YORK-ANTWERP RULES

SECOND EDITION

OTHER TITLES IN THIS SERIES:

Shipbuilding Contracts
SECOND EDITION
by Malcolm A. Clarke
1992

Time-Barred Actions
SECOND EDITION
Edited by Francesco Berlingieri
1993

Liability for Damage to the Marine Environment
Edited by Colin de la Rue
1993

THE YORK-ANTWERP RULES

THE PRINCIPLES AND PRACTICE OF GENERAL AVERAGE ADJUSTMENT IN ACCORDANCE WITH THE YORK-ANTWERP RULES 1994

SECOND EDITION

BY

N. GEOFFREY HUDSON, M.A.

of the Inner Temple, Barrister-at-Law
Member and Past Chairman of the Association of Average Adjusters
Ancien Président de l'Association Internationale des Dispacheurs Européens
Membre Titulaire du Comité Maritime International

FOREWORD BY LORD DONALDSON OF LYMINGTON

PUBLISHED UNDER THE AUSPICES OF
THE COMITÉ MARITIME INTERNATIONAL

LLP

LONDON NEW YORK HONG KONG
1996

LLP Limited
Legal & Business Publishing Division
27 Swinton Street
London WC1X 9NW

USA AND CANADA
LLP Inc.
Suite 308, 611 Broadway
New York, NY 10012, USA

SOUTH EAST ASIA
LLP (Far East) Limited
Room 1101, Hollywood Centre
233 Hollywood Road
Hong Kong

First published in Great Britain 1991
Second edition published 1996

British Library Cataloguing in Publication Data
A catalogue record for this
book is available from
the British Library

ISBN 1-85978-026-1

Text set in 10 on 12pt Plantin by
Interactive Sciences, Gloucester
Printed in Great Britain by
WBC Print Ltd, Bridgend,
Mid-Glamorgan

FOREWORD

BY LORD DONALDSON OF LYMINGTON

In the Foreword to the first edition of this work I wrote:

> "Charterparties and bills of lading, like the ships themselves, come in many shapes and sizes and are subject to differing national laws. They also display widely varying degrees of complexity and intelligibility. But they are likely to have at least one thing in common—a simple clause providing for the settlement of general average in accordance with the York-Antwerp Rules.
>
> General average itself is of very great antiquity. As Geoffrey Hudson points out, it is designed to concentrate the minds of shipowners, masters and crews upon saving ship and cargo in time of peril without regard to sectional interests. It seeks to achieve this objective by the subsequent redistribution of the burden of loss and expense upon general equitable principles. However the detailed application of those principles can give rise to differences of opinion. Hence the York-Antwerp Rules, almost universally adopted by contract in the interests of international uniformity.
>
> However the interests of the shipping and insurance industries have called for something more than common rules. They have called for an expert corps of professionals in whom they can have total confidence and whose task is to interpret and apply these rules uniformly throughout the world and, in addition, to provide a swift and economical 'alternative dispute resolution' process. That need has been met by the average adjusters of the maritime nations.
>
> Geoffrey Hudson is a world renowned expert in this field who, unlike some experts, can explain to others the mysteries of which he is a master. I know this to be true, because his was the directing mind when at Hamburg in 1974 I was the spokesman for the British team taking part in the conference which revised the York-Antwerp Rules 1950. In this book he makes his unique fund of knowledge available to a wider public and it gives me great personal pleasure to have the opportunity of welcoming it and congratulating him."

I see no reason to change a word. Indeed this edition serves to emphasise the author's talent for explaining the esoteric mysteries of general average in the context of the York-Antwerp Rules. The need for it arises out of the birth of the 1994 version of those Rules at the CMI Conference in Sydney.

One of the great strengths of the York-Antwerp Rules lies in the fact that, unlike international Conventions, they can be revised to take account of changed commercial circumstances without the involvement of governments. On this occasion the principal change involved was the emergence of pollution liabilities as a major hazard for commercial shipping. However, the opportunity was taken to make other revisions.

Having taken a leading part in the evolution of the 1974 Rules and been Chairman of the Conference drafting committee in 1994, Geoffrey Hudson is uniquely well placed to compare, contrast and comment on the two versions. That the 1994 Rules have, thus far, proved more controversial than their predecessors is no fault of his.

If to know all is to forgive all, a reader of this edition who studies the author's explanations of the conflicting pressures which led to the compromises adopted by the Conference will be admirably placed to approach the 1994 Rules in a spirit of forgiveness and even of acceptance.

January 1996 JOHN F. DONALDSON

PREFACE TO THE SECOND EDITION

It has always been fashionable in some sections of the maritime community to treat the subject of general average as if it were shrouded in mystery. "Arcane", "out-dated" and "incomprehensible" are just some of the epithets which have been thrown about when the subject is discussed.

One of the objects of this book has been to draw aside the veil and reveal the essential truth, which is that general average is as relevant today to the safety of ships and the problems attending the transportation of goods by sea as it was 2,000 years ago—perhaps even more so, having regard to the high concentration of capital invested in a modern maritime adventure.

The York-Antwerp Rules, which govern the adjustment of general average in virtually all cases, are unique in that they constitute an international legal system based upon consensus, rather than legislation. This consensus operates in two ways:

- — The York-Antwerp Rules apply because the parties agree to their incorporation in charterparties and contracts for the carriage of goods by sea;
- — the Rules, being under the guardianship of the Comité Maritime International, a body of private international lawyers with no axe to grind, are accessible to change at the behest of interested parties.

At the latest Conference of the CMI held in Sydney in October 1994, a number of changes were made in order to bring the Rules up to date and to tackle certain contemporary problems, particularly those relating to environmental damage in the context of general average.

The desirability of reporting these changes, now enshrined in the York-Antwerp Rules 1994, provides the occasion for a second edition of this book. However, in the hope that knowledge leads to understanding, I have expanded the text in order not merely to report the changes that were made and the improvements achieved, but also to demonstrate as far as possible the reasons why these changes were made and how they contribute to the aim of achieving safety at sea.

In carrying out this task, I have been warmly sustained by the support extended to me by Professor Allan Philip, President, and Professor Francesco

Berlingieri, President ad honorem of the Comité Maritime International, and I am grateful to them and their colleagues for agreeing to co-sponsor this work. I also wish to acknowledge with thanks the permissions given by the Association of Average Adjusters to reproduce herein the Rules of Practice relating to general average, as well as references to and excerpts from the Opinions of the Advisory Committee; by the Corporation of Lloyd's to print the text of Lloyd's Standard Form of Salvage Agreement—LOF 1995, and by the Association Internationale de Dispacheurs Européens to quote some of its more important Resolutions and to refer in some detail to reports from its working groups.

The law and practice as stated herein is believed to be correct as at December 1995.

18 January 1996 N. GEOFFREY HUDSON

ABOUT THE AUTHOR

Geoffrey Hudson, M.A. (Oxon) is a barrister and consultant average adjuster, having been for many years a partner of Ernest Robert Lindley & Sons, one of the leading firms of international average adjusters. He has been both Chairman of the Association of Average Adjusters and President of the International Association of European Average Adjusters (AIDE). He is a Titulary Member of the Comité Maritime International and currently Chairman of the Executive Committee of the British Maritime Law Association. He has contributed to several publications including *Lloyd's Maritime and Commercial Law Quarterly*. He is the author of *The Insurance of Average Disbursements*, *The Institute Clauses* (2nd edition) and co-author of *The Marine Claims Handbook*.

CONTENTS

GLOSSARY

ABBREVIATIONS

The following abbreviations are employed in the text:

AAA	Association of Average Adjusters
AAA of the US	Association of Average Adjusters of the United States
ADF	Association des Dispacheurs Françaises
AIDE	Association Internationale des Dispacheurs Européens
AMC	Amercian Maritime Cases
BIMCO	The Baltic and International Maritime Council
BMLA	British Maritime Law Association
CMI	Comité Maritime International
COGSA	Carriage of Goods by Sea Act
GA	General Average
ILU	Institute of London Underwriters
IMO	International Maritime Organization
ISC	International Sub-Committee
ISU	International Salvage Union
IUMI	International Union of Maritime Insurance
LOF	Lloyd's Open Form of Salvage Agreement
PA	Particular Average
UNCTAD	United Nations Conference on Trade and Development
USMLA	United States Maritime Law Association
YAR	York-Antwerp Rules

BIBLIOGRAPHY

The following are the major titles referred to herein:

Arnould, *A Treatise on the Law of Marine Insurance and Average*, 2nd ed., 1857.

Buglass, *Marine Insurance and General Average in the United States*, 2nd ed., 1981.

Carver, *Carriage by Sea*, 13th ed. by Colinvaux, 1982.

Congdon, *General Average: Principles and Practice in the United States of America*, 2nd ed., 1923.

Darling & Smith, *LOF 90 and the New Salvage Convention*, 1990.

"From the Chair", Addresses by Chairmen of the Association of Average Adjusters 1873–1976.

Hudson & Allen, *Marine Claims Handbook*, 4th ed., 1984.

Lowndes, *The Law of General Average*, 1st ed., 1873.

Lowndes & Rudolf, *The Law of General Average and the York-Antwerp Rules*, 10th ed. by Donaldson, Staughton and Wilson, 1975.
11th ed. by Wilson and Cooke, 1990.

Rudolf, *The York-Antwerp Rules*, 1926.

Selmer, *The Survival of General Average*, Oslo, 1958.

Stevens, *An Essay on Average*, 4th ed., 1822.

TABLE OF CASES

TABLE OF MATERIALS

ISSUED BY AVERAGE ADJUSTERS' ASSOCIATIONS

GENERAL AVERAGE—ANCIENT AND MODERN

"O hear us when we cry to Thee
for those in peril on the sea"

The stirring words of the well-known hymn remind us that the transport of the world's produce over the oceans from one country to another is still a hazardous undertaking. Despite all the advances in ship construction and marine engineering, and the technical sophistication of modern navigational equipment, the sea continues to take its toll on the ships and cargoes which ply their trade on the great waters. Any system which has as its object the prevention of loss by maritime peril therefore deserves the support and understanding of all who earn their living by seaborne trade.

General average is such a system. It has to do with losses suffered and expenses paid by the parties to a common maritime adventure in order to avert a peril which threatens it. Furthermore, the system provides within itself for the equitable redistribution of the cost of the loss prevention measures by dividing that cost over the value of the property involved.

In this respect the system of general average has a great deal in common with maritime salvage: at root both are a form of ransom from total loss, but whereas salvage has to do with the payment of a reward for the exertions of a party who stands outside the common maritime adventure, general average is concerned to regulate the position as between the parties to the adventure *inter se*. Of the two systems, that of general average is by far the older and, as we shall see when we examine their inter-relationship,[1] it is also more flexible and sophisticated.

THE ORIGIN OF GENERAL AVERAGE

Historical records tell us that systems of general average, involving a contribution from the interests involved in a common maritime adventure, have been in existence since the earliest days of seaborne traffic. The object of the system was to encourage ship masters and others who sailed with them to exert themselves to save the ship and its cargoes whenever a peril threatened the joint adventure. The prime example is the consent given by the owners of

1. See commentary on Rule VI, p. 125.

cargo to the ship master to make a judicious and timely sacrifice of their property, in the knowledge that their loss would be made good to them by rateable contribution from the other interests on the completion of the voyage.

Legal recognition of this consent, accorded the status of custom, appears in Justinian's Digest, and reads as follows:

"The Rhodian Law provides that if in order to lighten a ship merchandise is thrown overboard, that which has been given for all shall be replaced by the contribution of all."[2]

Sir James Allan Park opined that although the above-quoted extract from the Digest of Justinian was promulgated in A.D. 553, the law of the sea on which this passage was based may well have been in existence since the ninth century B.C. Readers of the New Testament will know that on St. Paul's journey as a prisoner to Rome, his ship was wrecked on the coast of Malta. It is recorded in the Acts of the Apostles that the Master, after consulting with the merchants, ordered the tackle on deck to be jettisoned, unfortunately without avail.[3] This was a general average act, even though it failed in its aim to save the maritime adventure.

GENERAL AVERAGE IN THE MIDDLE AGES AND AFTER

Despite the collapse of the social and economic regimes that had been preserved for so long by the Roman empire, the customs of seafarers changed little, and the notion that a sacrifice of goods or other property for the common safety should be made good by a general contribution, was one of the customs that was common to all recorded sea law. Of course these customs developed in different ways in different times and trades, as is evidenced from the records of decisions which survived and which have been analysed with great diligence by writers in the nineteenth and early twentieth centuries. These records include;

- The Rolls of Oleron, which date from the late eleventh century.
- The *Consolado del Mare*, which consolidate the customs of seafarers in the western Mediterranean.
- The *Farmannalog*, which is a codification of Norse sea law established about 1270 under the authority of the Norwegian king Magnus Haakonson.
- The ordinance of Amsterdam, ascribed to a conference of shipowners and merchants in that port in 1407.

2. Justinian, Digest, book XIV, title 2, "de lege Rhodia de jactu".
3. Acts, ch. 27, vv. 14–20.

The Laws of Visby, which were a kind of compilation of existing sea law derived from earlier sources.

The customs of Mediterranean origin emphasise that before a sacrifice of property could be made in time of peril, there had to be a measure of consultation between the master and the merchants who accompanied their cargoes. Perhaps because of this real community of interest, it was also common for the master and merchants to agree to bring into contribution other kinds of losses and expenses which had as their object the successful prosecution of their joint adventure. In this category there were such expenses as the engagement of a pilot, or the hire of lighters when a ship arrived deeply laden at her port of destination. Ultimately, two different classes of expenditure were distinguished: those which derived from an accident which threatened the adventure, as when the ship was driven into a port of refuge; and those which were incurred merely for the inconvenience of the voyage. The former came to be included within general average, whereas the latter class of expense became known as *petty average*, which under the Prussian maritime code of 1727, for example, was borne in the proportion of one-third to ship and two-thirds to cargo.

With the increase in commerce that accompanied the Renaissance, merchants no longer considered it necessary to accompany their goods and were prepared to rely upon the confidence they reposed in the master of the ship, backed by the legal rights which they enjoyed under the bill of lading concept. Even so, the laws of many Mediterranean countries continued to provide that there should be consultation between the master and members of the crew in order to justify making a sacrifice of property or engaging upon a general average act.

These formal remnants from olden times demonstrate the extent to which the institution of general average was founded upon the consensus of the parties to the adventure. In the author's opinion, this is significant since, as we shall see, the development and refinement of the basic principles of general average that have taken place in the nineteenth and twentieth centuries, through the adoption of the York-Antwerp Rules, resulted from the influence of commercial interests, rather than the dictate of governments.

GENERAL AVERAGE IN ENGLISH LAW

Beginning with the *Ordonnance de la Mer* of 1681, the majority of European countries proceeded to publish codes of maritime law which incorporated provisions as to general average. This has not been the route followed in the common law countries. No code of general average exists in England or the United States. Since the earliest times, English law and practice have developed hand in hand: even now the records of decisions in the courts of law combined with the Rules of Practice of the Association of Average Adjusters (which in many instances are derived from the customs of Lloyd's) provide in themselves an adequate working system, based upon knowledge acquired by actual experience.

However, there is also a statutory definition of general average which is provided in section 66 of the Marine Insurance Act 1906, reading as follows:

> "(1) A general average loss is a loss caused by or directly consequential on a general average act. It includes a general average expenditure as well as a general average sacrifice.
> (2) There is a general average act where any extraordinary sacrifice or expenditure is voluntarily and reasonably made or incurred in time of peril for the purpose of preserving the property imperilled in the common adventure.
> (3) Where there is a general average loss, the party on whom it falls is entitled, subject to the conditions imposed by maritime law, to a rateable contribution from the other parties interested, and such contribution is called a general average contribution."

Examples of general average sacrifices and expenditure under English law

The following are examples of sacrifices and expenditure which may be admitted in general average under English law and practice:

Sacrifices

CARGO AND FREIGHT

1. Jettison from under deck.
2. Jettison from on deck, provided that on-deck stowage is in accordance with the recognised custom of the trade in which the ship is engaged.
3. Damage by water or other means used to extinguish a fire on board ship.
4. Discharge and reshipment of cargo for the purpose of floating a stranded ship when in a position of peril.

SHIP'S MATERIALS

5. Masts, spars, sails or rigging cut away for the common safety.
6. Chains and anchors slipped to avert a threatening peril.
7. Damage to a vessel's machinery, ropes, winches, windlass and other gear sustained in endeavours to float a stranded ship when in a position of peril.
8. Damage sustained in the efforts to extinguish a fire on board or in the process of jettisoning cargo.

Expenditure

9. Expenses incurred in floating a stranded ship if in peril.
10. Inward expenses entering a port of refuge to repair damage to ship.
11. Cost of discharging cargo at a port of refuge for the common safety or to repair damage to ship.
12. Cost of warehousing, warehouse rent on cargo, reshipment of cargo and outward expenses leaving the port of refuge, but only when the cause of the vessel putting into port has been to repair damage which is itself the consequence of a general average act.

VARIANCE OF THE LAWS AND PRACTICES IN DIFFERENT COUNTRIES

The examples of general average sacrifices and expenditure set out above are typical, and most of them would be the subject of allowance in general average according to the law and usages of all maritime nations. However, as the laws of different countries have developed in different directions, there are variations. In examples 10 and 12 it will be seen that the inward expenses are allowed when entering a port of refuge to repair particular average damage or damage caused by general average sacrifice, whereas the outward expenses of leaving the port of refuge are only allowed in general average when the ship had put into the port in order to repair damage caused by general average sacrifice. In all other jurisdictions, both inward and outward port charges are allowed when a ship enters a port of refuge, even to repair particular average damage.

It is in this area, namely as to the extent of the expenses incurred in and consequential upon a vessel's resort to a port of refuge, that the greatest diversity can be found in the laws and practices of different countries. In general, the laws of most European countries favour the admission in general average of expenses at a port of refuge which have as their object the continuation of the voyage in good safety. Anglo-Saxon jurisprudence, on the other hand, looks to the attainment of safety as the object of a general average act, so that once the common adventure is in a position of safety, no further allowance can be made in general average. As we shall see, one of the features of the York-Antwerp Rules has been to harmonise the divergent practices of different countries on the treatment of expenses incurred at a port of refuge.

Of equal importance in the preparation of a general average adjustment is the ascertainment of the values of the interests which will contribute to the general average allowances. Once again it has to be said that prior to the introduction of the York-Antwerp Rules there was very little uniformity between the laws and practices of different countries on the method of establishing the values for contribution.

On one aspect, however, the laws of all maritime countries are consistent: namely, that the state of facts to be taken into account for the purposes of the general average adjustment, and hence the law to be applied in the absence of any agreement of the parties to the contrary, is that which obtains at the time and place where the common maritime adventure terminates. That is, of course, in the great majority of cases, at the port of destination where the cargo is to be discharged from the ship and delivered to the receiver in accordance with the terms of the contract of carriage.[4] Of course, cases do occur when events beyond the control of the parties cause the premature termination of the adventure, as for example, the outbreak of war causing the port of discharge to be blockaded by an enemy, damage to the ship causing her to be a commercial total loss, etc.; and in such circumstances, the general average is to be adjusted in accordance with the law and the state of facts prevailing at the place where the voyage is frustrated or abandoned.

Since, absent any agreement by the parties to the contrary, the process of adjustment is to be determined according to the law of the country in which the adventure ends, it will be appreciated that during the enormous expansion of commerce in the middle of the nineteenth century, shipowners and merchants became increasingly uncertain as to their rights and liabilities whenever a case of general average occurred. Consider, for example, a voyage from London to Copenhagen, Stockholm, Danzig and St. Petersburg in the 1850s. If during that voyage general average sacrifices and expenditures were incurred, it could be that four different adjustments would have to be drawn up according to the laws of Denmark, Sweden, Prussia and Russia in order to obtain a true picture of the liability of each cargo interest to pay its general average contribution.

It was precisely this kind of situation that fuelled the clamour for uniformity which led ultimately to the establishment of the York-Antwerp Rules.

4. In English law, see *Simonds* v. *White* (1824) 2 B. & C. 805; *Lloyd* v. *Guibert* (1865) L.R. 1 Q.B. 115.

THE YORK-ANTWERP RULES—VEHICLE FOR UNIFORMITY

The York-Antwerp Rules occupy a unique position in international maritime law. Unlike the Hague Rules, which regulate the law on the carriage of goods by sea, and the various Conventions relating to the limitation of shipowners' liability (to name but two examples), they depend not upon Convention, still less upon statute, but upon their voluntary acceptance by the maritime community. Although in a certain number of instances,[1] they have been imported into domestic legislation, the all but universal application of the York-Antwerp Rules in cases of general average has come about by their being incorporated by reference into bills of lading, contracts of affreightment and marine insurance policies. Yet in spite of the purely consensual nature of their application, they have succeeded where other attempts to achieve international uniformity have failed. As was said by Professor Knut Selmer, a by no means sympathetic critic: "It may safely be said that general average is the field of maritime law where the international unification effort has succeeded to the greatest degree."[2]

THE QUEST FOR UNIFORMITY

It all began with an open letter—now famous—addressed in May 1860 to the maritime countries of Europe by the National Association for the Promotion of Social Science under the signature of Lord Brougham and the Chairmen of Lloyd's, the London General Shipowners' Society, various Chambers of Commerce and other bodies representing shipping, mercantile and underwriting interests in the United Kingdom. The following sentence reflects the tenor of the letter as a whole and illustrates the aim of its authors:

"The system of general average is one which, to prevent confusion and injustice, pre-eminently requires that the same principles should be acknowledged amongst the chief maritime nations."

1. The 1974 Rules were introduced into legislative forms in the Soviet Union and the countries of Scandinavia. The 1994 Rules are expected to be incorporated into the domestic legislation of Norway during 1996.
2. *The Survival of General Average* (Oslo 1958), p. 58.

As a result of that letter a conference assembled at Glasgow in 1860 and adopted a number of resolutions (called "The Glasgow Resolutions") which, it was intended, should assist parliamentary draftsmen to draw up a Bill "with a view to its being enacted into a law by the legislative authorities of several nations of the world".

The York Rules 1864

The next step took place at York in September 1864 when the third International General Average Congress met to discuss the draft Bill and other suggestions towards achievement of uniformity in the adjustment of general average, and at the end of its labours, 11 Rules (known as "The York Rules") were agreed to. Once again, a resolution was adopted calling upon interested parties to take such measures as to persuade the legislatures in each country concerned to pass a Bill into their domestic law; but, pending legislation, it was recommended that clauses should be introduced into bills of lading and charterparties, reading:

> "All claims for general average to be settled in conformity with the international general average rules framed at York in 1864."

The York and Antwerp Rules 1877

In the climate of those days, however, there was no great rush to follow this proposal, and were it not for the perseverance of the reformers their idea to achieve uniformity by operation of contract might have been attended with as little success as their efforts to provoke legislation. The reformers, fortunately, persisted, and at a further conference held in Antwerp in 1877 where the York Rules were amended and a twelfth Rule added to them (thus becoming "The York and Antwerp Rules"), a definite date was adopted for the incorporation thereof into bills of lading, charterparties and policies of insurance, namely 1 January 1879. Despite a cool reception at Lloyd's, the movement for reform gathered momentum, and in 1881 at a conference of the Association for the Reform and Codification of the Law of Nations, it was reported that "the Rules have become all but universally adopted".

The York-Antwerp Rules 1890

From this time onwards, it may safely be said that the York-Antwerp Rules had arrived, and that hereafter discussion was centred not so much on the method for achieving uniformity, but rather upon the development of the Rules as an efficient instrument of commerce. The next move in this direction took place in 1890 on the initiative of the Association of Average Adjusters who drafted a report for submission to the conference of the Association for the Reform and Codification of the Law of Nations, held at Liverpool in 1890. The majority of these proposals were adopted but, despite the fact that the number of Rules was expanded to 18, they retained their existing format as a group of Rules dealing with specific points where experience had demonstrated a need for uniformity. Perhaps in recognition of this lack of cohesion, the Liverpool Conference agreed to add, as Rule XVIII, a "catch-all" provision that, except as provided in the other 17 Rules, the adjustment would be drawn up in accordance with the law and practice that would have governed, had there been no reference to the York-Antwerp Rules in the contract of affreightment.[3]

At a conference at Antwerp in 1903, a recommendation was made to add a further Rule providing that "rights to contribution in general average shall not be affected though the danger which gave rise to the sacrifice, or expenditure, may have been due to default of one of the parties to the adventure; but this shall not prejudice any remedies which may be open against that party for such default". Perhaps because this Rule was couched in very general terms, or perhaps because it did no more than embody existing law, it was not generally adopted in contracts of affreightment, and its inclusion into the general body of the York-Antwerp Rules had to wait until the introduction of the lettered Rules in 1924.

Between 1890 and 1924, when the Rules were next revised, there were developments which appeared to favour the preparation of an international code of general average which should form the basis for legislation. This idea was introduced at a conference of the International Law Association[4] in 1910 and as a result of the initiative of a Mr Dowdall a questionnaire was sent to representatives of a number of leading maritime countries. From the replies to this questionnaire Mr Dowdall collated a summary of the law of general average applying in Belgium, France, Germany, the Netherlands, Norway, the United Kingdom and the United States of America, and thereafter it was but a short step to produce a draft code of general average, which was circulated under the auspices of the International Law Association in early 1914.

The York-Antwerp Rules 1924

The intervention of the first world war delayed consideration of the Dowdall draft code, but was not responsible for its demise, which was due to an almost total absence of enthusiasm for the idea of codification on the part of the mercantile and business communities. Fortunately, the revival of interest sparked off by this debate was successfully diverted towards a further revision of the York-Antwerp Rules, and this movement was assisted by the publication in early 1924 of two draft texts, one produced by the French branch of the

3. Text of Rule XVIII of the 1890 Rules, Appendix 2, p. 327.

4. The Association for the Reform and Codification of the Law of Nations was renamed the International Law Association in 1895.

International Law Association and the other by the Association of Average Adjusters, which, although prepared independently, agreed substantially on most of the changes which were considered desirable. It was also significant that both the French and British texts included (in very similar terms) statements of general principle. These proposals were laid before an International Conference at Stockholm later in 1924, and the great majority of them were adopted; the statements of principle became the present lettered Rules of the York-Antwerp Rules.

Unfortunately, the marriage of general principle to specific example was not an easy one, and by 1928 the honeymoon was over. In that year, in the famous *Makis* case,[5] an experienced English judge (Mr Justice Roche) found himself rather at sea in the construction of the Rules. Although he concluded that the lettered Rules were the general rules and the numbered Rules were particular rules, he could not bring himself to accept that a case for general average could be made out by reference to the numbered Rules alone. At a stroke of the judicial pen, the intention of the draftsmen had been reversed. It was left to the pragmatism of English commercial men to redress the balance by the so-called "Makis" agreement, under which leading shipowners and underwriters agreed in 1929 to restore precedence to the numbered Rules.

The 1924 Rules also failed to attract unreserved approval in the United States. American shipowners, unconsciously anticipating the result of the *Makis* case, considered that Rule A was drafted in a manner insufficiently wide to encompass the allowances that they would expect to be made at a port of refuge, and they had other reservations as well. In the event, most American shipping companies claused their bills of lading to provide only partial application of the York-Antwerp Rules 1924, along the following lines:

> "General average shall be adjusted, stated and settled, according to Rules one to fifteen inclusive, seventeen to twenty two inclusive and Rule F of York-Antwerp Rules 1924 . . . "

The York-Antwerp Rules 1950

The review process was repeated after the second world war in much the same manner as before, save that the task was delegated by the International Law Association to the Comité Maritime International (CMI). In the event, the changes made at the 1949 Amsterdam Conference were not substantial. Indeed, the only important amendments were:

(a) the introduction of the Rule of Interpretation, to resolve the difficulty created in the Anglo-Saxon countries by the *Makis* decision;

5. *Vlassopoulos* v. *British & Foreign Marine Insurance Co. (The Makis)* [1929] 1 K.B. 187; 34 Com. Cas. 65.

(b) an alteration in the wording of Rule F to permit the allowance in general average of substituted expenses (other than those specified in Rule X(d)) up to the savings achieved in general average expenses, but without regard to any savings enjoyed by other interests; and
(c) a change in the method for establishing the amount to be made good in general average for sacrificial damage of goods.

The new edition of the Rules was known as the York-Antwerp Rules 1950, that being the year in which the changes made at the Amsterdam Conference were ratified by the International Law Association.

The York-Antwerp Rules 1974

Perhaps because of the paucity of the changes made at the previous review, a number of influential voices were heard in the latter part of the 1960s, calling for a new look at the ancient institution of general average. Some, including a number of underwriters who seemed to regard general average adjustment merely as a cumbersome means of transferring sums of money from one underwriter's pocket to another, called for a radical curtailment of the allowances available in general average, in preparation possibly for its eventual abolition.[6] Others, including average adjusters, recognised that there was much which could be done to simplify general average procedures and the process of adjustment, and set about creating the climate for international action.

In September 1967 the Association Internationale des Dispacheurs Européens (AIDE) set up a Commission, under the chairmanship of Dr Schadee of Rotterdam, to study proposals for the simplification of the YAR. This Commission reported to successive Assemblies of the AIDE in 1969 and 1971.

Parallel studies—not limited to the YAR, but ranging over the whole field of general average—were undertaken by the General Average Committee of the International Union of Marine Insurance (IUMI). That Committee reported to its parent body in March 1969 and the Summer of 1970.

Some of the recommendations coincided; on others there was no agreement. The second report of the AIDE Commission commented on the IUMI proposals, and remarked a number of them which went too wide to be dealt with in the YAR: the reduction in the number of small general average adjustments, by the introduction of an attainable franchise, was one example. On this topic, a better solution appeared to be the introduction of a clause in hull policies whereby hull underwriters would respond for the whole

6. 1970 Report of the IUMI General Average Committee, para. 5A.

of the general average expenditure incurred by their assured, up to a certain sum, without calling upon cargo or other interests to contribute.[7]

This activity culminated at the Conference set up by the Comité Maritime International at Hamburg in April 1974. At this Conference the emphasis was firmly placed upon the simplification of the Rules and the technique of adjustment. As the Chairman of the International Sub-Committee, Mr W. Birch Reynardson, said in his final report:

> "The concept of general average should not be allowed to be shrouded in academic mystique. It is a simple idea of great antiquity which has been followed in other branches of the law maritime, for example in the sphere of liability of cargo carried by sea, namely that losses incurred during the maritime adventure should be apportioned equitably between ship and cargo. But if this apportionment is to operate satisfactorily, then the principles upon which it is based must be clear and simple. If not, then unnecessary costs and delays will ensue."

Several important changes were approved by the Hamburg Conference. Apart from a small change of a clarificatory nature to the text of Rule D, the lettered Rules remained unaltered, but significant and far-reaching changes were made within the framework of the numbered Rules. The alterations of substance were:

— a new Rule VI, bringing within general average expenditure incurred on account of salvage, was introduced in place of an old Rule concerning damage to or loss of sails.

— Rules X and XI were amended in order to exclude from general average the cost of cargo handling and expenses incurred at a port of call or loading, when the accident giving rise to such expenses had occurred prior to the common adventure. Such cases had previously been described as "artificial general average", and while cargo interests could, and very often did decline to pay their share of contribution in such cases, it appeared to be quite anomalous that the expenses incurred in these circumstances should remain within the ambit of general average.

— Rule III, relating to the allowance of damage sustained in the course of fire extinguishing operations, was amended in a manner designed to simplify the calculation of the allowances.

— The Rules relating to substituted expenses were further amended so that the extra cost of towage to destination, or transhipment and forwarding of cargo would in appropriate cases be allowed up to the saving in general average expenses, without it being necessary to have regard to the savings to other interests.

7. The subsequent amendment of Institute Time Clauses, Hulls (1.10.69 form) with the introduction of a deductible franchise applying to "all claims" substantially reduced the attractiveness of this solution, at any rate as far as the U.K. insurance market was concerned.

— The calculation of the contributory values and amounts made good for loss and damage to cargo would henceforth be made on invoice, rather than market, values.

The 1990 amendment to the 1974 Rules

A further step was taken at the Conference of the Comité Maritime International held in Paris in June 1990. On that occasion the terms of Rule VI, dealing with salvage, were substantially revised in compliance with a request from the International Maritime Organization to bring general average allowances into line with the understandings underlying the International Convention on Salvage 1989, and those forms of salvage agreement, such as LOF 1990, which incorporated the essential features of that Convention. The text of the Rules incorporating this amendment were known as the York-Antwerp Rules 1974, as amended 1990.

INTRODUCTION TO THE YORK-ANTWERP RULES 1994

At the Paris Conference of the CMI in June 1990 the delegates participating in the meetings on general average, having attended to the immediate task in hand—the formulation of an amendment to Rule VI of the York-Antwerp Rules—were invited to express their views on the question whether or not the time was ripe for a wider review of the law of general average and a prospective revision of the York-Antwerp Rules. Having debated the topic, a straw poll produced an affirmative answer, and this was duly reported to the Executive Council of the CMI in order to enable them to set the wheels in motion.

THE PREPARATORY WORK OF THE COMITÉ MARITIME INTERNATIONAL

The first step was the appointment of a working group under the Chairmanship of Mr David Taylor, Honorary Secretary of the Association of Average Adjusters. In addition to the chairman, the working group consisted of Mr Douglas Adams, New York; Mr Jaap Gerritzen, Rotterdam; Mr Kazuhiro Harada, Tokyo; Mr Geoffrey Hudson, London; M. Pierre Latron, Paris; Mr Bent Nielsen, Copenhagen; Mr Lloyd Watkins, London, and Mr Geoffrey Brice, Q.C., in attendance as a special adviser. The group met in May 1991 in order to prepare a preliminary report and questionnaire. This provided a very brief background to the development of the York-Antwerp Rules and then added the following important rider:

> "The current examination of the law of General Average and the York-Antwerp Rules is not inspired by any call for the abolition of General Average, nor by any significant criticism of the present position. Nor is it either a response to the results or conclusions of any particular study or initiative. Rather it is inspired by the wish, by critical periodical examination, to consider the validity of the present regime in the modern fast-developing context, where not only is traditional documentation being substituted by electronic data, but techniques of carriage of goods by sea are continuing to develop rapidly, types of trades are changing and new financial practices are developing."

After placing emphasis on the important contribution made by the general average system towards safety at sea and summarising those parts of the system not dealt with in the York-Antwerp Rules which may be regulated by national law, the report concluded with a questionnaire in two parts.

Part A of the questionnaire sought information both as to the legal basis for the operation of the general average system and also as to legal or technical developments which might have an impact on the contemplated revision of the law of general average in each of the countries to which the questionnaire would be addressed.

Part B of the questionnaire sought the opinion of national Maritime Law Associations on a wide range of matters, ranging from the general principles of law and practice to specific proposals for the amendment of the York-Antwerp Rules. In this context detailed questions were asked as to the possible introduction of new provisions relating to the following subjects:

(a) currency of the adjustment and rates of exchange;
(b) tug (or pushboat) and barges;
(c) inclusions or exclusions in the list of contributory interests;
(d) reapportionment of differential salvage awards/settlements;
(e) non-separation agreements;
(f) general average franchises;
(g) environmental protection measures;
(h) contribution of freight when vessel in ballast;

and as to matters relating to general average which could fall outside the York-Antwerp Rules:

(a) general average absorption clauses in hull policies;
(b) standard forms for general average security; and
(c) optional bill of lading or charterparty clauses.

Some twenty national Maritime Law Associations replied to the questionnaire, and it was evident from their replies that the constituent members of the CMI were totally convinced of the usefulness of the general average system and its relevance to the all important question of safety at sea. In the opinion of the British Maritime Law Association it was considered "particularly apposite that the present study should come at a time when there is little demand from commercial interests for the abolition or radical curtailment of the general average system, since the absence of controversy creates the right climate to propose improvements which it is hoped will be beneficial to all concerned with maritime commerce."

The responses to the questionnaire were analysed by the working group in January 1992 and a synopsis of the views expressed was circulated to national associations in March 1992, together with an invitation to send delegates to a full meeting of the International Sub-Committee fixed for December 1992—this interval being designed to allow time for full consideration of the issues raised in the preliminary papers.

THE INTERVENTION OF UNCTAD

At about the same time as CMI initiated its activity, the United Nations Conference on Trade and Development (UNCTAD) began to look into the question of general average. In fact, it had been on the UNCTAD agenda for a considerable time, having been deferred some years previously in favour of an investigation into charterparties. In November 1991 a preliminary review of general average by the UNCTAD secretariat[1] was submitted to the XIIIth session of the Working Group on International Shipping Legislation. Having debated the report, the working group decided

> "to request the UNCTAD secretariat to approach, in close consultation with the CMI, the insurance industry (including IUMI) and international organisations representing commercial parties involved with general average, to study the extent to which insurance arrangements could simplify the general average system."

Those considering the report were invited specifically to focus upon (i) the advantages and disadvantages of the use of absorption clauses in hull policies, and (ii) the costs to the respective parties of any new insurance arrangements.

The AIDE was one of the bodies who responded to this invitation. Their reply took the form of a report of a small working party which was issued under the title: "International Collaboration with a view to simplifying the general average system". This report was delivered to the Director of the UNCTAD Shipping Division in April 1992, with copies sent to CMI and IUMI.

ASSOCIATION INTERNATIONALE DES DISPACHEURS EUROPÉENS

Following an exchange of correspondence between the then Presidents of CMI and AIDE, Professor Francesco Berlingieri and Dott. Carlo Mongrandi, it was agreed that both organisations would work closely together in their review of general average and the York-Antwerp Rules. At its General Assembly at Regensburg in September 1991 the AIDE passed a resolution defining its role as follows:

> "It was agreed that, as representing the profession of average adjusters, AIDE should continue to place its expertise at the disposal of those who will make the decisions as to what amendments, if any, should be adopted in the review of the York-Antwerp Rules and in other areas affecting the adjustment of general average. Any recommendations made by AIDE in this respect should have as their object the maintenance of the principles of general average, the avoidance of ambiguity and the limitation of the areas of potential dispute."

1. UNCTAD document TD/B/C.4/ISL/58 dated 19 August 1991.

It was recognised that the influence of the AIDE was likely to be limited to the extent that its expertise will be acceptable to national Maritime Law Associations. Consequently, in its consideration of the York-Antwerp Rules AIDE should consider and offer texts for potential amendments to the Rules in two rather differing situations:

— in areas where AIDE may recommend amendments in order to achieve uniformity of practice, avoid abuses and assist clarity of interpretation.
— in areas where it is perceived that there may be a desire for change, even though no such change is recommended by AIDE.

The AIDE appointed an International Sub-Committee comprising members from eighteen countries represented within the Association. The author of this book was appointed chairman of this committee. Specific areas of study were allocated to seven working groups, A–G, whose reports were considered by the ISC together with other material—CMI papers, previous reports of AIDE working groups, and so on. Two meetings of the International Sub-Committee were held, the first at Travemünde in October 1992, and the second at Woodbridge in May 1993. A comprehensive report, the influence of which should not be underestimated, was presented to the next General Assembly, held in Prague in September 1993. In areas where the ISC was unanimous or where there was a clear consensus, the ISC made a number of recommendations which were approved by the General Assembly, but where opinion was divided, the subjects were left open for decision by Resolution of the General Assembly. Copies of the AIDE Report, together with the Resolutions passed by the General Assembly, were then delivered to the chairman of the CMI committee and the Secretariat of UNCTAD.

FURTHER ACTIVITY LEADING TO THE CMI CONFERENCE AT SYDNEY, OCTOBER 1994

The proceedings of the International Sub-Committee of the CMI followed a somewhat similar pattern to that of the AIDE but on a rather more extended time-scale, in order to allow national Maritime Law Associations time to formulate their own views. What indeed was most stimulating was the way in which these associations seized upon and developed the topics for new studies, and in particular the questions of the allowance or non-allowance in general average of liabilities, costs and expenses relating to environmental damage and measures taken for its avoidance, the application of general average to tugs and barges, rates of exchange and the currency of adjustment, the use (or not) of general average franchises and absorption clauses in hull policies, and the question of time limits in relation to the production of documents.

Two meetings of the International Sub-Committee were held, the first in Brussels in December 1992 and the second in Paris in December 1993. The purpose of the first meeting, as stated by the chairman, was to consider the March 1992 report of the working group and to identify the main issues and proposals which had been raised by national associations in response to that report and to the wide-ranging questionnaire sent with it. Following that meeting, a report from the International Sub-Committee was circulated to national associations, which made specific reference to the proposals and ideas which were in circulation and invited further comments, particularly in reply to a further questionnaire on the subject of general average in relation to environmental issues. Armed with the further papers presented by national associations in response to this request, the second meeting of the International Sub-Committee reviewed all the proposals on a rule-by-rule basis and drew up a series of recommendations.

The final report of the International Sub-Committee was issued on 9 May 1994. Attached thereto as appendix I was a detailed report on the proceedings of the ISC at its December 1993 meeting, summarising the debate on each proposal, and as appendix II, a series of texts:

The York-Antwerp Rules 1974 as amended 1990.
Proposals considered by the ISC, subdivided:

— Recommended.
— Not recommended.
— Deferred for further consideration.

Suggestions made in the AIDE Report.

One might have thought that this was sufficient paperwork in advance of the CMI Conference fixed for Sydney in October 1994. But there was more to come.

UNCTAD

In March 1994 UNCTAD issued its further report entitled "The Place of General Average in Marine Insurance Today".[2] The report can be seen as a monument to the work of the UNCTAD Secretariat in collating the material furnished by governments of developing countries as well as that obtained through collaboration with the insurance industry and commercial interests,

2. UNCTAD document SDD/LEG/1.

including the CMI, AIDE and IUMI, whose co-operation was generously acknowledged. The report was laid out in four chapters:

Chapter I This dealt with the insurance aspect generally. After reviewing the virtual uniform coverage provided by marine insurance markets worldwide for general average contributions and the cover provided under Protection and Indemnity Club rules for cargo's contributions not recoverable by reason of a breach of the contract of carriage, the report went on to examine in more detail the extent to which uneconomic general average cases can be settled promptly by hull underwriters through the use of absorption clauses, without calling upon other interests to contribute.

Chapter II This looked at the incidents which lead up to cases of general average, attempted (on not very adequate evidence) to draw conclusions regarding the distribution of general average cases over the age, type and flag of the ships concerned, as well as the overall distribution of the cost between ships and cargoes. Not unexpectedly, there was also a section criticising the extent of the time taken by the general average process.

Chapter III This summarised comments made by governments and commercial institutions in the developing countries with regard to the problems encountered in those countries in the provision of general average security and in obtaining the finance to effect settlement when the adjustment is completed.

Chapter IV This chapter was probably the most useful section of the report. Headed "Insurance and other arrangements to simplify the operation of general average", it drew heavily upon the report of the AIDE working party of April 1992 (referred to on page 17 above) for a number of valuable suggestions, listed under the following headings:

A. Elimination of small general averages.
B. Simplification of procedures for the provision of general average security.
   1. Standardisation of forms utilised in the provision of security.
   2. Elimination of the need for "double-banked" security.
   3. Inclusion of an undertaking to pay in contracts of carriage.
   4. Encouragement of market agreements whereby cargo underwriters undertake to provide the appropriate security documentation subsequent to release of the goods.
   5. Combining the collection of security for both salvage and general average.

C. Encouragement of a more prompt settlement of general average contributions.

IUMI

Member Associations of the International Union of Marine Insurance received a report from a working party on general average dated July 1994, in anticipation of the IUMI Conference held in Toronto in September 1994. There were three documents:

— A report, entitled "General average and its impact on marine insurance". This comprised a detailed statistical analysis which attempted, as it said, "to steer clear of legal technicalities, which so often cloud the understanding of what for insurers is basically an economic exercise in re-allocating the cost of certain kinds of expense and loss".

— A commentary on the proposals for provision of the York-Antwerp Rules as set out in the report of the CMI International Sub-Committee dated May 1994. Some of the comments were extremely apposite, particularly those pertaining to the options to be debated at Sydney relative to the environmental issue; others, giving the impression that there was a "considerable momentum" directed at the expansion of general average, fell wide of the mark but may nevertheless have had an unfortunate influence upon the attitude of marine insurers' representatives at Toronto and subsequently.

— A questionnaire addressed to member associations.

The IUMI papers came too late to have a direct influence on the preparatory work for the CMI Conference, but they may well have strengthened the insurance industry's traditional reluctance to support many of the proposals for reform.

THE CMI CONFERENCE AT SYDNEY, OCTOBER 1994

The Conference occupied five working days, Monday to Friday 3–7 October 1994. As there were three important topics—of which general average was one—to be discussed concurrently, most of the work was done by an expanded International Sub-Committee. After introductory statements, mostly from the observers present, the ISC got to work on Monday afternoon and passed quickly through the proposed amendments by the end of the afternoon session on Tuesday. This left Wednesday for the work of the drafting committee, after which the ISC reviewed the proposed amendments again (in one instance reversing a vote previously taken), whereupon the completed text was submitted to a formal rule-by-rule vote by the Conference in plenary session. At the end of the proceedings, the following resolution was unanimously approved:

"The delegates representing the National Associations of Maritime Law of the states [listed in the resolution]:

1. Having noted with approval the amendments which have been made to the York-Antwerp Rules 1974 as amended 1990.
2. Propose that the new text be referred to as the York-Antwerp Rules 1994.
3. Recommend that the York-Antwerp Rules 1994 should be applied in the adjustment of claims in general average as soon as practicable after 31st December 1994."

It would be extremely difficult to trace a consistent pattern in the cross-patch of conflicting opinions expressed during the course of the debates at Sydney. If it were possible to do so, it would be found that in the background, while the clarification and simplication of existing Rules and practices would always be desirable, no encouragement would be given to any tendency to expand the scope of general average; whereas in the foreground there was perceived an urgent need to solve problems relating to the admissibility (or otherwise) of liabilities for environmental damage and costs incurred in order to prevent or minimise the same, when related to a general average act.

The important changes which were made include the following:

— The introduction of a Rule Paramount which provides that in no case shall there be any allowance for sacrifice or expenditure unless reasonably made or incurred.

— The issue of environmental liabilities and the cost of avoidance measures was settled by a composite amendment:

  — to Rule C excluding any allowance for "losses, damages or expenses incurred in respect of damage to the environment or in consequence of the escape or release of pollutant substances from the property involved in the common maritime adventure";

  — adding a new Rule XI(d) providing for the allowance of the cost of measures undertaken to prevent or minimise damage to the environment when incurred as part of certain specified general average operations.

  Although offered as a workable compromise which should be acceptable to both property underwriters and P. & I. Clubs, and approved as such by substantial majorities at the Sydney Conference, it may yet take some time for all to appreciate the benefits which will accrue to the maritime community as a result of the clarification of the position which arises in serious situations involving not only peril to ship and cargo but also potential damage to the environment.

— A new Rule B has been inserted in an attempt to advance the cause of uniformity when general average situations arise in a convoy consisting of tug and tow(s) or push-boat and barges.

- — Two additional paragraphs have been added to Rule E with the object of reducing delays in the preparation of adjustments. These provide that notice of any claims in general average shall be given to the average adjuster within 12 months of the end of the voyage and permit him to estimate the extent of any allowance or contributory value for which he has not received such notification or sufficient supporting evidence.
- — A Non-Separation wording has been added in Rule G providing that when the cargo or part thereof is forwarded to destination from a port of refuge, rights and liabilities in general average shall remain as nearly as possible the same as they would have been in the absence of such forwarding.
- — Rules II, V and VIII have been redrafted in such a way as to make it clear that any allowances made under these rules for loss or damage are confined to the property involved in the common maritime adventure.
- — Rule IX has been redrafted to bring in cases when cargo is necessarily used for fuel for the common safety.
- — Mails and passengers' accompanied private motor vehicles have been added to the list of interests exempted from contribution in Rule XVII.
- — The period that general average interest will continue to run has been extended to three months after issue of the adjustment.

The following proposals were *not* adopted at the Sydney Conference:

- — To rephrase Rule I, on the grounds of equity and to reflect modern practice, in positive terms, thus: "Jettison of cargo, wherever stowed, shall be made good as general average when made for the common safety".
- — A proposal to abolish "new for old" deductions in toto.
- — A proposal to delete the second paragraph of Rule XIV, with the object of eliminating from general average any allowance for the cost of temporary repairs of accidental damage.
- — A proposal to substitute "at the time of delivery under the contract of carriage" for "at the time of discharge" in both Rules XVI and XVII.
- — Either of the two proposals tabled to introduce into Rule XXI new material regulating the currency to be adopted for the adjustment and the rates of exchange to be utilised for this purpose.

Further details, with explanations, will be provided in the chapters which follow examining each rule separately.

RULE OF INTERPRETATION

In the adjustment of general average the following Rules shall apply to the exclusion of any Law and Practice inconsistent therewith.

Except as provided by the Rule Paramount and the numbered Rules, general average shall be adjusted according to the lettered Rules.

EVOLUTION

As we have seen, the York-Antwerp Rules until 1890 consisted of a set of Rules which dealt only with specific instances in those areas where the laws and practices of various countries had differed and where, for that reason, international uniformity was desirable. These Rules were numbered in no particular sequence and could not be said in any way to comprise a code of general average.

As if to emphasise this position, an additional Rule was added in 1890, which provided as follows:

"*Rule XVIII. Adjustment*

Except as provided in the foregoing rules, the adjustment shall be drawn up in accordance with the law and practice that would have governed the adjustment had the contract of affreightment not contained a clause to pay general average according to these rules."

This Rule XVIII was rescinded in 1924 when the lettered Rules were introduced. The purpose of the lettered Rules was to supplement the particular provisions of the numbered Rules and to furnish a general framework acceptable to the international maritime community. However, at that time, no provision was made to govern the relationship between the lettered and numbered Rules, and this deficiency was exposed shortly afterwards in the leading case of *Vlassopoulos* v. *British & Foreign Marine Insurance Co.*[1]

In that case the shipowner claimed in general average, *inter alia*, the cost of handling on board and discharging cargo at the port of loading in order to

1. *Vlassopoulos* v. *British & Foreign Marine Insurance Co.* (*The Makis*) [1929] 1 K.B. 187; 34 Com. Cas. 65.

effect repairs to the vessel's foremast which had been damaged by an accident in loading. An arbitrator had found as facts that the vessel and cargo were not in any danger, but that the repairs effected were necessary to enable the adventure to be safely completed. On this aspect, Roche J. held that, as a matter of construction, the lettered Rules constitute the general principles which are to be applied, to which the numbered Rules were subservient.

Consequently, the shipowner's claim for the expenses that would otherwise have been met under Rules X and XI was denied on the ground that the prerequisite of peril under Rule A was not present. The implications of this judgment caused consternation in shipping and insurance markets, particularly in the United Kingdom, and as a result leading British shipowners and underwriters concluded an agreement, which became known as the "Makis" agreement, which read as follows:

> "In consequence of the *Makis* decision, questions have arisen as to the intention of the parties in framing the York/Antwerp Rules, 1924, and it is desirable to set doubt at rest by agreeing that the Rules shall be construed as if they contained the following provision:
>
> 'Except as provided in the Numbered Rules 1 to 23 inclusive, the Adjustment shall be drawn up in accordance with the Lettered Rules A to G inclusive.' "

This agreement, which effectively reversed the decision in the *Makis* case, continued to govern the practice of adjustment in the United Kingdom, and when the York-Antwerp rules were next revised at the Amsterdam Conference in 1949, the British delegation proposed the introduction of a Rule of Interpretation, as follows:

> "In the adjustment of general average the following lettered and numbered Rules shall apply to the exclusion of any Law and Practice inconsistent therewith.
>
> Except as provided by the numbered Rules, general average shall be adjusted according to the lettered Rules."

This was approved without dissension.

During the run-up to the 1974 Hamburg Conference and the 1994 Sydney Conference, when the topic of general average was being debated at many different levels, voices were heard, chiefly among academic commentators, suggesting that the Rule of Interpretation be reversed so that allowances should not be made under the numbered Rules unless the criteria set out in Rule A were also satisfied.[2] However, such arguments were clearly not sufficiently influential to persuade national delegations to press for any change, and with the exception of a consequential amendment proposed by the drafting committee at Sydney to accommodate a reference to the Rule Paramount, the Rule of Interpretation has not been altered since its inception.

2. See Tetley, *Cargo Owners' Obligations in General Average* (1988) 19 J.M.L.C. 90, in which the paramountcy of the numbered Rules is censured as "an anomaly, if not an enormity". His argument appears to take no account of the fact that the numbered Rules were agreed by international conferences and put into effect some 60 years before the lettered Rules were introduced.

COMMENTARY

First paragraph

This provides for the application of the York-Antwerp Rules in the adjustment of general average, to the exclusion of any law and practice which is inconsistent. In fact, certain of the Rules go beyond the mere calculation of allowances and the apportionment of the same over the contributory values, e.g. Rule E which refers to the duties of the parties to give timely notice of their claims and to furnish promptly the relevant documentation when called upon to do so, and Rule XXII, which is specific on the treatment of general average deposits. Such Rules, not having to do with the adjustment of general average, may conflict with mandatory law or with laws which are applied on grounds of public policy in various countries. Although such instances are likely to be rare, it could reasonably be expected that a court of competent jurisdiction would apply mandatory, statutory or public policy laws notwithstanding a contrary provision in the Rules.[3] On the other hand, as between the parties to the contract, e.g. bill of lading, charterparty or policy of insurance, it is submitted that the laws of contract and/or private obligations would respect the provision to exclude any law and practice inconsistent with the Rules, at least so far as they concerned the rights and obligations of those parties in general average.

"... to the exclusion of any Law and Practice inconsistent therewith." Since the whole object of the York-Antwerp Rules is to override the jumble of inconsistencies which would otherwise apply under the national laws governing the adjustment of general average, these words are essential. However, the governing law, which in practically all maritime countries means the law which obtains at the place where the adventure ends (see Rule G) is not wholly excluded and such law may be used to fill the gaps, if required, in the framework provided by the York-Antwerp Rules.

Second paragraph

This is the "Makis" agreement, reworded in 1994 to include reference to the Rule Paramount. The original intention was to give precedence to the numbered Rules, so that those allowances in general average which have as their object the completion of the adventure (such as those under Rules X(b) and (c) relating to the cost of storing and reloading cargo in order to enable repairs to the ship to be effected that are necessary for the safe prosecution of the voyage) retain their authority even though the incurring of the expense would not constitute a general average act under Rule A.

3. See the dictum of Feinberg C.J. in *The Eagle Courier* quoted on p. 29.

Surprisingly, despite the unambiguity of the Rule of Interpretation, some courts in the U.S.A. have had difficulty in accepting the proposition stated above. In the Fifth Circuit in *The Orient Transporter* [4] the Court of Appeals appeared to ignore the Rule of Interpretation and held that in the absence of a situation of peril, Rules X and XI providing for the admission of expenses at a port of refuge were not applicable. This decision was strongly criticised by influential writers,[5] and subsequently, when the same point came up for decision in the Second Circuit, the outcome was different.

This was the case of *The Eagle Courier*,[6] which was chartered under a voyage charterparty providing for general average to be payable according to the York-Antwerp Rules 1950 and to be settled in New York. In pursuance of that charter the vessel loaded a cargo of wheat at Port Arthur, Texas, for Leningrad via Rotterdam for bunkers. Whilst navigating in the English Channel, a bump was felt, followed by metallic scraping noise from the stern. However, the vessel arrived safely in Rotterdam and moored to a buoy where, after bunkering, a diver's examination was held, which disclosed that the propeller had received extensive damage to the blades and had slackened on the taper. The vessel was therefore shifted to a berth for the discharge of cargo and afterwards to a drydock where the propeller shaft was replaced and the spare propeller fitted; the cargo was then reloaded and the vessel continued to Leningrad where the cargo was delivered without further incident.

A general average adjustment was prepared in which was admitted in general average the cost of discharge, storage and reloading of the cargo, and the wages and maintenance of the crew and fuel and stores consumed during the extra period of detention in Rotterdam. Cargo interests declined to pay, alleging that the vessel was never in peril within the terms of Rule A of the York-Antwerp Rules, and in the U.S. District Court, S.D.N.Y., summary judgment was given in favour of cargo on the ground that neither the vessel nor the cargo were in any peril at the time the expenditures were incurred: that the voyage could not have been completed without effecting repairs was deemed to be irrelevant.

This decision was reversed in the U.S. Court of Appeals, Second Circuit. The court heard argument by counsel not only for the plaintiffs and defendants, but also for the AAA of the US as *amicus curiae*. After referring to *The Star of Hope*[7] and *Hobson* v. *Lord* [8]—cases which demonstrated the recognition by U.S. courts of general average arising out of extraordinary expenses incurred for the joint benefit of ship and cargo—Feinberg C.J. reviewed the history of the York-Antwerp Rules and the way in which the Rule

4. *The Orient Transporter*, 1974 AMC 2593.

5. See Allen, "Peril in The Fifth Circuit" (1976) 7 J.M.L.C. 409; Buglass, *Marine Insurance and General Average in the United States* (2nd ed.), p. 183.

6. *Eagle Terminal Tankers Inc.* v. *Ingosstrakh* (*The Eagle Courier*), 1981 AMC 137.

7. *The Star of Hope* (1869) 76 U.S. 203.

8. *Hobson* v. *Lord* (1876) 92 U.S. 397.

of Interpretation formalised the effect of the "Makis" agreement. As to the York-Antwerp Rules, he said:

> "Although they have not been formally sanctioned on an inter-Governmental basis, and thus lack the force of law, the Rules reflect an important consensus of the international shipping industry and merit 'full judicial cognisance', at least insofar as they do not conflict with statutory or other policies of equal or greater importance."

Against this background, the Court of Appeals correctly applied the Rule of Interpretation and held that the expenses claimed were admissible in general average in accordance with Rules X(b) and XI(b) of the York-Antwerp Rules 1950. It is to be hoped that this decision of the Second Circuit will be preferred to that of the Fifth Circuit if the effect of the Rule of Interpretation should again come before the United States courts.

The reference to the Rule Paramount

This is dealt with more fully in the chapter which follows, but for the present it may be observed that the introduction of the Rule Paramount has in effect created a three-tiered hierarchy within the Rules:

— the Rule of Interpretation and the Rule Paramount;
— the numbered Rules;
and finally at the bottom of the pile
— the lettered Rules.

RULE PARAMOUNT

In no case shall there be any allowance for sacrifice or expenditure unless reasonably made or incurred.

EVOLUTION

This Rule was introduced in 1994. The proposal for its introduction emanated from the United States[1] who wished to add a third and fourth new paragraphs to the existing Rule of Interpretation and re-title all four paragraphs as "the Rule of Interpretation and Rules Paramount".

The proposed new third paragraph would read:

"There shall be no allowance in general average for sacrifice or expenditure unless reasonably made."

The proposed fourth paragraph would read:

"In no event shall there be an allowance in general average for pollution liability or clean-up of pollutants."

In the debates at Sydney, the United States proposals became detached from the Rule of Interpretation, and that relating to the exclusion of pollution liabilities was voted down in favour of the compromise package presented by the British delegation—see the section headed "The Environmental Issue" on page 52.

Although not receiving much support at the meeting of the International Sub-Committee in December 1993, the proposal for a Rule Paramount applying the concept of reasonableness to all subsidiary Rules was approved at the Sydney Conference, subject only to a minor change of wording.

COMMENTARY

This is all that remains of a substantial package of proposals from the United States which, if adopted, would have restricted in several instances allowances

1. CMI document GENAV-42.

for ship and cargo sacrifices, reintroduced certain unsatisfactory wordings swept away in the 1974 improvements and created a number of practical difficulties for adjusters. See observations on Rules III, IV, V, X(a) second paragraph and XIV.

Although not presented as a "package", the U.S. proposals appeared to have been put forward in response to the UNCTAD thesis for restraining the ambit of general average, or possibly as an attempt to defuse even more radical proposals for its curtailment.

The Rule was conceived in direct reaction to the English case of *The Alpha*.[2] The facts of the case were very simple. The vessel ran aground on a sand bank in the River Zaire and she with her cargo were in a position of peril. The master caused the engines to be used in efforts to refloat, but in so doing the water-cooling system became clogged up and substantial damage, costing US$800,000 to repair, was done to the main engine and auxiliaries. At the trial in the Commercial Court, cargo interests contended that the refloating efforts undertaken by the master were quite remarkably unskilful and that the master's negligence in this respect contributed substantially to the damage sustained. Hobhouse J. accepted this contention on the facts of the case, but held that since Rule VII does not use the word "reasonably", all the plaintiffs had to prove was—

1. that the damage was done when the vessel was aground and in a position of peril;
2. that the damage was done by trying to refloat the vessel;
3. that the damage arose from an actual intention to float the ship at the risk of such damage.

The argument presented, which presumably found favour with the majority of the delegates at Sydney, was that since, by reason of the Rule of Interpretation, the requirement of reasonableness contained in Rule A could not be imported into Rule VII, a Rule Paramount was needed in order to achieve the desired result.

In the opinion of the British delegates at Sydney, the judgment in *The Alpha* was correct. The importation, by operation of the Rule Paramount, of a test of reasonableness in an *Alpha* type situation will now make it necessary for the average adjuster to examine the cost of repairing the damage sustained in the efforts to refloat in order to separate the cost of repairing damage resulting from the efforts "reasonably" made from the rest of the damage which *ex hypothesi* would be "unreasonably" made. Such an exercise would require the average adjuster—as well as those subsequently wishing to criticise his adjustment—to examine with the benefit of hindsight the actions of a shipmaster taken in the agony of the moment. This kind of judgment by

2. *Corfu Navigation Co. and another* v. *Mobil Shipping Co. Ltd. and others (The Alpha)* [1991] 2 Lloyd's Rep. 515.

hindsight is strongly disapproved in English law[3] and it is submitted that the incorporation in the York-Antwerp Rules of this Rule Paramount may throw up an irreconcilable conflict of interpretation, particularly when related to the making of a general average sacrifice.

When is a sacrifice "reasonably made"?

The concept of reasonableness does not sit easily with the making of a sacrifice. Numerous examples could be given, but two may suffice:

— *Prima facie* it is the duty of the master, as servant of the carrier, to care for the cargo which has been placed in his custody and it does not appear to be reasonable that he should throw it overboard unless that cargo presented a danger to itself or to other property. But if the danger presents itself to *all*, then its jettison is sanctioned by the law maritime when undertaken as a general average act. Where the York-Antwerp Rules apply, the jettison has to satisfy Rule A and to be "intentionally and reasonably made . . . for the common safety for the purpose of preserving from peril the property involved in a common maritime adventure". In other words, the purpose of the jettison, to preserve the *whole* of the property, provides its justification.

— Similarly, it is not reasonable in the ordinary way of things for a master or a member of the crew deliberately to damage the ship, and if done without justification, such would be an act of barratry. So, once again, one has to look at the purpose of the act for its justification, but also, applying the Rule Paramount, at the manner in which it is performed, having regard to all the circumstances of the case. The test must be what a reasonable shipmaster would do in those circumstances: the more immediate the peril at the time of the act, the greater latitude in judging after the event whether the act was reasonable.

Similar problems may well arise in practice in other instances which the authors of the Rule Paramount may neither have intended nor anticipated. In particular, there may be difficulties in the application of Rule F, and in regard to salvage settlements and the treatment of costs under Rule VI. These will be examined in the chapters commenting on these Rules.

3. For the most recent (at the time of writing) of many judicial statements to this effect, see *The Star Sea* [1995] 1 Lloyd's Rep. 651 at p. 658, where Tuckey J. said in relation to an allegation of negligence on the part of a shipmaster in charge of fighting a fire: "I bear in mind that his actions are not to be judged with the benefit of hindsight and that we all make mistakes, particularly in an emergency such as that created by fire."

RULE A

There is a general average act when, and only when, any extraordinary sacrifice or expenditure is intentionally and reasonably made or incurred for the common safety for the purpose of preserving from peril the property involved in a common maritime adventure.

General average sacrifices and expenditures shall be borne by the different contributing interests on the basis hereinafter provided.

EVOLUTION

This Rule, together with the other lettered Rules, was introduced into the scheme of the York-Antwerp Rules at the 1924 Stockholm Conference.

The wording of the first paragraph bears a close resemblance to the definition of general average contained in section 66(2) of the (U.K.) Marine Insurance Act 1906, which reads:

> "There is a general average act where any extraordinary sacrifice or expenditure is voluntarily and reasonably made or incurred in time of peril for the purpose of preserving the property imperilled in the common adventure."

This similarity is not accidental. Indeed, the Drafting Committee set up to prepare the text for the 1924 Conference had proposed the U.K. statutory definition with only one difference, namely the substitution of "common maritime adventure" for the words "common adventure".

The variations adopted by the 1924 Conference, although slight, must therefore be considered as significant:

(1) "when, and only when" has been substituted for "where" after the words "there is a general average act". The added emphasis imparted by these words suggests that the Rule A definition of a general average act was intended to be exhaustive. Indeed, prior to the introduction of the Rule of Interpretation in 1950, there were grounds for considering that Rule A conflicted with those of the numbered Rules (particularly Rules X and XI) which were specifically designed to achieve uniformity of practice in cases where the object

of the general average allowances is not the attainment of safety, but the safe completion of the voyage.[1]

(2) The word "intentionally" was substituted for the word "voluntarily". Rudolf reported that the Conference, in deciding to adopt the word "intentionally", selected it as emphasising more clearly the idea of deliberate choice.

(3) In place of "in time of peril for the purpose of preserving the property imperilled . . . " the Conference substituted "for the common safety for the purpose of preserving from peril the property involved . . . ".

No change was made in the text of Rule A in 1949 or 1974. In 1994, however, the second paragraph was added. This had previously been Rule B and was transferred to Rule A in order to make space for a new rule governing tug and tow situations.

COMMENTARY

First paragraph

Rudolf tells us[2] that the feeling of the Stockholm Conference was clearly in favour "of not restricting the operations of general average only to such cases where the danger was immediate and imminent". This would explain why the words "in time of peril" were removed from the English definition and were replaced by the words "for the common safety", which already appeared in many of the numbered Rules and were thought to be widely understood.

Since the concept of general average has its origin in the attainment of safety from a position of peril, we need to construe parts of the text more closely:

" . . . for the common safety for the purpose of preserving from peril . . . "

Peril

It is submitted that the Rule A definition differs from the English law definition contained in section 66(2) of the Marine Insurance Act 1906 in this respect, namely, that it is not necessary in order to constitute a general average act that it should be made at a time when the peril is physically present, so to speak, provided that the act is undertaken for the purpose of preserving the property from a peril which threatens it, or which would threaten it if the act were not performed.

So, in *Watson* v. *Fireman's Fund Insurance Co.*,[3] which was a claim under a cargo insurance policy governed by English law, Rowlatt J. held that damage

1. See commentary on the Rule of Interpretation and the "Makis" agreement, p. 26.
2. Rudolf, *The York-Antwerp Rules 1924*, p. 42.
3. *Watson* v. *Fireman's Fund Insurance Co.* [1922] 2 K.B. 355; 12 Ll.L.Rep. 133.

caused to the plaintiffs' goods by steam applied to the hold of a ship to quench a non-existent fire was not a general average loss, since the peril of fire which the master thought to exist, was not present. For the position under the York-Antwerp Rules 1924, the leading case is *Vlassopoulos* v. *British & Foreign Marine Insurance Co.*[4] In that case, the second of two claims made by the shipowner was for the expense incurred in putting into Cherbourg as a port of refuge. The aspect of peril was questioned, as if Rule A applied, and in this respect Roche J., allowing the claim, said: "It is not necessary that the ship should be actually in the grip, or even nearly in the grip, of the disaster that may arise from a danger. It would be a very bad thing if shipmasters had to wait until that state of things arose in order to justify them doing an act which would be a general average act." On the other hand, as the learned judge was right to stress, "the peril must be real and not imaginary, [and] it must be substantial and not merely slight or nugatory. In short, it must be a real danger."

The words "for the purpose of preserving [the property] from peril" explain and clarify the expression "for the common safety", and it has been said that wherever the phrase "for the common safety" appears in the text of the York-Antwerp Rules, it has to be interpreted in this way. However, this appears to beg the question, much argued by commentators on the Rules, whether there can be a general average act when measures are taken by the master or other responsible person to avert a peril which he believes to threaten the adventure, but in fact does not. It is submitted below that this question is largely theoretical, and that the solution in borderline instances is to be found not by the illumination of hindsight, but by considering whether at the time it was performed the act was "intentionally and reasonably made or incurred . . . for the *purpose* of preserving the property from peril".

" . . . intentionally and reasonably made or incurred . . . "

In *Athel Line* v. *Liverpool & London War Risks Association*[5] two ships of the Athel Line were sailing in convoy from Bermuda to the United Kingdom and were ordered by the convoy Commadore to return to Bermuda on account of the convoy ahead of them having been attacked by an enemy raider. While obedience to lawful orders does not signify an intention on the part of the master, Tucker J. found it unnecessary to decide whether a general average act must be the act of the master. It now seems clear on the authority of *Australian Coastal Shipping Commission* v. *Green*,[6] in which the decisions made to call in tugs were taken on orders from the shipowners' office, that the act need not be

4. *Vlassopoulos* v. *British & Foreign Marine Insurance Co.* [1929] 1 K.B. 187; 34 Com. Cas. 65.

5. *Athel Line* v. *Liverpool & London War Risks Association* [1944] K.B. 87; 77 Ll.L.Rep. 132.

6. *Australian Coastal Shipping Commission* v. *Green* [1971] 1 Q.B. 456; [1971] 1 Lloyd's Rep. 16.

that of the master, provided it is made by the shipowner or his servant or agent having authority to do so. As Tucker J. summed it up in the *Athel Line* case: "the Rule [A] clearly envisages the exercise by someone of his reasoning powers and discretion applied to a particular problem with freedom of choice to decide to act in one out of two or more possible ways, and the language is quite inappropriate to describe the blind and unreasoning obedience of a subordinate to the lawful orders of a superior authority".

However, the making of the sacrifice or the incurring of the expenditure must be done "reasonably". This means that the master or other person making the decision must have reasonable grounds for believing that the sacrifice or expenditure will avert a peril that threatens the adventure or will preserve the property from an existing peril. Thus, in the instance frequently cited in regard to a non-existent peril, namely of a vessel putting into a port of refuge in order to carry out a survey for suspected damage, it is submitted that the question is not whether such damage exists or if it does, whether repairs have to be made to it that are necessary for the safe prosecution of the voyage, but whether the master had reasonable grounds for believing that the adventure would be imperilled if he failed to take that course of action. To take any other view would involve judging the master's decision with the benefit of hindsight and might inhibit those in command of vessels from acting with proper discretion when they considered it reasonable to do so.

The editors of Lowndes & Rudolf (11th ed.) take a different view. At section A.55 they state that if a vessel puts into port after stranding in order to obtain a diver's survey or other inspection to ensure that it is safe to proceed on the voyage, and is permitted so to proceed without repairs at that time, it follows that the common adventure was not in peril and that the entry into port was not a general average act. The author can trace no authority for this assertion and whilst it may represent the position which would obtain if English law were to govern the adjustment, it cannot be accepted as correct when the York-Antwerp Rules apply. Indeed, there is a long-standing practice to the contrary, based upon the desire of commercial and insurance interests to encourage shipowners and masters of ships to take proper and appropriate measures to ensure the safety of ships which have suffered damage on the voyage.

Another, not dissimilar question frequently debated in earlier days on a matter of principle was whether the alleged general average act had to be successful in its aim of saving the property. Of course, the totality of the acts done with this object must succeed, at least to the extent of saving *some* of the property, else there would be no fund to contribute. However, there is nothing in the Rule A definition of a general average act which requires that any particular act, or any single item of sacrifice or expenditure, shall be shown to have contributed to the ultimate success of the whole operation. Indeed, the case of *Australian Coastal Shipping Commission* v. *Green*[6] provides us with a catalogue of quite remarkably unsuccessful acts.

To end with a final illustration, let us consider the cost of engaging an aircraft to search for a missing or overdue vessel. In *The American Farmer*,[7] R.A.F. Coastal Command were requested to locate the ship, damaged by collision in mid-Atlantic. This was accomplished, but when the aircraft crew sighted the stricken ship, she was already being attended by two other vessels. Hence the despatch of the plane, of itself, achieved nothing; nevertheless R.A.F. Coastal Command were held to be entitled to a salvage reward, as were the other parties whose services had contributed more to the success of the salvage effort. Nowadays a searching aircraft is more commonly engaged on contract terms, and provided that the adventure was in fact threatened by a "real and substantial" peril, the reasonable cost of the aircraft charter will be allowable in general average within Rule A, irrespective of the success of the search.

Second paragraph

When first introduced at the 1924 Conference in Stockholm, the opening words read: "General average sacrifices and *expenses* . . . " Originally intended to form part of Rule A, the Conference decided that it should form a separate Rule B in order to link Rule A, defining a general average act, with the Rules which followed including, of course, the numbered Rules. If this was the intention, it was unsuccessful, as became apparent when the *Makis* case[8] was decided.

In 1994 the text was transferred back into Rule A, and the opportunity was taken to substitute "expenditures" for the word "expenses" for the sake of consistency.

7. *The American Farmer* (1947) 80 Ll.L.Rep. 672.

8. *Vlassopoulos* v. *British & Foreign Marine Insurance Co.* [1929] 1 K.B. 187; 34 Com. Cas. 65.

RULE B

There is a common maritime adventure when one or more vessels are towing or pushing another vessel or vessels, provided that they are all involved in commercial activities and not in a salvage operation.

When measures are taken to preserve the vessels and their cargoes, if any, from a common peril, these Rules shall apply.

A vessel is not in common peril with another vessel or vessels if by simply disconnecting from the other vessel or vessels she is in safety; but if the disconnection is itself a general average act the common maritime adventure continues.

EVOLUTION

This Rule was new in 1994, having been adopted by the Sydney Conference in place of the previous "connecting rule" which has now been transferred to and forms the second paragraph of Rule A.

The idea for a Rule to cover tug and tow situations was developed more or less simultaneously by working parties within the AIDE and the British Maritime Law Association with the object of promoting uniformity of practice in an area where the jurisprudence of different countries had developed in different directions. In their examination of the subject both working parties found a valuable precedent in the Rhine Rules, which govern the great majority of transports on the Rhine and adjoining rivers.

The text of Rhine Rule XXV reads as follows:

"Convoys

1. For the purpose of this Rule, a convoy is considered to be a group of vessels coupled with each other in such a way that none of the vessels has any freedom of independent movement.
2. When measures are taken to preserve a vessel and/or some or all vessels of such convoy and their cargo from a common peril, Rules I to XXIV shall be applied accordingly. A vessel forming part of a convoy is not in common peril with another vessel of that convoy, if by a mere uncoupling of the connection with such other vessel she can be placed in safety.
3. If a common peril exists, Rules I to XXIV shall be applied as much for the profit as to the charge of those concerned in the vessels of the convoy and their cargoes.

4. For the calculation of contributory values and allowances the vessels will be considered 'the vessel' and the total cargo carried in those vessels will be considered to be 'the cargo' in the sense these words bear in Rules I to XXIV."

COMMENTARY

The promoters of the new rule were concerned at the variety and inconsistency of the legal regimes applying in different countries to the transport of goods by barge, and in the various commercial instruments regulating the towage or other propulsion of those barges. An AIDE working group, appointed to investigate how far, if at all, general averages can be applied to tugs, tows and their cargoes, reported in 1985 having found little guidance in national legislation, confusion in the case law and inconsistency in the wording of towage contracts. It concluded, however, that even in the absence of contractual provisions, the carriage of cargoes on seagoing barges under tow is capable of giving rise to situations which justify the application of general average rules.[1]

In the United States and Canada there has been a substantial increase in the carriage of goods by barge, not merely on the Great Lakes and river systems, but also seagoing on the west coast. The case law, unfortunately, is inconsistent: each case appearing to have been settled on its own particular facts. On the other hand, there is a wealth of detailed commentary in a number of valuable papers prepared by eminent average adjusters in the United States and Canada which demonstrates that, despite the legal complexities, the adjusting profession has succeeded in establishing a number of accepted and uniform practices.

Law and Practice in the United States and Canada

In the *J.P. Donaldson*[2] (1897) a tug was towing two barges under a contract of towage between the tug owner and the barge owner. Each of the barges had her own master on board. During a storm, the barges were released in order to prevent the tug from driving ashore and both barges stranded. The parties agreed that there was a general average situation as between the barges and their cargoes, but the United States Supreme Court ruled that the right of contribution in general average could not extend beyond each barge and her cargo.

1. Report of AIDE working group on the carriage of goods by barge, XIIIth General Assembly, Venice, 1985.
2. *The J.P. Donaldson* (1897) 167 U.S. 599.

Per contra, in *Sacramento Navigation Company* v. *Salz*[3] (1927) the Supreme Court held that for contract of affreightment purposes a tug and tow in common ownership should be deemed to be one vessel. However, a few years later, in 1934, the District Court for the Southern District of New York, in *The Mohican*,[4] rejected the "Flotilla Doctrine" so far as general average was concerned in a case where only one barge was damaged and in peril as a consequence of the casualty.

If by that time it seemed that the law was confused, that confusion was further compounded in the case of *S.C. Loveland Company* v. *U.S.A.*[5] in 1963. In that case two barges were in tow of a tug, all of the same ownership, transporting cargo under a contract of affreightment. As a result of the tug grounding, the first barge in tow, "Loveland 33", struck the stranded tug and shortly afterwards the second, "Loveland 32", struck the "Loveland 33". As a result the "33" sustained substantial damage and she was voluntarily put aground in order to prevent her from sinking. The District Court for the eastern district of Pennsylvania held that the general average arising from the voluntary stranding, temporary repairs and the refloating of the "Loveland 33" was incurred for the common safety of the entire venture, so that contribution must be made by the tug and both barges as well as by cargo. In its judgment, the court distinguished the case of the *J.P. Donaldson* from the present case by reason of the ownership of the vessels and in the type of contract involved: "In *Donaldson* one party owned the tug and another the barges, and the contract was by A to tow the barges of B. Here tug and barges were all owned by libellant and the contract was not to tow barges but a contract of affreightment."

However, despite the uncertainty at law, there is a generally accepted practice in the United States when dealing with flotillas or tug and tow units.[6] In the first place a vessel which is not itself in peril will not be expected to contribute to sacrifices made and/or expenses incurred to save another vessel which is in peril. Secondly, in deciding which units of a flotilla will contribute in general average, one must look to the question of peril rather than to the contract of transportation.[7] "It matters not that the tug and barge are of the same ownership and provide a transportation service under a contract of affreightment, or whether the barge owner has contracted with the cargo owner to transport his goods and separately entered into a contractual arrangement to provide the necessary locomotion."[8] This practice was approved in 1966 by the AAA of the US Committee on Rules of Practice, with

3. *Sacramento Navigation Co* v. *Salz*, 1927 AMC 397.
4. *The Mohican*, 1934 AMC 112.
5. *S.C. Loveland Company* v. *U.S.A.*, 1963 AMC 260.
6. See Leo A. Walsh, Chairman's Address to the Association of Average Adjusters of the United States, 1986.
7. Buglass, *Marine Insurance and General Average in the United States* (2nd ed.), p. 285.
8. Leo A. Walsh, *loc. cit.*

the qualification that where all the units of a flotilla are in peril, salvage assistance rendered to tow the tug and the barges to a place of safety will be treated as general average and contribution will be due from the tug, barges and cargo carried therein.[9]

In Canada, the question of common peril was examined in *Northland Navigation Co.* v. *Paterson Boiler Works* (the "Sea Comet").[10] In that case the "Sea Comet" was towing a barge loaded with 11 steel buoys. Heavy weather was encountered during the voyage, which caused the tug's main engine to malfunction, and because of this the tug, being unable to control the tow, released the tow line. The tug reached safety, but the barge went aground. Efforts to refloat the barge with her cargo were unsuccessful. The owners of the barge gave notice of abandonment to their insurers, and subsequently the cargo was separately salved. An adjustment was prepared showing the cost of the attempted refloating of the barge as general average up to the time notice of abandonment was given, and the cost of salving the cargo as a special charge thereon. However, the cargo interests argued that the tug should be brought in to contribute to the general average expenses, but the court held that the safety of the tug was not involved; the adjustment was therefore correct.

In salvage situations where the services have been rendered to both the tug and her tow, the practice in British Columbia is to follow any award which is made showing the separate vessels to contribute upon the basis of their respective values, but the position is different when services are rendered and charged for in accordance with a local usage, whereby the first tug to arrive and assist is entitled to double the daily rate of hire for the first 24 hours of assistance, thereafter at normal hourly rates. When services are rendered to more than one vessel on this basis, there is a local practice to divide the cost equally between vessels in the first instance, and then as between each vessel and its cargo on an apportionment over values.[11] This system is known as "Common User Apportionment", and is acceptable by underwriters in the local markets.

Norway

The leading case is *The Alppi*.[12] An unmanned barge (the "Alppi") was being towed by the tug "Bjørn Eskil". The convoy got into difficulties and the tug's master, judging the position to be one of extreme peril for both tug and tow,

9. AAA of the US Committee on Rules of Practice, General Average—Tug and Tow, 22 September, 1966.

10. *Northland Navigation Co.* v. *Paterson Boiler Works (The Sea Comet)* (1983) 2 C.F. 59.

11. See K.W. Hext, Chairman's Address to the Association of Average Adjusters of Canada, 1984.

12. *The Alppi* (1989) Nordiske Domme i Sjøfartsanliggender (Nordic Maritime Law Report) 397. The author is grateful to Johannes Woxholt, average adjuster in Oslo, for information respecting this case.

cut adrift the "Alppi", which was totally lost. The town court approved an adjustment which treated the loss of the "Alppi" as a general average sacrifice, but this decision was overturned by the Appeal Court, which held that there was no community of interest in the general average sense between tug and tow. In reaching this conclusion the court stated that it had been unable to find any precedent in either Norwegian or foreign cases and expressed the opinion that if a general average situation between tug and tow had been considered internationally desirable, it would have expected this to have been recognised when the York-Antwerp Rules (which form part of Norwegian law) had last been revised (in 1974).

Conclusion

In the opinion of the author the uncertainty and confusion revealed in the law cases reviewed above entirely justifies the decision of the 1994 Sydney Conference to introduce a new rule into the scheme of the York-Antwerp Rules in an effort to achieve uniformity on the vexed questions of community of interest between tug and tow and what constitutes a situation of common peril. However, it has to be emphasised that except in Scandinavia and other countries, where the York-Antwerp Rules 1994 may be expected to form part of the domestic legal systems, the attainment of uniformity will depend upon the introduction of the YAR 1994 by reference into towage contracts as well as into contracts for the carriage of goods by barge.

RULE C

Only such losses, damages or expenses which are the direct consequence of the general average act shall be allowed as general average.

In no case shall there be any allowance in general average for losses, damages or expenses incurred in respect of damage to the environment or in consequence of the escape or release of pollutant substances from the property involved in the common maritime adventure.

Demurrage, loss of market, and any loss or damage sustained or expense incurred by reason of delay, whether on the voyage or subsequently, and any indirect loss whatsoever, shall not be admitted as general average.

EVOLUTION

The text agreed at the 1924 Stockholm Conference read as follows:

"Only such damages, losses or expenses which are a direct consequence of the general average act shall be allowed as general average. Damage or loss sustained by the ship or cargo through delay on the voyage, and indirect loss from the same cause, such as demurrage and loss of market, shall not be admitted as general average."

At the 1949 Amsterdam Conference the Rule was reconsidered and amended, so that it read:

"Only such losses, damages or expenses which are the direct consequence of the general average act shall be allowed as general average.

Loss or damage sustained by the ship or cargo through delay, whether on the voyage or subsequently, such as demurrage, and any indirect loss whatsoever, such as loss of market, shall not be admitted as general average."

The amendment was designed to make it clear that the consequences of delay occurring after the completion of the voyage were equally inadmissible in general average, as were the consequences of delay during the voyage. The intention was to close the door to the argument that as the 1924 Rule referred only to delay on the voyage, and did not mention subsequent delay, it could be said that the consequences of subsequent delay might be admitted in general average in some circumstances. So far as English law is concerned, that argument had been rejected in *Wetherall & Co.* v. *London Assurance*.[1] In that

1. *Wetherall & Co.* v. *London Assurance* [1931] 2 K.B. 448; 36 Com. Cas. 181.

case a ship had been placed off-hire for a period of repairs after the end of the voyage, during which repairs of sacrificial damage were effected. The shipowner claimed in general average the loss of hire for the period of time that the vessel was off-hire for those repairs. That claim was denied.

There was no change in 1974.

The Rule was substantially altered in 1994, chiefly by the insertion of a new (second) paragraph excluding from general average any losses, damages or expenses incurred in respect of damage to the environment or in consequence of the escape or release of pollutant substances from the property involved in the common maritime adventure.

The alteration in the third paragraph consisted of a rearrangement of the 1974 text to take into account that in the English case of *Czarnikow* v. *Koufos*[2] loss of market had been held to be a direct, and not an indirect loss.

COMMENTARY: THE RULE AS TO CONSEQUENCES

Lowndes and Rudolf state that the terms of Rule C reproduce the English common law *as it was then understood*. However, since that time English law has moved on. As Lord Denning M.R. said in *Australian Coastal Shipping Commission* v. *Green*,[3] "At the time when the Rules were made in 1924, all lawyers thought that they could tell the difference between 'direct' and 'indirect' consequences. The distinction had been hallowed by the great authority of Lord Sumner in *Weld-Blundell* v. *Stephens*[4] . . . Naturally enough, therefore, the framers of the York-Antwerp Rules used it too. But forty years later the Privy Council poured scorn upon it [in *The Wagon Mound*[5]]." After commenting on this decision, Lord Denning continued: "In these circumstances I propose to go back to the concept, as I understood it in 1924, when the York-Antwerp Rules were made. 'Direct consequences' denote those consequences which flow in an unbroken sequence from the act: whereas 'indirect consequences' are those in which the sequence is broken by an intervening or extraneous cause. I realise that this is not very helpful: because the metaphor of 'breaking the chain' of causation means one thing to one man and another thing to another. But still we have to do the best we can with it."

This last-quoted passage has led the editors of Lowndes & Rudolf to suggest that the test of remoteness of damage in general average cases, having crystallised at 1924, is now different from the test of remoteness at common law. In the earlier English law cases as to the consequences of a general average

2. *Czarnikow* v. *Koufos* [1969] 1 A.C. 350; [1967] 2 Lloyd's Rep. 457.
3. *Australian Coastal Shipping Commission* v. *Green* [1971] 1 Q.B. 456; [1971] 1 Lloyd's Rep. 16.
4. *Weld-Blundell* v. *Stephens* [1920] A.C. 956.
5. *The Wagon Mound* [1961] A.C. 388; [1961] 1 Lloyd's Rep. 1.

act, two slightly differing tests were cited. The first is the test of Lowndes who, after referring to the general rule as to remoteness of damage, as laid out in "Mayne on Damages" (3rd ed., p. 39):

"The first, and in fact the only enquiry in all these cases is, whether the damage complained of is the natural and reasonable result of the defendant's act; it will assume this character if it can be shown to be such a consequence as in the ordinary course of things would flow from the act, or, in cases of contract, if it appears to have been contemplated by both parties",

went on to say:

"applying this Rule more closely to general average, it may be thought that, since we have to determine *quod pro omnibus datum est*, and since giving must always imply an intention to give, what we have here to ascertain must be, what loss at once has in fact occurred, and likewise must be regarded as the natural and reasonable result of the act of sacrifice? Or, in other words, what the shipmaster would naturally, or might reasonably have intended to give for all when he resolved upon the act? If then, upon the act of sacrifice any loss ensues, which the master did not in fact bring before his mind at the time of making the sacrifice, it would have to be considered whether it were a loss of which he naturally might or reasonably ought to have taken account."

The second test was proposed by Ulrich in his work *Grosse-Haverei*:

"General average comprises not only the damage purposely done to ship and cargo, but also (1) all damage or expense which was to be foreseen as the natural (immediate) consequence of the first sacrifice, since this unmistakenly forms part of that which was *given* for the common safety; (2) all damage or expense which, though not to be foreseen, stands to the sacrifice in relation of effect to cause, or, in other words, was its *necessary* consequence. Not so, however, those losses or expenses which, though they would not have occurred but for the sacrifice, yet, likewise, would not have occurred but for some subsequent accident."

CASES

It may be convenient to consider the English law cases in two categories; first, those touching upon consequences generally, and secondly those involving liabilities to third parties.

Generally as to consequences

In *McCall* v. *Houlder Bros.*[6] a vessel put into a port of refuge with damage to her propeller. There were no facilities for storing the cargo, which was perishable, and so the vessel was tipped by the head in order to effect the propeller repairs. In consequence some water escaped through a broken pipe and damaged some of the cargo. The damage to the cargo was allowed in general average,

6. *McCall* v. *Houlder Bros.* (1897) 66 L.J.Q.B. 408; 2 Com. Cas. 129.

since the tipping was held to be a general average act undertaken for the preservation of both ship and cargo.

In *Anglo-Argentine Livestock Agency* v. *Temperley*[7] the vessel was carrying livestock from the River Plate to England. On the voyage she sprang a leak and the vessel put in to Bahia (in Brazil) as a port of refuge. In consequence of this, as the master knew, the landing of the animals in England would be prohibited under an Order in Council then in force, and in the event they were taken to Antwerp, where the market price was less than in England. Bigham J., approving the Lowndes test, allowed the loss on sale as a direct and immediate consequence of the general average act of putting into Bahia.

In *Anglo-Grecian Steam Trading Co.* v. *Beynon*[8] a ship which was holed and immobilised by fouling a mooring chain was taken under tow to a place where she could be safely beached. In fact, owing to the parting of the tow-ropes in bad weather, the vessel took the ground in a place which had not been intended, and the question for decision was whether the damage she sustained by grounding could be allowed in general average. Roche J., applying the Ulrich test, found that "although the grounding on the rocks was not at any rate foreseen as either a necessary or even a probable consequence by the pilot, yet it was not a subsequent accident unconnected with the grounding".

In each of these cases the York-Antwerp Rules 1890 applied, and since they pre-dated the introduction of the lettered Rules, they should be taken to illustrate the application of English law principles to the question of remoteness of damage.

In *Eisenerz GmbH* v. *Federal Commerce and Navigation Co. Ltd.*[9] the cargo consisted of metal ingots of different specifications, which had to be discharged at a port of refuge in order to enable damage to the ship to be repaired. After the repairs, the cargo was reloaded, but at destination it was found that ingots of different specifications had become mixed. On being sued under the bill of lading, the shipowners defended the claim by arguing that the loss due to admixture was allowable in general average under Rule XII, but the judge found as a fact that the admixture was due to a failure on the part of the master and the general average surveyor to control the stacking of the ingots at the port of refuge. The loss was therefore not a direct consequence of the general average act. It is submitted that the result of the case would have been different if it had been found as a fact that owing to the limited facilities at the port of refuge, some degree of admixture would inevitably have taken place or should have been foreseeable.

Comparison may be made with an instance of a loss properly allowable in general average cited by Lord Tenterden in his book on Shipping:

7. *Anglo-Argentine Livestock Agency* v. *Temperley* [1899] 2 Q.B. 403; 4 Com.Cas. 281.

8. *Anglo-Grecian Steam Trading Co.* v. *Beynon* (1926) 24 Ll.L.Rep. 122.

9. *Eisenerz GmbH* v. *Federal Commerce and Navigation Co. Ltd. (The Oak Hill)* [1970] 2 Lloyd's Rep. 332, affirmed [1975] 1 Lloyd's Rep. 105.

"So, if, to avoid an impending danger, or to repair the damage occasioned by a storm, the ship be compelled to take refuge in a port to which it was not destined, and into which it cannot enter without taking out a part of her cargo, and the part taken out to lighten the ship on this occasion happens to be lost in the barges employed to convey it to the shore, this loss also, being occasioned by the removal of the goods for the general benefit, must be repaired by general contribution."[10]

Liabilities to third parties

In *Austin Friars S.S. Co.* v. *Spillers & Bakers*[11] a ship was in danger of sinking and in order to bring her into dock it was expected by both the master and the pilot that she might strike against a pier in the course of that manoeuvre. The ship did strike the pier and caused damage to it. Bailhache J., after referring to section 66 of the Marine Insurance Act 1906 and quoting with approval both the Lowndes and Ulrich tests, held that the liability of the shipowner in tort to the owners of the pier was properly to be admitted in general average, as well as the damage sustained by the ship.

This case was followed by *The Seapool*,[12] where the facts were similar. In that case the York-Antwerp Rules 1924 applied to the adjustment of general average, although Langton J. relied upon the terms of Rule A, rather than Rule C, in support of his judgment in favour of the shipowners' claim.

Another instance of the admission in general average of claims for tortious liability arose from the efforts to refloat a ship which had stranded close to a canal bank in the St. Lawrence Seaway. In the efforts to refloat, an excessive wash was created which caused damage to the properties of a number of riparian owners. The amounts paid by the shipowner in settlement of those claims were admitted in general average without objection by any party to the adjustment.

Liability under contract

Australian Coastal Shipping Commission v. *Green*[13] concerned two cases where the shipowners' servants or agents had hired tugs on the terms of the U.K. Standard Towage Conditions to assist their vessels in distress. In both cases the tugs, whilst assisting the vessels in distress, had their propellers fouled by broken tow-ropes, as a result of which in one case the tug, being without

10. *Abbott on Shipping* (5th ed.), p. 346; (13th ed.), p. 630; quoted with approval by: Cresswell J. in *Hallet* v. *Wigram* (1850) 9 C.B. 580 at p. 608; Mathew J. in *McCall* v. *Houlder Brothers* (1897) 2 Com. Cas. 129; Denning M.R. in *Australian Coastal Shipping Commission* v. *Green* [1971] 1 Lloyd's Rep. at p. 21.

11. *Austin Friars S.S. Co.* v. *Spillers & Bakers* [1915] 3 K.B. 586; 20 Com. Cas. 100 and 342.

12. *The Seapool* [1934] P. 53; 47 Ll.L.Rep. 331.

13. *Australian Coastal Shipping Commission* v. *Green* [1971] 1 Q.B. 456; [1971] 1 Lloyd's Rep. 16.

usable anchors, grounded and became a total loss; and in the other case the tug was saved only by the exertions of salvors.

In both cases the tug owners claimed an indemnity from the shipowners under Clause 3 of the U.K. Standard Towage Conditions; and the shipowners paid and claimed in general average: in the first case, legal costs incurred in successfully defending the claim of the tug owners; and in the second case, the amount of the salvage remuneration incurred by the tug owners.

Mocatta J. held in favour of the shipowners' claims in both cases, and his judgment was affirmed by a strong Court of Appeal. Lord Denning M.R. held that in each case the contract made by the shipowners with the tug was a general average act; that the terms of the U.K. Standard Towage Conditions were reasonable, and that the amounts which the shipowners would have to pay under the indemnities required by the contract flowed in unbroken sequence from the general average act. Lord Denning did not approve of that part of the Ulrich test which suggests that when, after a general average act, there is a "subsequent accident" which results in loss or damage, it breaks the chain of causation. In Lord Denning's words: "in both cases before us, the master, when he engaged the tug, should have envisaged that it was distinctly possible that the tow-line might break and foul the propeller. When it happened, therefore, it did not break the chain of causation." Phillimore and Cairns L.JJ., however, considered that the last sentence of the Ulrich test was inapplicable in this case, since it refers only to instances where the general average act is a sacrifice.

Lord Denning was at pains to emphasise that the amounts payable by the shipowners in terms of the contract must be reasonable. As he said, "if the indemnity clause had been unreasonable and such that the master ought never, in justice to the cargo-owners, to have agreed to it, then I think that the expenditure would not flow from the general average act."

THE ENVIRONMENTAL ISSUE

The new second paragraph enshrines the first part of the compromise proposal put forward by the British Maritime Law Association to deal with the vexed question of environmental liabilities and avoidance measures. At one extreme stood the United States proposal to introduce a second Rule Paramount which would have stated baldly that "in no event shall there be an Allowance in general average for pollution liability or clean-up of pollutants", without indicating how the cost of environmental damage avoidance measures would be treated. At the other end of the spectrum were those who advocated no change, either in Rule C or anywhere else. This polarisation reflected the positions respectively of property underwriters and P. & I. Clubs: the argument of the former being that property underwriters would not be willing in present circumstances to accept any obligation to meet pollution or environmental liabilities through the back door, whereas the latter, relying upon the English law decisions in *Austin Friars* v. *Spillers & Bakers* and *The Seapool*, considered that the 1974 text of the YAR effectively nodded through the admission of all liabilities to third parties resulting from a general average act.

The environmental issue was first raised in the CMI document entitled "Chairman's Preliminary Report and Questionnaire" dated 3 July 1991, and the study which followed rapidly divided the issue into two questions: whether or not to admit in general average

— a. liabilities for pollution or other environmental damage resulting from a general average act, and

— b. the cost of measures taken to avoid environmental damage, particularly when such measures were required as a condition of entering or remaining at a port or place of refuge.

As an addendum to the report of the CMI International Sub-Committee issued in July 1993, a questionnaire on the subject was sent out to national Maritime Law Associations and also to members of the AIDE Sub-Committee.

The replies from the latter source showed that in the common law countries there was no shortage of authority to justify the allowance in general average of liabilities to third parties arising out of a general average act, even though the liabilities were for pollution or other environmental damage. However, the responses from France, Germany and Italy indicated that in those countries there would be no allowance in general average in any case of liabilities incurred or damages sustained to the environment. The British response may have been influenced by the reference which appears in the 10th and 11th editions of Lowndes & Rudolf to an arbitration in a case where in order to refloat a stranded tanker a quantity of oil was jettisoned, giving rise to a claim for pollution. In the arbitration the shipowners' claim to admit in general average the cost of settling their liability for oil pollution was allowed, being both the direct and foreseeable consequence of the jettison.

Similar replies were given by AIDE members regarding the allowance in practice of the cost of measures taken to avoid pollution or environmental damage, save that in France and Germany the cost of such preventive measures was considered to be admissible in general average if imposed by public authorities as a precondition to a vessel's entry into, remaining at or departure from a port of refuge within the terms of Rule X of the York-Antwerp Rules.

Such was the foundation upon which the BMLA built their compromise proposal to exclude from general average all environmental damage liabilities, but to allow the cost of environmental damage avoidance measures in certain restricted circumstances.

During the final twelve months prior to the Sydney Conference, it became clear that the trend towards the exclusion of environmental damage liabilities had become virtually irresistible. There were two main reasons for this:

— the moral ground; that the institution of general average should not be seen to encourage the deliberate pollution of the environment, and
— the practical ground; that the determination of environmental liabilities, including clean-up costs, damages for restitution and economic losses, would lead to unconscionable delay in the issue of a general average adjustment.

The amendment originally proposed by the BMLA included a direct reference to "liabilities" in both the existing first paragraph as well as the new second paragraph of the Rule, but this was perceived by some delegates and observers as creating an apparent expansion in the area of non-environmental damages. The compromise solution ultimately favoured was to match the words in the exclusion for environmental damage to the words in the existing first paragraph, i.e. "losses, damages or expenses". In answer to a direct question, Lord Donaldson of Lymington, the leader of the British delegation, expressed the opinion that these words were wide enough to comprehend all liabilities for environmental damage, whereupon the U.S. delegation issued a unilateral statement in the following terms:

"The Delegation of the United States of America understands that the proposed York-Antwerp Rules 1994 exclude allowances in general average in respect of liability in consequence of the escape or release of pollutant substances from the property involved in the common maritime adventure."

The second part of the BMLA proposal regarding environmental damage concerned the circumstances in which the cost of measures to prevent or minimise damage to the environment would be allowed when undertaken as part of the general average act. For the sake of clarity of interpretation, it was essential that this provision should appear in a numbered rule,[14] so that in the event of any inconsistency, its wording should take precedence over the general exclusion contained in Rule C. The U.S. delegation, who had originally proposed that pollution liabilities should be excluded in a Rule Paramount, objected to the British proposal, arguing that it would leave open the possibility of the admission of damage sustained by third parties through the operation of the numbered Rules. This argument was met by amending Rules II, V and VIII by specifying that the admission of consequent loss or damage in the circumstances set out in those rules should be limited to "the property involved in the common maritime adventure". The effect of this is that claims for loss or damage suffered by third parties in consequence of a sacrifice (Rule II), a voluntary stranding (Rule V) or a general average discharge of cargo, fuel or stores (Rule VIII) can no longer be argued to arise

14. See Rule XI(d), p. 183 *et seq.*

under those numbered Rules; they can only be entertained by applying Rule C with all its newly acquired rigour.[15]

GENERAL EXCEPTIONS

The third paragraph (previously the second paragraph) continues to express in general terms the kinds of loss or damage which, although consequent on a general average act, shall not be admitted in general average. These exceptions are:

"Demurrage"

This means specifically any claim for demurrage which is payable under a voyage charterparty by reason of time expended by the ship which is involved in the general average act. Examples would be:

- additional time spent at a port of loading in consequence of discharging part cargo for the common safety and afterwards reloading it;
- a delay in the commencement of loading under a subsequent charterparty by reason of the necessity to effect repairs of sacrificial damage sustained to ship.

However, the exclusion does not extend to demurrage on other vessels chartered by the shipowner for the purpose of a general average operation, e.g. storage of cargo in barges at a port of refuge.

"Loss of market"

This is a heavy and, in the author's opinion, a rather unfair exclusion. It would have the effect of denying the admission in general average of a claim for financial loss suffered by an owner of cargo as a result of losing his market in consequence of the ship having to put into a port of refuge, such as was the case in *Anglo-Argentine Livestock Agency* v. *Temperley*.[16]

"Loss, damage or expense incurred by reason of delay . . . "

Once again, this exclusion probably hits owners of cargo fairly frequently by denying claims for the deterioration of perishable commodities by reason of the ship's detention in a port of refuge. However, the exclusion also follows

15. See the example given in the commentary on Rule V, p. 119.

16. See facts and citation on p. 50. The opinion stated in the text is maintained, notwithstanding a contrary view expressed in the 11th edition of Lowndes & Rudolf.

English law in extending to losses of time charter hire suffered by shipowners during repairs to the ship. Such losses may occur:

- — during the voyage; see *The Leitrim*[17] (a case heard prior to the introduction of the lettered rules);
- — after the end of the voyage; see *Wetherall & Co.* v. *The London Assurance*[18] (a case decided under the York-Antwerp Rules, 1924).

" . . . any indirect loss whatsoever . . . "

This rarely used exclusion is none the less desirable, in that it provides justification for the exclusion of some of the more fanciful claims which an average adjuster from time to time receives.

17. *The Leitrim* [1902] P. 256.
18. *Wetherall & Co.* v. *London Assurance* [1931] 2 K.B. 448; 36 Com. Cas. 181.

RULE D

Rights to contribution in general average shall not be affected, though the event which gave rise to the sacrifice or expenditure may have been due to the fault of one of the parties to the adventure, but this shall not prejudice any remedies or defences which may be open against or to that party in respect of such fault.

EVOLUTION

This Rule had its origin in the text of a Rule recommended for adoption at a Conference held in Antwerp in 1903, which read:

"Rights to contribution in general average shall not be affected though the danger which gave rise to the sacrifice, or expenditure, may have been due to default of one of the parties to the adventure; but this shall not prejudice any remedies which may be open against that party for such default."

Although accepted by the Conference, the Antwerp Rule 1903 was not generally introduced into contracts of affreightment, possibly because it did no more than embody existing law in most, if not all, maritime countries.

The text of the Antwerp Rule 1903 was reintroduced and adopted at the Stockholm Conference in 1924, with the substitution of the word "event" for "danger", and "fault" for "default".

In 1974, the reference to "defences . . . to" was added to supplement "remedies . . . against".

In its work prior to the Sydney Conference, the AIDE subjected both the terms and the practice applying under Rule D to hard and critical scrutiny. A working group under the chairmanship of Mr Jan Sandström of Gothenburg was commissioned to study and report as to whether there was a need for revision or amendment of Rule D, particularly in view of the entry into force of the Hamburg Rules. In his analysis of the position Mr Sandström observed:

"The law of general average and the law of the carriage of goods by sea have developed quite separately. The basic concepts behind the two branches of the law are quite different and there seems to be good and valid arguments in favour of the opinion that they should not be confused and that the question of GA contributions should be dealt with and disposed of before the second question, deciding whose fault it was that the circumstances of the general average situation existed. It seems further that since the Hamburg Rules tilt the scales against the carrier on the question of presumed fault, commercial interests should at least consider, as a matter of equity, whether the concerned in cargo ought to acknowledge their obligation to pay their general average contributions before seeking to exercise their rights of recourse. In this context it is also interesting to note that whereas a cargo claimant, who has suffered damage, has to suffer the burden of commencing legal proceedings in order to exercise his right of recourse against the carrier, the cargo objector, who claims to exert his right to decline to pay his general average contribution, has merely to sit on his hands and wait to be sued."

and later in his report:

"Article 24.2 of the Hamburg Rules expressly recognises that the cargo interest seeking recourse may already have paid his general average contribution or his proportion of salvage. Hence a clause in the contract of carrier creating an obligation to pay general average contribution before seeking recourse could not be objected to on the ground that it contravened the Hamburg Rules."

On the whole, members of the International Sub-Committee, recognising the limitations of their mandate as representatives of a service industry, were inclined towards a more cautious report, but in the event the AIDE General Assembly, by a majority, passed a resolution recommending that consideration be given, on the grounds of equity and to accelerate the settlement of general average cases, to an amendment to Rule D to make rights of recourse subject to settlement under an adjustment.

Although there was a fair deal of sympathy with this idea, it was not in harmony with the stricter views prevailing at Sydney, and no national delegation was prepared to promote it further.

As stated in Lowndes and Rudolf, Rule D does not alter the common law of England. However, its importance lies in the fact that it makes it abundantly clear that when a general average situation exists the sacrifices made and expenditure incurred which qualify as general average shall be the subject of an adjustment even though the general average situation would not have arisen but for the fault of the claimant.

EFFECT OF THE FAULT OF THE CLAIMANT

When sacrifices have been made and expenditure incurred by the shipowner, he will not be entitled to recover cargo's contribution to those sacrifices and expenditures where the event giving rise to the general average act was due to his *actionable* fault, that is to say when the event was one which would entitle the cargo interest to counter-claim under the contract of carriage. In English common law, this meant that when the event giving rise to the general average was an excepted peril under the contract of carriage, the shipowner could recover, whereas if the event was one for which the shipowner was liable, he could be unable to recover. As Lord Hannen said in *The Carron Park*[1]:

"Negligence for which he [the shipowner] is not responsible is as foreign to him as to the person who has suffered by it."

This principle was subsequently approved and confirmed in the case of *Milburn* v. *Jamaica Fruit Importing Co.*[2]

When the Hague-Visby Rules apply to the contract of carriage, the doctrine is different, and the shipowner will only be entitled to recover when the event that gives rise to the general average act is not due to unseaworthiness, or if due to unseaworthiness, he (the shipowner) can demonstrate that he exercised due diligence before and at the beginning of the voyage to provide a seaworthy ship; *and* that the event was one of those for the consequences of which the shipowner is exonerated from liability under Article III, r. 1.

Thus, for example, if the vessel strands and is in a position of peril, general average sacrifices and expenditure incurred to refloat her will be general average and cargo's proportion will be recoverable if the stranding was due to an error in navigation; not so, however, if the stranding was due to the failure of the steering gear owing to a defect in it which was in existence at the beginning of the voyage, and which the shipowner, by the exercise of due diligence, should have found and corrected.

As to the burden of proof, a cargo interest seeking to decline payment of a general average contribution on the ground of unseaworthiness has to produce positive evidence:

(a) that the vessel was unseaworthy, and
(b) that the unseaworthiness was causally connected with the general average.

If he establishes both these propositions, the burden of proof then shifts to the carrier who will have to prove that he had exercised due diligence to make the vessel seaworthy.[3]

The fact that the concerned in cargo or other innocent party may decline to pay its general average contribution does not, however, invalidate the shipowner's claim in general average as regards his insurances: subject to the law governing the insurance, the shipowner will be able to recover under his hull policy his claims for sacrifice of ship and ship's proportion of general average expenditure. Under English law, a claim under a time policy on ship for loss, damage or expense proximately caused by an insured peril will not be vitiated by the vessel's unseaworthiness unless the shipowner has been guilty of

1. *The Carron Park* (1890) 15 P.D. 203; 6 Asp. M.C. 543.
2. *Milburn* v. *Jamaica Fruit Importing Co.* [1900] 2 Q.B. 540; 5 Com. Cas. 346, affirming 4 Com. Cas. 331.
3. N. G. Hudson, Chairman's Address to the Association of Average Adjusters, 1973; reprinted in *From the Chair*, p. 103. This paragraph respecting the burden of proof was quoted with approval by Buglass, *Marine Insurance and General Average in the United States* (2nd ed.), p. 301.

sending the ship to sea in an unseaworthy condition at the commencement of the risk, with knowledge and privity of that unseaworthiness. Hence, in a large majority of cases, an adjustment will be required in order to show the claim upon the shipowner's hull insurances.

In the event of the cargo interests having justifiable grounds for declining to pay their general average contribution on account of a breach of the contract of carriage, a shipowner who has entered his vessel in a P. & I. Club will almost certainly be entitled, subject to the Club Rules, to claim reimbursement for cargo's proportion of his general average expenditure not recoverable solely by reason of such breach.

WHERE THE FAULT IS THAT OF A PARTY OTHER THAN THE CLAIMANT

Here a different situation applies. The claimant is clearly entitled to have his loss or expense admitted in general average, but he will also enjoy a concurrent right to recover his loss or expenditure as damages from the party at fault.

If the party at fault is the shipowner, a cargo claimant is likely to repudiate the general average adjustment, even though he may appear as a creditor in the final balance; consequently, in this event, the shipowner is not precluded from collecting the contributions due from his hull underwriters, nor from such other cargo interests as are unaffected by the shipowner's wrongdoing or who have not raised it as a defence. Following this logic, it would appear to make no difference whether the claim in damages of the cargo claimant is settled before or after the issue of the general average adjustment. If before, the shipowner is entitled to retain the contributions of the other parties, as contributions to the loss which he had settled; if after the issue and liquidation of the general average adjustment, the cargo claimant will be obliged to give credit for the general average contributions which he has received towards his loss under the general law as to mitigation of damages.

If the fault is that of a shipper or charterer, for example, for having presented for shipment dangerous cargo without giving notice, the position in practice is more akin to that where a recovery is sought from a third party not involved in the common maritime venture; the only difference being that any general average contribution due from and in fact paid by the party at fault should be credited against the amount sought to be recovered by way of damages.

POSITION IN THE UNITED STATES

The Harter Act 1893 provided that if a shipowner had exercised due care to make the vessel seaworthy, neither he, the vessel, her agent nor her charterers would be liable for damage or loss arising from (*inter alia*) faults or errors in navigation, or in the management of the vessel. However, the Supreme Court in the case of *The Irrawaddy*[4] held that this apparent exoneration from liability did not have the effect of entitling the shipowner to claim a contribution in general average arising out of an accident due to his servants' negligence. It is therefore general practice to include in all bills of lading issued for shipments to and from the United States a clause designed to remedy this position. This is the "Jason Clause", so called after the case in which the Supreme Court pronounced its validity.[5] The effect of the judgment in *The Jason* was that:

(a) the Clause was valid and entitled the shipowner to collect general average contribution from cargo;
(b) the cargo owners had a right to contribution from the shipowner for sacrifices of cargo, and
(c) the cargo owners were not entitled to recover contribution from the shipowner towards their loss without also contributing to the shipowner's losses and expenditure.

Now, by virtue of the Carriage of Goods by Sea Act 1936, the shipowner's position has been somewhat ameliorated, in that the unseaworthiness of the vessel (if due diligence has not been exercised) is only relevant if the loss or damage results from it. However, contracts of affreightment for voyages to and from United States ports will continue to include a general average negligence clause, generally referred to as the "New Jason Clause", which reads as follows:

"Where the adjustment is made in accordance with the law and practice of the United States of America, the following clause shall apply:

> 'In the event of accident, danger, damage or disaster before or after the commencement of the voyage, resulting from any cause whatsoever, whether due to negligence or not, for which, or for the consequences of which, the carrier is not responsible, by Statute, contract or otherwise, the goods, shippers, consignees or owners of the goods shall contribute with the carrier in general average to the payment of any sacrifices, losses, or expenses of a general average nature that may be made or incurred and shall pay salvage and special charges incurred in respect of the goods.' "

4. *The Irrawaddy* (1898) 171 U.S. 187.
5. *The Jason* (1908) 225 U.S. 32.

RULE E

The onus of proof is upon the party claiming in general average to show that the loss or expense claimed is properly allowable as general average.

All parties claiming in general average shall give notice in writing to the average adjuster of the loss or expense in respect of which they claim contribution within 12 months of the date of the termination of the common maritime adventure.

Failing such notification, or if within 12 months of a request for the same any of the parties shall fail to supply evidence in support of a notified claim, or particulars of value in respect of a contributory interest, the average adjuster shall be at liberty to estimate the extent of the allowance or the contributory value on the basis of the information available to him, which estimate may be challenged only on the ground that it is manifestly incorrect.

EVOLUTION

The first paragraph of the present text formed the original Rule, which was introduced in 1924, and remained unaltered until 1994.

At the Hamburg Conference in 1974 it was proposed to add a further paragraph reading: "Thereafter the onus of proof is upon the party refusing to contribute in general average to show that he is not liable to contribute." This proposal was not accepted, not because it was incorrect but because it was thought to trespass upon the province of Rule D.

In the run-up to the Sydney Conference in 1994, attention was focused upon the problem which had arisen from time to time when parties claiming in general average failed to give timely notice of their intention to claim or, having done so, failed to produce adequate evidence in support of their claim in spite of being requested to do so. The average adjusters on the CMI International Sub-Committee were invited to give their attention to this problem with a view to recommending whether or not it would be feasible to impose a cut-off, either by a provision in the York-Antwerp Rules or otherwise. This was a shrewd move, since average adjusters were only too frequently blamed for the length of time taken to produce average adjustments due not to their inefficiency, but to the dilatoriness of the parties in producing essential evidence. The AIDE passed the question to one of their working groups and in the event the General Assembly at Prague in September 1993 approved a proposal to recommend the following text as an addition to Rule E:

"All parties claiming in general average shall give notice in writing to the average adjuster of their claims in general average within 12 months of the date of the termination of the common maritime adventure.

If this requirement is not complied with, or if after having been requested by the average adjuster to furnish particulars of the claims of which notice has been given, any of the parties shall fail within 12 months of such request to supply the required particulars, the average adjuster shall be at liberty to estimate the extent of the claims admissible in general average on the basis of the information then available to him, which estimate may be challenged only on the ground that the average adjuster has acted unreasonably.

The parties shall also furnish the average adjuster with particulars of the value of their interests within 12 months of their having been requested for the same, failing which the average adjuster shall determine the contributory value on the basis of the information available to him, and the party concerned may not challenge the estimated value thus arrived at."

By the time the Sydney Conference took place the BMLA, conscious that the proposal had gathered considerable momentum in the meantime, undertook to propose a shorter version prepared by the drafting committee appointed by the ISC in December 1993, and incorporating so far as possible the same features as had been recommended by the AIDE After debate and a relatively minor amendment (referred to below in the Commentary) the proposal was accepted by a substantial majority.

COMMENTARY

The 1924 Rule (the present first paragraph) had been criticised for stating a truism, in that it merely repeated settled law in all countries. However, in the opinion of the author it is desirable to include this statement of principle in the text of the York-Antwerp Rules, and it certainly assists the average adjuster in his task for two important practical reasons:

1. It requires the claimant to produce documentary evidence of the matters relied upon to justify his claim, and
2. It reduces the number of opportunities for argument when the evidence is insufficient to justify allowance in general average.

The "cut-off" provisions

The cut-off provisions—paragraphs two and three—introduce an element of compulsion, backed by what may turn out to be an inadequate sanction. Even so, the author suspects that they will not be universally popular. Indeed it is quite remarkable the number of occasions when, either through incompetence or for some financial reason that can only be guessed at, commercial interests have been curiously dilatory in putting forward claims, whether for amounts to be admitted in general average or for reduction of their contributory values. That this dilatoriness seriously inconveniences other parties to the general average appears not to worry the defaulters one iota. New procedures will have to evolve to deal with the cut-off provisions:

1. Notification

The shipowner will effectively have given his notice of a claim in general average by the appointment of an average adjuster; and that state of affairs will be made known to all cargo interests either by a declaration of general average, where that is the recognised procedure, and/or by a demand for general average security accompanied by the appropriate forms, e.g. an average bond and/or an underwriters' guarantee. In practice, one or more of these documents, or the correspondence covering them, will surely mention the name and address of the nominated average adjuster. Thereafter, in terms of the Rule, the parties so advised have 12 months, measured from the date of the termination of the common maritime adventure, in which to give notice in writing to the average adjuster of any loss or expense in respect of which they claim contribution in general average.

2. Evidence in support of a claim and particulars of contributory value

In practice, the average adjuster will check the information supplied as soon as he receives the general average security documents. In most cases—particularly when those documents include a Lloyd's form of average bond (LAB 77), to which a valuation form is attached—he may expect a copy of the commercial invoice to be supplied by the cargo receiver, but if this is not forthcoming, it will clearly be prudent for the average adjuster to make a prompt request for this document. Similarly, the average adjuster will be responsible in all cases where other documents before him, e.g. ship's log books or surveyors' reports, have indicated that some cargo may have suffered loss or damage, to make a prompt request for particulars of the same. In both instances a new 12 month period will start to run, during which time the cargo receiver or his underwriter must furnish particulars of the value of his cargo and/or evidence in support of any claim.

If the average adjuster does not receive satisfactory information as to value or evidence in support of any potential claim within 12 months of his requesting the same, the Rule states that he shall be at liberty to estimate the extent of the allowance or the contributory value on the basis of other information which may be available to him, so as to enable him to complete the adjustment without any further delay. There has to be a safeguard of course, and this is provided in the closing words of the Rule which state that if the average adjuster, being without the requested information, has been obliged to assess the contributory value of one or more interests, or the extent of any claim, on the basis of "the information available to him", his estimate may be challenged if it is "manifestly incorrect".

There was a serious discussion at the Sydney Conference as to how this right of challenge should be expressed. In the text recommended by the International Sub-Committee, which was in effect an abbreviation of the proposal originally recommended by the AIDE, the only ground of challenge was that the average adjuster had acted unreasonably in arriving at his estimate. The delegates at Sydney preferred an objective, rather than subjective, test and the counter-proposal was that the adjuster's estimate could be challenged when it was "grossly incorrect". In reply to this, it was pointed out that this test provided no guidance for the average adjuster, since *ex hypothesi* he would have no information before him by which to judge whether his estimate was widely or only narrowly different from the true figure. Hence the Conference settled for "manifestly incorrect", which expression, in the opinion of the author, must mean incorrect on the basis of information known to the average adjuster, not that which was withheld from him.

RULE F

Any additional expense incurred in place of another expense which would have been allowable as general average shall be deemed to be general average and so allowed without regard to the saving, if any, to other interests, but only up to the amount of the general average expense avoided.

EVOLUTION

This Rule, in common with the other lettered Rules, was introduced in 1924. However, although the other lettered Rules restated the generally accepted law of all maritime countries, the principle of substituted expenses expounded by Rule F was by no means hallowed by the jurisprudence of all nations.

The position under English law was particularly critical. In *Wilson* v. *Bank of Victoria*[1] the Court of Queen's Bench held that the purchase of coals to work the auxiliary engine of a sailing ship, incurred in place of the greater expense of repairing masts and spars damaged in a storm, should not be made the subject of general average contribution, since it was the shipowner's duty under the contract of affreightment to adopt the most economical course available to him. On the other hand, in *Lee* v. *Southern Insurance*[2] the principle of substituted expenses was applied to a claim under a policy of insurance on freight for the cost of forwarding cargo to destination by rail from a port where the voyage had been abandoned; judgment was given for only so much of the rail freight as would properly have formed a charge on the freight if the cargo had been reloaded and forwarded by sea.

This uncertainty as to the direction which English law was taking caused the Association of Average Adjusters to adopt two Rules of Practice in 1876 in order to chart a fair course in those circumstances where the saving of expenses could be clearly demonstrated, *viz*:

1. *Wilson* v. *Bank of Victoria* (1867) L.R. 2 Q.B. 203; 2 Mar. L. C. 449.
2. *Lee* v. *Southern Insurance Co.* (1870) L.R. 5 C.P. 397.

AAA Rule of Practice F14 (previously B16)

"*Towage from a port of refuge*

That if a ship be in a port of refuge at which it is practicable to repair her, and if, in order to save expense, she be towed thence to some other port, then the extra cost of such towage shall be divided in proportion to the saving of expense thereby occasioned to the several parties to the adventure."

AAA Rule of Practice F15 (previously B17)

"*Cargo forwarded from a port of refuge*

That if a ship be in a port of refuge at which it is practicable to repair her so as to enable her to carry on the whole cargo, but, in order to save expense, the cargo, or a portion of it, be transhipped by another vessel, or otherwise forwarded, then the cost of such transhipment (up to the amount of expense saved) shall be divided in proportion to the saving of expense thereby occasioned to the several parties to the adventure."

This was pretty stern stuff, given the judicial disapproval of the principle of substituted expenses expressed in *Wilson*'s case. The reference to the division of the extra costs in proportion to the savings occasioned to the several parties to the adventure reflected English law and practice as to the treatment of expenses incurred at a port of refuge, which at that time was to allow in general average the cost of putting in to the port of refuge and discharging the cargo, but to treat the cost of storing the cargo as a special charge thereon, and its reloading, together with the outward port charges, as a special charge on freight.[3]

The Association of Average Adjusters, fortified by their own practice, duly presented a text based upon the above-quoted Rules of Practice as one of their proposals at the 1890 Liverpool Conference, which was agreed without a dissenting vote. After the renumbering of the Rules, this became Rule X(d) of the York-Antwerp Rules 1890:

"If a ship under average be in a port or place at which it is practicable to repair her, so as to enable her to carry on the whole cargo, and if, in order to save expenses, either she is towed thence to some other port or place of repair or to her destination, or the cargo or a portion of it is transhipped by another ship, or otherwise forwarded, then the extra cost of towage, transhipment, and forwarding, or any of them, (up to the amount of the extra expense saved) shall be payable by the several parties to the adventure in proportion to the extraordinary expense saved."

Since under the preceding paragraphs of Rule X the expenses of storing and reloading cargo, as well as the outward port charges, were now all within the ambit of general average, the reference in Rule X(d) to the saving to the various parties of the adventure had a new significance. Henceforth, as was made clear by Mr Charles McArthur in introducing the subject at the Liverpool Conference, regard must be had not only to the savings in general

3. For the way in which English law and practice developed in this respect, see the history and development of Rule X, p. 149.

average expenditure, but also to the saving (if any) in the cost of repairs to the ship.

Over the years that followed, the equity of allowing in general average items of expenditure on the basis of savings achieved to general average was so much accepted that the statement of principle contained in Rule F was approved by the Stockholm Conference, notwithstanding the absence of support for it according to the laws of England, Germany and the Netherlands.

The 1924 text of Rule F read as follows:

> "Any extra expense incurred in place of another expense which would have been allowable as general average shall be deemed to be general average and so allowed, but only up to the amount of the general average expense avoided."

It will be noted that in this text there is no reference to the savings (if any) to interests other than general average. This question came up for discussion at the 1949 Amsterdam Conference, at which the majority supported the principle that in considering the savings achieved by the adoption of a substituted course, regard should be had only to the general average expenses avoided by taking that course, and that savings to other interests, e.g. in the cost of repairs, should be disregarded. A similar amendment was made at the same time in Rule XIV, where it deals with the allowance as a substituted expense of the cost of temporary repairs effected to accidental damage, but Rule X(d) was left unaltered. Some looked upon this result as a fair working compromise: others considered it an insupportable inconsistency. In 1974 the latter view prevailed, and Rule X(d) was entirely deleted.

Since 1974, therefore, all substituted expenses are to be treated in accordance with the principle set forth in Rule F. This includes the cases of towage from a port of refuge to destination, and the cost of transhipment and forwarding of cargo from a port of refuge, both of which had previously been specifically provided for under Rule X(d), as well as the cost of temporary repairs of accidental damage specifically provided for under Rule XIV.

In the run-up to the Sydney Conference of 1994, the AIDE appointed a working group under the chairmanship of Mr Howard Myerson to examine Rules F and XIV in the light of present day practice and current criticisms. Three of the questions considered in relation to Rule F were:

— What is the meaning to be given to the word "extra" in the phrase "any extra expense"? Should the word "extra" be replaced by the word "extraordinary"?

All were agreed that, however described, the expenses to be taken into consideration were such that would not have been incurred in the ordinary way in the performance of the contracted voyage, and two members of the group therefore favoured substituting "extraordinary" for "extra" in order to emphasise this point. The majority, however, were against any change, and their view was supported later when the CMI Sub-Committee proposed that for the avoidance of doubt the word "extra" should be changed to "additional". This change was subsequently approved by the Sydney Conference.

— Should Rule F be amended so as to make provision for consideration to be given to *losses* sustained in substitution for general average expenses?

The discussion on this question is summarised below.

— Should Rule X(d) (as it was under the York-Antwerp Rules 1950) be reinstated?

Despite the arguments favouring the reinstatement of this Rule advanced by a number of average adjusters, no proposition to this effect was moved at any stage of the debates within AIDE or CMI.

THE QUESTION OF SUBSTITUTED LOSS

Despite the suggestion having been put forward at each of the Conferences from 1924 onwards, the majority opinion has invariably been to exclude any reference to *loss*, either as part of the substituted claim, or in the calculation of the amount saved. This means that, in terms of Rule F, the claim to be considered and the amount of the savings have to be calculated solely by reference to *expenses* which have been incurred, or which would have been incurred. Generally speaking, "expense" comprises those allowances which qualify as general average expenditure, but when calculating the expenses which have been or would have been incurred during the prolongation of a voyage or a period of detention in port, it is the practice to include the figures for the consumption of bunker fuel, even though for other purposes the consumption of bunkers (unless specially replaced during the voyage) is treated as a general average sacrifice.

Cases do, however, arise when claims are put forward in general average for losses which have been accepted by one of the parties to the adventure, on the understanding that those suffering the loss should be made whole by a general contribution. Let us assume a case where a cargo is consigned to two different receivers, both of whom are willing to accept delivery of their cargoes at the port of refuge instead of at final destination. Receiver A incurs additional expense in having the goods sent to destination by rail, whereas receiver B suffers a financial loss through having to sell the goods at a discount to reflect their lower value at the port of refuge. By their actions, receivers A and B have saved the general average community the expense of storing and reloading their cargoes, and it is equitable that the financial losses suffered by each of them should be made good up to the amount of the general average expenses saved.

By British practice, at least between 1902 and 1924, the loss suffered by receiver B on the sale of his cargo in these circumstances would have been considered as allowable by way of substitution up to the amount of the expense saved proportionately by the "several parties to the adventure", on the same principle as was then provided under Rule X(d).[4] Indeed, the Rule of Practice still stands, but although its application would have been distinctly arguable until the introduction of the Rule of Interpretation in 1950, it is now clearly inconsistent with the text of Rule F.

In practice, therefore, the only fair way to bring receiver B's loss into contribution is to do so by seeking the consent of the other parties to the adventure by special agreement. If all parties agree, such a derogation from the strict terms of Rule F can in practice be applied when the circumstances warrant it.

INTERPRETATION

"Any additional expense"

If the text of the lettered Rules had been introduced with headings (as are the numbered Rules), the heading to Rule F would be *Substituted Expenses*. The expression "additional expense" is intended to indicate that the substituted course which has been undertaken has resulted in additional financial outlay which would not have been incurred in the ordinary way. In the discussion on this rule which took place in the AIDE International Sub-Committee prior to the Sydney Conference, it was suggested that the expression which had been utilised from 1924 onwards—"any extra expense"—did not adequately convey this element of extraordinariness, and consequently it should be replaced by the words "any *extraordinary* expense".

This suggestion did not commend itself to AIDE members, who considered that the French text—"*toute dépense supplémentaire*"—more accurately conveyed the required meaning.[5] The CMI Sub-Committee took the point and accordingly recommended that the English text should read "any additional expense" in order to align itself with the French version.

The use of the word "extraordinary" in this context would have implied that the substituted expense, in order to qualify for consideration under Rule F, would have to be something quite out of the ordinary course—not merely resulting in additional financial outlay, but also extraordinary in kind. Of course, some substituted expenses do fall within this category—towage to destination, for example—but not every kind of substituted expense can be so characterised.

4. Rule of Practice F16 (previously B18), Appendix 4, p. 358.
5. See the observation to this effect in the first edition of this book.

The substitution of "additional" for "extra" in the English text does not involve any change in the practice which has evolved in the treatment of substituted expenses since 1924. Excluded from consideration will be:

— an expense which qualifies for admission in general average in its own right; and
— an expense to which the shipowner is committed in the ordinary course of performing his obligations under the contract of carriage, i.e. a normal voyage expense.

"Additional expense" construed in relation to repair charges

When a ship is at a port of refuge with damage, then unless the damage sustained by the ship is of such a magnitude as to render her a commercial total loss, or is such that the cost and time that would be expended on repairs would be so great as to entitle the shipowner to abandon the voyage, it is the obligation of the shipowner under the contract of carriage to proceed to repair the ship so that she may safely prosecute the remainder of the voyage.[6] The cost of the accidental damage repairs is for the account of the shipowner or his hull underwriter, and it might be thought at first glance that there was no part of the cost of such repairs which could be brought into the general average account. However, this is not the case, since the practice of adjusters has identified a number of areas in which the cost of repairs may be enhanced by reason of measures taken in order to save time on repairs, and if such enhanced costs exceed what may be considered to be the reasonable cost of repairs, the resultant excess cost is in practice treated as an "additional expense" under Rule F.

It is not every enhancement in cost that is to be considered as "additional". It is submitted that in order to qualify for consideration under Rule F, the incurring of the expense has to be motivated by a desire to save time, and is not one to which the shipowner is committed by circumstances beyond his control or which he would in any case adopt as part of his normal repairing practice.

The following instances in which the cost of repairing the ship may be enhanced with a consequent saving of time on repairs were examined in a recent report by an AIDE working group[7]:

1. Movements of the vessel in port and docking/undocking at night-time or on holidays

The usual practice of adjusters is to treat any additional cost for night-time or holiday movements in port or in docking the ship to be normal to the

6. Carver, *Carriage by Sea* (13th ed.), sect. 1236 and cases there cited.
7. Report of AIDE working group on Rules F and XIV presented as a discussion paper at the XVth General Assembly, York 1989.

operation charged for, on the ground that the shipowner or master has virtually no option but to accept the berthing or docking slot offered to him.

2. Overtime of shore labour on repairs

The extra cost of overtime, being the differential between the overtime rate and the normal working rate for the number of hours worked, is in practice accepted as a substituted expense, provided that the shipowner was in a position to exercise the choice of having the work done in normal hours or in overtime.

3. Overtime of crew engaged on repairs

Prior to 1994, provision used to be made for the allowance of such overtime payments under Rule XI(d), but in practice little use was made of this provision, perhaps because of the difficulty of demonstrating any saving to general average by the crew working overtime on repairs. However, despite the rescission of old Rule XI(d), allowance may still be made under Rule F for the cost of crew's overtime on non-GA repairs, to the extent that a saving can be shown in time-based charges which would otherwise have been incurred and allowed in general average.

4. Cost of air-freighting spare parts

When air transport was in its infancy, there was a practice to treat as a substituted expense the additional cost of air-freight on spare parts over and above the cost of surface freight. This practice was supported by the case of *Western Canada Steamship Co.* v. *Canadian Commercial Corporation*,[8] a decision of the Supreme Court of Canada under the York-Antwerp Rules 1924. In that case a replacement tailshaft was flown by a chartered aircraft from the United Kingdom to Singapore in 1947. Cargo interests contested the admission in general average of the excess cost of air carriage over sea carriage, but the Court ruled in favour of its allowance as an extra expense under Rule F.

It is submitted that the best guide to correct practice is still as stated by an AIDE Committee in 1969: "In your Committee's opinion air-transport by scheduled flight is now an ordinary measure, but the stage has not been reached where this is also the case in respect of charter-transports." This practice has now been formally approved in the United States since 1991, when Rule of Practice XXI was amended to read:

8. *Western Canada Steamship Co.* v. *Canadian Commercial Corporation* [1960] 2 Lloyd's Rep. 313.

"The cost of ordinary air freight on repair parts shall be allowed as part of the reasonable cost of repairs. The cost of any extraordinary shipments by air, such as chartered aircraft or similar means, shall be dealt with by the Adjuster considering (1) the reasons for such shipment and/or (2) the saving resulting therefrom. The Adjuster shall insert a note in the average statement in explanation of the allowances or charges made."

5. *Employment of riding repairers*

In some cases, the engagement of riding repairers will cost no more than shore labour. Even when the cost is greater, there will be instances where the employment of riding repairers is normal and reasonable, for example where the vessel is trading on a scheduled service.

6. *Employment of a superintendent or an agent to expedite repairs*

In Anglo-Saxon countries, the cost of employing a superintendent to expedite repairs is invariably treated as part of the cost of the repairs, and will be allowed as part of a particular average claim to the extent that the charge is reasonable. However, in some continental countries, e.g. France, Denmark, and Germany, a different practice has evolved whereby part of the cost of superintendence may be considered within Rule F when the ship is repaired at a port of refuge, to the extent that the employment of a superintendent has expedited the repair. The evolution of this practice no doubt reflects the influence of domestic hull insurance markets which do not recognise the cost of superintendence in the settlements made under hull policies for particular average claims.

When an enhanced repair cost is admissible by these criteria as a substituted expense, the allowance made in general average is limited to the saving in general average expenses. However, there may also be savings in relation to the claims that may be stated on the hull insurances—see later in this commentary, under the phrase "without regard to the saving, if any, to other interests".

" . . . in place of another expense which would have been allowable as general average . . . "

To fall within the terms of the Rule, there must be another course of action available to the shipowner which if followed would give rise to a general average expense. This may be any expense admissible in general average under the terms of the numbered Rules or of Rule A. If the alternative course of action would be allowed under Rule A or when it comprises wages and maintenance of crew incurred during the prolongation of a voyage or a period of detention allowable under Rule XI, the expense must be reasonable in order to qualify in general average.

For this reason it is sometimes argued that there must be some point at which the "other" expense becomes unreasonable, and hence it should not rank in full in justification of the substituted expense. In the first edition of this book it was submitted that this argument is circular and self-defeating. Now, since 1994, we have to consider it afresh, in the context of the Rule Paramount.

The effect of the Rule Paramount

The Rule Paramount provides that "in no case shall there be any allowance for sacrifice or expenditure unless reasonably made or incurred". In relation to Rule F, does this provision apply only to the expense actually incurred, or does it also attach to the "other" expense which was *not* incurred? The promoters of the Rule Paramount certainly entertained no doubt as to their intention. The United States delegation to the Sydney Conference had proposed, in addition to the Rule Paramount, an amendment to Rule F to make it clear, in the words of their explanatory paper, "that the expense substituted for would have been one that a reasonable shipowner would have incurred". Under their proposal, the opening words of Rule F would have read:

> "Any extra expense incurred in place of another expense which would have been *reasonably incurred and* allowable as general average . . . "

In the event, once the Rule Paramount had been voted and approved, the Rule F proposal was withdrawn. Conceivably its proposers considered that it was no longer necessary, although their explanatory paper conveyed a contrary impression.

As a matter of strict interpretation, it is the author's opinion that the Rule Paramount succeeds in qualifying the alternative expense which was not incurred since, as set out in the words of the Rule, that "which would have been allowable as general average" must satisfy the requirements laid out in the York-Antwerp Rules as a whole, including the Rule Paramount, Rule A, Rule C and the numbered rules. However, having said that, we need to consider whether there is likely to be any change in practice, and this may involve us in a reappraisal of the theory of substituted expenses.

Comparison of the available options

Although Rule F is phrased in terms which refer to the incurring of the expense, its application in practice presupposes a choice between two (and sometimes more) different courses of action. If one of those courses of action, say to effect permanent repairs in the port of refuge, would open the door to allowances in general average under Rules X(b) and X(c) for the cost of discharging, storing and reloading cargo and under Rule XI(b) for the wages and maintenance of crew and fuel and stores consumed during the extra detention for repairs, then we have a benchmark by which to measure the effect, so far as general average is concerned, of any alternative course of action. Let us suppose that the alternative course of action is to forward the cargo to destination, and that this is the course adopted. If the extra cost of forwarding cargo exceeds the general average allowances which would have been made if permanent repairs had been effected at the port of refuge, this will tend to show that the latter course would have been the "more reasonable" so far as the general average is concerned, and the allowance under Rule F will be limited to this figure. On the other hand, if the extra cost of forwarding cargo turns out to be the lesser figure, then that is the amount allowed in general average, and the reasonableness or otherwise of the cost of the alternative ceases to be of any importance. For these reasons it appears to the author that the advent of the Rule Paramount will have little, if any, impact in practice upon the allowances which may be made under Rule F.

Let us now examine some typical examples of substituted expenses which frequently arise in practice:

Forwarding cargo to destination

This option occurs most commonly when a ship is at a port of refuge with substantial damage which will take a long time to repair. In many instances, particularly when the ship is in liner service, all parties will benefit from a decision to forward the cargo to destination, and the fact that the extra cost of this operation can be redistributed rateably through the medium of a general average adjustment is undoubtedly to the advantage of the commercial community.

The equity of allowing for the redistribution of the extra cost of transhipment and forwarding up to the expense thereby saved has been recognised in the practice of British adjusters since 1876 and in the York-Antwerp Rules since 1890.[9]

The operation may be performed by different means, depending upon the circumstances of each case, for example by discharging from ship to shore, thence to forwarding vessel; alternatively by direct transhipment. The forwarding itself may be performed by a vessel in the same liner service, or by a vessel or vessels specially chartered for the purpose, or by overland transport. The treatment of the expense, however, follows the same pattern throughout:

9. AAA Rule of Practice F15 and Rule X(d) of the York-Antwerp Rules 1890, quoted p. 68.

1. Discharge of cargo at port of refuge	— General average if necessary for the common safety or repairs to ship necessary for safe prosecution of voyage (Rule X(b)). — Otherwise forms part of the substituted expense.
2. Loading cargo on forwarding vessel(s) or land conveyance(s)	— Substituted expense.
3. As an alternative to 1 and 2, direct transhipment	— Substituted expense.
4. Carriage to destination, either:	
— by chartered vessel(s) for voyage	— Chartered freight, inclusive of demurrage if incurred and commissions form part of the substituted expense.
— by time chartered vessel(s)	— Time charter hire plus bunkers consumed form part of the substituted expense.
— by vessel(s) in same liner service	— Usually the line will make no charge for freight, treating the carriage as part performance of the original contract, but may claim for diversion and/or extra detention of forwarding vessel, which allowable as part of the substituted expense.
— by vessel(s) in competitive service	— Substituted expense.
— by overland conveyance(s)	— Allowable as a substituted expense, subject to deduction of any inland transit costs normally paid by the original carrier.
5. Discharge of cargo at destination	— In principle forms part of the substituted expense, but see below regarding deductions for expenses not incurred.

Having arrived at the total cost of transhipment and forwarding, the next step is to deduct the normal voyage expenses which by reason of the substituted operation the original carrier has not incurred. When all the cargo has been forwarded, these will consist of the wages and maintenance of crew and fuel and stores consumed from leaving the port of refuge until the time when the discharge of cargo would have been completed, port charges at port(s) of destination and the cost of discharging the cargo, to the extent normally payable by the carrier. When only part cargo has been forwarded, the normal cost of its discharge will be deducted, together with wages and maintenance, fuel and stores and port charges but only to the extent that the vessel's itinerary has been shortened by the forwarding of part cargo.

After deducting the non-incurred voyage expenses, we have the figure which represents the extra cost of transhipment and forwarding. Generally speaking, this will be the amount claimable as the "additional expense" under Rule F, although in some circumstances it may be proper to take account of other additional items of expense incurred by the shipowner or time charterer in consequence of the decision to forward the cargo.

The allowance in general average will be for the additional expense so arrived at, "but only up to the amount of the general average expense avoided", that is to say, not exceeding the expense which would have been incurred and allowed in general average if the cargo had not been forwarded but had been taken to destination in the original carrying ship after repairs; but omitting, of course, any expense which has been incurred and allowed in general average, particularly having regard to the operation of any Non-Separation agreement under the Rules prior to 1994 or the Non-Separation Clauses in Rule G of the 1994 Rules.

Broadly speaking, whenever the cost of discharging the cargo has been allowable in general average, the main general average expenses avoided will be for the cost of its storage and reloading, but there may be other non-incurred expenses to take into account.

EXAMPLE

Vessel A struck submerged object and put back to port of refuge R. Necessary to drydock A for repairs necessary for the safe prosecution of the voyage and to discharge all cargo for this purpose. After discharge, all cargo forwarded to destination D by vessel B chartered in for voyage: all cargo interests duly advised.[10] On completion of repairs, A sailed from R under new fixture.

Timing of events	
Putting back to R	occupied 4 days
Discharge of cargo	6
On repairs and until leaving R	40
	50 days

Times saved	
Reloading cargo at R	would have taken 6 days
Regaining position	4
On remainder of voyager, R–D	10
Discharging cargo at D	4
	24 days

10. As to the necessity of advising cargo interests when the York-Antwerp Rules 1994 apply, see the Non-Separation Clauses in Rule G, p. 93 *et seq*.

Daily costs

Wages and maintenance of crew: 1,000
Consumption of fuel and stores: at sea 3,000; in port 500.

An adjustment under the York-Antwerp Rules 1994 will show:

		Cost of Forwarding	General Average	Remainder
Expenses incurred				
Inward port charges at R	£10,000	—	£10,000	—
Discharge of cargo at R	50,000	—	50,000	
Loading on forwarding vessel B	80,000	80,000		
Paid under B's charterparty				
Lumpsum freight	160,000	160,000		
Commission	5,000	5,000		
Demurrage	10,000	10,000		
Wages and maintenance	50,000	—	50,000	
Fuel and stores putting back to R	12,000	—	12,000	
Fuel and stores consumed at R (includes 40 days on repairs, attracting a moiety of the charge: See Rule XI(b), second para.)	23,000	—	13,000	10,000
Outward port charges at R (in ballast)	5,000			5,000
Discharge of cargo ex vessel B at D	45,000	45,000		
	£450,000	300,000	135,000	15,000
Credit voyage expenses saved				
Wages and maintenance, 14 days	£14,000			
Fuel and stores at sea	30,000			
Fuel and stores at D	2,000			
Port charges at D	14,000			
Normal cost of discharge at D	40,000			
	£100,000	CR 100,000		
Extra cost of forwarding		£200,000	200,000	
Fully compensated by GA expenses saved, viz:				
Storage of cargo at R	£100,000		£335,000	£15,000
Reloading cargo at R	80,000			
Wages and maintenance, 10 days	10,000			
Fuel and stores at R and regaining position	15,000			
Outwards port charges (with cargo)	10,000			
	£215,000			

Repatriation of part crew at a port of refuge

A shipowner may decide that instead of incurring the heavy cost of paying and maintaining a full crew on board the vessel during an extended period at a port of refuge he will repatriate all but the essential crew members and replace them later, shortly before the vessel is ready to proceed on the voyage. When this is done it is customary to treat the cost of the crew's repatriation and replacement as a substituted expense allowable in general average up to the saving in cost of the wages and maintenance of the repatriated crew members for that extended period. But, it might be argued, in some circumstances it would not have been reasonable to incur the cost of the wages and maintenance of a full crew during the whole time the vessel was detained; in which case it appears to the author that the cost of the crew's repatriation and replacement would qualify as a direct admission in general average.

Drydocking with cargo on board

In normal circumstances a ship has to be fully discharged so as to reduce her deadweight as much as possible before drydocking. However, when drydocking for repairs at a port of refuge, it may be decided that instead of discharging all the cargo for the purpose of preparing to drydock, the ship may be permitted to drydock with all or part of her cargo on board provided measures are taken to accommodate the additional deadweight. This may involve preparing additional blocks and supports, and the drydock owner may require an indemnity against the possibility of damage being sustained.

In these circumstances it is accepted practice for the additional cost of drydocking with cargo on board to be treated as a substituted expense and allowed in general average up to the saving in the cost of discharging, storing and reloading that cargo, which would otherwise have been allowable under Rules X(b) and X(c).[11] The additional expense will certainly involve the cost of extra preparation of the drydock, but it may also include the cost of additional insurances taken out to cover the extra risks of damage to (a) the ship; (b) the drydock; and (c) cargo on board. In this respect the shipowner should be advised to consult his hull insurers and his P. & I. Club to ascertain whether they will be willing to accept these risks without additional premiums, but if chargeable such premiums will form part of the additional cost of the operation, so far as the shipowner is concerned. As to the treatment of the cost of such extra premiums, there appears to be some difference in practice: some adjusters charging the premiums where the risk of damage or liability would fall; others (including the author) preferring to rely upon the natural construction of the words in Rule F: "any additional expense . . . shall be . . . allowed without regard to the saving, if any, to other interests."[12]

11. The practice was approved in the United States in *Bowring* v. *Thebaud*, 42 Fed. Rep. 794.

12. These matters were discussed by the AAA Practice Committee at a meeting on 2 August 1983.

Before leaving this topic, it is worth observing that before the judgment of the House of Lords in *The Bijela*,[13] the practice of treating the cost of drydocking with cargo on board as a substituted expense was, at least in theory, susceptible to the same kind of argument as was employed by the Commercial Court to disallow the cost of temporary repairs of accidental damage under Rule XIV, namely that since the ship could be drydocked with cargo on board, it was no longer possible to contend that the discharge of that cargo was necessary "to enable damage to the ship to be repaired" within the terms of Rule X(b). However, for the reasons cogently expressed by Lord Lloyd of Berwick, the substituted expense provisions contained in the York-Antwerp Rules cannot now be assailed by this argument.

Towage to destination

Another example can be found among the many scenarios in which it may be decided to tow the vessel with her cargo to destination. If this decision is taken in order to save expense at a port of refuge at which it is practicable to repair, then it is clear that the extra cost of towage to destination, that is to say, after crediting the normal voyage expenses saved, qualifies as a substituted expense. But what if the decision to tow the vessel to destination is taken by the shipowner when the vessel is disabled at sea? In many instances it can be said that the exercise of this option has combined to achieve the safety of the adventure and the completion of the voyage at a cost which can be measured against the equally available and reasonable option of towing the vessel to a port of refuge where she can be repaired before continuing the voyage. There is, however, another case. Let us suppose that a vessel breaks down in mid-Atlantic on a westbound voyage, and that the nearest ports with appropriate repair facilities are alternatively in the United Kingdom or the east coast of the United States. A tug is despatched to aid the stricken vessel and, theoretically at least, she might be ordered to tow the disabled ship either eastwards or westwards, were it not for the shipowner's obligation to prosecute the contracted voyage, which obligation effectively rules out the eastbound option. In these circumstances, it would be idle to view the extra cost of the towage to destination as a substituted expense, and in practice that cost is invariably allowed as a direct admission in general average under Rule A. Note, however, that despite the inapplicability of Rule F, the amount to be allowed in general average is limited to the *extra* cost, credit being given against the cost of towage for the normal voyage expenses saved.

If there is no practical alternative to the extra expense, then it cannot be allowed as a substituted expense within the terms of Rule F, and its admissibility in general average will have to be considered, if at all, under one

13. See *The Bijela* (H.L.) [1994] 2 Lloyd's Rep. 1, more closely examined in the context of Rule XIV, p. 204 *et seq*.

of the other Rules. If the alternative course of action would lead to the abandonment of the voyage, then the "other" expenses which may be ranked in justification for the substituted expense will be limited to those allowable under Rules X(c) and XI(b), up to the date of the abandonment of the voyage or the date of completion of discharge of cargo if the abandonment takes place before that date.

" . . . without regard to the saving, if any, to other interests . . . "

When, under the previous Rule X(d)—abolished in 1974—it was necessary to divide the cost of the substituted expense in proportion to the "savings to the several parties to the adventure", it was necessary to consider the nature and extent of the expenses that had been saved. By a Rule of Practice of the Association of Average Adjusters[14] it was declared "that the saving of expense . . . is limited to a saving or reduction of the actual outlay, including the crew's wages and provisions, if any, which would have been incurred at the port of refuge, if the vessel has been repaired there, and does not include supposed losses or expenses, such as interest, loss of market, demurrage, or assumed damage by discharging".

Under Rule F, it is not necessary to consider what other savings there may be in addition to the savings achieved in general average. There may have been savings to other interests and in particular in the cost of repairs, but the general average adjuster is not concerned with them. Only if an adjustment is prepared for the dual purpose of stating the general average and for showing the claim upon the vessel's hull and machinery underwriters, is the adjuster concerned with the saving in repair costs, and then only to the extent that the substituted expenses exceed the savings in general average. So far as the practice of British adjusters is concerned, this point was clearly brought out by an Opinion of the Advisory Committee in August 1954, in answer to an enquiry as to the treatment of the extra cost of overtime of shore repairers whilst a vessel is under repair in drydock at a port of refuge. To the question whether the saving in drydock dues should be taken into account before considering the saving of general average allowances for wages and maintenance etc., the Advisory Committee replied that in their opinion "the cost of the overtime represents an extra expense incurred within the terms of Rule F and, as such, forms a first charge on the general average saving without regard to the savings, if any, to other interests, e.g. drydock dues".[15] At about the same time a similar enquiry was considered by a meeting of Scandinavian adjusters, who delivered a unanimous opinion to the same effect.

14. Rule of Practice F17 (previously B19), Appendix 4, p. 358.

15. AAA Advisory Committee Opinion No. 28 dated 13 August 1954 (confirmed 5 February 1990).

RULE G

General average shall be adjusted as regards both loss and contribution upon the basis of values at the time and place when and where the adventure ends.

This rule shall not affect the determination of the place at which the average statement is to be made up.

When a ship is at any port or place in circumstances which would give rise to an allowance in general average under the provisions of Rules X and XI, and the cargo or part thereof is forwarded to destination by other means, rights and liabilities in general average shall, subject to cargo interests being notified if practicable, remain as nearly as possible the same as they would have been in the absence of such forwarding, as if the adventure had continued in the original ship for so long as justifiable under the contract of affreightment and the applicable law.

The proportion attaching to cargo of the allowances made in general average by reason of applying the third paragraph of this Rule shall not exceed the cost which would have been borne by the owners of cargo if the cargo had been forwarded at their expense.

EVOLUTION

When introduced in 1924, Rule G comprised only the first two paragraphs set out above. The second two paragraphs (the "Non-Separation Clauses") were added in 1994.

The first paragraph reflects in part the important step towards uniformity taken firstly by the adoption of Resolution No. 9 at the 1860 Glasgow Conference and confirmed in Rule X of the York Rules 1864 (subsequently renumbered as Rule XVII in 1890), the opening words of which provided that "contribution to a general average shall be made upon the actual values of the property at the termination of the adventure".[1]

English law is similar as to the place of adjustment, meaning by that expression the place at which account is taken of the parties' rights and liabilities in general average. In *Simonds* v. *White*,[2] Abbott C.J. said:

1. See the evolution of Rule XVII, p. 225 *et seq.*
2. *Simonds* v. *White* (1824) 2 B. & C. 805.

"The shipper of goods tacitly, if not expressly, assents to general average as a known maritime usage, which may, according to the events of the voyage, be either beneficial or disadvantageous to him. And by assenting to general average he must be understood to assent also to its adjustment at the usual and proper place; and to all this it seems to us to be only an obvious consequence to add that he must be understood to consent also to its adjustment according to the usage and law of the place at which the adjustment is to be made."

In *Lloyd* v. *Guibert*,[3] the Court of Exchequer Chamber laid down:

"The adjustment of a general average at the port of discharge, according to the law prevailing there, is binding upon the shipowner and the merchant, as they must be taken to have assented to adjustment being made at the usual and proper place, and, as a consequence, according to the law of that place."

In *Wavertree Sailing Ship Co.* v. *Love*,[4] it was contended on behalf of cargo that the statements of the law pronounced in these two cases obliged the shipowner to have the average statement drawn up by an adjuster at the port of discharge, but the Privy Council held that a shipowner may make up the statement himself, and is not bound to employ an average adjuster either there or anywhere else.

The second paragraph of Rule G reflects that judgment, in the same terms that were suggested in the Dowdall draft code.

The third and fourth paragraphs were added at the Sydney Conference in 1994. These are the "Non-Separation" and Bigham Clauses which were previously submitted for agreement by the parties on a case-by-case basis in order to justify the preparation of the adjustment as if the common maritime adventure continued notwithstanding that the cargo, or part of it, was to be forwarded to its destination(s) by other means.

COMMENTARY

One virtue of the Rule is to dispose of a moot point in English law. Whereas there had never been any doubt that cases of general average sacrifice were to be adjusted at the termination of the adventure (on the grounds that if the other property failed to arrive at destination, then surely that which was sacrificed would also have been lost), it had been strenuously argued by Lowndes that in a case of general average expenditure, the adjustment should be made according to the state of facts at the time when the outlay was incurred.

In *Chellew* v. *Royal Commission on the Sugar Supply* (*The Penlee*)[5] general average expenditure was incurred on account of a resort to a port of refuge,

3. *Lloyd* v. *Guibert* (1865) L.R. 1 Q.B. 115.
4. *Wavertree Sailing Ship Co.* v. *Love* [1897] A.C. 373; 8 Asp. M.C. 276.
5. *Chellew* v. *Royal Commission on the Sugar Supply* (*The Penlee*) [1922] 1 K.B. 12; 27 Com. Cas. 1; 15 Asp. M.C. 393.

but both ship and cargo were totally lost by a subsequent accident before reaching destination. Sankey J. and a strong Court of Appeal held that by virtue of the words quoted above in Rule XVII of the York-Antwerp Rules 1890 there could be no adjustment, since the adventure terminated with the total loss of ship and cargo, at which time the values were nil. Although the case was decided under the York-Antwerp Rules, Sankey J. gave it as his opinion that the position was the same under English law, namely that the state of facts for the adjustment of general average expenditure is that which obtains at the termination of the adventure.

Expenditure differs from sacrifice, of course, in that once the expenditure has been made, it is so much money lost to the party who disbursed it. Hence the practice that has grown up over many years of insuring general average disbursements (but not sacrifices), the cost of which is allowable in general average in accordance with Rule XX.

" . . . as regards both loss and contribution . . . "

"Loss" in the expression "loss and contribution" comprehends both sacrifice and expenditure. Since the word "loss" is used elsewhere in the Rules in the sense of physical loss, a better word in this context would probably be "admissions".

" . . . the basis of values at the time and place when and where the adventure ends"

When does the adventure end? To answer this question we have to consider several differing sets of circumstances:

1. When cargo is delivered at the port or place named in the bill of lading

This is the simplest case: when the goods are delivered from the carrying vessel at the port named in the bill of lading, and the contractual voyage is co-terminous with the common maritime adventure. Where there is only one port of discharging, it is generally held that the adventure ends on the last day of discharging at the named port of destination. However, the writers of textbooks appear to be confused when a vessel has on board cargoes destined for a number of different ports of discharging. In the opinion of the author, the adventure ends, as regards each separate bill of lading holder, when the cargo consigned to him is discharged from the ship. The reason for this is because the York-Antwerp Rules are imported into each of the separate contracts evidenced by the bills of lading, and as respects each bill of lading holder, the adventure ends when his goods are discharged. It is accepted that the state of facts existing at that time governs the adjustment of the general average occurring during the period that his cargo was on board the ship, i.e. when it formed a part of the community of interest, but the question arises whether events that take place after the discharge of his cargo, e.g. such as might affect the contributory value of the ship, will affect the adjustment. The general practice of adjusters in approaching this problem is to adopt as the values for contribution the value of cargoes at each of the ports to which they are consigned, and the value of the ship at the last port of discharging.

EXAMPLE

A ship loads cargo at port A for discharge at X, Y and Z. While proceeding up the channel at the entrance to port X, the ship strands and sustains damage by the stranding and efforts to refloat. She is then escorted into X by tugs, and after discharge of the cargo destined for X, a divers' examination reveals substantial damage to the ship, which has to be repaired in order that she may prosecute the remainder of the voyage. In the adjustment of the general average, the allowances are separated between those to which all cargo will contribute, namely the cost of refloating, damage repairs to the ship and the extra cost of the tug services, whereas the cost of discharging, storing and reloading the cargoes consigned to Y and Z plus the allowances under Rule XI during the extra period of detention at X for the repairs necessary for the safe prosecution of the voyage will be the subject of contribution between ship and the cargoes destined for Y and Z.

On berthing at Y, the ship strikes the quay and sustains damage to her shell plating, the repairs to which are deferred until after the end of the voyage. This affects the value of the ship for its contribution not only to the adjustment which concerns the cargoes destined for Y and Z, but also that which concerns the cargo discharged at X.

Whilst proceeding between Y and Z, a fire occurs on board and damage is sustained to certain of the cargo consigned to Z both by fire and the means used to extinguish it. The contribution to this second general average will, of course, be made only by the ship and the cargo consigned to Z, but the adjustment of the first general average will be affected since the values on which the ship and the Z cargo will contribute to it will be reduced by their respective contributions to the second general average.

The case is rather different when the goods are discharged from the carrying vessel in order to be on-carried to the destination named in the bill of lading by another vessel or other conveyance. In this case the contractual obligations of the carrier extend beyond the point in time and place where ship and cargo separate.

Although on principle it might be thought that the adventure continues as regards any particular parcel of cargo so long as the transit continues to the destination named in the bill of lading, we have here an instance where, by operation of the Rule of Interpretation, the general words in Rule G are overridden by the specific provisions of Rules XVI and XVII, which require the extent of loss and contributory values of cargo to be established at the time of discharge from the carrying ship, rather than at the time of delivery of the cargo to the receiver at destination.

2. When in consequence of accident the ship puts into a port of refuge or returns to her port of loading, and the voyage is abandoned there

In short, the adventure ends at the time and place when and where the voyage is abandoned, and it is the state of facts as of that time and place that will form the basis of the adjustment.

So far as English law is concerned, this follows from the case of *Fletcher* v. *Alexander*,[6] in which a ship carrying a cargo of salt from Liverpool to Calcutta stranded shortly after sailing, and in order to refloat her a substantial quantity of salt had to be jettisoned. Thereafter the ship limped back to Liverpool where it was established that the damage, both to the ship and to the salt which remained on board, was so substantial that the voyage was abandoned. The cargo owner claimed that the amount to be made good for the jettison should be based upon the value for which the salt could have been sold in Calcutta, but Bovill C.J. held that although as a general rule the place of adjustment was the port of destination, in this case the adventure came to an end when the voyage was broken up in Liverpool, and it was upon those facts and the law which applied there that the adjustment should be prepared.

In what circumstances is the shipowner or carrier entitled to abandon the voyage?

In order to answer this question, it is prudent to remind ourselves of the carrier's obligations, which were well expressed by Kennedy J. in *Hansen* v. *Dunn*[7] in a passage which touches upon other aspects of the shipowner's responsibilities when a ship has been obliged to put into a port of refuge, and which therefore merits setting out in full. The learned judge first quoted from *Abbott on Shipping*[8]:

"Where a ship is damaged and obliged to put into an intermediate port for repairs, it is the duty as well as the right of the Shipowner, if he can repair his ship without unreasonable sacrifice and within reasonable time, to repair his ship and carry the goods to their destination. This is the purpose for which he has been entrusted with the cargo, and this purpose he is bound to accomplish by every reasonable and practicable method."

He then continued:

6. *Fletcher* v. *Alexander* (1868) L.R. 3 C.P. 375; 3 M.L.C. 69.
7. *Hansen* v. *Dunn* (1906) 11 Com. Cas. 100.
8. *Abbott on Shipping* (14th ed.).

"If he so determines to fulfil his contract, it is his duty, whilst the repairs are being done, to take all reasonable means to preserve the cargo from deterioration. If, on the other hand, the circumstances are such that the shipowner is justified in not repairing his ship, or are such that, even if the ship is eventually repaired, it is not, with a due regard to his own interest and the interest of the owner of the cargo, reasonably practicable, owing either to the length of time which the repairs will take or the perishable nature of the cargo, or to the expense involved, or all or any such reasons, that the carriage of the cargo should be completed in the ship when repaired, then the shipowner is at liberty to tranship and carry the cargo to its destination in another bottom and so earn the freight. He is not bound to employ another vessel to complete the voyage at his own loss. But if he chooses, because he deems it best and for his own advantage, to pursue this course, he must, when he has been entrusted with a perishable cargo, which is daily incurring on shipboard an increase of deterioration, use all reasonable promptitude in procuring the transhipment, and take all reasonable means to prevent, or at least to minimise, the deterioration of the cargo until the transhipment is effected. Lastly, if the Shipowner decides neither to repair nor to tranship, it is his duty with the greatest dispatch which the circumstances, reasonably considered, admit, to inform the owner of the cargo, or his agents on the spot, in order that he or they may not be unreasonably hindered in the protection of his interests, and the perishable cargo may not be unnecessarily damaged by the lapse of time before the owner or his agents have it placed at his or their disposition."

This quotation is also relevant in a marked degree to the situations envisaged in paragraph 4, which follows.

Under English law, a shipowner will be released from his obligation to carry on the voyage when the vessel has sustained such damage in consequence of excepted perils that she is a commercial total loss (*Moss* v. *Smith*[9]). Such a situation arises when the cost of repairing the damage exceeds the value of the ship when repaired plus the freight at risk (if any) for the voyage (*de Cuadra* v. *Swann*[10]). The extent of the repairs to be considered in this connection are those that are necessary to complete the voyage (*Kulukundis* v. *Norwich Union*[11]).

Somewhat later, English law developed the concept of frustration of contract. This arises when, without fault on either side, performance of the contract becomes impossible by reason of some supervening event. Such supervening event could be the destruction of the thing which is the subject matter of the contract (*Taylor* v. *Caldwell*[12]), the non-happening of an event which was predicated as the basis of the contract (the cancellation of a Jubilee) or the happening of an event which destroys the purpose of the contract. When a contract is deemed to be frustrated, both parties are discharged from further performance.

There is clearly an overlap between cases where the voyage is abandoned and instances when the contract of carriage is frustrated. But there is a difference, because if the facts are such that the shipowner has the right to

9. *Moss* v. *Smith* (1850) 9 C.B. 94.
10. *de Cuadra* v. *Swann* (1864) 16 C.B.(N.S.) 772.
11. *Kulukundis* v. *Norwich Union* [1937] 1 K.B. 1; 55 Ll.L.Rep. 55.
12. *Taylor* v. *Caldwell* (1863) 3 B. & S. 826.

abandon the voyage, he may if he wishes elect to continue with it, for example by repairing his ship at an expense greater than its value when repaired, and in these circumstances he will be deemed to have waived his right to abandon the voyage (*Assicurazioni Generali* v. *Bessie Morris*[13]). On the other hand, if a ship has been chartered to carry a particular cargo to a particular place within a certain time, and the vessel runs aground with the result that the time elapsed in refloating and repairing the ship makes it impossible for the charterers to fulfil the purpose for which the voyage was undertaken, then the doctrine of frustration applies and both parties are discharged from further performance: this was the case in *Jackson* v. *Union Marine*,[14] which concerned the carriage of a cargo of rails from Newport to San Francisco to be used in the construction of a railway.

When the voyage is justifiably abandoned or the circumstances are such as to frustrate the contract of affreightment, the shipowner or carrier is relieved from further responsibilities under the contract of carriage. However, as indicated in the extract cited above from the judgment in *Hansen* v. *Dunn*, he remains under an obligation to take care of the goods entrusted to him and also has the responsibility to notify the concerned in cargo of the circumstances which have occurred and to obtain their instructions as to its further care and ultimate disposition. Because of this, there are particular provisions in Rules X(c) and XI(b) which cater for the allowance of the cost of storage of cargo and the wages and maintenance of crew from the date of abandonment until the completion of discharge of the cargo.[15] By virtue of the Rule of Interpretation, these particular provisions override the generality of Rule G.

3. *When part cargo is left behind at the port of refuge*

In *Hill* v. *Wilson*[16] the "*Virago*" left Riga with 1,893 tons of general cargo in November 1876, bound for Hull. She stranded in the Baltic and after jettison of about 30 tons of cargo she succeeded in refloating and put into Copenhagen as a port of refuge. About 1,643 tons of cargo belonging to the plaintiffs was found to be damaged and was sold there; the balance of the cargo, being sound, was either forwarded to Hull in other ships belonging to the owners of the "*Virago*" or reloaded onto that vessel after repairs and delivered in due course. The shipowners procured an adjustment of the case in Copenhagen which in accordance with Danish law charged the plaintiffs with freight *pro rata itineris peracti*. This would not have been chargeable against the plaintiffs under English law: hence the action. Lindley J. held that in order to uphold the Danish adjustment the shipowners would have to show (i) that the voyage was in fact terminated at Copenhagen; and (ii) that it was so terminated by

13. *Assicurazioni Generali* v. *Bessie Morris* [1892] 2 Q.B. 652; 7 Asp. M.C. 217.
14. *Jackson* v. *Union Marine* (1874) L.R. 10 C.P. 125; 2 Asp. M.C. 435.
15. See commentaries on Rules X(c) and XI(b), pp. 167 and 180.
16. *Hill* v. *Wilson* (1897) 4 Asp. M.C. 198.

agreement or by necessity, i.e. by such circumstances beyond the shipowners' control as rendered the completion of the voyage impossible, either physically or from a business point of view. On point (i) the learned judge found as a fact that, *vis-à-vis* the plaintiffs' cargo which was sold at Copenhagen, the voyage had terminated there, but as to point (ii) the shipowners had failed to show either agreement or necessity.

Although *Hill* v. *Wilson* had primarily to do with the place where the adjustment was to be prepared, the finding that the voyage had been terminated at Copenhagen as regards the cargo left behind and sold there, whereas the voyage continued in being for the cargo which was carried on to Hull is, in the author's opinion, highly persuasive in considering where "the adventure ends" in terms of Rule G, at least when English practice is applied. Furthermore, the case can be seen as an extension of the principle laid down in *Fletcher* v. *Alexander*,[17] and the result is consistent with the author's opinion expressed in paragraph 1.

On the other hand, it has to be reported that a majority of the AAA Advisory Committee[18] took a different view in a matter submitted to them in 1968 under the York-Antwerp Rules 1950, concerning the amount to be made good and the contributory value of goods damaged by sacrifice and sold short of destination. In their 1950 texts, Rules XVI and XVII referred to the "termination of the adventure", and the majority of the Committee considered those words to apply to the adventure as a whole and to refer to the total abandonment of the voyage short of destination. Consequently, in their opinion in the event of the voyage (with other cargo) being completed to original destination(s), the amount to be made good to cargo damaged by sacrifice and necessarily sold at an intermediate port should be the difference between the sound (market) value on the last day of discharge of the vessel at the intended destination and the net proceeds of sale. Furthermore, if subsequently on the voyage with the remainder of the cargo there was a further general average or salvage, the amount made good for the cargo left behind and sold at the intermediate port should be reduced by the proportion of contribution payable by the interests actually involved therein.

In the opinion of the author, this goes too far. While the logic appears relentless, it is based on the false premise that the adventure continues for goods which have been left behind and sold or otherwise disposed of, and a false analogy with a loss by jettison. This was also the opinion of one of the members of the 1968 Advisory Committee, Mr D. G. Milburn, whose minority report returns to first principles and deserves to be reproduced in full:

"It is established by the case of *Fletcher* v. *Alexander* that where a vessel puts back to her port of loading and there discharges cargo, which is not reloaded, the adventure is

17. *Fletcher* v. *Alexander* (1868) L.R. 3 C.P. 375; 3 M.L.C. 69.
18. AAA Advisory Committee Opinion No. 34 dated 7 May 1968.

brought to an end, and the adjustment is to be prepared on the basis of values at that time and place. In my view the same principle applies where cargo is discharged at an intermediate port short of destination, and is not carried on, and the common adventure is terminated, so far as such cargo is concerned, at the time and place of separation.

The alternative suggested, namely that the adventure in goods left behind does not terminate until the vessel reaches the intended destination with the balance of the cargo, is not only illogical: it raises a number of practical difficulties which in many cases will lead to greater complication in the preparation of the adjustment. This is not an encouragement to those who seek the simplification of general average.

There is a clear distinction to be drawn between a case where cargo is left behind at an intermediate port, whether by reason of general average damage, particular average damage or a combination of both, and a case of jettison. In the case of jettison the physical property is lost at the time of the jettison and the cargo owner has an inchoate right to receive his made good thereon, subject to the safe arrival of the rest of the adventure. This right is in law a "chose in action" and forms part of the property at risk: it travels, so to speak, with the rest of the adventure and carries the risks of the adventure with it. Thus the amount to be made good for jettison is subject to deduction on account of subsequent particular average losses and liability for salvage charges under the doctrine of hypothetical salvage.

This line of reasoning cannot apply where goods are left behind at a port of refuge since the goods remain physically in existence. They cannot be called upon to contribute on any value other than that which they have in fact (with the addition of made good, if any) at the time and place where they part company with the ship; their right to receive made good cannot be assessed on the basis of a "loss of voyage" which is not the direct consequence of the general average act, and they do not, of course, bear the future perils which may attend the ship and other cargo from which they are separated."

Now, since the changes made to Rules XVI and XVII in 1974, the questions of the amount to be made good and the contributory value of damaged cargo which is sold short of destination have largely been taken out of contention.

The second paragraph of the Rule XVI states:

"When cargo so damaged [i.e. by general average sacrifice] is sold [and this must apply either at destination or short of destination] and the amount of the damage has not otherwise been agreed, the loss to be made good in general average shall be the difference between the net proceeds of sale and the net sound value as computed in the first paragraph of this Rule [i.e. ascertained by reference to the commercial invoice]." (Author's comments in square brackets.)

The fourth paragraph of Rule XVII states:

"Where cargo is sold short of destination, however, it shall contribute upon the actual net proceeds of sale, with the addition of any amount made good as general average."

In some cases, because of lack of market or restrictions against importation at the port of refuge, the goods left behind there are subsequently forwarded to destination as the best way to realise value. The above quoted provisions of Rules XVI and XVII will not apply in these circumstances, and assuming that the adventure has been terminated at the port of refuge, Buglass tells us that the value of the goods there is to be deduced from the value realisable at destination; under the 1974 and 1994 Rules the contributory value of sound goods will be their invoice value less the cost of forwarding.[19]

4. When the voyage is interrupted (but not abandoned) at the port of refuge, and cargo is forwarded to its destination by other vessel(s) or means of conveyance

The cargo or a part of it, may be transhipped at a port of refuge and carried forward to destination in a number of different circumstances. As we have seen, this may occur after the voyage has been abandoned at the port of refuge, either by the shipowner in exercise of his option to do so in order to earn freight, or at the instance of the concerned in cargo. In either case, however, by reason of the abandonment of the voyage, there is a termination of the common maritime adventure, and the events which occur thereafter are of no concern to general average. In particular, there are no grounds upon which the cost of the transhipment and forwarding can be considered in general average, since the community of interest has been brought to an end.

If the voyage has not been abandoned, and the cargo is forwarded by the shipowner or carrier in exercise of a liberty to tranship under the bill of lading, the case is different. In these circumstances, while the community of interest has been brought to an end, the contract of carriage subsists. This means, in practical terms, that the shipowner can exercise his lien for general average at destination and under English law this is the proper place for adjustment. On the other hand the goods, or some of them, may be transhipped and forwarded at the expense of their owners in exercise of their right (where this exists) to take delivery at the port of refuge on full payment of any freight due thereon, or simply because this enables them to meet their commercial obligations.

In either case, at least part of the motivation for the forwarding of cargo in these circumstances will be the saving of time, and since time means money in terms of general average allowances (just as it does in other respects), consideration will have to be given to the cost of forwarding as a substituted expense under Rule F.[20]

However, prior to the 1994 version of the Rules there was a lacuna in that, although it was in the interest of all parties to forward the cargo to its destination(s) in these circumstances, the "community of interest" (ship and cargo) was deemed to be broken from the time the goods were discharged from the original carrying vessel. To meet this situation it became the all but universal practice in such circumstances to require the merchant to provide, in consideration of the release of his goods, not merely the customary forms of general average security, but also his adherence to a "Non-Separation Agreement". The purpose of the agreement was to provide that the owners of

19. Buglass, *Marine Insurance and General Average in the United States* (2nd ed.), p. 278; see *The Eliza Lines*, 102 Fed. Rep. 184.

20. See commentary on the cost of forwarding cargo, pp. 76–80.

the goods released would contribute to the general average expenses incurred and those which would have been incurred if there had been no forwarding and the voyage had continued after the ship had been repaired.

The "Non-Separation Clauses"

The third and fourth paragraphs of Rule G import into the 1994 Rules the essence of the forms of Non-Separation Agreement previously in use, having been approved by the leading markets as follows:

The British formula was:

"Standard Form of 'Non-Separation Agreement' as agreed between Representatives of Shipowners, Underwriters and Average Adjusters in December 1967
It is agreed that in the event of the vessel's cargo or part thereof being forwarded to original destination by other vessel, vessels or conveyances, rights and liabilities in general average shall not be affected by such forwarding, it being the intention to place the parties concerned as nearly as possible in the same position in this respect as they would have been in the absence of such forwarding and with the adventure continuing by the original vessel for so long as justifiable under the law applicable or under the Contract of Affreightment.

The basis of contribution to general average of the property involved shall be the values on delivery at original destination unless sold or otherwise disposed of short of that destination; but where none of her cargo is carried forward in the vessel she shall contribute on the basis of her actual value on the date she completes discharge of her cargo."

This form was also considered and approved by a working group of AIDE.[21]

A similar form was approved by the American Institute of Marine Underwriters in September 1988:

"Non-Separation Agreement
In the event that the cargo or any part thereof is forwarded to its original destination by the vessel owner or charterer using other vessels or land conveyances, rights and liabilities in General Average shall not be affected, it being the intention of the parties that they shall be, as nearly as possible, in the same position as if there had been no forwarding and the adventure had continued in the original vessel as long as justified by law and the contract of affreightment.

Contribution to General Average shall be based upon values at the original destination except that cargo not forwarded to destination shall contribute on its value where disposed of and the vessel, if it carries none of the cargo to destination, shall contribute on its value at completion of discharge. Rule XVII York/Antwerp Rules, 1974, if applicable, remains fully in force.

It is understood that the amount charged to cargo under this agreement shall not exceed what it would cost the cargo owners if cargo was delivered to them at the port of refuge and forwarded by them to destination."

21. Report of AIDE working group presented at the Vth General Assembly, Genoa, 1969, pp. 111–112.

The last paragraph of this text, sometimes called the "Bigham Clause",[22] became customary in the United States in order to avoid the possibility that the concerned in cargo might be called upon to contribute in general average more than it would cost him to forward the cargo to destination at his own expense.

The question whether or not to include a Non-Separation provision in the Rules of 1994 was first raised in the chairman's report and questionnaire of July 1991 and provoked warm debate in the International Sub-Committees of both the AIDE and CMI. In favour of inclusion it was argued that the practice of utilising standard forms was now so widespread that it deserved to be crystallised in the YAR, thus reducing paperwork and avoiding the use of irregular wordings; while the main argument to the contrary was that in principle the question should be left to the parties to the adventure to decide. On the drafting of the Non-Separation Clauses there was little controversy, the text proposed by the BMLA receiving general approval. At the Sydney Conference, however, two changes were made:

- The sentence regulating the time and place for ascertaining the values of the contributing interests was transferred to Rule XVII;
- The following words were added:
  "subject to cargo interests being notified if practicable . . . "

The purpose of these additional words is rather hard to divine. Presumably if notification is not made when it would have been "practicable" to do so, the clause will not apply. This seems to be unfair, since the real consideration for the retention of the general average allowances accruing to the shipowner during the repair of the ship is the earlier delivery of the cargo at its destination. On the other hand, the notification will provide cargo receivers with early news as to the arrival of their goods by the substituted vessel or conveyance, and will also afford them the opportunity of considering (if they have the right to do so) whether to demand delivery at the port of refuge. As to the practicability of notification, the author envisages that in virtually every case the most strenuous efforts will be made to notify all cargo interests of the decision made to forward cargo and invoke the Non-Separation Clauses: no average adjuster will wish to take the risk of being the first to report that communication with cargo interests is impracticable.

Can the cargo owners demand delivery at the port of refuge?

In the U.S.A. and Canada it is settled law that cargo owners who have paid the full freight or who agree to pay any balance of freight due can demand delivery of their goods at an intermediate port provided that facilities exist for it to be discharged and made available to them. Receipt of a notice from the carrier

22. So called after the firm of attorneys who drafted it.

proposing that cargo should be forwarded from the port of refuge instead of being delivered by the original carrying vessel will therefore alert the cargo owner to the position and provide him with the opportunity of deciding whether or not to take delivery at the port of refuge. Prior to the insertion of the Non-Separation Clauses in Rule G, the cargo owner would have been similarly alerted by receiving a request to sign an average bond with a Non-Separation Agreement attached to it.

This is what happened in a case before the Canadian courts under the York-Antwerp Rules 1974; *Ellerman Lines* v. *Gibbs Nathaniel Ltd.* (*The City of Colombo*).[23] The ship, with cargo destined for Toronto and Hamilton, was detained at Montreal in order to repair substantial damage sustained by the main engines. Shipowners advised all cargo interests accordingly, adding that they proposed to forward the cargo to destination provided that if in addition to the customary average bond the cargo receivers would agree to the terms of the standard Non-Separation Agreement. The defendants declined this agreement and instead demanded delivery of their goods at Montreal. The shipowners (inadvisedly, as it turned out) refused to do this and claimed that the goods remained subject to their right of lien. The defendants therefore applied to the Federal Court of Canada for an injunction requiring the shipowners to deliver the goods at Montreal, and this was granted by the court subject to the provision of an average bond which *did not* include a Non-Separation Agreement. The subsequent action was brought by shipowners in an attempt to recover the general average contribution which would have been due from the defendants on the same basis of adjustment as applied to all the other cargo interests who had signed the Non-Separation Agreement. In the trial division of the Federal Court, the judge was not satisfied that there had been grounds for a declaration of general average, since neither cargo nor the ship had been in peril, and even if there had been a good case of general average, the cargo owners were fully justified in requiring that their cargo be delivered in Montreal on payment of full freight. Shipowners appealed to the Federal Court of Appeal where Stone J., relying fairly heavily on *Eagle Terminal Tankers* v. *Ingosstrakh*,[24] correctly applied the Rule of Interpretation and concluded that a general average situation existed at Montreal under Rule XI(b) by reason of the vessel's detention for the repair of engine damage necessary for the safe prosecution of the voyage. However, on the issue of delivery of cargo at Montreal, the judge, following the American cases of *The Julia Blake*[25] and *The Domingo de Larrinaga*,[26] upheld the decision in the court below and approved the following statement of the law:

"Neither general contract law nor admiralty law obliges a cargo owner to keep his cargo aboard a ship until the ultimate destination provided for in the bill of lading is reached

23. *Ellerman Lines* v. *Gibbs Nathaniel Ltd.* (*The City of Colombo*), 1986 AMC 2217.
24. *Eagle Terminal Tankers* v. *Ingosstrakh* (*The Eagle Courier*), 1981 AMC 137.
25. *The Julia Blake* (1882) 107 U.S. 418.
26. *The Domingo de Larrinaga*, 1928 AMC 64.

if he pays in full the freight charges provided for therein for the entire voyage and requests off-loading at any intermediate port where the ship has docked and facilities are available."

It has been suggested that *The City of Colombo* throws doubt on the validity of a Non-Separation Agreement in circumstances when the cargo owner may legally demand delivery of his goods at the port of refuge. In fact this was not in issue, since the defendant had specifically dissented from its terms. However, the question may well arise in the future whether in those jurisdictions where intermediate port delivery can properly be demanded effect will be given to the Non-Separation Clauses contained in Rule G, so far as concerns contribution to the additional allowances due to the shipowner for the wages and maintenance of his crew, etc., at the port of repair. It is submitted that the fact that the cargo owner has a right to take delivery at the intermediate port ought not to affect the contractual obligation of the cargo owner, imported via the incorporation of the York-Antwerp Rules 1994 into the contract of carriage. However, it might not appear reasonable that the cargo owner should be asked to pay a contribution to expenses incurred after the termination of the community of interest, in addition to the expenses which he had incurred in taking delivery. Another point which would be difficult to overcome would be that *ex hypothesi* the "applicable law" would find the termination of the adventure to be justifiable, so far as that particular cargo was concerned.

Restrictions upon the applicability of the Non-Separation Clauses

The ship must be "at any port or place in circumstances which would give rise to an allowance in general average under the provisions of Rules X and XI". This could be paraphrased by the shorthand expression "when the ship is *under average*". She may have put into a port of refuge or put back to her port of loading for the common safety, or be in any port or place with damage sustained during the voyage which requires repairs which are necessary for the safe prosecution of the voyage. The reference to Rules X and XI should be interpreted widely, as if it read "either Rule X or Rule XI, or both of them".

Cargo interests must be notified if practicable. This has already been commented upon.

The alternative course of action available to the parties if the cargo were not forwarded to destination would have to be a continuation of the adventure in the original ship "for so long as justifiable under the contract of affreightment and the applicable law". This is a limitation upon the "rights and liabilities in general average" (and thus the extent of the allowances that can be made) remaining "as nearly as possible the same as they would have been in the absence of such forwarding". Thus, if the alternative was to retain the cargo on board the ship or in storage at the port of refuge while the original ship was being repaired, and this extended over so long a period of time that the commercial object of the adventure would be frustrated, then the allowances which could be made for the period of the ship's detention would be limited to the extent which would be considered proper and reasonable by the law governing the contract of carriage.

If it can be shown that it would have been cheaper for the cargo interests (or any of them) to have taken delivery of their goods at the port of refuge and forwarded the same to destination, compared with their proportion of the allowances which would fall to be made "as nearly as possible the same as they would have been in the absence of . . . forwarding", then the fourth paragraph of Rule G (the "Bigham Clause") will limit the amount chargeable to cargo to such lesser expense. The likelihood that this will occur in practice is extremely remote.

The effect of the Non-Separation Clauses, when applicable, is to preserve the shipowner's allowances for the wages and maintenance of crew and other detention expenses during the period of repairs and sometimes even further, up to the date when the ship would have regained her position (at which time the general average allowances made "in the absence of . . . forwarding" would cease). It is, however, submitted that the Non-Separation allowances should be limited to expenses which are *actually incurred* by the shipowner or charterer and should exclude any expenses which are properly chargeable to the vessel's next engagement. The figures set out in the Example on pages 78–79, which also show how the cost of forwarding cargo is treated under Rule F, illustrate this proposition.

Prior to 1994 it was not infrequently found that the provisions of the so-called standard forms of Non-Separation Agreement were not apt to cover the particular circumstances in which the parties found themselves. When this was the case, it was very often the task of the average adjuster to draft a special agreement, incorporating a Non-Separation provision, in order to suit the needs of the situation. It is envisaged that, notwithstanding the introduction of the Non-Separation Clauses into Rule G, cases will continue to arise which will exercise the ingenuity and diplomacy of the average adjuster to find a solution, in partial derogation of the York-Antwerp Rules, which will satisfy the conflicting interests of the parties.[27]

27. Two such instances are referred to in the Chairman's Address to the Association of Average Adjusters of the United States by Mr W. A. Carlson in October 1977.

RULE I

JETTISON OF CARGO

No jettison of cargo shall be made good as general average, unless such cargo is carried in accordance with the recognised custom of the trade.

EVOLUTION

Perhaps the most significant thing about this Rule is that it says nothing at all about the allowance in general average of cargo jettisoned from under-deck: the reason being that since the very earliest days[1] the jettison of under-deck cargo for the common safety has been recognised by the law and practice of all countries as the prime example of a general average sacrifice.

Conversely, the law as it developed in various countries of the world displayed considerable differences as to the allowance in general average, if any, for the jettison of cargo carried on deck.[2]

Consequently, in a desire to secure uniformity, the following text was adopted at the 1864 York Conference:

"Rule I. Jettison and Deck Cargo

A jettison of timber or deals, or any other description of wood cargo, carried on the deck of a ship in pursuance of a general custom of the trade in which the ship is then engaged, shall be made good as general average, in like manner as if such cargo had been jettisoned from below deck.

No jettison of deck cargo, other than timber or deals, or other wood cargo, so carried as aforesaid, shall be made good as general average.

Every structure not built in with the frame of the vessel shall be considered to be a part of the deck of the vessel."

In 1877, however, no doubt owing to the influence of the greater number of continental delegates present, the Antwerp Conference reversed the provision for allowance of jettison of timber cargoes carried on deck, so that the Rule read:

1. See Justinian, Digest XIV.2.1. "The Rhodian Law decrees that if in order to lighten a ship merchandise has been thrown overboard, that which has been given for all shall be replaced by the contribution of all."

2. See Rudolf, pp. 62–63.

"Rule I. Jettison of deck cargo

No jettison of deck cargo shall be made good as general average. Every structure not built in with the frame of the vessel should be considered to be a part of the deck of the vessel."

In the 1880s a number of cases on the question were decided in the English courts, as a result of which it could be stated with certainty that so far as English law was concerned a jettison of a deck cargo carried in accordance with a recognised custom of the trade, and not in violation of the contract of affreightment, was within general average.[3]

At the Liverpool Conference of 1890, therefore, the British Association of Average Adjusters proposed an amendment to Rule I accordingly, but this proposal was not accepted.

As a result of this, those engaged in the timber trade resorted to the expedient of issuing charterparties and bills of lading providing for the adjustment of general average in accordance with the York-Antwerp Rules 1890, "but excluding the word 'No' in Rule I". It was not until the 1924 Stockholm Conference, therefore, that a modified version of the British proposal was accepted and the present text emerged, without reference to what constitutes the deck of a vessel.

No changes were made in the Rule at the Conferences of 1949 or 1974.

At the Sydney Conference of 1994, the British delegation proposed on the grounds of equity and modern practice to reverse the emphasis of Rule I so that it would read:

"Jettison of cargo, wherever stowed, shall be made good as general average when made for the common safety."

Some delegations opposed this, perceiving the proposal as an unwarranted expansion of general average; others approved in principle, but considered the amendment unnecessary. In the event the proposal was lost by a narrow margin.

COMMENTARY

" . . . the recognised custom of the trade"

In English law there is little in the way of authority to establish what constitutes a recognised custom of the trade. Apart from two early cases in which a usage or custom was asserted and not denied,[4] it is established that a practice to insert in the bill of lading a liberty to stow on deck does not of itself establish a usage or custom of the trade.[5]

3. See *Johnson* v. *Chapman* (1865) 19 C.B.(N.S.) 563; *Wright* v. *Marwood* (1881) 7 Q.B.D. 62; *Burton* v. *English* (1883) 12 Q.B.D. 218; *Strang* v. *Scott* (1889) 14 App. Cas. 601; also AAA Rule of Practice F1, Appendix 4, p. 354.

4. *Gould* v. *Oliver* (1837) 4 Bing. N.C. 134 (timber from Quebec); *Milward* v. *Hibbert* (1842) 3 Q.B. 120 (pigs from Ireland).

5. *Dixon* v. *Royal Exchange Shipping Co.* (1886) 12 App. Cas. 11 (cotton from New Orleans).

In practice, therefore, it has to be decided as a matter of fact in each case, wherever the cargo is stowed, whether the location of the stowage is a proper place for the cargo to be carried in accordance with the custom of the trade.

When the York-Antwerp Rules were reviewed by the CMI International Sub-Committee in 1973, no recommendation was made to amend this Rule with reference to the practice of carrying containers on deck "because it was felt that generally a custom to carry containers on deck was already held to exist".[6] It is submitted that at the present time it is a recognised custom in virtually all trades to carry containers on deck for both deep sea and coastal voyages, and that this applies both to ships which are custom-built for the trade and those which have been adapted for the purpose.

6. In *Du Pont de Nemours International* v. "*Mormacvega*", 1972 AMC 2366; [1973] 1 Lloyd's Rep. 267, it was held in the District Court (S.D.N.Y.) that a custom had not been proved in 1967 to carry containers on deck; however to do so at that time did not amount to an unreasonable deviation: hence the carrier was entitled to limit his liability under U.S. COGSA.

RULE II

LOSS OR DAMAGE BY SACRIFICES FOR THE COMMON SAFETY

Loss of or damage to the property involved in the common maritime adventure by or in consequence of a sacrifice made for the common safety, and by water which goes down a ship's hatches opened or other opening made for the purpose of making a jettison for the common safety, shall be made good as general average.

EVOLUTION

This rule had its origin in a negative resolution passed by the 1860 Glasgow Conference, which read:

"(3) That the damage done to cargo by chafing and breakage, resulting from a jettison of part of the remainder of the cargo, ought not to be allowed in general average."

One of the reasons prompting this resolution was the practical difficulty of establishing what claims by chafing and breakage may have resulted from cargo being disturbed in its stowage by the efforts of those undertaking the jettison, and what was the result of accidental damage or normal handling.

At the 1864 York Conference principle was preferred to practical convenience, with the result that the Glasgow Resolution was reversed and a paragraph was added to affirm the established practice of allowing damage caused by water going down the hatches during a jettison. The text was:

"*RULE II. Damage by Jettison*

Damage done to goods or merchandise by water which unavoidably goes down a ship's hatches opened, or other opening made, for the purpose of making a jettison shall be made good as general average, in case the loss by jettison is so made good.

Damage done by breakage or chafing, or otherwise from derangement of stowage consequent upon a jettison, shall be made good as general average."

At the 1877 Antwerp Conference the two paragraphs in the Rule were brought into line by adding at the end of the second paragraph the phrase "in case the loss by jettison is so made good".

At the 1890 Liverpool Conference it was decided to broaden the Rule so as to bring within its framework not only damage sustained to cargo in consequence of an act of jettison, but also damage, both to ship and cargo, caused by any other sacrifice made for the common safety or consequential upon such a sacrifice being made. Both the text and the title were changed, so as to read:

"RULE II. Damage by Jettison and Sacrifice for the Common Safety.

Damage done to a ship and cargo, or either of them, by or in consequence of a sacrifice made for the common safety, and by water which goes down a ship's hatches opened or other opening made for the purpose of making a jettison for the common safety, shall be made good as general average."

No alteration was made in the 1924, 1950 or 1974 versions of the York-Antwerp Rules.

At Sydney in 1994, the title was again changed and the opening words of the Rule were amended to read: "*Loss of or damage to the property involved in the common maritime adventure* by or in consequence of . . . " This amendment sprang from two separate initiatives, the reasons for and purposes of which are explained in the commentary below.

COMMENTARY

In the first edition of this book, commenting upon the 1974 version of the Rule, it was noted that the text referred only to "damage" and not to "loss". Furthermore, the only interests referred to were ship and cargo, and for these reasons it was felt that the wording of the Rule was less than perfect, in that in the event of, e.g. a loss of cargo or damage to a container sustained in consequence of an act of sacrifice, justification would have to be sought in terms of Rule A, as qualified in Rule C. In the run-up to Sydney, therefore, the BMLA proposed that the opening words of the Rule should read simply: *Loss or damage sustained* in consequence of . . . " This proposal was supported by the CMI International Sub-Committee as a drafting amendment since no change of substance, nor of practice, was intended.

At Sydney, the U.S. delegation, in the course of arguing their case for the exclusion from general average of all pollution liabilities by means of a Rule Paramount, objected to the British recommendation for the improvement of Rule II on the ground that, absent a Rule Paramount, it would leave the door open to the admission of third party claims for damages for, *inter alia*, pollution consequent upon the jettison of oil. The problem was referred to the drafting committee who promptly proposed to shut the door by inserting "the property involved in the common maritime adventure" after "Loss of or damage to . . . " This solution—which was also applied in Rules V and VIII—was adopted by the conference.

"to the property involved in the common maritime adventure"

Although these words were designed to exclude any allowance under these numbered Rules II, V, and VIII for loss or damage sustained by parties not involved in the common maritime adventure, it is submitted that they are intentionally wide enough to comprise:

- all physical property, irrespective of its ownership, which is legitimately[1] on board the vessel at the time of the general average act. This will include containers, charterers' bunkers and equipment, as well as navigational and other equipment hired for its purpose. Whether in practice the benefit of this provision will also extend to the stocks of duty-free and other shops on board a passenger vessel will probably depend on the terms of the contract with the owner or franchise holder.
- freight at risk.[2]

Some goods legitimately on board the ship may be exempted from paying general average contribution[3] and might for this reason be thought to fall outside the common maritime adventure. But this is not so. In an adjustment prepared in 1931 in accordance with the 1924 Rules a considerable quantity of passengers' baggage, which had been damaged by measures taken to extinguish a fire which had occurred on a passenger/cargo liner, was properly made good as general average sacrifice, notwithstanding that passengers' baggage which was unaffected was exempted from contribution by Rule XVII. In an article published on the case,[4] a commentator wrote:

"This apparent anomaly is to be explained by the fact that while the parties to the contract of affreightment and their underwriters may for convenience and the saving of expense agree to exempt passengers' baggage from liability to contribution they cannot take away the right of any [other] party to claim compensation in general average for damage done to their property by the measures taken to save the common adventure in time of a peril."

As to losses of freight, Rule XV, as we shall see,[5] provides for the admission in general average of any such loss arising from damage to or loss of cargo "either when caused by a general average act, or when the damage to or loss of cargo is so made good". The intention is to make good in general average the freight element at carrier's risk on goods which are the subject of allowance for sacrifice. However, the wording of that Rule is rather obscure and in some instances in the past has been subject to a more generous interpretation than was intended by the draftsman. For example, the editors of Lowndes and Rudolf considered that Rule XV would cover a loss of freight at carrier's risk

1. One case of illegitimacy is instanced in Rule XIX. See *post*, p. 247.
2. Cf. The International Convention on Salvage 1989, Art. 1 (definitions).
3. As instanced in the final paragraph of Rule XVII, *post*, p. 228.
4. *The Comorin*, Lloyd's List of 30 November 1931.
5. *Post*, p. 213.

on cargo left behind at a port of refuge which had to be discharged in order to bring the vessel within her loadline to compensate for the additional weight of water absorbed by other cargo as a result of a fire extinguishing operation.[6] Since 1994 however, it is the author's opinion that justification for the allowance in these circumstances can be found within Rule II.

6. Lowndes & Rudolf (11th ed.), sect. 15.09.

RULE III

EXTINGUISHING FIRE ON SHIPBOARD

Damage done to a ship and cargo, or either of them, by water or otherwise, including damage by beaching or scuttling a burning ship, in extinguishing a fire on board the ship, shall be made good as general average; except that no compensation shall be made for damage by smoke however caused or by heat of the fire.

EVOLUTION

The second Resolution passed by the 1860 Glasgow Conference read:

"That the damage done to ship, cargo, and freight, in extinguishing fire, shall be allowed in general average."

This was approved without very much alteration by the 1864 York Conference, so that the Rule then read:

"Damage done to a ship and cargo, or either of them, by water or otherwise, in extinguishing a fire on board the ship, shall be general average."

It is to be noted that both the Resolution and the Rule differed from the then current practice of British average adjusters, who excluded from contribution the damage caused to goods by water poured upon them to extinguish a fire, possibly on the ground that, unlike a case of jettison, no particular package or packages had been selected for the sacrifice. As Lowndes tells us, the practice of British adjusters until 1873 was that if a hole was cut in the deck of a ship in order to pour water down into the hold and quench the fire, the cost of repairing the deck was allowed in general average, but the damage done to the goods by the water poured upon them was not allowed. This practice was totally disapproved by Quain J. in *Stewart* v. *West India and Pacific Steamship Co.*,[1] in which the learned judge said:

"It is to be hoped that in future there will be no difference between law and custom on this point [the allowance in general average of damage done to cargo by pouring on water to extinguish a fire] and that average adjusters will act on the law as now declared, and that bills of lading will also be framed in accordance with it."

1. *Stewart* v. *West India and Pacific Steamship Co.* (1873) L.R. 8 Q.B. 88; 1 Asp. M.C. 528.

In consequence of this decision, the AAA, at their 1873 General Meeting, passed a Rule of Practice "that damage done by water poured down a ship's hold to extinguish a fire be treated as general average".[2]

The old guard took their small revenge the following year by persuading the 1874 General Meeting of the AAA to pass another Rule of Practice modifying the above. This read:

"That goods in a ship which is on fire, or the cargo of which is on fire, affected by water voluntarily used to extinguish such fire, shall not be the subject of general average if the packages so affected be themselves on fire at the time the water was thrown upon them." [3]

At the 1877 Antwerp Conference, Richard Lowndes successfully moved an amendment to the 1864 Rule, by which the following wording was added:

" . . . except that no compensation be made for damage done by water to packages which have been on fire."

Two further amendments were made at the 1890 Liverpool Conference, so that the Rule then read;

"Damage done to a ship and cargo, or either of them, by water or otherwise, including damage by beaching or scuttling a burning ship, in extinguishing a fire on board the ship, shall be made good as general average; except that no compensation shall be made for damage to such portions of the ship and bulk cargo, or to such separate packages of cargo, as have been on fire."

Those who favoured the second amendment clearly thought that when a fire had broken out in a cargo carried in bulk, no allowance should be made for extinguishing damage sustained by any of the cargo in those compartments where the fire had taken hold. So far as English law is concerned, that view was held to be too sweeping, since in *Greenshields Cowie & Co.* v. *Stephens & Sons*,[4] Lord Alverstone C.J. said:

"[It was] contended that each hold constituted a 'portion' of bulk cargo, and that no contribution could be claimed under this rule in respect of damage by water to the coal in the three holds which were on fire. I think it is quite impossible to read the clause in that way."

No alteration to Rule III was made at the Conferences of 1924 or 1949, and during the years that preceded the 1974 Hamburg Conference, it became apparent that there were differences in the practice of average adjusters in different countries in deciding:

(a) what was a "portion" of the ship or of a bulk cargo which had been on fire, and

2. This Rule of Practice (F2) still stands; see p. 355.
3. This Rule was rescinded in 1968.
4. *Greenshields Cowie & Co.* v. *Stephens & Sons*, in the Court of Appeal; [1908] 1 K.B. 51; 13 Com. Cas. 91; 10 Asp. M.C. 597 (citation at p. 600); affirmed in the House of Lords on the "inherent vice" issue.

(b) whether, and to what extent, damage by smoke should be allowed as general average.

In connection with the latter, it was averred that in many cases when carbon dioxide gas was applied to a compartment which had been properly sealed for the purpose of suppressing a fire, the generation of smoke was thereby increased and liable to affect the packages in the compartment with greater intensity. This view was denied by other experts, and many of the variations in practice appeared to depend upon the opinion of the cargo surveyors attending the case. Furthermore, the practice of allowing in general average the enhancement of damage by smoke in consequence of efforts to extinguish fire had been disapproved in the United States in the case of *Reliance Marine Insurance Co.* v. *New York & Cuba Mail Steamship Co.*[5]

In the run-up to the 1974 Hamburg Conference, the BMLA proposed two amendments to solve these problems by:

(a) deleting the exclusion that no compensation should be made for damage to "such portions of the ship and bulk cargo, or to separate packages of cargo, as have been on fire", and
(b) to add, in its place, a new exclusion for damage by smoke or heat, however caused.

Since the main thrust of the Hamburg Conference was to encourage simplification of general average procedures, these amendments were adopted.

In the meetings of the International Sub-Committee preparatory to the Sydney Conference, the United States M.L.A. tabled proposals for further amendment, one of which would have had the effect of reinstating the exclusion of damage "to such parts of the ship or bulk cargo, or to such separate packages of cargo, as have been on fire". This was denounced as totally regressive and so heavily mauled in committee that at the Conference itself the U.S. delegation withdrew this proposal, whilst maintaining the other of its proposals, namely to substitute "heat of the fire" for the single word "fire" in the existing text. This latter amendment was approved.

COMMENTARY

In consequence of (a)—the first of the 1974 amendments mentioned above —cargo surveyors no longer need to make a separation of water-damaged cargo into parcels suffering water damage only and those which have additionally been touched by fire. The other parties to the adventure will not now have to pay for the additional labour cost involved in making this

5. *Reliance Marine Insurance Co.* v. *New York & Cuba Mail Steamship Co.* (1896) 70 Fed. Rep. 262; 77 Fed. Rep. 317.

separation, nor, if it has been overlooked, will the average adjuster have to rely on guesswork. No longer is it necessary to explore the realm of semantics to decide what is a "portion" of a bulk cargo, or whether there is a distinction between a package which is charred and one which is scorched. The second amendment, (b), has also been beneficial, since the exclusion for damage by smoke, however caused, has succeeded where argument had failed in bringing about uniformity of practice.

The reason for the "heat of the fire" amendment was explained at Sydney by a member of the U.S. delegation by reference to a case in which water was applied to extinguish a fire in the engine room of a reefer ship. This water put the refrigerating machinery out of operation and as a result the temperature in the refrigerated spaces rose and a quantity of foodstuffs went bad. An adjustment was prepared, admitting into general average, *inter alia*, the value of the condemned foodstuffs. This was objected to by certain debtor interests on the ground that under the 1974 text of Rule III this was "damage by . . . heat however caused". It was to avoid a recurrence of this spurious kind of objection that the amendment was moved and passed.

Although in the course of these various amendments the scope of the Rule has been widened, it still does not embrace every circumstance which may arise in practice in cases of fire or the danger of fire. So, in the interpretation of this Rule III it is to be noted:

(i) The Rule applies to "damage"; not "loss and damage". Although the word "damage", when applied to cargo, may cover instances where such damage renders the goods a constructive total loss, allowance for the loss sustained by jettisoning cargo which is on fire (provided it is not in a state of wreck) requires Rule A, and possibly also Rule I, for its justification.

(ii) Damage to property which is not "cargo" would need to be justified under Rule A, and loss of freight under Rule XV.

More importantly, Rule III deals only with damage done in extinguishing *fire*. As Wright J. said in *Tempus Shipping* v. *Louis Dreyfus*: "Mere heating which has not arrived at the state of incandescence or ignition is not within the specific word 'fire' ".[6] So, if a cargo has overheated and there is a real danger of its catching fire, measures reasonably taken to prevent the outbreak of fire will fall, not under Rule III, but under Rule A.[7] On the other hand, if the master has misjudged the situation and has applied water to goods in the

6. *Tempus Shipping Co.* v. *Louis Dreyfus* [1930] 1 K.B. 699 at p. 708; 36 Ll.L.Rep. 159 at p. 169.

7. See *The Knight of St. Michael* (1898) 8 Asp. M.C. 360; 3 Com. Cas. 62. In that case Barnes J. found that there was "an actual existing state of peril of fire" even though at the time the measures were taken to avert that peril there had been no actual outbreak of fire.

mistaken belief that there was a fire in the hold, when none existed, nor even any danger of fire, this is not a general average situation at all, the element of peril being absent.[8]

8. See *Watson* v. *Fireman's Fund Insurance Co.* [1922] 2 K.B. 355; 12 Ll.L.Rep. 133.

RULE IV

CUTTING AWAY WRECK

Loss or damage sustained by cutting away wreck or parts of the ship which have been previously carried away or are effectively lost by accident shall not be made good as general average.

EVOLUTION

This Rule had its origin in a resolution passed at the 1860 Glasgow Conference, which read:

"That the loss sustained by cutting away the wreck of masts accidentally broken ought not to be allowed in general average."

At the 1864 York Conference the terms of this Resolution were slightly enlarged and brought into the text of the York Rules. The Rule then read:

"Loss or damage caused by cutting away the wreck or remains of spars, or of other things which have previously been carried away by sea-peril, shall not be made good as general average."

No change was made at any of the subsequent revisions of the York-Antwerp Rules until 1974. At that time it was considered by some that the Rule, which clearly demonstrated its origin from the days of sailing ships, was obsolete and should be deleted. However, it was decided to retain the Rule, and a more up-to-date wording was adopted, omitting any reference to spars. The grounds for its retention were that, apart from serving a function in a limited number of cases, it also sets out a principle which was not expressed elsewhere in the York-Antwerp Rules.

At the Sydney Conference in 1994 the United States Delegation proposed that the Rule should be rescinded and the following be adopted in its place:

"Rule IV—Allowance for Sacrifice.
When the ship or cargo or other property on board the ship sustains a combination of sacrificial damage and damage which is not general average the amount made good in general average under any of these Rules shall not exceed the net increase in repair or replacement costs resulting from the sacrificial damage."

In support of this proposal, the U.S. working paper[1] declared:

"The philosophy behind this recommendation is the same as that behind current Rule XVIII(b), i.e., what has been lost by accident cannot be sacrificed.

If this revision is accepted, it would mean that if a part must be replaced because of the accidental damage alone, the mere fact that it also suffered damage in, say, refloating or fire extinguishing efforts, would not qualify any part of the replacement cost for an allowance in general average.

Also, if both sacrificial and accidental damage require drydocking and other so-called "common charges," the allowance in general average would be limited to the amount by which the sacrificial damage *increased* the time on drydock, etc."

The delegates clearly thought that this was altogether too much to swallow at one gulp, and the proposal was decisively rejected.

COMMENTARY

Historically, it would not be totally accurate to say that the Rule expressed a principle; rather, it was originally designed to avoid the difficulty of determining what value, if any, attached to the remains of a mast or spars which, having carried away by sea-peril, had to be cut adrift for the common safety. Rudolf states that the practice in England, Belgium and Scandinavia was therefore to exclude from allowance in general average any part of the mast or spars which had previously carried away, even though some part of the spars might have been saved had it not been decided to cut them all adrift for the common safety.

The present text of the Rule, it is submitted, would not support such a severe practice. Indeed, the 1974 text has brought the Rule closer to principle. "Parts of the ship which . . . are effectively lost by accident . . . " is simply a more up to date way of saying "parts of the ship which are in a state of wreck". The Rule in its present form has to do with the reality of the sacrifice, and excludes from general average only those parts of a ship which are as good as lost at the time when the decision is made to cut them away.

For example: a ship is lying at anchor when a storm blows up, and the master, being concerned that the anchors might drag and the ship might be blown onshore, decides to weigh the anchors and make out to sea for the common safety. One anchor is successfully weighed, but the other has caught on some underwater obstruction and cannot be freed. The cable is therefore allowed to run out and is lost, together with the anchor. Although the slipping of the cable is an act performed for the common safety, there is no sacrifice, either of the anchor or the cable, if the facts are such that both anchor and cable would be irretrievable even in the absence of the emergency. In that

1. CMI document GENAV 47.

event both would be effectively lost by sea peril, through the anchor being caught on a snag prior to the decision to let go the cable.

On the other hand, if despite the emergency, time had permitted the cable to be buoyed, and afterwards the anchor and cable could be recovered, the cost of its recovery and reconnection to the ship would be allowable in general average, not as sacrifice, but as a general average expenditure; the reason being that the subsequent successful recovery of the anchor and cable would demonstrate that their loss was not irretrievable.

One of the amendments effected in 1974 was to substitute the words "sustained by" for "caused by" in the phrase that previously read "loss or damage *caused by* cutting away wreck . . . " Even as amended, the wording of this part of the Rule is criticised by Lowndes & Rudolf,[2] on the ground that consequential damage to a part of the ship not previously affected by the accident could be caused by the cutting away of wreck. The case is instanced of a broken mast on an auxiliary sailing vessel which was cut away for the common safety, and as a consequence of being cut away caused damage to the propeller. In the opinion of the author the editors of Lowndes & Rudolf are correct in stating that the damage to the propeller should not be excluded, but it is submitted that this conclusion can be justified not only on principle, but also on the construction of the Rule in its present wording.

2. Lowndes & Rudolf (11th ed.), sect. 4.15.

RULE V

VOLUNTARY STRANDING

When a ship is intentionally run on shore for the common safety, whether or not she might have been driven on shore, the consequent loss or damage to the property involved in the common maritime adventure shall be allowed in general average.

EVOLUTION

At the 1860 Glasgow Conference there was a heated debate between those who would allow the damage caused by voluntary stranding as a matter of principle, and those who would disallow it on the ground of uncertainty of proof. In the event, the Resolution passed by the Conference was vague and inconclusive:

"That, as a general rule in the case of the stranding of a vessel in the course of her voyage, the loss or damage to ship, cargo or freight shall not be the subject of general average, but without prejudice to such a claim in exceptional cases, upon clear proof of special facts."

At the 1864 York Conference the wording was altered:

"When a ship is intentionally run on shore because she is sinking or driving on shore or rocks, no damage caused to the ship, the cargo and the freight, or any or either of them, by such intentional running on shore, shall be made good as general average."

No alteration was made to the terms of the Rule at the 1877 Antwerp Conference.

Thus far the Rule dealt only with two situations where, contrary to principle, it was intended to exclude from general average damage caused in consequence of voluntary stranding, the purpose of the exclusion being to reduce the opportunities that were thought to exist for fraud and abuse, and not any point of principle. In this respect it followed the old custom of Lloyd's, which read:

"The custom of Lloyd's excludes from general average all damage to ship or cargo resulting from a voluntary stranding. This Rule does not necessarily exclude such damage as is done by beaching or scuttling a burning vessel to extinguish the fire."

At the 1890 Liverpool Conference two alterations were made:

(a) the circumstances of exclusion were narrowed to apply to those cases where a ship would *inevitably* sink or drive on shore or on rocks, and
(b) a new sentence was added to make it clear that in all cases where the exclusions did not apply, the damage caused by voluntary stranding should be made good in general average.

At the 1924 Stockholm Conference, the exception of the ship's inevitably sinking was removed from the Rule, and at the 1949 Amsterdam Conference it was made clear that even when the sole remaining exception applied, namely that the vessel would inevitably drive on shore or on rocks, the damage caused by refloating the vessel should nonetheless be allowed.

The 1950 Rule then read:

> "When a ship is intentionally run on shore, and the circumstances are such that if that course were not adopted she would inevitably drive on shore or on rocks, no loss or damage caused to the ship, cargo and freight or any of them by such intentional running on shore shall be made good as general average, but loss or damage incurred in refloating such a ship shall be allowed as general average.
>
> In all other cases where a ship is intentionally run on shore for the common safety, the consequent loss or damage shall be allowed as general average."

In 1974 the Rule was recast in such a way as to remove the remaining exception, namely that no damage would be allowed in general average when the circumstances were such that the vessel would inevitably have driven onto the shore or rocks. This amendment eliminates the necessity to decide, when the peril of stranding is present, whether the facts are such that the vessel will *inevitably* strand. The author has had experience of such a case, under the 1950 Rules, when a vessel was torn adrift from her moorings by the surge of an extraordinary river flood and, being without motive power, was driven inexorably towards the sea by the flood waters: in that case, however, it was not inevitable that the vessel would strand, since other dangers were also present, namely of violent collision with other vessels and/or contact with the harbour installations.

It is submitted that the Rule as it stands is consistent with principle.

However, in the proceedings of the CMI International Sub-Committee prior to the Sydney Conference of 1994, the USMLA tabled a proposal to revert to the wording as it was in 1950. There was a total absence of support for this proposal, which was accordingly withdrawn. The only change made at Sydney was to add the words "to the property involved in the common maritime adventure" after "the consequent loss or damage" in order to prevent any potential claims for liability to third parties (and particularly for pollution damages) from being admitted under this Rule.[1]

1. See commentary headed "The Environmental Issue", p. 52 *et seq*.

COMMENTARY

"... intentionally run on shore for the common safety"

The meaning of the expression "intentionally run on shore" and the extent of "the consequent loss or damage" are illustrated in the case, under the 1890 Rules, of *Anglo-Grecian Steam Trading Co. Ltd.* v. *T. Beynon & Co.*[2]

In that case the vessel's propeller became entangled with the mooring chain of a buoy, which rendered both the vessel's engines and steering inoperable. It was therefore decided to beach the vessel and for that purpose two tugs were engaged to tow her to a particular bay where the pilot considered that she could safely be beached. However, the vessel took the ground unexpectedly in a place not intended by the pilot and, the tugs' tow ropes parting in trying to hold the ship against the wind and tide, she carried against some rocks and sustained substantial damage to her bottom. Shipowners brought an action to recover cargo's contribution to this damage under Rule V of the 1890 Rules. Roche J. held that the vessel was run ashore for the common safety, and that the beaching was intentional, even though the vessel had grounded sooner and at a different place than was intended. Furthermore, since there was no intervening negligence on the part of anyone, the damage sustained to the vessel's bottom by striking the rocks was the direct and immediate consequence of the general average act.

"... consequent loss or damage to the property ... adventure"

This expression is certainly wide enough to encompass a loss sustained by cargo and a loss of freight resulting, not only from the action of beaching the vessel, but from the measures taken to refloat her subsequently. For example, following a collision in which the vessel was holed she is voluntarily stranded on a sandbank. After the crew has effected temporary repairs to patch the hole, both ship and cargo may be considered technically to be in safety, at least so far as the peril of sinking is concerned. Nevertheless, it may be necessary to lighten the ship in order to enable her to refloat, and the loss of cargo by jettison for this purpose, together with the corresponding loss of freight if the same be at the shipowners' risk, is properly admissible in general average in the terms of Rule V.

On the other hand, if as a result of the voluntary stranding loss or damage is sustained by parties who are not involved in the common maritime adventure, it has now been made abundantly clear since the 1994 amendment to the Rule that any claim in respect of such loss, damage or expense cannot be brought within general average by virtue of this Rule V. Such claims will therefore have to be tested by the terms of Rule C. For example, suppose a

2. *Anglo-Grecian Steam Trading Co. Ltd.* v. *T. Beynon & Co.* (1926) 24 Ll.L.Rep. 122.

vessel, having been holed by striking a submerged object, is run ashore for the common safety, and in so doing:

(a) fouls the moorings of a fishing boat, which consequently breaks adrift and is wrecked;
(b) runs over an oyster bed, and
(c) in going aground, broaches one of her bunker tanks, which spills oil onto an adjoining beach.

The outcome will be:

(a) The claim for the loss of the fishing boat will be admissible in general average provided that the loss can be shown to have been the direct consequence of the general average act, as provided in the first paragraph of Rule C;
(b) The claim of the owner of the oyster bed for damages in tort will be excluded from general average since it is "in respect of damage to the environment" within the second paragraph of Rule C; and
(c) Similarly, the cost of cleaning up the beach, directly incurred by the shipowner, would be an "expense incurred . . . in consequence of the escape or release of [a] pollutant substance" and likewise excluded.

RULE VI

SALVAGE

(a) Expenditure incurred by the parties to the adventure in the nature of salvage, whether under contract or otherwise, shall be allowed in general average provided that the salvage operations were carried out for the purpose of preserving from peril the property involved in the common maritime adventure.

Expenditure allowed in general average shall include any salvage remuneration in which the skill and efforts of the salvors in preventing or minimising damage to the environment such as is referred to in Article 13 paragraph 1(b) of the International Convention on Salvage 1989 have been taken into account.

(b) Special compensation payable to a salvor by the shipowner under Article 14 of the said Convention to the extent specified in paragraph 4 of that Article or under any other provision similar in substance shall not be allowed in general average.

EVOLUTION

This rule was introduced in 1974 in place of an obsolete rule regarding loss or damage to sails. The object was to ensure that payments made by the parties to adventure on account of salvage would be allowed as general average, and apportioned as such over the values obtaining at the termination of the adventure whenever the salvage services were undertaken for the common safety. This was indeed in accordance with the law and practice in virtually all the countries of continental Europe and also in the United States of America, but English law was different, as is explained in more detail in the commentary below, and it was precisely because English law and practice was so much out of line with that which obtained in the rest of the world that, once again, the York-Antwerp Rules were used as the vehicle for achieving uniformity.

The text which was agreed by the Hamburg Conference was as follows:

"*Salvage remuneration*

Expenditure incurred by the parties to the adventure on account of salvage, whether under contract or otherwise, shall be allowed in general average to the extent that the salvage operations were undertaken for the purpose of preserving from peril the property involved in the common maritime adventure."

The British delegation, recognising their responsibility to introduce a text to correct what was, after all, a peculiarity of the English system, had submitted a draft, the opening words of which were: "The aggregate of the liabilities incurred by the parties to the adventure . . . ". The expression "the aggregate of the liabilities" was thought to be both clumsy and confusing, as it might possibly be construed as if it had some connection with liabilities *of the salvor*. The view was expressed in debate that the opening words of the draft meant no more than "all expenditure", and in the final text the word "all" was also dropped as being mere surplusage.

In 1990 the Rule was substantially amended at a Conference of the CMI held in Paris, the subject having been added to the conference agenda at relatively short notice at the request of the Secretary General of the International Maritime Organization (IMO), following the adoption of a resolution to that effect by the conference convened in London in April 1989 to approve the text of a new International Convention on salvage.[1]

No change was made to the Rule at the Sydney Conference in 1994.

THE INTERNATIONAL CONVENTION ON SALVAGE 1989

At the heart of the Convention, in Article 8, lies the obligation, which attaches equally to the salvor and to the master of the salved vessel and the owners of property, "to exercise due care to prevent or minimise damage to the environment" in the course of the salvage operations. Damage to the environment is defined in Article 1(d) as "substantial physical damage to human health or to marine life or resources in coastal or inland waters or areas adjacent thereto, caused by pollution, contamination, fire, explosion or similar major incidents".

In return for the acceptance of this obligation, it is provided in Article 13.1(b) that one of the criteria to be taken into account in fixing a salvage reward will be "the skill and efforts of the salvor in preventing or minimising damage to the environment".

Article 13.2 follows English law in providing that payment of the reward will be made by the salved ship and other property in proportion to their respective salved values. However, if the national law should require payment to be made by only one of such interests, for example by the shipowner, this will be recognised subject to the right of recourse of the party making the payment against the other interests for their respective shares, e.g. by their contribution in general average.

It will be remembered that the 1910 Convention made no provision as to who was the debtor for any salvage reward.

1. See Darling and Smith, *LOF 90 and the new Salvage Convention*, where the text of the Convention is reproduced (Appendix B, pp. 153–164). The resolution requesting the amendment of the York-Antwerp Rules is contained in Attachment 2 of the Final Act of the Conference.

When there has been a threat of damage to the environment and the salvage service has been unsuccessful, or succeeds only to a limited extent, the salvor will be entitled, as an exception to the "No Cure—No Pay" principle, to "special compensation", which will be paid by the shipowner (Article 14). This "special compensation" may be assessed at three different levels:

(a) If there has been a threat of damage to the environment which (by implication) the salvor was unable to avert, he will be entitled to recover his out-of-pocket expenses reasonably incurred in the salvage operation and a fair rate for equipment and personnel actually and reasonably employed therein (referred to hereafter as "his expenses").
(b) If the salvor's efforts have prevented or minimised damage to the environment, he may recover his expenses plus an uplift of up to 30 per cent.
(c) The extent of the uplift in the circumstances envisaged in paragraph (b) may however be increased to not more than 100 per cent. of the salvor's expenses if the tribunal considers it fair and just to do so.

Furthermore, the expenses will be payable for the whole period of the salvage operation; they will not be limited to any particular part of the operation, let alone that part during which there was a threat to the environment. However, "expenses" as defined in Article 14.3 (summarised in paragraph (a) above) does not include any element of profit.[2]

The Convention will apply to any salvage operations except to the extent that a contract otherwise provides expressly or by implication (Article 6.1). The authority to conclude salvage contracts is vested in the master for the shipowner's interest, and in the master or the shipowner on behalf of the property on board (Article 6.2).

A salvor of life remains unentitled to any remuneration from the persons whose lives are saved, but when the saving of life forms part of the service rendered on the occasion of the accident giving rise to a claim for salvage, the salvor of life will be entitled to a fair share of the remuneration awarded for the salvage of property or for the prevention of environmental damage.

The Convention will enter into force on 14 July 1996, i.e. one year after its acceptance by Italy, the 15th country to do so. In England, however, the Convention has already come into effect, as from 1 January 1995, by virtue of the Merchant Shipping (Salvage and Pollution) Act 1994.

What the Convention does *not* state is how the payments, whether under Article 13 for a salvage reward or Article 14 for "special compensation", are to be funded. This all-important question had in fact been hammered out in principle as long ago as 1980, when Lloyd's Form of Salvage Agreement was amended in order to provide for the first time for payments outside the

2. So decided by Clarke J. in *The Nagasaki Spirit* [1995] 2 Lloyd's Rep. 44.

principle of "no cure—no pay" when a salvor had been unsuccessful in salving a laden tanker. Under this agreement, originally undertaken by London market underwriters and the International Group of P. & I. Clubs and subsequently followed in all leading markets, property underwriters continued to pay for conventional salvage rewards, even though the cost might be higher by reason of the salvor's efforts to avoid environmental damage, and P. & I. Clubs would pay the amounts awarded when the salvage efforts had been unsuccessful (the "safety net"). This market understanding was extended informally when the proposals for a new Salvage Convention were debated at a CMI Conference in Montreal in 1981, and for this reason it is sometimes referred to as the "Montreal compromise". The agreement was subsequently formalised by its principal parties after the issue of an amended Lloyd's Form of Salvage Agreement on 5 September 1990.

It is to be noted that the relationship between Article 13 and Article 14 is purely mathematical. To be recoverable under the "safety net", the expenses incurred by the salvor need not have had as their object the prevention or minimising of environmental damage. Indeed, they might have no such connection at all. The only relevant criteria are that there had been a threat of damage to the environment, and that the salvor had failed to earn a sufficient reward under Article 13. It was these factors which, more than any other, rendered necessary the 1990 amendment to Rule VI (see comments hereafter).

LLOYD'S FORM OF SALVAGE AGREEMENT

LOF 1990 AND LOF 1995

It was expected that because of the need to attract 15 ratifications or accessions it would be many years before the 1989 Salvage Convention came into force. The industries concerned (particularly the salvage industry) were not prepared to wait that long. The Lloyd's working party (which represents all commercial organisations interested in salvage) therefore made an early decision in 1990 that the process should be accelerated with the introduction in that year of a new Form of Lloyd's Salvage Agreement, known as LOF 1990. This form gave life to the Convention by the simple device of incorporating into the Agreement the relevant parts of Articles 1, 8, 13 and 14. The same process was adopted in the updating of the French Contrat d'Assistance Maritime and other forms of salvage agreement.

Lloyd's Form of Salvage Agreement was further amended to come into effect concurrently with the enforcement in England of the 1989 Convention. This form is known as LOF 1995.[3]

3. The text of LOF 1995 is reproduced as Appendix 5, p. 361.

Consequently when LOF 1990, LOF 1995, or other appropriately amended salvage form has been agreed by the parties, the essential parts of the 1989 Convention, in particular the duty of the salvors and the owners of property to exercise due care in the conduct of a salvage operation to prevent or minimise damage to the environment, and the extended "safety net", take effect by contract.

It is worth noting that under Article 1 (the "definitions" Article):

(a) Salvage operations may take place not only in navigable waters, but in any other waters whatsoever.
(b) "Vessel" means any ship or craft, or any structure capable of navigation, and
(c) Property includes freight at risk.

These definitions extend the concept of salvage as previously applied in English law.

Also noteworthy is Article 6.2:

> "The master shall have the authority to conclude contracts for salvage operations on behalf of the owner of the vessel. The master or the owner of the vessel shall have the authority to conclude such contracts on behalf of the owner of the property on board the vessel."

This provision, now part of English law, puts to rest the vexed question whether the master had authority to bind the owners of other property to a salvage contract as an "agent of necessity"—a question disputed by owners of cargo in the case of *The Choko Star*.[4]

THE INTER-RELATIONSHIP OF SALVAGE AND GENERAL AVERAGE

In essence, both salvage and general average are forms of ransom from total loss. By the law maritime of all countries the cost of redemption from total loss is to be borne by the interests which have been saved.

The points of similarity are:

1. The property, to be the subject of the salvage or general average, must be in peril.

The extent of peril required to justify an act as general average is discussed in the chapter on Rule A.[5] For salvage, English law appears to recognise that a service may be rewarded as salvage in circumstances which are closer to the

4. *The Choko Star* [1990] 1 Lloyd's Rep. 516.
5. See *ante*, p. 35 *et seq*.

theory of "common benefit" than to "common safety". In *The Troilus*[6] the vessel was towed by a sister ship from a port of refuge where she was able to lie in physical safety but at which she could not effect repairs, to her port of destination at which repairs could be effected. The House of Lords held that this service was rewardable as salvage. Lord Porter, in delivering the judgment of the House, said:

"The solution of the question whether a ship has reached a place of safety must, I think, depend upon the facts of each case, one of which is the facility for repairs at the place in question, and another, the possibility of safely discharging and storing the cargo and sending it on to its destination and the danger of its deterioration. It is not a sufficient answer to say that she can lie in a particular position of physical safety. It must be remembered that in every voyage of a merchant ship carrying cargo the interests of both ship and cargo have to be borne in mind."

2. The property which is imperilled must be saved by the exertions of those engaged, otherwise there is no fund to pay for them.

In the Salvage Conventions of 1910 and 1989 this is expressed by stating that services which do not have a "useful result" will not earn any reward.

For general average, Bovill C.J. said in *Fletcher* v. *Alexander*[7]:

"If, after the jettison or the matter which is the subject of general average has arisen, the remainder of the goods are totally lost, and so no benefit accrues to the owners of the other goods from the jettison, no contribution can be claimed."

3. If successful, the exertions made to save the imperilled property create a legal right to charge the property saved to pay an amount of money for saving it. However, the similarity ends there, since the nature of the right and the time at which it can be exercised differ.

The main points of difference are:

1. In a claim for salvage, the exertions which are to be rewarded are those of persons who are strangers to the community of interest. In English legal theory, they are "volunteers" who are entitled to a reward from the salved property by reason of their voluntary efforts.

In general average, it is the duty of those on board the ship to exert themselves for the safety of the ship and cargo. There is no question of reward; the system of general average being concerned with the equitable redistribution within the community of interest of the cost, whether in terms of sacrifices

6. *The Troilus* [1951] A.C. 820; [1951] 1 Lloyd's Rep. 467; affirming 83 Ll.L.Rep. 195. See also *The Glaucus* (1948) 81 Ll.L.Rep. 262, in which the cost of towage to a second port of refuge was likewise rewarded as salvage. In that case Willmer J. said: "Quite apart from the physical danger, there is this to be added, that until somebody got her to a place where the necessary repairs could be executed she was completely immobilised. It is no use saying that this valuable property, worth something approaching a million pounds, is safe, if it is safe in circumstances where nobody can use it. For practical purposes, it might just as well be at the bottom of the sea. For these reasons, therefore, I am satisfied that the *Glaucus* must be regarded as being throughout in a position of danger . . . "

7. *Fletcher* v. *Alexander* (1868) L.R. 3 C.P. 375; 3 M.L.C. 69.

made or expenses incurred, of the measures considered necessary for the common safety and/or a safe outcome of the adventure.

2. In a case of salvage, the salvor has a maritime lien on the property saved, which attaches at the time and place where the salvage services terminate. For general average contributions, the shipowner's remedy, recognised in most jurisdictions, is a possessory lien which he cannot exercise until the termination of the adventure. As stated in the chapter on Rule G,[8] the adventure terminates at the time and place at which the carrier is obliged to effect delivery of cargo under the contract of carriage, i.e. at destination, unless circumstances arise which entitle him to abandon the voyage short of destination, or cause the adventure to be frustrated.

3. For both salvage and general average it is necessary to make an assessment of the values which have been saved. In a salvage case this is done to assist the tribunal in the assessment of the reward and, when it is part of the tribunal's function to do so, to determine how much each interest will pay. In general average, the purpose is to assess the values on which each interest will contribute. Moreover, there are differences in the manner in which these values are calculated:

(a) For the reasons given in paragraph 2, the values in a salvage case are assessed at the time and place where the salvage services terminate, whereas for general average the values are assessed when and where the common maritime adventure ends.

(b) In assessing the value of a vessel under time charter, the English law of salvage requires that the enhancement of the vessel's value by reason of her trading under a beneficial charter,[9] and possibly also the disadvantageous effect of her trading under an unprofitable charter, should be taken into account. In general average, by virtue of Rule XVII of the York-Antwerp Rules, the beneficial or detrimental effect of the charterparty is disregarded.

(c) In the adjustment of general average, amounts made good for general average sacrifice are added to the physical values at the termination of the adventure in order to arrive at the values for contribution.

THE ADMISSION OF SALVAGE PAYMENTS INTO GENERAL AVERAGE ADJUSTMENT

1. Continental Europe

In several jurisdictions, e.g. the Netherlands, Greece, France and Spain, the shipowner is mandatorily or at the option of the salvor the debtor for the

8. See *ante*, p. 83 *et seq*.
9. *The Castor* [1932] P. 142; 18 Asp. M.C. 312.

salvage remuneration. Even when this is not the case, most (and probably all) continental systems provide that the salvage award or remuneration is shared among the parties to the adventure in accordance with the provisions which apply in those countries relating to general average contribution—see, for example, Italian Code of Navigation, Article 497. This was recognised in a resolution approved by the General Assembly of the Association Internationale des Dispacheurs Européens (AIDE) at Antwerp in 1965 reading (in translation):

"The Assembly considers than when the salvage reward has already been divided by an arbitrator or by a tribunal between ship, freight and cargo, the average adjuster may treat the reward as general average and establish another apportionment on the basis of the actual values which after verification are admitted in the general average adjustment."

2. United States

The principle is that when salvage services are engaged or accepted by the master to save the adventure from a common peril the amounts so paid are apportioned as general average in the same manner as any other extraordinary disbursement voluntarily incurred for the common benefit.[10]

This principle was upheld by the Court of Appeals (Second Circuit) in *Amerada Hess Corporation* v. *Mobil* (*The Mobil Apex*).[11] This case was decided under the 1950 Rules, the court being satisfied that the performance of the salvage services fell within the definition of general average contained in Rule A.

3. United Kingdom

English law has for many years viewed the position differently. Since the case of *The Raisby*[12] it has been held that where there is no salvage agreement, or even where there is a salvage agreement but it does not fix the amount of remuneration, the liability of the shipowner does not extend beyond the proportion due in respect of his interest in ship and freight. Since that case, it has never been questioned that the liability of salved interests to the salvors is individual. Thus, when salvage services were rendered by volunteers, the practice was to exclude them altogether from the general average adjustment; they would either lie where they fell as awarded by the tribunal, or if the tribunal had made a lump sum award, that would be apportioned over salved values separately from any general average apportionment.

The position was however considered to be uncertain when the salvage services had been rendered under an agreement on a "no cure—no pay" basis,

10. See *Congdon on General Average* (2nd ed.), p. 106.
11. *Amerada Hess Corporation* v. *Mobil* (*The Mobil Apex*), 1979 AMC 2406.
12. *The Raisby* (1885) 10 P.D. 114; 5 Asp. M.C. 473.

such as Lloyd's Form of Salvage Agreement. In this connection, an opinion given by counsel to the Association of Average Adjusters in 1942 said:

"The interests salved are, of course, bound to discharge their several liabilities *to the salvors* on the basis of contract of salvage; i.e., on the basis of their respective values at the termination of the services. But it does not follow that *as between themselves* they are not bound to adjust their rights and liabilities under the York-Antwerp Rules . . . " (emphasis supplied by counsel).

The reference to the York-Antwerp Rules enabled the Association of Average Adjusters in that year to pass a Rule of Practice, which still stands and is now numbered C1:

"Expenses for salvage services rendered by or accepted under agreement shall in practice be treated as general average provided that such expenses were incurred for the common safety within the meaning of Rule A of the York-Antwerp Rules 1924 or York-Antwerp Rules 1950."

Although the adoption of this Rule of Practice enabled average adjusters in the United Kingdom to fall into line with their professional colleagues elsewhere, it could not be said to be an ideal solution. A number of admiralty lawyers were against it; it was not binding on average adjusters, and cases did arise where adjusters exercised their discretion to disregard it, particularly when there had been a substantial change in the value of ship or cargo as between the time when the salvage services were terminated and the time when the voyage was completed; and most importantly, it did not apply to maritime salvage in the absence of any contract or agreement, e.g. salvage of a derelict.

Hence the importance of Rule VI to the profession in the United Kingdom.

COMMENTS ON THE 1990 AMENDMENT

It will be noted that the Rule is now divided into two sections: the first section (a) setting out the circumstances in which salvage expenditure is allowed in general average, and the second section (b) dealing with the exclusion from general average of special compensation payable to a salvor by a shipowner under Article 14 of the International Convention or any provision (such as that contained in LOF 1990) similar in substance.

Looking at the first paragraph of section (a), it is to be noted that two amendments have been made since the introduction of the Rule in 1974:

— The words "in the nature of salvage" have been substituted for "on account of salvage", thus widening the circumstances for admission to include expenditure arising under contracts in the nature of salvage.
— The rather ambiguous provision that salvage expenditure would be allowed "*to the extent that* the salvage operations were undertaken for

the purpose of preserving from peril the property involved in the common maritime adventure" has been amended by the substitution of the introductory words "provided that . . . " in place of "to the extent that . . . ".

The second paragraph of section (a) makes it clear that the admission in general average will comprise the whole of any reward made in accordance with the terms of Article 13.1 of the 1989 Convention, inclusive of any additional element in recognition of the skill and efforts of the salvors in preventing or minimising environmental damage. In certain countries in the continent of Europe doubts had been expressed about the correctness of so doing under the 1974 text of Rule VI, since the avoidance of damage to the environment was not something done for the purpose of preserving the *property* at risk. Hence the necessity to spell out the admission in general average of the whole of the salvage reward inclusive of any element of enhancement by reason of efforts to avoid environmental damage.

Section (b) makes clear the exclusion as specifically requested by the 1989 Salvage Conference. In some quarters it was doubted whether the exclusion was necessary, but those who expressed this view had evidently failed to take into account that the salvor's expenses on which the special compensation will be based under Article 14 are not limited to expenses incurred in order to avoid environmental damage, and indeed may not have been incurred with that purpose at all.

THE PROBLEM OF DIFFERENTIAL SETTLEMENTS

Since the introduction of Rule VI in 1974, problems have arisen when ship and cargo interests have made separate settlements with the salvors at different levels of remuneration; also when separate lawyers' bills are put in by the parties who have been separately represented in the salvage proceedings. Do the differences lie where they fall, or do all the settlements and all the legal costs incurred go into the general average "melting pot" in order to be apportioned over all the contributing interests?

In Anglo-Saxon jurisprudence, there is legal authority in favour of a general apportionment. In *The Jason,*[13] it was held in the U.S. Court of Appeals (Fifth Circuit) (and their decision in this respect was not disputed when the case went to the U.S. Supreme Court), that payments to salvors which were agreed upon by different interests on different dates and even under differing beliefs as to the state of facts at the time, were all to be brought into general average contribution. As the court said:

13. *The Jason* (1910) 162 Fed. Rep. 56, 178 Fed. Rep. 414.

"The contract the ship's agent did make was really this: The Merritt Company was to get 40 per cent of the salved value of the vessel, and whatever the court or agreement might allow on the salved value of the cargo; but the company was to salve both vessel and cargo. The agreement was one. The compensation only was not fully agreed on. It must be found that this agreement was reasonable considering the time of year and probability of hurricanes, the dangerous nature of the coast and the likelihood of loss of cargo by melting. The truth is that a high charge was made for the hull because it seemed unlikely that there would be much cargo left. It was not the cargo owner that made the original and essential bargain. It was the ship's agent; but the cargo owner ratified that bargain and united in sacrificing something for the common benefit when he paid money to the salvors. It seems to me, therefore that this salvage expense, however or whenever liquidated, was something done for common benefit, and therefore should under American law be brought into the general average adjustment."

In the United Kingdom support is given to this view by an opinion of the AAA Advisory Committee.[14] The submission to the Committee recognised that the incidence of differential payments to salvors was likely to increase in view of the growing tendency for ship and cargo (and sometimes also separate cargo interests) to furnish separate and independent security to the salvors. When this occurs, it is more than likely that each interest separately guaranteed will enjoy the benefit of separate legal representation, thus increasing the opportunity for separate interests to "go it alone" in their dealings with the salvors. Instances were given: when one interest or a group of interests has successfully appealed the original award, whereas the other interests have not; and when one interest has made a separate deal with the salvors prior to arbitration, leaving the other with the alternatives of coming to terms with the salvors or proceeding to arbitration. Similarly in regard to costs: for example, when one interest or group of interests has unsuccessfully appealed the original award, and has in consequence to pay the whole of the costs of the appeal.

The Advisory Committee was unanimously of the opinion "that Rule VI is mandatory as between the parties to a contract of affreightment providing for adjustment of general average according to York-Antwerp Rules 1974. The Committee accordingly takes the view that subject to the overall requirement of reasonableness in the amounts claimed by the parties to the adventure, differential expenditure, including costs, on account of salvage should be allowed in general average and apportioned as such."

The Advisory Committee however added a rider:

"The Committee are of course concerned at the anomalies which may arise from the application of Rule VI as above, but feel that the solution lies, partly at least, in closer co-operation between the salved interests in the negotiation of settlements with salvors and/or in decisions as to the lodging of appeals."

The practice of adjusters is generally to give effect to the Rule in accordance with its intentions.

14. AAA Advisory Committee Opinion No. 40 dated 1 July 1983.

However, as stated in the first edition of this book, the subject of the treatment of differential settlements continued to arouse strong passions[15] and among the papers circulated to the International Sub-Committees preparing for the Sydney Conference were two which demonstrated that influential adjusters in Belgium and Canada would prefer differing salvage payments and separately incurred legal costs to be excluded from general average and allowed to lie where they fall. This view was again expressed by the Belgian delegation at Sydney, but it was pointed out in debate that if all parties so agreed that they would settle on terms separately negotiated with the salvors and pay their own costs, they were free to derogate by that agreement from a strict application of Rule VI. In the event Rule VI was confirmed without amendment by an overwhelming majority.

EFFECT OF THE RULE PARAMOUNT

The unexpected (in some quarters) adoption at Sydney of the Rule Paramount has stimulated a re-think as to the philosophy underlying Rule VI. Fortunately, the studies undertaken in the past few years had already provided lawyers and adjusters with a ready-made source of reference. Take, for example, the views expressed by members of Working Group D reporting to the AIDE International Sub-Committee:

F-X. Albertini (France): "When a master whose vessel is in peril signs a salvage contract, he does so in the name of and for the whole community; ship and cargo. If the contract provides for the salvage reward to be fixed by arbitration, the whole community must, in consequence, submit itself to this procedure. No single party should disengage himself from this obligation which has been taken on for his account by the master. It flows logically from this that if certain parties deal directly and for their individual account with the salvor [prior to the arbitration] the expense which they incur while thus individually engaged in the fragmentation of the community will have to be integrated into the general average *(so long as it is not excessive)*." [Emphasis supplied].

J.J.H. Gerritzen (Netherlands): "In my conception salvage is a school example of general average in that it is directed to the preservation of ship and cargo. The fragmentation arises if the applicable law provides for separate liabilities vis-à-vis salvors, but that does not alter the nature of the services, nor does it change the quality of salvage as a general average act. I have always allowed all "fragments" of the salvage remuneration and [consequent] costs in general average, *provided the amounts were reasonable*." [Emphasis again supplied].

J.A. Macdonald (United Kingdom): "The essence of general average is the community which exists between the participating interests: they sink or swim together. Where

15. For the competing arguments, see: D. J. Wilson, Address from the chair to the General Meeting of the AAA, May 1988, reprinted in *Hull Claims Analysis*, vol. 5, p. 69; N. G. Hudson, "A question of differentials", *Hull Claims Analysis*, vol. 5, p. 188; AIDE reports of working groups re Rule VI, delivered to the XVth and XVIth General Assemblies, York, 1989, and Regensburg, 1991.

one party uses his commercial muscle to obtain an advantageous settlement, this is of course perfectly understandable but should not be sanctioned by the general average: there lurks the suspicion that what the salvor may lose in one differential settlement he may attempt to compensate for in dealing with another, possibly less muscular, interest."

It will be apparent from these extracts, written well before the passage of the Rule Paramount, that their authors considered the reasonableness of each individual settlement, and each individual set of costs, to be an essential component in the practical application of Rule VI. As an example of what is generally considered to be unreasonable is frequently instanced the case where one party, without good reason, appeals against an arbitration award which has been accepted by the other parties, loses, and is obliged to pay both his own and the salvors' costs of appeal.

In the opinion of the author, therefore, the passage of the Rule Paramount should not have any effect upon the practice of average adjusters in their careful examination of all individual settlements and sets of costs and expenses in salvage cases, although it may conceivably provide critics with a pretext for formulating unreasonable objections to an adjustment subsequent to its issue.

RULE VII

DAMAGE TO MACHINERY AND BOILERS

Damage caused to any machinery and boilers of a ship which is ashore and in a position of peril, in endeavouring to refloat, shall be allowed in general average when shown to have arisen from an actual intention to float the ship for the common safety at the risk of such damage; but where a ship is afloat no loss or damage caused by working the propelling machinery and boilers shall in any circumstances be made good as general average.

EVOLUTION

This Rule had its origin in 1890, when the British Association of Average Adjusters, having recently passed a Rule of Practice to the same effect, introduced the following text, which was duly approved by the Liverpool Conference:

"Damage to Engines in Refloating a Ship
Damage caused to machinery and boilers of a ship which is ashore and in a position of peril, in endeavouring to refloat, shall be allowed in general average, when shown to have arisen from an actual intention to float the ship for the common safety at the risk of such damage."

At the 1924 Stockholm Conference it was proposed in part to widen the scope of the Rule so that any damage done to ship or cargo which was brought about by working the machinery and boilers in efforts to refloat a ship which was ashore and in a position of peril should be allowed in general average, but with a proviso that no such loss or damage should be allowed when the ship was afloat. The Conference did not approve the first, positive, part of the proposed amendment, but they accepted the second, restrictive, part of it, so that the following words were added at the end of the 1890 text: " . . . but where a ship is afloat no loss or damage caused by working the machinery and boilers shall be made good as general average".

Further amendments were made at the 1949 Amsterdam Conference:

(a) The title was changed to read "Damage to Machinery and Boilers".
(b) The wording of the second part of the Rule was further expanded so that it read: " . . . but where a ship is afloat no loss or damage caused

> by working the machinery and boilers, including loss or damage due to compounding of engines or such measures, shall in any circumstances be made good as general average".

The reference to "compounding of engines" was short-lived, since by 1974 it was recognised that this was a measure infrequently resorted to and, as it applied only to steam-driven engines, was likely to become obsolete. Hence the words "including loss or damage due to compounding of engines or such measures" were deleted.

Meanwhile, practical experience had exposed a weakness in the 1950 text in regard to the interpretation of the word "machinery". If it was correct to interpret "machinery" widely in the first part of the Rule, so as to include damage to auxiliary engines, pumps, etc., in efforts to refloat, then the word "machinery" in the second part of the Rule would have to be given an equally wide interpretation, which would have the effect of excluding damage to auxiliaries in any circumstances where the ship was afloat: for example, in fighting a fire. In order to correct the position, the 1974 Hamburg Conference made the following small, but important, changes:

(a) In the first part of the Rule, the wording was changed to read: "Damage caused to *any* machinery . . . "
(b) In the second part of the Rule, the exclusion for loss or damage where a ship is afloat was confined to that which was caused "by working the *propelling* machinery and boilers".

There was no proposal to amend the Rule in 1994.

COMMENTARY

" . . . ashore and in a position of peril . . . "

It is not every grounding of a ship which places her in a position of peril. Many ships are constructed so as to be able to lie safely on the bottom, provided it is flat and even and clear of obstruction. On the other hand, many modern purpose-built vessels are constructed to very close tolerances and are more susceptible to structural damage whilst ashore than their counterparts of previous years.

Some guidance is afforded by the following cases in the English courts:

1. In *Trafalgar Steamship Co.* v. *British & Foreign Marine Insurance Co.*[1] the vessel took the ground shortly after leaving Buenos Aires. She remained aground for about two hours and after working her engines ahead and astern,

1. *Trafalgar Steamship Co.* v. *British & Foreign Marine Insurance Co.*, *Shipping Gazette*, 18 November 1904.

she ultimately refloated, largely on account of a rise in the water. Channell J. found that the vessel was not in peril. He said:

"It seems to be an extremely common thing to go through this soft mud and occasionally to stick, and the evidence is very clear that you will not have any wind that will cause any damage to you from being aground, which will not, some 12 hours, it is said, before that wind comes to you, have raised the water so as to get you off. It seems, therefore, that, although, I suppose, people would generally say that in anything that can be called an open roadstead to be aground is to a certain extent to be in peril, yet in this particular place it rather seems that that is not so; it is a place where the water is shallow, where vessels habitually disregard it; they do not appear to wait until there is a southerly wind to raise the water, and it is not in practice considered to be a danger."

2. *Daniolos* v. *Bunge & Co.*[2] was another case where the ship was found not to be in peril. She had taken the ground on her port side while sailing up the channel in the Randers Fjord. After refloating with tug assistance, she was caught by the current and wind so as to take the ground again on her starboard side, being in effect pressed against the bank of the channel by the prevailing wind. The factors which influenced Goddard J. in deciding that the vessel had not been in any real danger were, firstly that this had happened in an inland waterway with no substantial danger of the vessel bumping on the bottom in rough seas; the bank against which the vessel was held was soft; and that, although the ship had sustained some damage, it was no more than to be expected and was not of a character which in the opinion of the judge exposed the cargo to any danger.

3. In *Charter Shipping Co.* v. *Bowring Jones & Tidy*[3] the vessel ran aground shortly after leaving the quay at Jacksonville. Engines were worked ahead and astern but without success, and the vessel was eventually refloated with tug assistance after being aground for about three hours. Roche J. found that the vessel had been in peril. In his judgment he said:

"It is said, in the first place, that the vessel was not in a position of peril, that she was in no real danger, that she was in inland waters 20 miles from the sea, and that it was merely a matter of rising water and, if necessary, the assistance of a tug to get her off. The danger was not very great, but still I am satisfied that there was a position of peril within the meaning of the rule; the danger was real and substantial enough to necessitate the use of the engines; and the risk of damage which was undergone, and the damage, if any, which resulted from their use and other circumstances, was damage within that rule of the York-Antwerp Rules."

It is not possible to deduce any general principle even by a close reading of these cases. That all three of them were borderline cases is obvious, otherwise they would not have been litigated.

In the author's experience the following factors have to be considered by the average adjuster in order to form an opinion whether or not the ship and cargo are in a position of peril whilst aground:

2. *Daniolos* v. *Bunge & Co.* (1937) 59 Ll.L.Rep. 175.
3. *Charter Shipping Co.* v. *Bowring Jones & Tidy* (1930) 36 Ll.L.Rep. 272.

1. The nature of the bottom on which the vessel is aground. Obviously if a ship is aground on a rocky shore, she will be more likely to sustain damage than if she were aground on a sandbank. The nature of the bottom has also to be considered jointly with factors 2, 3 and 4.
2. The position of the vessel relative to the ground, and the nature of the stresses likely to be set up if the vessel is "working" in that position.
3. The effect of tide. For example, if the vessel takes the ground forward at high tide, the effect of the falling tide will be to leave the stern of the vessel unsupported to a greater or smaller degree, depending upon the extent of the tide.
4. The effect of wind and weather, e.g. to drive the vessel more firmly aground, or to cause her to bump on the bottom.
5. The proximity of the grounding position to other potential sources of danger, e.g. a vessel aground close to a navigable channel may present a collision hazard.

" . . . when shown to have arisen from an actual intention to float the ship . . . at the risk of such damage . . . "

These words are retained from the original text of the 1890 Rule. The object of the draftsman was presumably to ward off any opposition to his motion by showing that the circumstances in which the proposed allowances could be made for damage caused to machinery and boilers would be limited to those which could be demonstrated to constitute a voluntary sacrifice. In the first edition of this book, the author asked rhetorically whether the presence of these words suggested a higher standard of proof in the case of damage caused to machinery and boilers than in other cases of sacrifice of ship. This question has now received judicial consideration in the case of *The Alpha*,[4] together with a re-examination of the relationship between this Rule VII and lettered Rules A, C and E. In that case the ship with cargo was aground in a position of peril and substantial damage was sustained by the main and auxiliary engines having overheated due to the sea water circulating system becoming clogged by sand during efforts to refloat. Cargo interests denied the shipowner's claim for contribution under the York-Antwerp Rules 1974, arguing, *inter alia*, that the master's conduct in the way the efforts to refloat were undertaken was so unskilful as to be unreasonable. In the Commercial Court Hobhouse J. accepted that on the evidence this was the case, but he held that in accordance with the Rule of Interpretation, the specific provisions of Rule VII, which do not include a test of reasonableness, applied to the exclusion of Rule A. However, since Rule VII did not detract from Rules C and E, the burden of

4. *Corfu Navigation Co.* v. *Mobil Shipping Co. & Ors.* (*The Alpha*) [1991] 2 Lloyd's Rep. 515.

proof remained with the shipowner, who must prove that the damage claimed was the direct consequence of the general average act.

In terms of Rule VII, therefore, the shipowner had to prove:

> "(1) That the damage was done when the vessel was aground and in a position of peril;
> (2) that the damage was done while trying to refloat the vessel;
> (3) that the damage arose from an actual intention to float the ship at the risk of such damage."

These requirements were satisfied, and judgment was given for the plaintiff shipowner.

Unfortunately, one of the consequences of the publicity given to the *Alpha* judgment was to highlight the absence of any overall requirement of reasonableness within the scheme of the York-Antwerp Rules, thus prompting a movement which led eventually to the introduction of the Rule Paramount. How this will affect the adjustment of a claim in an "Alpha" type situation under Rule VII of the 1994 Rules is difficult to foresee, but in the author's opinion it will require a much more minute examination of the facts on a case-by-case basis.[5]

" . . . but where a ship is afloat no loss or damage caused by working the propelling machinery and boilers shall in any circumstances be made good as general average"

This is another instance in which allowance in general average is denied, not on principle, but to avoid some supposed difficulty in establishing the facts which would justify allowance in general average.

Indeed, Rudolf[6] revealed that there was a considerable difference of opinion among the delegates to the Stockholm Conference on the merits of this exclusion. He went on to say that it was evidently the view of some of the delegates that when damage was caused to a vessel's engines by being strained in attempting to avoid running ashore, this should be treated as general average.

Unfortunately, the exclusion cuts much deeper. Suppose a shipmaster is faced with a fire in the cargo and, being unable to contain it with the means at his disposal, orders the engines to be forced at full power in order to attain the safety of a port of refuge where fire fighting facilities exist. The author has had experience of such a case in which the resultant damage to the vessel's main engines was excluded from allowance under the terms of this exception. In that case, a submission was also made to the vessel's hull underwriters to ascertain if they would accept the damage as particular average, but in the event no recovery could be made from this source, since in the opinion of

5. See commentary on the Rule Paramount, p. 31 *et seq.*
6. Rudolf, *The York-Antwerp Rules*, p. 73

counsel, English law governed the contract of insurance, and by that law the damage to the main engines would have been admitted in general average, were it not for the reference to the York-Antwerp Rules in the policies of insurance.

In the author's opinion, this exclusion is both unnecessary and unfair.

RULE VIII

EXPENSES LIGHTENING A SHIP WHEN ASHORE, AND CONSEQUENT DAMAGE

When a ship is ashore and cargo and ship's fuel and stores or any of them are discharged as a general average act, the extra cost of lightening, lighter hire and reshipping (if incurred), and any loss or damage to the property involved in the common maritime adventure in consequence thereof, shall be admitted as general average.

EVOLUTION

This Rule was introduced in 1890, the text then being:

"When a ship is ashore and, in order to float her, cargo, bunker coals and ship's stores, or any of them are discharged, the extra cost of lightening, lighter hire and re-shipping (if incurred), and the loss or damage sustained thereby, shall be admitted as general average."

The 1890 text did not contain reference to a requirement that the ship should be in peril, nor that the discharge should be for the common safety. In the United Kingdom this omission was seen as a mere oversight, and consequently the draft prepared for the 1924 Stockholm Conference included a reference to both these requirements being present in order to justify the allowance of the cost of discharging in general average. However, as Rudolf reports, several delegates preferred the old Rule, arguing that if a vessel were aground, no discouragement should be put in the way of the master in relieving her from that abnormal situation as expeditiously as possible. In the event, a compromise wording was adopted, continuing to omit any reference to peril or to common safety, but instead inserting a provision that the discharge must be done "as a general average act".

No changes were made to the Rule in 1950 or 1974.

In 1994 the text was altered; the words "the loss or damage sustained thereby" being replaced by "any loss or damage to the property involved in the common maritime adventure in consequence thereof". The object of this amendment was to prevent any potential claims for liability to third parties (and particularly for pollution damages) which might arise in consequence of the discharge or reshipping of cargo, fuel or stores from being admitted under this Rule.[1]

COMMENTARY

"discharged as a general average act"

As a matter of interpretation the use of the words "as a general average act" import a reference back to the definition contained in Rule A under which, as we have seen, the purpose of the act must be for the common safety "for the purpose of preserving from peril the property involved in a common maritime adventure".

A case within the author's experience illustrates both this point and the significance of the word "extra" in the expression "extra cost of lightening, lighter hire and re-shipping (if incurred)". A vessel was chartered to carry a cargo of petroleum products to Iquitos, it being customary for charterers to discharge a part of the cargo into tank barges at a station short of final destination. Whilst proceeding up the River Amazon the vessel grounded at a point several miles before reaching the customary lightening point where the tank barges and attending tugs were stationed. In answer to the master's radio call for assistance, the charterers despatched two tank barges under tow to the point where the vessel had run aground, and sufficient cargo was discharged there, not only to enable the vessel to refloat but also to lighten her sufficiently to reach her final destination. The charterers claimed the extra cost (in terms of hourly rate of hire) of the tugs and barges for the time spent in proceeding from the usual lightening point to the place where the vessel had gone aground, and return. While this method of calculation was correct in that credit had properly been given against the total cost incurred for the normal charges of lightening the vessel, the question of allowance in general average turned upon whether the operation had been carried out "as a general average act", and this in turn involved an investigation as to whether the ship and cargo had been in a position of peril.

"any loss or damage to the property . . . in consequence thereof"

The discharge of cargo from a stranded vessel is frequently a hazardous operation, and any loss or damage to the property involved in the common maritime adventure which flows as a direct consequence of one of those hazards, or could reasonably be foreseen as likely to occur in the performance of the lightening operation will be admitted in general average. While this is no more than a restatement of the general principle set forth in Rule C, the number of instances in which such loss or damage can clearly be demonstrated

1. See commentary headed "The Environmental Issue", p. 52 *et seq.*

to be either the direct or foreseeable consequence of the lightening operation tends to support the view that in practice any loss or damage sustained in the operation of refloating a stranded ship which is in a position of peril will be brought into general average contribution, unless it be the result of a *novus actus interveniens*.[2] Such, almost certainly, was the view of the draftsmen of 1890.

Examples of such losses and damages admitted in general average are:

- — Loss of bulk cargo from grabs being used to discharge from the stranded vessel, and in the course of reloading, even though the grabs are in poor condition or improperly handled. The presumption is that the shipowner or his agent, faced with the necessity to hire equipment at short notice, would not have time to exercise much choice in the selection of equipment and personnel.
- — Damage to the stranded vessel's shell plating through contact with barges or other floating equipment being brought alongside or leaving the vessel.
- — Loss or damage sustained by cargo on board a lighter which strands owing to the irregular depths in the vicinity of the stranded vessel.

" . . . to the property involved in the common maritime adventure"

Since the 1994 amendment, the consequent loss or damage admissible in terms of this Rule VIII is limited to that suffered by property, including freight, which is within the community of interest.

For losses and damages sustained by third parties in consequence of the lightening operation, regard must be had to Rule C. For example, the liabilities incurred by the shipowner to make good losses and damages sustained by the lighters and other equipment hired by the shipowner to assist in the refloating operations will be admitted in general average, whether arising in tort or under the terms of the contracts by which the lighters or other craft were engaged.[3] On the other hand, liabilities arising from a spillage of fuel oil during the transfer to barge of the ship's bunkers will be totally excluded.

2. See the opinion of Lord Tenterden regarding the admission in general average of cargo lost in a barge employed to lighten a ship in order to enter a port of refuge, cited above, pp. 50–51.

3. For the admission in general average of payments due under indemnities imposed by the U.K. Standard Towage Conditions, see *Australian Coastal Shipping Commission* v. *Green* [1971] 1 Q.B. 456; [1971] 1 Lloyd's Rep. 16.

RULE IX

CARGO, SHIP'S MATERIALS AND STORES USED FOR FUEL

Cargo, ship's materials and stores, or any of them, necessarily used for fuel for the common safety at a time of peril shall be admitted as general average, but when such an allowance is made for the cost of ship's materials and stores the general average shall be credited with the estimated cost of the fuel which would otherwise have been consumed in prosecuting the intended voyage.

EVOLUTION

This Rule dates from 1890. At the time the text was:

"*Cargo, ship's materials and stores burnt for fuel*

Cargo, ship's materials and stores, or any of them, necessarily burnt for fuel for the common safety at a time of peril, shall be admitted as general average, when and only when an ample supply of fuel had been provided; but the estimated quantity of coals that would have been consumed, calculated at the price current at the ship's last port of departure at the date of her leaving shall be charged to the shipowner and credited to the general average."

In 1924 the reference to cargo was deleted both from the title and the text; the word "fuel" was substituted for "coals", and the credit for the value of the fuel which would have been consumed in the prosecution of the voyage (had not ship's materials and stores been burnt) was not expressly required to be debited to the shipowner. The rule then read:

"*Ship's materials and stores burnt for fuel*

Ship's materials and stores, or any of them, necessarily burnt for fuel for the common safety at a time of peril, shall be admitted as general average, when and only when an ample supply of fuel had been provided; but the estimated quantity of fuel that would have been consumed, calculated at the price current at the ship's last port of departure at the date of her leaving, shall be credited to the general average."

No change was made to the Rule at the Conferences of 1949 and 1974.

The omission between 1924 and 1994 of the earlier reference to cargo being burnt for fuel might seem to suggest that it was intended to remove this case from the ambit of general average, but this was not so. It was envisaged that the omission of the reference to cargo in Rule IX would have the effect that claims for cargo burnt for fuel for the common safety would henceforth be allowable under Rule A and would therefore no longer be subject to the restriction that allowance could be made only when an ample supply of fuel had been provided.

At its meeting in December 1993 the CMI International Sub-Committee had before it two proposals prepared quite independently by the British and United States Maritime Law Associations which sought to reintroduce the reference to cargo used for fuel. The thinking behind this was that since it was now quite feasible with the equipment of a modern tanker to transfer a quantity of a suitable oil from cargo tanks to bunker tanks, there was an increased likelihood that this means of supplementing a vessel's bunker supply might well be resorted to in some circumstances, and it was important to regulate by a numbered rule the relatively few occasions when this was done for the common safety. The BMLA proposal was the more radical. It read:

> "*Cargo, ship's materials and stores used for fuel*
>
> Cargo, ship's materials and stores, or any of them, necessarily used for fuel for the common safety at a time of peril shall be made good as general average and the general average shall not be credited with the estimated quantity of fuel which would otherwise have been consumed."

The text proposed by the USMLA had the same title and read:

> "Cargo, ship's materials and stores, or any of them, necessarily used for fuel for the common safety at a time of peril shall be made good as general average, but such an allowance may be made for the cost of ship's materials and stores when and only when an ample supply of fuel had been provided. The general average shall be credited with the value of the estimated quantity of fuel which would otherwise have been consumed in prosecuting the voyage."

Although the drafting committee was invited to look at these proposals with a view to submitting a joint text, it declined to do so on the ground that there were differences of substance between them, and both texts were therefore brought forward to the Sydney Conference. After debate, the BMLA suggested a compromise wording, conceding that credit should be made in general average for the estimated cost of the fuel which would otherwise have been consumed in prosecuting the intended voyage whenever the allowance was made for the cost of ship's materials and stores. This was the text finally approved.

COMMENTARY

The 1994 wording omits the proviso which had previously been expressed in the Rule since 1890 that allowance would be made for cargo, ship's materials and stores burnt for fuel "*when and only when an ample supply of fuel had been provided*". The object of the proviso was, of course, to exclude any claim which might arise owing to the fault of the carrier in failing to provide a sufficient quantity of bunkers for the voyage, or the stage of the voyage, on which the vessel was engaged at the time when the deficiency of fuel became manifest. When the claim was for cargo burnt for fuel in these circumstances, the remedy of the cargo owner would not lie in general average, but in an action under the bill of lading for short delivery. While no doubt this was a salutary provision in 1890, the delegates at Sydney were evidently persuaded that it was now otiose, and indeed had been ever since 1924, when Rule D was introduced. Modern thinking approves the separation of the notions of *peril* (which is a matter of fact) and of *fault* (which depends upon the interpretation given by the applicable law to the contract of carriage). However, since Rule D preserves the alternative (legal) remedies open to an aggrieved party, it is considered to be fair and just to the parties that the statement showing a claim in general average arising from any deficiency of fuel should set out all the relevant facts, including the material dates and distances, and particulars of fuel supplied and consumed.[1]

"Cargo . . . necessarily used for fuel"

The reformers of 1994 recognised that as the vast majority of ships are propelled today by oil engines, the relatively few cases which are likely to involve cargo being used for fuel will concern tankers; hence the expression "*used* for fuel". For the same reason, the most likely of a ship's "materials and stores" to be used for this purpose will be lubricating or other oils, and the author has had experience of such oils being used to eke out a diminishing supply of bunker fuel. It is also an essential ingredient in the interpretation of the Rule that the cargo or other materials shall have been *necessarily* used for fuel in the circumstances which have arisen; thus carrying the implication that such measures were taken as a last resort.

"for the common safety at a time of peril"

This is the only Rule where the expression "for the common safety" is supplemented by the additional words "at a time of peril". It is evident that these words were added by the 1890 draftsman for emphasis only, but no change was made in the 1994 redraft since delegations were enjoined by the chairman of the International Sub-Committee to avoid any unnecessary alteration of established wordings. In practice, despite the additional words "at a time of peril", the extent of the peril affecting the adventure is determined by the same tests as are applied in the interpretation of Rule A: it is not necessary that the ship should actually run out of bunkers before the decision is made to use cargo or ship's materials; it is sufficient that were this course not taken, there would be a real danger that she might do so. There is good reason

1. See Rule of Practice B9 of the AAA of the United Kingdom, Appendix 4, p. 349.

for the test being the same, since an analogous and rather more common class of claim is that for the cost of putting in to an uncontemplated port to take additional bunkers when there is a threat to the common safety arising by reason of deficiency of fuel: this situation does not fall within Rule IX, and claims in these circumstances have to be decided in terms of Rule A.

"the general average shall be credited with the estimated cost of the fuel which would otherwise have been consumed . . . "

This credit is only to be made to the general average when the subject of the allowance under Rule IX is for the cost of ship's materials and stores used for fuel. This disposes of the question, considered in the first edition of this book to be a moot point, whether a credit for the value of fuel which would otherwise have been consumed should be made against an allowance for cargo used as fuel. When the ship's materials which are used for fuel are the property of the shipowner and he is also the party responsible for the provision of fuel for the voyage, it is manifestly fair that the general average allowance in his favour should be reduced by the normal voyage expenditure saved. The position is not so clear when it is the time charterer who is responsible for the provision for fuel. Equity suggests that in those circumstances the amount credited to the general average should be charged to the charterer, not by reason of any imputation of fault, but merely because he is the party who has benefited in financial terms by the saving in normal fuel consumption. However, the rule does not say to whom the amount credited in general average shall be charged, and consequently when, as in the vast majority of cases, it is the shipowner's materials for which the allowance is made, it would seem that it will be for him to pursue his claim under the terms of the time charterparty for the amount by which his allowance in general average has been reduced.

RULE X

EXPENSES AT PORT OF REFUGE, ETC.

The Rule is divided into three sections dealing with different subjects, *viz*:

(a) port charges;
(b) handling or discharge of cargo, and
(c) storage and reloading cargo.

EVOLUTION

The Rule had its origin in Resolution No. 6 passed at the Glasgow Conference of 1860:

"That the expense of warehouse rent at a port of refuge on cargo necessarily discharged there, the expense of reshipping it, and the outward port charges at that port, ought to be allowed in general average."

The Resolution said nothing about the cost of entering a port of refuge, which was allowed in general average under the law and practice of all maritime countries when necessary for the common safety. However, at that time English law was alone in treating the expenses of storage and reloading of the cargo, and the outward port charges, in a manner different from that obtaining in other countries, namely by charging the storage expense specifically to the cargo, and the cost of reloading it and the outward port charges as a specific charge on freight.

The English law on these matters was clarified and refined in later cases[1] but at the 1864 York Conference the principle decided at Glasgow was expanded and incorporated into the York Rules, *viz*:

"*Rule VII. Port of Refuge Expenses*

When a ship shall have entered a port of refuge under such circumstances that the expenses of entering the port are admissible as general average, and when she shall have sailed thence with her original cargo or a part of it, the corresponding expenses of

1. *Atwood* v. *Sellar* (1879) 4 Q.B.D. 342; (1880) 5 Q.B.D. 286; 4 Asp. M.C. 283; *Svendsen* v. *Wallace* (1883) 11 Q.B.D. 616; (1884) 13 Q.B.D. 69 (C.A.); (1885) 10 App. Cas. 404; 5 Asp. M.C. 87, 232, 453.

leaving such port shall likewise be so admitted as general average; and whenever the cost of discharging the cargo at such port is admissible as general average, the cost of reloading and stowing such cargo on board the said ship, together with all storage charges on such cargo, shall likewise be so admitted. Except that any portion of the cargo left at such port of refuge, on account of it being unfit to be carried forward, or on account of the unfitness or inability of the ship to carry it, shall not be called on to contribute to such general average."

It is to be noted that the Rule did not deal in terms with the cost of entering into a port of refuge or with the cost of discharging the cargo, the allowance in general average of these expenses being governed by the national laws which continued to apply to the adjustment of general average (except insofar as varied by the adoption of the York Rules, of course).

At the 1877 Antwerp Conference, the text of the Rule was confirmed, apart from the exception contained in the last sentence, which was deleted.

At the 1890 Liverpool Conference the Rule was considerably expanded, besides being renumbered owing to the introduction at that time of new Rules VII, VIII and IX. From 1890 onwards, therefore, we have the present division into three sub-Rules.

RULE X(a)

When a ship shall have entered a port or place of refuge or shall have returned to her port or place of loading in consequence of accident, sacrifice or other extraordinary circumstances which render that necessary for the common safety, the expenses of entering such port or place shall be admitted as general average; and when she shall have sailed thence with her original cargo, or a part of it, the corresponding expenses of leaving such port or place consequent upon such entry or return shall likewise be admitted as general average.

When a ship is at any port or place of refuge and is necessarily removed to another port or place because repairs cannot be carried out in the first port or place, the provisions of this Rule shall be applied to the second port or place as if it were a port or place of refuge and the cost of such removal including temporary repairs and towage shall be admitted as general average. The provisions of Rule XI shall be applied to the prolongation of the voyage occasioned by such removal.

EVOLUTION

The first paragraph of Rule X(a) was created at the 1890 Conference by adding to that part of the existing text dealing with the cost of leaving a port of refuge a form of words intended to be declaratory of maritime laws governing the cost of entry into a port of refuge or return to a port of loading.

Apart from punctuation—two superfluous and misleading commas[2] which crept into the English text in 1950 being swept away in 1994—the text of the first paragraph has remained unaltered since 1890.

The second paragraph was added in 1950 and amended in 1974.

COMMENTARY

Paragraph 1

This paragraph is declaratory of the circumstances in which the expenses of entry into and departure from a port of refuge are allowable in general average. As we have seen, in its original version the Rule did not define in what circumstances the resort to a port of refuge gave rise to general average allowances, this question being dealt with according to the law and practice governing the adjustment. So far as English law is concerned, these circumstances were that the common safety of ship and cargo were threatened by some untoward event, and this no doubt influenced the drafting of the wording which was added in 1890 setting out the circumstances in which the expenses of entry and departure shall be allowed.

In the author's view, a correct interpretation of the Rule requires two conditions to be met:

1. The resort to the port or place must arise "in consequence of accident, sacrifice or other extraordinary circumstances".

"Accident" means any fortuitous event and may include, for example, the breakdown of a piece of machinery even though that was due to wear and tear. An accident is something which *may* happen, not something that *must* happen, but in looking, for example, at the consequence of a latent defect, the fact that the existence of the defect is unknown means that its consequence, when it does happen, is equally unforeseen. Mr J. T. Walker, reviewing this subject in his Address to the Association of Average Adjusters in 1949, distinguished between accident and inevitability. Considering the case of damage which comes into existence through wear and tear, he said:

"It is inevitable that sooner or later the affected part will disintegrate, but so also is it inevitable that all material and physical things shall at some time or other become useless for their purpose. Accident it seems to me is related not only to a physical happening, a physical change, but also to time and place. It may be a chance happening that the worn part should cease to function efficiently whilst the vessel is at sea during a contractual voyage. Even in such a case, had it been known and appreciated when the vessel set sail that the particular part was worn, could it be said that inevitably it would become so inefficient during the voyage as to imperil the whole property? So many factors may be operative between the date of sailing and the date of inefficiency, that

2. As to which, see 1st ed., p. 101.

the time of the breakdown becomes a matter of chance. There is always the straw which breaks the camel's back."[3]

However, in order to constitute an "accident", it is submitted that a wear and tear condition has ultimately to reach a point of breakdown, at a moment in time when a part which was previously functioning now fails to perform that function.

"Sacrifice" means a general average sacrifice as defined in Rule A. This implies an intentional deliberate act undertaken for the purpose of averting a peril threatening the common maritime adventure.

"Other extraordinary circumstances." These words provide the adjuster with a wide degree of latitude, but even so the number of cases that arise in practice where "other extraordinary circumstances", not amounting to an accident, render it necessary for the common safety to resort to a port or place of refuge, are relatively infrequent. Rudolf cites the serious depletion of the crew by their succumbing to an epidemic on board, and the author can occasion a case when the health and safety of the crew were seriously threatened by the escape of noxious gases from drums of tetra-ethyl lead which were broached in heavy weather. Also in this category are cases arising from shortage of bunkers, and even from the shortage of provision or drinking water if the effect of being on short rations was such as to affect the crew in the performance of their duties. However, it is submitted that for the circumstances to be extraordinary in such "shortage" cases, the deficiency in the bunkers or of the ship's supplies must come about through an accident or some unforeseen event, and not merely in consequence of under-provisioning.

2. The resort to the port or place of refuge must be necessary for the common safety.

The editors of Lowndes & Rudolf suggest that wherever the expression "for the common safety" appears in the numbered Rules, it has to be construed as if it were qualified by the words that follow that expression in Rule A: "for the purpose of preserving from peril the property involved in a common maritime adventure".[4]

In practice, remembering that the expression "port of refuge" has enjoyed a distinct and definable meaning long before the drafting of the York-Antwerp Rules, adjusters frequently rely upon the correlation between Rules X(a), X(b) and XI(b). In other words, the fact that it is found necessary at the port of refuge to effect repairs to the ship without which she cannot safely prosecute the remainder of the voyage will be sufficient to justify the resort to the port of refuge as a general average act. The logic of this analysis is that if the ship

3. Chairman's Address to the Association of Average Adjusters, 1949, p. 15, reprinted in *From the Chair*, p. 132.
4. Lowndes & Rudolf (10th ed.), sect. 680.

has sustained such damage at sea that its repair is necessary for the safe prosecution of the voyage, then while such damage remained unrepaired at sea, she must have been in a position of peril. This reasoning also accords with modern legal thinking on the question of peril whilst in the comparative safety of a port of refuge.[5]

This is entirely compatible with the duty of the master, where he has any choice in the matter, to select as an intended port of refuge a port or place at which the damage sustained by the ship can be efficiently and expeditiously repaired. This may not necessarily be the nearest port in terms of mileage; as Lowndes put it, "It is that port which, on the whole, in the actual circumstances of the ship, is the fittest place for repairing; convenience and cheapness being fairly balanced against the advantages of mere nearness".[6] Although it had to do with the master's duty under the contract of carriage to repair the ship without delay, the leading case is *Phelps (James) & Co.* v. *Hill.*[7] In that case the ship, having sustained damage on a transatlantic voyage, put into Queenstown (now Cobh) as a port of refuge. Consideration was given by the master and owners to effect permanent repairs either at Swansea or at Bristol. After consulting their underwriters, the shipowners decided to have the repairs effected at Bristol, since it was there that the vessel had been built. On the way to Bristol (and after passing Swansea) the ship came into collision with another vessel and sank. Cargo owners claimed their loss to be the consequence of an unjustifiable deviation, but the Court of Appeal held that there was no ground on which to upset the verdict of a jury that the shipowner was entitled to select Bristol as the appropriate port at which to effect repairs. The law is the same in the United States—*Kansas City Fire & Marine Insurance Co.* v. *Dan Arias Shrimp Co.*[8]

Resort to a port or place for survey

When there has been a serious casualty, such as a stranding, and the master has reason for thinking that the ship may have sustained underwater damage which could affect her seaworthiness, it is clearly right and prudent that he should proceed to a port or place where a diver's or other inspection can be made in order to ensure that the ship will be fit to prosecute the remainder of the voyage in safety. For the reasons given in the chapter on Rule A,[9] it is considered good practice to treat this situation as a resort to a port or place of refuge for the common safety, even if no damage be found.

5. See the dictum of Lort Porter in *The Troilus*, quoted on p. 126; also commentary on Rule XI.
6. Lowndes & Rudolf (11th ed.), sect. 10.21.
7. *Phelps (James) & Co.* v. *Hill* [1891] 1 Q.B. 605; 7 Asp. M.C. 42.
8. *Kansas City Fire & Marine Insurance Co.* v. *Dan Arias Shrimp Co.*, 1959 AMC 135.
9. *Supra*, p. 38.

Avoiding adverse weather conditions

Resort to a port or place merely for shelter to avoid impending bad weather does not qualify for allowance in general average, on the grounds that storms and gales are not infrequently encountered at sea, and do not constitute "extraordinary circumstances". Conversely, on coasts which are exposed to hurricanes and other extremes of weather, it may be safer for vessels to stand out to sea rather than risk the dangers of collision or stranding in port, and in those circumstances when undertaken for the common safety the act of standing out to sea will constitute a general average act.

"Port or place." The additional words "or place" were added in 1890. In a case not involving general average,[10] Scrutton L.J. opined that "place" following "port" must be interpreted as a *ejusdem generis* with "port" as a locality having some or many of the characteristics of a "port". In practice, such places as a recognised anchorage in a roads or fairway, or a sheltered bay or estuary, have all been treated as within the words "port or place". Torbay, for example, is frequently resorted to as a place of refuge.

"Corresponding expenses of leaving such port or place." In a case under the 1890 Rules,[11] Bigham J. held, *obiter*, that when ice had formed in the approaches to a port of refuge whilst the ship was detained there the cost of engaging an icebreaker for the outward passage did not form part of the "corresponding expenses" which the ship had incurred on her way into the port, when there was no ice. This observation is criticised by the editors of Lowndes & Rudolf, who consider that the expression "corresponding expenses" refers to the purpose of the expenses, i.e. to proceed outwards, and not to the cost involved.

Paragraph 2

The 1950 amendment had its origin in a Rule of Practice of the Association of Average Adjusters passed in 1949.[12] This provided for the admission in general average of the cost of removing the vessel from a first to a second port or place whenever the repairs that were necessary for the safe prosecution of the voyage could not be effected at the first port or place. The Rule of Practice applied when a vessel was "at any port or place in circumstances in which the wages and maintenance of crew during detention there for the purpose of repairs necessary for the safe prosecution of the voyage would be admissible in general average under Rule XI of the York-Antwerp Rules 1924". A similar form of words was proposed by the Dutch delegation at the 1949 Amster-

10. *Humber Conservancy Board* v. *Federated Coal & Shipping Co.*, 1927 29 Ll.L.Rep. 177 at p. 179; cf. *Maritime Insurance Co. Ltd.* v. *Alianza* [1907] 2 K.B. 660 at p. 663, where Walton J. considered the expression "port or ports, place or places in New Caledonia" in a policy of marine insurance.

11. *Westall* v. *Carter* (1898) 3 Com. Cas. 112.

12. AAA Rule of Practice C3, Appendix 4, p. 354.

dam Conference but, after being referred to the drafting committee, the text was amended so that the removal would apply only when a ship was at a port or place of refuge at which it was not possible to effect repairs. As this was seen to be restrictive on British practice, the Association of Average Adjusters passed a further Rule of Practice in 1957 to restore the status quo.[13]

In 1974 the paragraph was amended in order to make it clear that the cost of removal from a first to a second port of refuge would include the cost of towage and temporary repairs, when necessary for the purpose of such removal.

INTERPRETATION

"When a ship is at any port or place of refuge . . ."

As already noted, it is British practice to apply the provisions of the second paragraph of Rule X(a) whenever a vessel is at any port or place in circumstances in which the wages and maintenance of crew during detention there for the purpose of repairs necessary for the safe prosecution of the voyage would be admissible in general average under Rule XI. This interpretation has become increasingly important, since with the increasing size and sophistication of ships, many commercial ports are without adequate repair facilities, and when a vessel suffers a serious accident in, say, her port of loading, it may be essential for her to proceed to another port in order to effect the repairs which are necessary for the safe prosecution of the voyage.

"Because repairs cannot be carried out . . ."

When this paragraph was originally drafted, it was envisaged that the repairs which would be required in order to ensure that the vessel would be in a fit condition to continue the voyage would be permanent in nature. Furthermore, the accepted practice at that time (1949) in regard to the interpretation of the second paragraph of Rule XIV was that it could only be invoked when a ship was at a port or place where permanent repairs could have been effected; consequently no thought was given to a case such as *The Bijela*[14] in which the alternative to the carrying out of temporary repairs (sufficient for the safe prosecution of the voyage) was necessarily to remove the vessel to another port to effect permanent repairs. When *The Bijela* case was argued in the Commercial Court, it was part of the shipowner's submission that, in calculating the expenses saved by effecting temporary repairs at the port of refuge, the cost of removal allowable under the second paragraph of Rule X(a) could be taken into account. This submission was countered by the

13. AAA Rule of Practice C4, Appendix 4, p. 354.

14. *Marida Ltd.* v. *Oswal Steel (The Bijela)* (Com. Ct.) [1992] 1 Lloyd's Rep. 636; (C.A.) [1993] 1 Lloyd's Rep. 411; (H.L.) [1994] 2 Lloyd's Rep. 1.

argument that the second paragraph of Rule X(a) could not be applied in calculating the expenses saved, since the temporary repairs which were effected at the (first) port of refuge were all that were needed for the safe prosecution of the voyage. In the Court of Appeal and before the House of Lords, this submission was dropped, since it was only necessary to demonstrate that the cost of discharging, storing and reloading the cargo under Rule X(b) would have exceeded the cost of the temporary repairs effected. The result is that, under English Law at least, it cannot be said with certainty whether the word "repairs" in the context of the second paragraph of Rule X(a) means:

- — permanent repairs, or
- — repairs, either temporary or permanent, which can be described as "necessary for the safe prosecution of the voyage".

In the author's opinion, the second interpretation is probably the one which is more likely to be upheld if the question were to be argued in an English court, even though contrary to the intention of the original draftsman.

" . . . the provisions of this Rule shall be applied to the second port or place . . . "

"this Rule" means Rule X(a). The effect is that the expenses of entering and leaving both the first and second ports of refuge will be allowed in general average.

"and the cost of such removal including temporary repairs and towage shall be admitted as general average".

Removal expenses as such may include the cost of any necessary sea pilotage or tug escort services, and in appropriate cases the cost of additional premiums of insurance on the vessel by reason of her performing the removal passage in damaged condition. However, the cost of crew's wages and maintenance and fuel and stores consumed on the removal passage will be allowed on a different basis, i.e. to the extent that the voyage has been prolonged by reason of the resort to both the first and second ports of refuge—see Commentary on Rule XI(a).[15]

The words "including temporary repairs and towage" were added in 1974, largely in recognition of the fact that if incurred by salvors under Lloyd's Open Form, these expenses would be taken into account in assessing the salvage reward.[16] The reference to "temporary repairs" introduces yet a third category

15. *Ante*, p. 175.
16. See *The Glaucus* (1948) 81 Ll.L.Rep. 262; *The Troilus* [1951] A.C. 820; [1951] 1 Lloyd's Rep. 467; discussed on p. 126.

of repair envisaged by the second paragraph of Rule X (a). "Temporary repairs" in the context of a vessel's removal to another port or place means such repairs as are necessary to make the vessel fit for the removal passage, and in practice are likely to be much less extensive than such temporary repairs as would enable the vessel to obtain a certificate of seaworthiness for the remainder of the voyage.

Treatment of the cost of removal to a second port for repairs in other circumstances

When repairs which are necessary for the safe prosecution of the voyage *can* be carried out at the port of refuge, this will in nearly all cases be the course adopted, and it will only be in exceptional cases that a decision will be taken to remove the vessel to another port to carry out those repairs. Because of this, the practice of adjusters is to examine closely the reasons why, despite the availability of repair facilities at the port of refuge, it was decided to effect repairs elsewhere. Such reasons could be:

(a) Technical. If the facilities at the port of refuge are so inadequate or the workforce so notoriously inefficient that no surveyor or technical manager would seriously consider repairing the ship there, a decision to remove the vessel to an efficient shipyard in another port would be entirely justified. The inclination of adjusters in these circumstances would be to interpret the second paragraph of Rule X(a) as if it read: " . . . because repairs cannot *practicably* be carried out . . . ". In the run-up to the Sydney Conference in 1994, there was a proposal from the Netherlands M.L.A. that this practice should be recognised by an amendment to the Rule, but this attracted little support, the general feeling among the delegates being that when these circumstances apply, the adjuster can explain his treatment of the cost of removal by an explanatory note in his adjustment.

(b) Expense. When the vessel is removed from the port of refuge to another port in order to achieve a saving in the cost of repairs, the usual (and it is submitted, correct) practice is to treat the cost of the removal as part of the cost of the repairs effected.

(c) Delay. When the removal is undertaken in order to save time on repairs, Rule F can be invoked so as to allow in general average the cost of removal up to the savings in the cost of detention expenses (wages and maintenance of crew, port charges and fuel and stores etc.) under Rule XI.

In the event of there being savings in both time and the cost of repairs, Rule F, which applies "without regard to the savings, if any, to other interests", requires the adjuster to make the time savings a first charge on general average, leaving the balance (if any) of the cost of the removal expenses to be charged to the cost of repairs.

RULE X(b)

The cost of handling on board or discharging cargo, fuel or stores whether at a port or place of loading, call or refuge, shall be admitted as general average when the handling or discharge was necessary for the common safety or to enable damage to the ship caused by sacrifice or accident to be repaired, if the repairs were necessary for the safe prosecution of the voyage, except in cases where the damage to the ship is discovered at a port or place of loading or call without any accident or other extraordinary circumstance connected with such damage having taken place during the voyage.

The cost of handling on board or discharging cargo, fuel or stores shall not be admissible as general average when incurred solely for the purpose of restowage due to shifting during the voyage unless such restowage is necessary for the common safety.

EVOLUTION

This provision, as a separate sub-Rule, dates back to 1890. Prior to that time it had been provided as part of Rule VII of the York Rules 1864 and the York-Antwerp Rules 1877, that "whenever the cost of discharging cargo . . . is admissible as general average, the cost of reloading and stowing such cargo . . . shall likewise be so admitted". This left the question in what circumstances the cost of discharging the cargo would be allowed in general average to be decided according to the law and practice of the place of adjustment.

The matter was brought within the ambit of the Rules at the 1890 Liverpool Conference when the provisions of the previous Rule VII were subdivided, by providing that the cost of discharging cargo, whether at a port or place of loading, call or refuge, shall be admitted as general average in two separate circumstances:

1. when the discharging was necessary for the common safety; alternatively
2. when the discharging was undertaken to enable damage to the ship caused by sacrifice or accident during the voyage, to be repaired, if the repairs were necessary for the safe prosecution of the voyage.

Two amendments were made in 1924:

— The Rule was extended to allow the cost of handling on board, as well as the actual discharge of cargo, and also to cover those operations when applying to the shifting or discharge of ship's bunker fuel and stores, as well as cargo.

— The words "during the voyage", which qualified "sacrifice of accident", were deleted from the Rule. While this modification appeared to widen the circumstances justifying the allowance in general average of cargo handling for repairs, it is interesting to observe that 50 years later, in 1974, a similar, but more precise, restriction was reintroduced into the text.

No changes were made to the Rule in 1950, but in 1974 two additions were made, each of which have the effect of limiting the circumstances in which allowance can be made for the cost of discharging or handling cargo:

— At the end of the first sentence the following was added:
" . . . except in cases where the damage to the ship is discovered at a port or place of loading or call without any accident or other extraordinary circumstance connected with such damage having taken place during the voyage."

— An entirely new paragraph was added, reading:
"The cost of handling on board or discharging cargo, fuel or stores shall not be admissible as general average when incurred solely for the purpose of re-stowage due to shifting during the voyage unless such re-stowage is necessary for the common safety."

The effect of these two additions is discussed below.

No change was made in 1994.

COMMENTARY

Measures taken for the common safety when the vessel is in port

There is no doubt that the location of the vessel is an important factor in determining whether a ship is threatened by peril to an extent sufficient to justify the allowance in general average of the measures taken. For example, an engine malfunction may be such as to create a position of peril at sea, whereas, once the vessel is in port, or even in a sheltered estuary, the danger will have dwindled to insignificance. On the other hand, a vessel which has lost her propeller may still be in danger at a recognised roadstead if it is exposed to such conditions of wind and weather as might cause the vessel to drag her anchors and, being innavigable, run aground or come into collision with another vessel.

It has been suggested that when a ship is within the comparative safety of a port of refuge, the words "common safety" must relate to a situation of the utmost gravity, i.e. when ship and cargo are truly in the "grip of disaster". In the author's opinion this statement is misleading: it is not that when the vessel is in the comparative safety of a port the immediacy of the peril has to be greater, it is simply that because of the relative security of the vessel's location, there will be fewer occasions when peril threatens.

In other words, the standard as to the degree of peril that must threaten the adventure to justify a general average act remains the same, whether the vessel is at sea or at port. Of course, if the vessel is at sea, additional factors will be involved which may enhance the degree of peril beyond that standard, but this is immaterial.

Two common instances of perils arising whilst a vessel is in port, and likely to require cargo-handling operations, are:

1. Fire

Until the fire has been extinguished, and the master (in collaboration with the local fire-fighting authority) is able to stand down the crew and/or shore fire-fighters a situation of peril continues to exist. Hence the discharge or shifting on board of cargo in order to enable the fire-fighters to reach the seat of the fire or to minimise the risk of its spreading is allowable in general average, as is the cost of those measures, even when the fire is apparently extinguished, in order to make entirely certain that there is no danger of a further outbreak. In a case where an explosion occurred in a container on board a container ship, giving rise to a fire, the cost of discharging other containers was allowed in general average without objection by any party, when undertaken not only to reach the container in which the explosion had occurred, but also to reach and discharge for examination other containers stowed nearby in which quantities of the same chemical had been loaded.

2. Collision

A ship which has been holed in consequence of a collision occurring in port may be in as much danger of sinking or capsizing as a ship which has sustained similar damage at sea. Furthermore, a vessel may be in danger in a shallow berth if by reason of taking in water in one or more of her holds she were to take ground unevenly or be subject to undue stresses by reason of the additional weight taken on board. In these circumstances the discharge of cargo to restore the ship to an even keel or to reduce the extra stresses to normal, will be allowable under Rule X(b) as having been incurred for the common safety.

The above remarks apply with equal force to allowances for the wages and maintenance of crew and fuel and stores consumed during the extra period of detention incurred in consequence of these measures. See Rule XI(b).

Continuation of the allowances following the measures undertaken as a general average act

It follows from what has been stated above that in practice the situation of peril that necessitated the resort to the port of refuge is deemed to continue until the ship and cargo have been placed in a position where remedial measures can be taken. This, indeed, is the origin of the English practice to allow in general average not only the cost of entry into a port of refuge for the repair of accidental damage, but also the cost of discharging the cargo when necessary to effect such repairs, even though, as the current argument went, the fact that the vessel had then attained a position of safety required the cost of storing the cargo and reloading it, together with the outward port charges, to be charged to particular interests.

It was not until 1890 that it was considered necessary to state this in terms, even though it accorded with what had been the accepted practice in all maritime countries. The form of words was:

> " . . . to enable damage to the ship caused by sacrifice or accident to be repaired, if the repairs were necessary for the safe prosecution of the voyage."

The extent of damage to the ship, for repairs to be "necessary for the safe prosecution of the voyage", is the same as, if unrepaired, would give rise to a position of peril at sea.

In general, the discharging of cargo will be necessary to enable such damage to be repaired whenever it has to be undertaken for access to the part of the ship in need of repair, or when the vessel has underwater damage which requires the vessel to be drydocked. It is only in exceptional circumstances that a ship will be drydocked with cargo, or part cargo, on board, and if it would have been usual in those circumstances to discharge all the cargo before drydocking, then the extra cost of drydocking the vessel with cargo on board will be treated as a substituted expense under Rule F.[17]

The effect of the words "if the repairs were necessary for the safe prosecution of the voyage" was challenged in the case of *The Bijela*.[18] Cargo interests, disputing the allowance of the cost of temporary repairs of accidental damage under the second paragraph of Rule XIV, argued that the cost of discharging, storing and reloading cargo which would have been necessary in order to drydock the ship for permanent repairs and was admittedly saved by effecting the temporary repairs, could not in those circumstances have been allowed in general average because the permanent repairs would not then have been necessary for the safe prosecution of the voyage—the temporary repairs which were effected being all that was necessary for this purpose. This wholly

17. See commentary on drydocking with cargo on board, p. 80.

18. *Marida Ltd.* v. *Oswal Steel (The Bijela)* (Com. Ct.) [1992] 1 Lloyd's Rep. 636; (C.A.) [1993] 1 Lloyd's Rep. 411; (H.L.) [1994] 2 Lloyd's Rep. 1.

specious argument was accepted in the Commercial Court and by a majority of the Court of Appeal, but was finally over-ruled by the House of Lords.

Discovery of damage to the ship at a port of loading or call

In principle, in order that a port of call situation should qualify for general average allowance, both the detention at the port and the accident that gave rise to it should have occurred during the community of interest.

This principle was applied in the original 1890 version of Rule X(b), which required that the repairs that were necessary for the safe prosecution of the voyage, for which the cargo was to be discharged, had to be for damage caused by accident or sacrifice *during the voyage*. These words "during the voyage" were deleted in 1924, but the restriction was reintroduced in 1974 by the addition of the following exception to the first paragraph:

> " . . . except in cases where the damage to the ship is discovered at a port or place of loading or call without any accident or other extraordinary circumstance connected with such damage having taken place during the voyage."

It will be seen that the exception will not apply, even if the damage was caused on an antecedent voyage, provided that there is some accident or extraordinary circumstance which occurs during the community of interest. An example frequently given is of a fracture in a vessel's plating which was sustained prior to the loading of cargo but which remained unobserved until, after loading cargo, it had been brought below the water line.

On the other hand, the mere discovery of a latent defect would not constitute either an "accident" or an "extraordinary circumstance", and the cost of discharging any cargo necessary for access to the repair of the latently defective part would be caught by the exception and not allowed in general average.

There is a similar exclusion in Rule XI(b) in respect of the wages and maintenance of crew and fuel and stores consumed during a period of detention for the repair of such antecedent damage discovered at a port or place of loading or call.

Handling or discharge of cargo, etc. when incurred for the restowage of shifted cargo

The second paragraph of Rule X(b) excludes the cost of handling on board or discharging cargo, fuel or stores when incurred solely for the purpose of restowage due to shifting during the voyage unless such restowage is necessary for the common safety. This amendment was introduced in 1974. Up to that time the cost of restowing cargo at a port of refuge which had shifted during the voyage, giving rise to a position of peril at sea, was something of a contentious issue. Only in the United States of America was there a consistent practice (apart from the York-Antwerp Rules) to allow such expenses, and under the Rules, prior to 1974, that remained the practice in Pacific Coast ports.[19]

In a typical case, a vessel with a deck cargo of, say, timber encounters heavy weather as a result of which the deck stowage is disturbed, the vessel takes a pronounced list and is in danger of capsizing. Although in peril whilst bearing up for a port of refuge, safety is attained once she arrives in port. In these circumstances the restowage of the cargo, although necessary for the safe prosecution of the voyage, is not necessary for the common safety. Of course, in an exceptional case the vessel with her cargo may still be in a position of peril at her moorings, and if that be the fact the cost of restowage may be admitted in general average as having been incurred for the common safety.

The arguments for and against the admission of the cost of restowage of cargo in our typical case have been summarised as follows:

"They are generally regarded as not being allowable in general average because they were not incurred for the common safety, the ship being in safety within the port of refuge, and there are no other grounds upon which they can be allowed as general average under the York/Antwerp Rules. But they are nearer to general average in nature than they are to anything else. They are indeed incurred to enable the voyage to be prosecuted with safety in the same way as are repairs at a port of refuge. Some argue that if permanent repairs of accidental damage are not admissible in general average although they are necessary for the safe prosecution of the voyage, then the expenses of re-stowing deck cargo are likewise not admissible; but the essential difference between the expenses of particular average repair of accidental damage and the expenses of re-stowing deck cargo, is that the former is of permanent value to the shipowner and that the latter is of no permanent value to anybody."[20]

Reverting to our typical case, when the restowage of the shifted cargo is necessary for the safe prosecution of the voyage, but not for the common safety, the practice is to allow the inward and outward port charges under Rule X(a), and the wages and maintenance of crew and fuel and stores consumed during the prolongation of the voyage (Rule XI(a)) and for the period of extra detention until restowage is complete (Rule XI(b)), but the actual cost of restowing the shifted cargo, together with any necessary handling for access, is caught by the exclusion in Rule X(b), second paragraph.

If this cost has been incurred by the shipowner, he may have a right of recourse under the terms of the charterparty if the original stowing and

19. See Walter G. Hays, Chairman's Address to the Association of Average Adjusters of the United States, 1959; where he said: "Under any York/Antwerp Rules the Adjustment Committee of the Board of Marine Underwriters of San Francisco, serving in a market where lumber movement is a major underwriting factor, for several decades has consistently approved allowances in General Average for the expense of restowing."

20. M. H. Downes, Chairman's Address to the Association of Average Adjusters, 1959, p. 10.

lashing were the responsibility of the charterers or stevedores appointed by them, but he will be likely to be unsuccessful if the charterparty provides that these operations were to be performed under the supervision of the master. Shipowners faced with this category of expense should consult their P. & I. Clubs, some of whom as a last resort undertake to indemnify their members for this class of expense.

So far we have considered only the cost of restowing the shifted cargo, but what of other costs of handling or discharge for access to the cargo needing to be restowed? A working group of AIDE studying the effect of the second paragraph of Rule X(b) concluded that the cost of cargo operations for access to the shifted cargo was caught by the exclusion, just as was the cost of restowage itself. However, they argued that this was wrong in principle, since the analogous cost of handling cargo for access to accidental damage repairs was allowable under Rule X(b), so why not the cost of handling cargo for access to the restowage?

In the event, the General Assembly of AIDE went further than this, and resolved by a majority to recommend that when the York-Antwerp Rules were next revised, the second paragraph should be amended so as to allow in general average the cost of restowage of shifted cargo not only when necessary for the common safety, but also when necessary for the safe prosecution of the voyage.[21] This proposal was confirmed by the AIDE at the XVIIth General Assembly in Prague in 1993, and a resolution to this effect was moved by the Japanese delegation at the 1994 CMI Conference.[22] However, owing to the current mood of the delegates not to expand the field of general average at this time, the resolution was defeated.

RULE X(c)

Whenever the cost of handling or discharging cargo, fuel or stores is admissible as general average, the costs of storage, including insurance if reasonably incurred, reloading and stowing of such cargo, fuel or stores shall likewise be admitted as general average. The provisions of Rule XI shall be applied to the extra period of detention occasioned by such reloading or restowing.

But when the ship is condemned or does not proceed on her original voyage storage expenses shall be admitted as general average only up to the date of the ship's condemnation or of the abandonment of the voyage or up to the date of completion of discharge of cargo if the condemnation or abandonment takes place before that date.

21. Report of AIDE working group on Rule X(b) presented at the XIVth General Assembly, Bruges, 1987 and the Resolution there passed, pp. 81–82.

22. For the reasons stated in the Japanese M.L.A. paper submitted to the Conference (CMI document GENAV 48 *bis*).

EVOLUTION

This Rule, in its separate form, dates from 1890, when the text read:

"Whenever the cost of discharging cargo from a ship is admissible as general average, the cost of re-loading and storing such cargo on board the said ship, together with all storage charges on such cargo, shall likewise be so admitted. But when the ship is condemned or does not proceed on her original voyage no storage expenses incurred after the date of the ship's condemnation or of the abandonment of the voyage shall be admitted as general average".

At the 1924 Stockholm Conference three amendments of substance were made to the Rule:

1. Provision was made for the cost of storage and reloading of fuel and stores, as well as cargo, in line with sub-Rule X(b) admitting the cost of their handling and discharge from the ship.
2. Specific allowance was made for the cost of fire insurance (if incurred) as part of the cost of storage.

   This was further varied in 1950 when the words "including fire insurance, if incurred" were replaced by "including insurance, if reasonably incurred". This provision is commented upon below.
3. The allowance for storage expenses ashore, in the event of the ship being condemned or the voyage abandoned, was extended to the date of completion of discharge of cargo, if the condemnation or abandonment of the voyage had taken place before that date.

The alterations made in the text in 1974 were designed merely to tidy up the wording of the Rule, and no change in principle or practice was contemplated.

In 1994 a new sentence was added to the first paragraph to justify the allowance of wages and maintenance of crew, etc., during the period a ship is detained for reloading or restowing cargo discharged as a general average act.

COMMENTARY

When Rules X(b) and X(c) are read together, they envisage that in the ordinary way the whole cost of discharging, storing and reloading will be allowed in general average when the discharge was necessary for the common safety or to enable repairs to the ship necessary for the safe prosecution of the voyage to be effected.

However, the Rule also provides justification for the cost of storage and reloading of cargo, fuel or stores which have been discharged from a stranded ship as part cost of lightening under Rule VIII if, as frequently occurs, the contents of the lighters are discharged ashore and are reloaded after the ship has completed her repairs in the port of refuge.

"Costs of storage"

This comprehends the cost of transporting the cargo from the quay or other place to which they have been discharged from the ship and into the warehouse or other place of storage, as well as the warehouse rent and associated costs. If stored in the open, such items as quay rent, the hire and fixing of tarpaulins, the wages of watchmen or other provision for security, are all included.

"Insurance . . . reasonably incurred"

The arguments for and against the allowance in general average of the cost of fire insurance premiums were widely discussed by adjusters both before and during the 1924 Stockholm Conference. On the one hand, it was said that since a loss of cargo by fire in a warehouse would not fall to be admitted in general average, it was illogical to charge the premium to general average and its cost should fall upon the party for whose benefit the insurance was taken out. Furthermore, if the cargo were insured for marine risks occurring during the voyage, it would be expected that the insurance would cover a fire occurring whilst the cargo was discharged at a port of refuge. On the other hand, it was said that under the contract of carriage the shipowner continues to be under a duty to act reasonably and care for the cargo whilst it is in his custody as a bailee, and that in pursuance of that duty he is obliged to arrange for the cargo to be insured against fire whilst ashore. The latter view prevailed at the Stockholm Conference, and the controversy was stilled. Justification for the result (to allow the cost of fire insurance in general average) came later in the American case of *The Mormacmar.*[23] In that case cargo discharged at a port of refuge was lost owing to a fire in the warehouse and the shipowner, as carrier, was sued for the loss: it was held to be part of his duty to keep and care for the goods to place insurance on the goods whilst ashore against the risks of fire, collapse of structures and rising of navigable water.

In consequence it can be confidently stated that it is in the joint interest of both the shipowner and the cargo owner to ensure that unexpected risks which may affect the cargo whilst ashore are covered by insurance, even though the consequences of such risks are not themselves admissible in general average.[24]

23. *The Mormacmar,* 1947 AMC 1611; 1956 AMC 1028.

24. For the risks of loss and damage to cargo which are admissible in general average, see Rule XII, p. 189 *et seq.*

The premium of insurance will be allowable if reasonably incurred in the circumstances. Of course, in the case of a bulk cargo, a shipowner will be advised to ascertain, if he can, what insurances were already in place for the voyage, and whether the concerned in cargo wish to cover additional risks while the cargo is in storage at the port of refuge.

Application of Rule XI to the period of extra detention occasioned by the reloading or restowage of cargo discharged as a general average act

This provision was added at the instance of the U.S. delegation at the Sydney Conference in 1994. It closes what was perceived as a lacuna in the Rules, in that the wages and maintenance of crew, etc., necessarily incurred during extra periods of detention for the reloading and restowage of cargo discharged as a general average act were not previously allowable by express provision in the Rules. Two typical scenarios were outlined in the first edition of this book,[25] and the author remarked that in these circumstances it was then (1991) the usual practice to allow the extra periods of detention. Now we have a rule to justify the practice.

Condemnation of the ship and abandonment of the voyage

A. "Condemnation of the ship"

This applies when the ship is a constructive total loss in the commercial sense, such as to discharge the shipowner from his obligation as carrier of the goods to execute the necessary repairs and continue the voyage. In English law this position is attained if a vessel has sustained such damage on the voyage by excepted perils that the cost of salving and repairing her would exceed her value when repaired.[26]

B. "Abandonment of the voyage"

This expression comprehends two situations:

1. Where by reason of external events, such as damage to the ship sustained in consequence of excepted perils, the commercial purpose of the adventure is frustrated, e.g. when the extent of delay necessary to repair the ship would defeat the purpose for which she had been chartered.[27]

25. 1st edition, chapter on Rule XI(b), pp. 128–129.

26. *Moss* v. *Smith* (1850) 9 C.B. 103; *Assicurazioni Generali* v. *Bessie Morris S.S. Co.* [1892] 2 Q.B. 652; 7 Asp. M.C. 217.

27. *Jackson* v. *Union Marine Insurance Co.* (1873) L.R. 8 C.P. 572; (1874) L.R. 10 C.P. 125; 2 Asp. M.C. 435.

2. When the voyage is abandoned by agreement of both parties.

Although the cost of discharging cargo is dealt with under Rule X(b), it may be relevant in the present context to note that the cost of discharging may have to be treated differently when the voyage is frustrated, as compared with cases where the voyage is abandoned by agreement of the parties. In case A, when the ship is "condemned", it is evident that the shipowner will not wish to repair the ship. Hence, any allowance in general average for the cost of discharging the cargo under Rule X(b), and likewise the cost of storage of the cargo under Rule X(c), can only be justified when the discharge of cargo is necessary for the common safety: the reason being, of course, that *ex hypothesi* there is no question of effecting any repairs to the ship.

However, in cases under B relating to the frustration of the adventure or the abandonment of the voyage for reasons other than the extent of damage sustained by the ship, it may well be the shipowner's wish to have his ship repaired as soon as possible, in order to enable him to take up a further engagement. In case B.2, where the voyage is abandoned by agreement, it would be usual for the parties to the adventure, as part of their agreement, to stipulate whether the cargo owner will take delivery at the port of refuge, or whether the cargo will be forwarded to destination and if so, at whose expense and whether the Non-Separation Clauses contained in Rule G will apply.

In cases when the ship is condemned or the adventure frustrated, it is not unusual for the parties to take their time in deciding what is to be done with the cargo. Consequently, if it has not been necessary to discharge the cargo for the common safety, it may well remain on board during this period of delay and the shipowner, whether as bailee or under the contract of affreightment, remains under an obligation to care for it. This is the justification, if any is required, for the continuation of the allowance for storage expenses (and also for the wages and maintenance of the crew and fuel and stores consumed) beyond the date of the ship's condemnation or of the abandonment of the voyage and up to the date on which the cargo was finally discharged from the ship.

If all of the cargo has been finally discharged from the ship before the date of the ship's condemnation or of the abandonment of the voyage, it is submitted that the date on which general average allowances will cease will be that upon which the state of facts became manifest which justified the abandonment or evidenced the frustration of the adventure, e.g. the opening of tenders for repairs, which demonstrated that the cost of repairs would exceed the value of the ship when repaired or, when the voyage is abandoned by mutual consent of the parties, the date of that agreement.

RULE XI

WAGES AND MAINTENANCE OF CREW AND OTHER EXPENSES BEARING UP FOR AND IN A PORT OF REFUGE, ETC.

This Rule is divided into four sections which deal with:

(a) Wages and maintenance of crew incurred and fuel and stores consumed at sea, bearing up for a port of refuge and regaining position;
(b) Wages and maintenance of crew incurred and fuel and stores consumed whilst detained in port;
(c) The definition of wages for the purpose of this and other Rules, and
(d) The circumstances when measures taken to prevent or minimise damage to the environment will be allowed in general average.

EVOLUTION

The Rule had its origin in Resolution No. 8 passed at the Glasgow Conference of 1860:

"That the wages and provisions for the ship's crew ought to be allowed to the shipowner in general average, from the date the ship reaches a port of refuge in distress until the date on which she leaves it."

This Resolution reflected the law and practice of virtually all maritime countries, apart from England. Nothing was said in this or any other of the Glasgow Resolutions as to the wages and provisions of the crew for the period of time the ship was bearing up for a port of refuge or in distress at sea, possibly because of the differing views on this subject. In fact, the treatment of the wages and provisions of crew while the vessel was at sea continued to be governed by the applicable national law until the revision of the York-Antwerp Rules in 1924.

At the 1864 York Conference the following text was adopted as Rule VIII, to follow the then Rule VII of the York Rules, which dealt with port of refuge expenses:

"RULE VIII. Wages and maintenance of crew in port of refuge

When a ship shall have entered a port of refuge under the circumstances defined in Rule VII, the wages and cost of maintenance of the master and mariners, from the time of entering such port until the ship shall have been made ready to proceed upon her voyage, shall be made good as general average. Except that any portion of the cargo left at such port of refuge on account of its being unfit to be carried forward, or on account of the unfitness or inability of the ship to carry it, shall not be called on to contribute to such general average."

The exception in the second sentence, which appeared in identical terms in both the then Rules VII and VIII, was deleted when the text was reviewed in 1877, the first sentence remaining unchanged.

At the 1890 Liverpool Conference, the Rules were renumbered so that Rule VIII became Rule XI. The 1877 text was slightly amended in the interest of clarity, and a further sentence was added to deal with the situation if the ship was condemned or the voyage abandoned at the port of refuge:

"But when the ship is condemned or does not proceed on her original voyage, the wages and maintenance of master, officers and crew, incurred after the date of the ship's condemnation or of the abandonment of the voyage, shall not be admitted as general average."

As Rudolf tells us, this provision was found to be less than satisfactory, since it led to the temptation that shipowners might discharge their crews immediately following the abandonment of the voyage at a port of refuge, leaving no one, other than perhaps the master, to care for the ship and cargo. In order to correct the position, the following additional sentence was added to the text in 1924:

"In the event of the condemnation of the ship or the abandonment of the voyage before completion of discharge of cargo, wages and maintenance of crew, as above, shall be admitted as general average up to the date of completion of discharge."

The 1924 Stockholm Conference also adopted the proposal submitted by the Association of Average Adjusters to include in the Rules for the first time provisions for the allowance of the wages and maintenance of crew during the prolongation of the voyage occasioned by a ship entering a port of refuge, and also for the fuel and stores consumed both in this operation and whilst the vessel was detained in accordance with Rule XI. This became Rule XX, reading:

"Rule XX. Expenses bearing up for port, etc.

Fuel and stores consumed, and wages and maintenance of master, officers and crew incurred, during the prolongation of the voyage occasioned by a ship entering a port or place of refuge or returning to her port or place of loading shall be admitted as general average when the expenses of entering such port or place are allowable in general average in accordance with Rule X(a).

Fuel and stores consumed during extra detention in a port or place of loading, call or refuge shall also be allowed in general average for the period during which wages and maintenance of master, officers and crew are allowed in terms of Rule XI, except such fuel and stores as are consumed in effecting repairs not allowable in general average."

In 1950 Rule XI took on its present shape: the first paragraph of Rule XX became Rule XI(a); the previous text of Rule XI was redrafted together with the second paragraph of Rule XX and an additional paragraph regarding port charges, to become Rule XI(b), and sub-Rules (c) and (d) were added for the purposes of definition.

The text of Rule XI(a) was not altered in 1974 or 1994.

RULE XI(a)

Wages and maintenance of master, officers and crew reasonably incurred and fuel and stores consumed during the prolongation of the voyage occasioned by a ship entering a port or place of refuge or returning to her port or place of loading shall be admitted as general average when the expenses of entering such port or place are allowable in general average in accordance with Rule X(a).

COMMENTARY

English law and practice does not allow for the cost of the wages and maintenance of the master or members of the crew in any circumstances, except possibly during the detention at a port of refuge on account of the necessity to effect repairs to general average sacrifice.[1] The English view is that freight is "the mother of wages", and that the shipowner, having engaged the crew for the purpose of earning his freight, must bear the risk of a longer or shorter voyage.

American law and practice provides for the allowance of wages and maintenance of crew bearing up for a port of refuge and whilst detained in port, but on rather different terms than are provided in Rule XI. By United States practice (apart from the York-Antwerp Rules) the allowance commences when the vessel deviates from her normal course in order to bear up for the port of refuge and ceases when, any necessary repairs having been completed, the vessel is in a position to resume her voyage.

"Wages and maintenance of . . . crew" and "fuel and stores"

Wages are defined by sub-Rule XI(c), and it will be convenient for us to examine the meaning of each of the words in the expressions "wages and maintenance of crew" and "fuel and stores" in that context.[2]

1. See *per* Thesiger L.J. in *Atwood* v. *Sellar* (1880) 5 Q.B.D. 286; 4 Asp. M.C. 283.
2. *Post*, p. 181.

" . . . prolongation of the voyage occasioned by a ship entering a port or place of refuge . . . "

Two factors are evident by the use of the expression "prolongation of the voyage":

— that account is to be taken of the time and/or distance involved in regaining the vessel's normal course as well as the time and/or distance in bearing up for the port of refuge, and
— except in the case of the vessel returning to her port of loading or her previous port of call, the saving in time and/or distance resulting from the vessel regaining course at a point further advanced than the point at which she left it has also to be taken into account. This is best illustrated by a diagram:

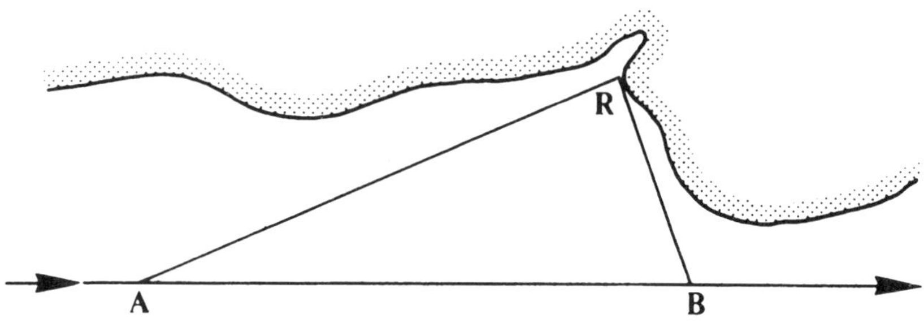

Supposing that A represents the point at which the ship begins to deviate from her normal course, R represents the port of refuge and B the point at which, after leaving the port of refuge, the ship regains her normal course, it is apparent that the extent to which the voyage has been prolonged by reason of her deviation to the port of refuge can be expressed as AR plus RB minus AB. This method of calculation is sometimes known as the "net deviation" or "triangulation" basis.

In order to calculate the allowance for wages and maintenance of crew for the extra time incurred in consequence of deviating to the port of refuge, it is customary to take the actual time elapsed from the point at which the vessel altered course in order to bear up for the port of refuge until arrival at the pilot station at that port, plus the time from dropping the pilot until the vessel's normal course is resumed, the time "from pilot to pilot" being within the calculation of the vessel's detention at the port of refuge. This fixes the time for AR plus RB, but it will be appreciated that the credit for the time AB has to be estimated on a theoretical basis. It is at this point that a difference in practice emerges. One practice is to apply the vessel's normal voyage speed (or her average voyage speed prior to the casualty) to the distance AB and credit the result of that calculation as the time saved. This produces a fair result when the vessel maintains her normal voyage speed in bearing up for the port of refuge and in regaining course, but it is open to objection when the vessel's resort to the port of refuge is undertaken at reduced speed owing to her partial disablement as a result of the casualty. In these circumstances a calculation of the time based on AR plus RB minus AB will result in the general average being charged with the vessel's slow steaming over a part of her normal course of the voyage, as well as for the extra distance covered by reason of putting into the port of refuge. The following figures will indicate this:

Assume the distances:
AR=204 nautical miles
RB=50 nautical miles
AB=230 nautical miles

and that the vessel's normal voyage speed is 12 knots and her disabled speed 6 knots; then if the vessel's deviation to the port of refuge is undertaken at normal speed:

AR + RB = 254 nautical miles at 12 knots: time taken	21 hrs 10 mins.
Less: AB = 230 nautical miles at 12 knots: time taken	19 hrs 10 mins.
Allowance in general average =	2 hrs 0 mins.

If the vessel proceeds to the port of refuge at her disabled speed of 6 knots, then:

AR = 204 nautical miles at 6 knots: time taken	34 hrs 0 mins.
RB = 50 nautical miles at 12 knots: time taken	4 hrs 10 mins.
	38 hrs 10 mins.
Less: AB = 230 nautical miles at 12 knots: time taken	19 hrs 10 mins.
Difference:	19 hrs 0 mins.

The alternative practice, when a vessel has put into a port of refuge at reduced speed, is first to calculate the extra distance which the vessel has covered by reason of putting into the port of refuge on each of the two legs AR and AB, separately. The method can be illustrated on our diagram by dropping a perpendicular from R to the line AB, joining it at point X, as shown below:

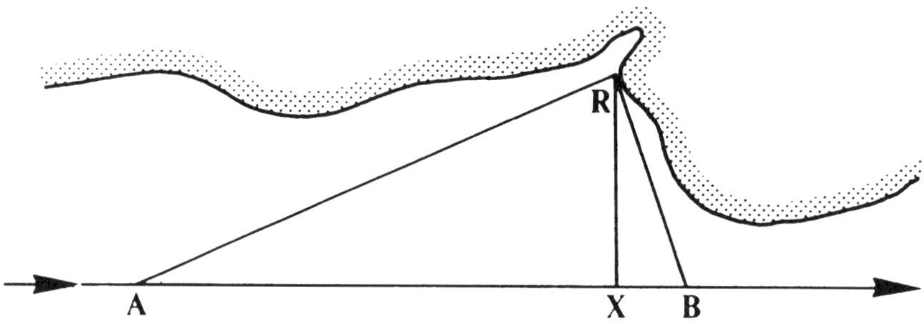

It will then be found that the distance AB is made up by

AX =	200 nautical miles
plus XB =	30 nautical miles
	230 nautical miles

Using these figures, we then calculate the prolongation of the voyage putting into the port of refuge:

AR (204) nautical miles) less AX (200 nautical miles)	
equals 4 nautical miles at 6 knots: extra time	40 minutes
RB (50 nautical miles) minus XB (30 nautical miles)	
equals 20 nautical miles at 12 knots: extra time	
	1 hour 40 minutes
Allowance in GA	2 hours 20 minutes

It is submitted that the latter practice is correct in principle, since it preserves the element of extra time *occasioned by* putting into a port of refuge, while excluding the element of extra time taken in prosecuting the normal cause of the voyage by reason of the vessel's disablement.

More arguable, however, is the element of time taken when a vessel is towed into a port of refuge by reason of her total disablement. In this case the usual practice is to allow for the leg AR the time actually taken under tow, plus regaining course RB as elapsed, less AB at the vessel's normal voyage speed, on the ground that the general average act was the engagement of the tug, and that all that has to be set off are the normal voyage expenses saved.

" . . . when the expenses of entering . . . are allowable . . . in accordance with Rule X(a)"

It is important to note that the allowances under this Rule XI(a) for wages and maintenance of crew and fuel and stores consumed during the prolongation of the voyage can be made only when such prolongation has been "occasioned" by:

- entering a port or place of refuge
- returning to a port or place of loading in the circumstances when the cost of entry is admissible in terms of Rule X(a), first paragraph; or
- removing to a second port for repairs in the circumstances set out in Rule X(a), second paragraph.

RULE XI(b)

When a ship shall have entered or been detained in any port or place in consequence of accident, sacrifice or other extraordinary circumstances which render that necessary for the common safety, or to enable damage to the ship caused by sacrifice or accident to be repaired, if the repairs were necessary for the safe prosecution of the voyage, the wages and maintenance of the master, officers and crew reasonably incurred during the extra period of detention in such port or place until the ship shall or should have been made ready to proceed upon her voyage, shall be admitted in general average.

Fuel and stores consumed during the extra period of detention shall be admitted as general average, except such fuel and stores as are consumed in effecting repairs not allowable in general average.

Port charges incurred during the extra period of detention shall likewise be admitted as general average except such charges as are incurred solely by reason of repairs not allowable in general average.

Provided that when damage to the ship is discovered at a port or place of loading or call without any accident or other extraordinary circumstance connected with such damage having taken place during the voyage, then the wages and maintenance of master, officers and crew and fuel and stores consumed and port charges incurred during the extra detention for repairs to damages so discovered shall not be admissible as general average, even if the repairs are necessary for the safe prosecution of the voyage.

When the ship is condemned or does not proceed on her original voyage, the wages and maintenance of the master, officers and crew and fuel and stores consumed and port charges shall be admitted as general average only up to the date of the ship's condemnation or of the abandonment of the voyage or up to the date of completion of discharge of cargo if the condemnation or abandonment takes place before that date.

DEVELOPMENT FROM 1950

At the 1949 Amsterdam Conference, as we have seen, Rule XI was expanded by the incorporation of the previous Rule XX, and the opportunity was also taken to redraft the essential provisions now contained in the first paragraph of Rule XI(b) so that, instead of hanging on the interpretation of Rule X, the circumstances governing the detention of the vessel in any port or place are spelled out as those that arise "in consequence of accident, sacrifice or other extraordinary circumstances which render that necessary for the common safety, or to enable damage to the ship caused by sacrifice or accident to be repaired, if the repairs were necessary for the safe prosecution of the voyage". An additional paragraph was also added to deal with port charges incurred during the vessel's detention.

At the 1974 Hamburg Conference a proviso was added to Rule XI(b) to exclude from general average any allowance for wages and maintenance etc. during detention of the vessel at a port or place of loading or call for the repair of damage which is merely discovered at that port, without any accident or other extraordinary circumstance connected with such damage having taken place during the voyage. The effect of this exclusion, designed to suppress cases of "artificial general average", has been considered in the commentary on Rule X(b).[3]

The opportunity was also taken in 1974 to redraft, for the sake of clarity, the paragraph relating to the date on which the general average allowances will cease when the ship is condemned or the voyage abandoned at the port of refuge. These circumstances have been the subject of comment in the section dealing with Rule X(c).[4]

In the examination of this Rule prior to the Conference of 1994 it was appreciated that the 1974 amendments—the prior damage exclusion and the redrafted paragraph dealing with the cessation of allowances—had failed to make reference to port charges. This was put right at the Sydney Conference and at the same time the five separate paragraphs were re-ordered into a more logical sequence.

COMMENTARY

Although the delegates at the Amsterdam Conference considered that they had produced a clear, yet all-embracing text to define the circumstances in which the detention of a ship will give rise to general average allowances, the first paragraph of Rule XI(b) remains somewhat obscure and presents practitioners with some difficulties in its interpretation.

In an effort to overcome these difficulties, let us focus separately on each of the following sets of circumstances:

3. See commentary on Rule X(b), p. 162.
4. See commentary on Rule X(c), p. 167.

1. Detention following entry of the vessel into a port of refuge or her return to the port of loading

In order to claim the benefit of the allowances for the vessel's detention, it is necessary to demonstrate that the vessel's entry into the port of refuge or her return to the port of loading occurred "in consequence of accident, sacrifice or other extraordinary circumstances which render that necessary for the common safety, or to enable damage to the ship caused by sacrifice or accident to be repaired, if the repairs were necessary for the safe prosecution of the voyage". This wording repeats the criteria governing entry to a port of refuge, or return to a port of loading, as set out in Rule X(a). Cases falling into this category form the great majority of the claims for detention expenses, and do not occasion many problems.

2. Detention at a port in consequence of some event which happens during the vessel's stay in that port

In this case, in order to claim the benefit of general average detention allowances, it appears to be necessary to demonstrate one or two alternative sets of circumstances:

— that the vessel was detained in consequence of accident, sacrifice or other extraordinary circumstances "which render that necessary for the common safety"; or

— that the vessel was detained to enable damage caused by sacrifice or accident to be repaired, if the repairs were necessary for the safe prosecution of the voyage.

The second of these circumstances is reasonably straightforward and the criteria to be applied are the same as those which will justify the allowance of detention expenses following the vessel's entry into a port of refuge or her return to a port of call in order to effect necessary repairs to damage sustained at sea.

It is in relation to the first set of circumstances under this paragraph that the problems of interpretation arise. Given that the vessel's detention arises in consequence of accident, sacrifice or other extraordinary circumstances, what is "that" which those events have to render necessary for the common safety? The simple answer is to say that "that" refers to the vessel's detention, but such an interpretation has to be rejected, since the detention of a vessel in port cannot, of itself, be necessary for the common safety. Two acceptable alternative interpretations remain: the first is that when considering a vessel's detention arising from accident, sacrifice or other extraordinary circumstances which have occurred in port, they must have created such a situation of peril that the vessel, if at sea, would have been justified in resorting to a port of refuge; the other, that the occurrence of these events is sufficient of themselves, and that the words "which render that necessary for the common safety" are ineffectual and should be ignored.

Another difficulty of interpretation arises by the use of the expression "the extra period of detention". Extra to what—to the vessel's normal expected stay in port, or to the period of detention which follows inevitably from the occurrence of the accident, sacrifice or other extraordinary circumstances?

When do detention allowances begin?

The problem is best illustrated by reference to cases of fires, which not infrequently occur whilst the loading of cargo is in progress. Given that the fire creates a position of peril such that, if the vessel was at sea, a resort to a port of refuge would be justified, there would be general agreement in practice that Rule XI(b) will justify some allowance being made for the wages and maintenance of crew etc. for a period of detention consequent upon the measures taken to extinguish the fire. But when do such allowances begin? United States practice is to commence such allowances at the time of the first act to extinguish the fire.[5] The author's preference is to commence the allowances at the time the vessel's normal operations, e.g. loading cargo, are suspended in consequence of the fire-fighting operations.

This brings us to the question of the extent of "voluntariness" which must be present in the detention in order to qualify for allowance under Rule XI(b), particularly when a vessel has been detained at some "place", not necessarily having the characteristics of a port of refuge or call. Rule XI(b) refers to "any port or place", but despite the apparent width of this expression, it is common practice not to allow the wages and maintenance of crew etc. during the period that a vessel is aground following an accidental stranding, even though the place where she has stranded is within the confines of a port. Similarly, the author has denied allowance for the wages and maintenance of crew etc. when, following the fracture of a vessel's tailshaft due to the propeller striking a mooring buoy whilst leaving port, the vessel was able to come to anchor and there waited 12 days pending the arrival of a tug to tow her to a more convenient port for repairs. On the other hand, if a vessel in peril is voluntarily stranded on a recognisable beach in order to avoid sinking, the element of "voluntariness" is clearly present and it would be churlish to deny an allowance for the wages and maintenance of crew etc. during the period that the vessel was detained there while undertaking temporary repairs to enable her to refloat and proceed to drydock.

5. Buglass, *Marine Insurance & General Average in the United States* (2nd ed.), p. 242.

When do detention allowances cease?

"*. . . until the ship shall or should have been made ready to proceed upon her voyage . . .*"

Shipowners not infrequently submit their claims for the wages and maintenance of crew etc. following a mishap which has occurred at sea, covering the full period of the vessel's incapacity from the time of breakdown until she has regained her course, conveniently ignoring the fact that the allowances which may be made in general average for the prolongation of the voyage and during the period of extra detention in port are distinct and separate, and do not necessarily form an unbroken continuum of time. The words "until the ship shall or should have been made ready to proceed upon her voyage" in Rule XI(b) are a salutary reminder that the period of extra detention in port is restricted to that which is necessarily and reasonably incurred in order to make the ship and cargo fit to proceed on the voyage after remedying the consequences of the accident, sacrifice or other extraordinary circumstances that gave rise to the extra detention.

Some latitude is allowed in the interpretation of the Rule. For example, the period of detention is extended to allow the ship to be surveyed after repairs by a competent surveyor (if one is reasonably available) and certified fit to proceed.

On the other hand, when the period of detention in port has been extended by circumstances unconnected with the average, it is clear that no allowance should be made for that period of time. Examples of additional delays which do not justify the continuation of allowances for a vessel's detention expenses under Rule XI(b) are stormy weather and fog, the continuation of any maintenance work or repairs for owners' account, crew changes or sickness. In an intermediate category stand such events as strikes, which in some instances may be entirely unexpected and in others of such a kind that they might be called an everyday event; also ice conditions, delay on account of which would not be allowable unless foreseeable at the time of entry into the port of refuge. There is no certain practice, either, in the case of a vessel being detained in order to provide security for salvors. According to Buglass,[6] it is American practice in such cases to allow the extra detention in general average, so far as reasonable. However, if the delay is due to the shipowner's lack of funds, this would clearly be unreasonable and non-allowable.

Port charges

The paragraph dealing with port charges has provoked some controversy in the past and is still, regrettably, unclear. At the 1949 Amsterdam Conference, the text before the International Sub-Committee read:

6. *Ibid.*, p. 243.

"Port charges incurred during the extra period of detention shall likewise be admitted as general average except that port charges incurred during repairs not allowable in general average shall be admitted in general average only if they would have been payable in consequence of the detention, whether repairs were effected or not."

An amendment moved by the representative of U.K. insurers was accepted, with the result that the exception now reads:

"Except such charges as are incurred solely by reason of repairs not allowable in general average."

In practice, port charges fall into two main broad categories:

(a) Specific charges for movements of the vessel, berth hire etc. In practice these are always treated in accordance with the purpose for which the vessel was moved or for which she was laid to that berth.
(b) General charges, not relating specifically to any particular purpose. It is as to charges of this nature that the adjuster requires guidance, and it is submitted that the original draft which was presented at the Amsterdam Conference, although rather clumsily worded, is in fact clearer in its intention than the one which replaced it.

Prior damage exclusion

The second paragraph of Rule XI(b) provides that no allowance will be made for the wages and maintenance of crew etc. during any detention for repairs of damage discovered at a port of loading or call without any accident or other extraordinary circumstances connected with such damage having taken place during the voyage. There is a similar exclusion in Rule X(b), and the reader is referred to the commentary in this connection.[7]

Position when the ship is condemned or does not proceed on her original voyage

When this is the situation, the wages and maintenance of crew etc. will be admitted as general average up to the date of the ship's condemnation or of the abandonment of the voyage, but if at that time the vessel still has cargo on board, the allowances will continue until the date of completion of discharge of cargo. This is similar to the provision in Rule X(c), to which the reader is referred.[8]

7. *Ante*, p. 162.
8. *Ante*, p. 167.

RULE XI(c)

For the purpose of this and the other Rules wages shall include all payments made to or for the benefit of the master, officers and crew, whether such payments be imposed by law upon the shipowners or be made under the terms or articles of employment.

COMMENTARY—WAGES AND MAINTENANCE OF CREW

This sub-Rule was introduced into the text approved at Amsterdam in 1949 in order to settle the question whether the word "wages" in the York-Antwerp Rules was to be construed as applying only to the crew's basic wages, or more generously as the cost to the shipowner of crewing the ship. In the event, a generous construction prevailed, and allowance is made on the basis that all payments by the shipowner to or for the benefit of the crew will be included. However, it is submitted that payments made to the crew on an irregular basis or to reward crew members for specific achievements, such as bonuses, performance payments and overtime for specific tasks, do not fall within the definition of wages. Compare the definition given by the Advisory Committee of the Association of Average Adjusters in connection with the expression "wages and maintenance" in the context of the Institute Time Clauses, Hulls:

"The term 'wages' comprises the gross amount of all those payments made by the shipowners to the members of the crew on a monthly, weekly or other periodic basis including leave pay, overseas allowance, etc. and the employers' contribution to state and other insurance and/or pension schemes which relate to those payments, and also payments of overtime to the crew in pursuance of their normal watchkeeping and/or other duties which may loosely be termed regular overtime."[9]

This may be the appropriate context in which to offer other definitions in regard to the allowances which fall to be made under Rule XI:

"Maintenance"

This comprises the cost of food and drink supplied for crew's meals and the cost of cabin laundry. In practice a figure is generally arrived at by aggregating the cost of provisioning and ship's laundry over a period of time, or over a number of voyages, and dividing the total over the number of man-days that the crew were on board, so as to arrive at a round figure per man, per day. Alternatively, for extended periods of general average detention, a claim may

9. AAA Advisory Committee Opinion No. 35 dated 15 September 1971.

be submitted, based upon the actual accounts for provisioning and laundry incurred during the vessel's detention.

Where by reason of the sacrifice or accident, for the repairs of which the vessel is detained, members of the crew cannot be accommodated on board for all or part of the time, the reasonable cost of accommodation ashore is allowable,[10] but not when the reason for their being lodged ashore is unconnected with the average.

"Crew"

Traditionally speaking, the crew of a ship comprises those persons who are engaged by the shipowner under articles to perform the functions of navigating and operating the vessel. This definition would exclude a supercargo, even if entered on the master's portage bill, who had been put on board by a charterer to perform certain supervisory functions in relation to the cargo. Similarly excluded are "cattlemen", whose function is to look after the animals on board.[11] In practice, cabin stewards on board a passenger liner, whose function is to look after the passengers, are treated as "crew", but not engineers specifically engaged to operate and maintain dredging machinery on a dredger, nor scientists, despite the fact their names were entered on the portage bill, engaged on a joint exploration/supply vessel on voyages to the Antarctic.

Calculation of the allowances for wages and maintenance of crew

The practice in the United Kingdom is to calculate the allowances for wages and maintenance of crew to the nearest half day[12] and in the United States to the nearest whole day,[13] whereas on the continent of Europe a more accurate calculation is made. Since other commercial calculations for periods of time, e.g. time charter hire, demurrage and the extent of detention in a claim for collision damages, are all calculated accurately, it is submitted that the Anglo-American practice is now archaic and should be abolished.

"Fuel and stores"

Within the context of Rule XI:

10. AAA Advisory Committee Opinion No. 22 dated 11 January 1951.
11. See *Anglo-Argentine Livestock Agency* v. *Temperley* [1899] 2 Q.B. 403; 4 Com. Cas. 281; 8 Asp. M.C. 595.
12. AAA Advisory Committee Opinion No. 5 dated 29 October 1941.
13. AAA of the US Rule of Practice XVIII.

Fuel

Allowance is made not only for the fuel required to drive the vessel's main engines at sea during the prolongation of the voyage, but also moves in port for general average purposes; also fuel to drive auxiliary engines supplying power for operational purposes at sea and "ship's ordinary purposes" whilst in port. Any separate consumptions for maintaining cargo ventilation and/or refrigeration, and for firing galley stoves are also allowed.

Stores

The term "stores" comprises all consumable stores for deck, engine room and cabin departments actually used for their required purposes during the period of allowance in general average.[14]

The exception in the second paragraph of Rule XI(b) for "such fuel and stores as are consumed in effecting repairs not allowable in general average" requires the adjuster to estimate and disallow the consumptions required for moves in port for purposes unconnected with the general average, as well as specifically for repairs not allowable in general average. However, it is common practice, when a generator is kept on load in order to supply light and power both for the purpose of repairs and for ship's ordinary purposes, for the adjuster to divide in moieties the consumption required to run the generator engine, on the principle of joint user.

RULE XI(d)

The cost of measures undertaken to prevent or minimise damage to the environment shall be allowed in general average when incurred in any or all of the following circumstances:

- (i) as part of an operation performed for the common safety which, had it been undertaken by a party outside the common maritime adventure, would have entitled such party to a salvage reward;
- (ii) as a condition of entry into or departure from any port or place in the circumstances prescribed in Rule X(a);
- (iii) as a condition of remaining at any port or place in the circumstances prescribed in Rule XI(b), provided that when there is an actual escape or release of pollutant substances the cost of any additional measures required on that account to prevent or minimise pollution or environmental damage shall not be allowed as general average;

14. AAA Advisory Committee Opinion No. 21 dated 25 August 1950.

(iv) necessarily in connection with the discharging, storing or reloading of cargo whenever the cost of these operations is admissible as general average.

EVOLUTION

This Rule was new in 1994. It takes the place of a previous rule dealing with the cost of overtime of crew engaged on accidental damage repairs or ship's maintenance during a period of general average detention, which stated that such overtime was allowable only as a substituted expense. That rule was rarely invoked, and in its absence any claim for crew's overtime in such circumstances will now fall to be considered under Rule F.[15]

The new Rule forms a limited exception to the principle expressed in the second paragraph of Rule C that there will be no allowance in general average for losses, damages or expenses incurred in respect of damage to the environment or in consequence of the escape or release of pollutant substances from the property involved in the common maritime adventure.

The environmental issue was raised at an early stage of the work preparatory to the Sydney Conference in the CMI preliminary report and questionnaire dated 3 July 1991. The subject was developed at the first meeting of the CMI International Sub-Committee in December 1992, and in view of the importance attached to the subject by the national representatives at that meeting a further questionnaire was prepared in collaboration with the AIDE and sent out to national Maritime Law Associations and AIDE councillors.

As stated in the chapter on Rule C,[16] the positions taken in the early stages of the discussion ranged from those who advocated a total exclusion from general average of all liabilities and expenses arising from pollution (see the United States proposal for a second Rule Paramount) and those who sought no change (a position stoutly defended by the P. & I. Clubs). Out of these conflicting views was born the compromise proposed by the British Maritime Law Association, under which losses, damages or expenses in respect of pollution and environmental damage were generally excluded by Rule C, whereas the cost of measures undertaken to prevent or minimise environmental damage would be allowed in the restricted circumstances set out in this rule. In its passage up to the floor of the Sydney Conference, the British proposal suffered from the opprobrium earned by most well designed compromises, being criticised by the protagonists at each end of this scale (hull underwriters and P. & I. Clubs) as conceding too much. However, the proposal attracted increasing support from national delegations as it progressed through the proceedings of the International Sub-Committee, and

15. *Ante*, p. 73.
16. Under the heading "The Environmental Issue", p. 52.

was finally approved at the Sydney Conference by an overwhelming majority.

COMMENTARY

The first and most important thing to note is that allowances under this Rule are limited to the *cost of measures* undertaken to prevent or minimise environmental damage when incurred in the circumstances set out in paragraphs (i)–(iv). Liabilities for damage to the environment, compensatory payments, clean-up costs etc. fall outside the rule, as do any consequences for failing to prevent environmental damage. Just as damages and liabilities are excluded, so is the cost of any guarantee or undertaking given to pay such liabilities if incurred.

Prior to the introduction of this Rule, there was no uniformity in the practice among adjusters in the leading maritime nations as to the treatment of environmental damage prevention measures in the circumstances now covered by this rule. The responses to the joint CMI/AIDE questionnaire of February 1993 showed the following disparities in practice under the 1974 Rules:

> *Would allow environmental damage prevention measures in all the circumstances which are now covered by Rule XI(d):*
> Canada, Holland, Sweden, U.S.A. and possibly Denmark.
> *Would allow the cost of such measures in the circumstances envisaged in paragraphs (ii), (iii) and (iv):*
> United Kingdom and Norway.
> *Would allow the cost of such measures only when imposed by public authorities as a pre-condition to a vessel's entry into, stay at or departure from a port of refuge:*
> Belgium, France and Germany.
> *Would not allow the cost of such measures in any circumstances:*
> Finland, Italy and Poland.

It will therefore be seen that the extent of the additional allowances which will in practice be made in general average as a result of the introduction of this rule into the scope of the York-Antwerp Rules will not be as great as some property underwriters have feared.

However, of much greater significance than the financial consequences should be the establishment of the clear line of demarkation between the expenses which it will be the responsibility of the shipowner to incur, possibly following the advice of his average adjuster, in the general interest, and the liabilities or potential liabilities as to which he should consult his P. & I. Club. Provided this Rule is brought into effect without reservation, we should see a substantial reduction in the number of instances of the "maritime-leper"-ships which are not permitted into a port or place of refuge because of potential liabilities and uncertainty as to who pays what.[17]

We will now examine each paragraph separately:

> (i) "As part of an operation performed for the common safety which, had it been undertaken by a party outside the common maritime adventure, would have entitled such party to a salvage reward."

As we have seen in the chapter on salvage,[18] Article 13.1(b) of the International Convention on Salvage, reproduced in LOF 1990 and 1995, provides that one of the criteria to be taken into account in fixing a salvage reward will be "the skill and efforts of the salvor in preventing or minimising damage to the environment". The effect of this, as regards the general average adjustment, is that the measures taken by the salvor to provide environmental protection will be reflected in the reward admitted into general average under Rule VI. The intention of this paragraph (i) is to ensure that when the salvage operation (to use that expression in its wider sense) is performed under a contract or on terms which do not include the "no cure—no pay" element, the cost of the environmental protection measures will likewise be brought into general average. Let us consider, for example, the case of lightening a stranded tanker in order to refloat her. If undertaken under LOF, the salvor would provide booms and skimmers to contain any possible spillage and the cost, together with the skill employed in the operation, would be reflected in the salvage reward. However, if the stranded tanker had been chartered by one of the oil majors, it would clearly be more convenient and cheaper for the charterer to provide the equipment and personnel for the transhipment operation. Under the rules prior to 1994 the cost of the transhipment vessel(s) would be admitted in general average under Rule VIII, but, under British practice at least, the cost of supplying and operating the booms, skimmers etc. would not. Now, this paragraph (i) ensures parity of treatment for such expenses.

Two requirements have to be met before the cost of the environmental damage prevention measures will be allowed under this paragraph:

— The services must be supplied as part of an operation undertaken for the common safety, e.g. refloating a stranded ship which is in a position of peril or in connection with a fire-fighting operation;

17. Under the current version (1/11/95) of the Institute Time Clauses, Hulls, London market underwriters have extended the Pollution Hazard Clause to cover loss or damage to ship caused by governmental action to prevent a pollution hazard or damage to the environment or threat thereof, when resulting from damage to the ship caused by an insured peril. It can therefore be seen that hull underwriters have a substantial inducement to reduce the number of instances when a ship is declared a "maritime leper". Despite this, the ITC Hulls 1/11/95 specifically exclude ship's proportion of any claim in general average for "expenses or liabilities incurred in respect of damage to the environment, or the threat of such damage, or as a consequence of the escape or release of pollutant substances from the vessel, or the threat of such escape or release" (clause 10.5.2). The cover can, however, be reinstated by means of a "buy-back" clause, but its effect is limited to cases to which the YAR 1994 apply.

18. *Ante*, p. 121.

— The operation must be such that, had it been performed by a party outside the common maritime adventure, such party would have been entitled to a salvage reward.

(ii) "As a condition of entry into or departure from any port or place in the circumstances prescribed in Rule X(a)."

This is probably the most common case, where a port or local authority requires certain anti-pollution or environmental damage preventive measures to be taken as a condition of entry into a port of refuge; likewise as a condition of leaving the port of refuge. It will be noticed that the proviso which applies in case (iii), namely where there is an actual escape of pollutant substances the cost of additional measures required on that account shall not be allowed as general average, does *not* apply to the expenses required as a condition of entry or departure; and for a very good reason since, if it did, the clear line of demarkation would be blurred, with a potential increase in the number of instances when vessels in peril are detained awaiting permission to enter a port of refuge while property and liability underwriters argue as to their respective responsibilities.

(iii) "As a condition of remaining at any port or place in the circumstances prescribed in Rule XI(b), provided that when there is an actual escape or release of pollutant substances the cost of any additional measures required on that account to prevent or minimise pollution or environmental damage shall not be allowed as general average."

This is really self-explanatory. If it is a condition of entry into a port of refuge that an oil boom shall be placed round the ship, it is most unlikely that the port authority will allow it to be removed whilst the vessel is in the port, whereas if an actual spillage takes place in port the cost of any additional measures required on that account are nothing to do with the general average.

(iv) "Necessarily in connection with the discharging, storing or reloading of cargo whenever the cost of those operations is admissible as general average".

This paragraph is intended to deal with the extra cost of precautionary measures required on account of the discharge or other operations of hazardous or pollutant cargoes.

SUMMARY OF TREATMENT OF ENVIRONMENTAL DAMAGE PREVENTION MEASURES

The following is an extract from the report made to members of the BMLA and AAA by the average adjusters who formed part of the British delegation at Sydney, dealing with the cost of measures undertaken to prevent or minimise damage to the environment:

When the measures are incurred	Treatment under the YAR 1994
(a) as part of a salvage operation, earning the contractor an enhanced salvage reward under Art. 13.1(b) of the International Salvage Convention 1989	Allowable by Rule VI(a), para. 2
(b) as part of an operation for the common safety rendered as a contract service or by one of the parties to the adventure	Allowable by Rule XI(d)(i)
(c) as a condition of entry into a port of refuge, whether there has been a spillage or merely a threat of spillage	Allowable by Rule XI(d)(ii), provided Rule X(a) is also satisfied
(d) as a condition of remaining in a port of refuge, when there is no spillage or merely a threat of spillage	Allowable by Rule XI(d)(iii), provided Rule XI(b) is also satisfied
(e) in a port of refuge when there is an actual spillage	Excluded by Rule XI(d)(iii), to the extent that the cost is additional to that payable under the preceding paragraph
(f) necessarily in connection with the discharge, storing or reloading of cargo	Allowable by Rule XI(d)(iv), provided Rule VIII or Rules X(b) and X(c) are satisfied
(g) specifically in order to protect vulnerable locations in the vicinity, e.g. beaches, fish farms, etc.	Excluded by Rule C

All shipowners' liabilities to third parties or imposed by competent authorities for pollution, damage to the environment, clean-up expenses etc., even when caused by a deliberate act undertaken for the common safety, will likewise be excluded by Rule C.

One aspect which is not spelled out in the Rules concerns the cost of providing a guarantee or guarantees to a third party or competent authority. In the opinion of the writer this aspect should be governed by the practice of adjusters to charge the cost of the guarantee (if raised) to the party on whom the guaranteed obligation or liability would fall. Hence any general guarantee to pay for pollution liabilities or clean-up costs would be chargeable to the shipowner or his P. & I. Club. Only if a port authority requires a guarantee to undertake and pay for environmental protective measures, as a condition of entry into or remaining at a port of refuge, can the cost of the guarantee be considered within general average.

RULE XII

DAMAGE TO CARGO IN DISCHARGING, ETC.

Damage to or loss of cargo, fuel or stores sustained in consequence of their handling, discharging, storing, reloading and stowing shall be made good as general average, when and only when the cost of those measures respectively is admitted as general average.

EVOLUTION

The old British practice, prior to 1883, was not to make any allowance in general average for loss of or damage to cargo caused by discharging it at a port of refuge. This was enshrined in a Custom of Lloyd's, reading: "Damage done to cargo by discharging it at a port of refuge, in the manner and under the circumstances customary at that port, is not allowed as general average."

This practice contrasted with that which obtained in a number of other countries, and also with the universal practice of allowing in general average the loss or damage to cargo sustained in consequence of its discharge as part of the operation of refloating a stranded ship.[1]

At the Conferences of 1860, 1864 and 1877 the British view prevailed despite mounting opposition.

The Glasgow Resolution read:

"4. That the damage done to cargo, and the loss of it and the freight on it, resulting from discharging it at a port of refuge in the way usual in that port with ships not in distress, ought not to be allowed in general average."

The York Rule 1864, unchanged in 1877, read:

"Damage done to cargo by discharging it at a port of refuge shall not be admissible as general average in case such cargo shall have been discharged at the place and in the manner customary at that port with ships not in distress."

During the 1880s average adjusters in England began to take a less restrictive view about the allowances that ought to be made in general average, and in 1883 a Rule of Practice was adopted that, whenever the cost of discharging, storing or reloading cargo was allowable in general average,

1. See Rule VIII, Evolution, p. 141.

damage necessarily done to cargo in the course of those operations should likewise be allowed.[2]

No doubt as a result of this change in heart, the 1890 Liverpool Conference reversed the effect of the previous Rule. The new text was as follows:

"Damage done to or loss of cargo necessarily caused in the act of discharging, storing, reloading and stowing, shall be made good as general average when and only when the cost of those measures respectively is admitted as general average."

The 1924 Stockholm Conference made two amendments to this text:

1. The word "necessarily" in the expression "necessarily caused in the act of . . . " was deleted.
2. The wording of the Rule was extended to include fuel and stores as well as cargo in the subjects to be made good, and a reference to handling in the list of operations, to accord with similar amendments made in Rule X(b).

No changes were made in 1950 or 1974.

In 1994 the Sydney Conference approved a British proposal that the words "caused in the act of" should be replaced by "sustained in consequence of their . . . ".

COMMENTARY

Until the amendment of 1994, the text of the Rule continued to bear the stamp of its original authors, whose intention was that it should be construed restrictively to loss or damage caused "in the act of" the operations listed. Rudolf[3] gave examples, such as the breakage of packages in slings, leakage of liquids through the casks being strained, damage by hooks etc., and then went on to say that the Rule "does not extend to loss or damage to cargo by fire in a warehouse in which it has been stored, or by the sinking of a lighter conveying the goods ashore or by shifting of packages in heavy weather during the completion of the voyage owing to indifferent stowage in the hold". Loss or damage arising in these circumstances could not be allowed in general average under the 1924 wording.

There was an interesting, but rather confusing, debate on this subject at the 1949 Amsterdam Conference. The preparatory text had proposed that the expression "caused in the act of" should be replaced by "caused by", thus extending the area of allowance under Rule XII to include loss or damage which, although not caused by the physical process of handling etc., followed in consequence of those acts. By the time the subject came up for discussion

2. The Rule accepted in 1883 was rescinded in 1968. The present Rule of Practice is now numbered F18, Appendix 4, p. 358.

3. Rudolf, *The York-Antwerp Rules 1924*, p. 87.

on the floor of the Conference, some delegations had had second thoughts. The Belgian delegation proposed that the wording should be "directly caused by", instancing a consignment of frozen meat being discharged at a port of refuge where no cold storage is available. Other delegates, while not going so far as to deny the reasonableness of making allowance in such a case, clearly thought that it would be the thin end of the wedge and that the use of the expression "caused by" would open the door to the admission of claims for the deterioration of perishable (non-refrigerated) cargoes, which would conflict with and (because of the Rule of Interpretation) override Rule C. In the event, the 1924 text was left unchanged.

Reference to the 1949 debate shows that the delegates did not wish to disturb the practice that had grown up under the 1890 and 1924 texts, whereby loss or damage to cargo that occurs as a direct or foreseeable consequence of its discharge at a port of refuge where facilities are inadequate is admitted in general average. The following were instances:

— damage to cargo through the leakage of rainwater through the roof of a warehouse;
— damage to cargo through exposure to weather on account of insufficiency of storage under cover, and
— pilferage, in so far as petty thieving would be more or less inevitable at the port or place where the cargo is landed.[4]

It is difficult to see, at this distance in time, how this practice could be justified under the 1924 phraseology: "caused in the act of . . . ". In more recent times it has become apparent that there were differences in practice, some adjusters construing "in the act of" as restricting allowances to claims for loss or damage caused in the physical process of handling, discharging, storing, reloading and stowing, and others, either relying on old practices such as those referred to in the preceding paragraph or by applying the principle enshrined in Rule C, who preferred a more generous approach.

It was for these reasons that the BMLA proposed at Sydney that Rule XII be amended by substituting "in consequence of their" for "in the act of". The object of the amendment was to ensure that claims for loss or damage under Rule XII should be dealt with in accordance with the same rule as to consequences as is applied in the context of Rule C, thus making for consistency and uniformity of practice. This time there was no confusion in the debate, and the amendment was approved with only one dissentient vote.

It can now be stated with reasonable confidence that allowances for loss or damage that is the direct or foreseeable consequence of the handling, discharging, storing, reloading and stowing of cargo, fuel or stores, when the cost of those measures is allowed in general average, can be fully justified when

4. See Lowndes (6th ed.), p. 42; (10th ed.), sect. 753; cf. 11th ed., sect. 12.11.

the York-Antwerp Rules 1994 apply. These will include those instances, referred to above, when loss or damage has been sustained as a result of the inadequacy of the facilities at the port of refuge, but not such loss or damage as is the result of some supervening event, such as fire in a warehouse, its structural collapse, flooding owing to an unexpected rainstorm, conspiratorial theft or robbery with violence.

In a slightly more controversial category stand acts of negligence or breach of duty. Is it permissible to argue that a certain degree of negligence is to be expected when goods are handled at a port of refuge? Possibly, yes; but the author would prefer to superimpose a different test: if the act or omission were the result of mere incompetence or inefficiency, such as could reasonably have been foreseen, then there is no breakage in the "chain of causation", but if it amounts to that which Anglo-Saxon jurisprudence would characterise as a breach of a "duty of care", that would be a supervening event.

This question was considered under the previous wording of Rule XII in a Canadian case: *Eisenerz GmbH* v. *Federal Commerce and Navigation Co. (The Oak Hill)*.[5] In that case a cargo of pig iron, of different grades, was forced discharged, and at some stage during the discharge, storing and reloading, pig iron of different grades became intermingled. The Supreme Court of Canada held that the master (and perhaps also the general average surveyor) had been negligent in failing to supervise the stevedores who had undertaken these tasks, and consequently the charterers were entitled to recover their claim in full, and not merely for the ship's proportion of the general average allowance under Rule XII.

5. *Eisenerz GmbH* v. *Federal Commerce and Navigation Co. (The Oak Hill)* [1970] 2 Lloyd's Rep. 332; [1975] 1 Lloyd's Rep. 105.

RULE XIII

DEDUCTIONS FROM COST OF REPAIRS

Repairs to be allowed in general average shall not be subject to deductions in respect of "new for old" where old material or parts are replaced by new unless the ship is over fifteen years old in which case there shall be a deduction of one third. The deductions shall be regulated by the age of the ship from the 31st December of the year of completion of construction to the date of the general average act, except for insulation, life and similar boats, communications and navigational apparatus and equipment, machinery and boilers for which the deductions shall be regulated by the age of the particular parts to which they apply.

The deductions shall be made only from the cost of the new material or parts when finished and ready to be installed in the ship.

No deduction shall be made in respect of provisions, stores, anchors and chain cables.

Drydock and slipway dues and costs of shifting the ship shall be allowed in full.

The costs of cleaning, painting or coating the bottom shall not be allowed in general average unless the bottom has been painted or coated within the twelve months preceding the date of the general average act in which case one half of such costs shall be allowed.

EVOLUTION

It was traditional British practice, in adjusting claims for the cost of repairs to ship, both for general and particular average, to apply a very simple set of deductions to the cost of repairs in all cases where old material had been replaced by new. The custom to apply these deductions to the cost of repairs was given judicial approval in 1879.[1] Even as late as 1906, the (U.K.) Marine Insurance Act stated that the measure of indemnity under a policy of marine insurance should be, when the ship has been repaired, "the reasonable cost of repairs, less the customary deductions . . . ".[2] The customary deductions, which applied to all repairs, other than to damage sustained on a vessel's maiden voyage, were fixed at one-sixth for chain cables and one-third for all

1. See *Aitchison* v. *Lohre* (1877) 2 Q.B.D. 501; (1878) 3 Q.B.D. 558; 4 Asp. M.C. 11, 168.
2. Marine Insurance Act 1906, s. 69(1).

other repairs and replacements, except for anchors and materials and stores that had not been put into use, which were allowed in full.

With the introduction of iron and steel ships, it became apparent that the customary deductions were altogether too severe, and in 1884 the Association of Average Adjusters set up a committee to take technical advice and recommend a progressive scale of deductions depending upon the age of the ship. This scale was approved by the Association in 1887 as a Rule of Practice,[3] and this formed the basis of a new York-Antwerp Rule XIII in 1890.[4]

In 1924 only minor changes of detail were made in the text.

In the run-up to the Amsterdam Conference, it was agreed at the committee stage that the deductions of one-third or one-sixth (as the case might be) should be limited to the cost of the materials or parts, rather than the full cost of repairs including the cost of installation. Some delegations continued to argue for wider deductions in accordance with their national practices and in the event, after the matter had been referred to the drafting committee, the following was added to the text:

"The deductions shall be made from the cost of new material or parts, including labour and establishment charges, but excluding cost of opening up."

The inclusion of this paragraph in the text of Rule XIII triggered an important change in practice—see commentary below.

The replies to the CMI questionnaire which preceded the 1974 Hamburg Conference showed strong support for the total abolition of new for old deductions from the cost of repairs. However, during the Conference itself a counter-proposal, based on an AIDE report,[5] to retain a greatly simplified set of deductions, which would apply only to ships over the age of 15 years, was ultimately accepted by the Conference.[6]

At the Sydney Conference in 1994, there was once again a proposal (from Brazil) to abolish new for old deductions, but this time it was defeated by a substantial majority. There was also a proposal that the fourth and fifth paragraphs, which deal with the costs of drydock charges, shifting the ship and bottom treatment, should be transferred to Rule XVIII. Although this would be a more logical location for these paragraphs, some delegates thought that a change might lead to confusion, and the proposal was allowed to lapse.

3. AAA Report 1887, pp. 68–69.

4. See Appendix 2, pp. 312–319, for the successive texts of Rule XIII.

5. Report of AIDE working group on Rule XIII presented at the IVth General Assembly, Rotterdam, 1967, pp. 131–137. See also the debate on the *Report re Simplification of General Average* presented at the VIth General Assembly, Gausdal, 1971, at pp. 52–53.

6. At the final voting at the Hamburg Conference, the proposal to abolish new for old deductions, being the most radical, was, by Continental practice, put first. The result of this vote being a tie, the motion was deemed to be lost; whereupon the alternative motion for a simplified set of deductions was put to the vote and carried.

COMMENTARY

The theory underlying the deductions made from the cost of repairing sacrificial damage to ship is that when new materials or parts have been put into a ship in place of old materials or parts, the ship has been improved, and consequently it would be unfair to call upon cargo to contribute in general average to this element of improvement. In the days of wooden ships, which were built to last up to 50 years or more, there was an element of justice in this theory.

However, with the advent of iron and steel ships, it was apparent that the customary deduction of one-third of the cost of all repairs other than anchors and cables was too severe: hence the detailed table of progressive deductions introduced into the York-Antwerp Rules in 1890. Some notion of the importance attached at this time to amending the previous practice can be gleaned from the fact that when Rule XIII was introduced into the York-Antwerp Rules in 1890, there was no rule governing the amount to be allowed for sacrificial damage to ship generally. This had to wait until the introduction of Rule XVIII in 1924.

At the present time it must seriously be doubted whether there is any enhancement in the value of a ship by reason of the replacement of an old part by a new one. Ships are now built for trading within an expected lifetime, typically 20 or 25 years, and virtually all parts of the ship, other than such items as are clearly recognised to be subject to wear and tear or deterioration, are constructed to last for that length of time. In the practical notes which follow, reference is made to the replacement of an engine bedplate. If the ship is over 15 years old, the renewal of the bedplate will attract a deduction of one-third from the cost of the bedplate in its condition when it is finished and ready for installation. An engine bedplate is designed to last at least as long as the normal expected trading life of a ship and, being a non-moving part, is not subject to wear and tear. Consequently, if an engine bedplate is fractured and needs to be renewed in consequence of efforts made to refloat a stranded ship after 15 years of service, the fact that the ship will then be fitted with a new bedplate will not in any way enhance the life expectancy of the ship or its value to her owner.

PRACTICE

When considering the cost of sacrificial damage repairs to a ship which is over 15 years of age at the time of the general average act, it is necessary to make a close examination of the repair accounts in order to ascertain what is "the cost of the new material or parts when finished and ready to be installed in the ship". In practice, average adjusters need to be advised in this respect by consulting engineers or surveyors, whose experience enables them to furnish an accurate estimation of the cost involved. The experts regularly consulted by average adjusters for this purpose are frequently referred to as "marking surveyors", from the fact that (before the days of photocopying) they were originally invited to "mark" the original repair accounts with their comments.

After the alteration to Rule XIII in 1950, whereby the deductions were limited to the cost of new material or parts, including labour and establishment charges, but excluding the cost of opening up, it became apparent to adjusters in the United Kingdom that marking surveyors were not totally consistent in the way in which they approached their estimations of the cost involved. In consequence of this, two of the leading firms of U.K. average adjusters combined to draft a "directive to marking surveyors" in order to secure uniformity of practice in the offices of the surveyors whom they regularly consulted. Subsequently, the directive was approved by the Advisory Committee of the Association of Average Adjusters,[7] and was also accepted in the interests of uniformity by at least one major firm of marine consultants in the United States.

The directive stated:

> "In applying Rule XIII of the York/Antwerp Rules 1950 deductions new for old in accordance therewith shall be made only when, but in all cases where, old material is replaced by new. The deductions shall be confined to the cost of the new material, the cost of the manufacture of the new article from the new material and the cost of such final preparation of the new material for the new article as may be necessary for fitting or otherwise. All other costs, including the actual fitting costs, shall be allowed in full together with the cost of preparing any old material for the fitting of the new article and the cost of removal of the old article.
>
> Costs of transport of new material or new parts shall be allowed in full except such local transporting costs as occur upon the repairers' or manufacturers' premises or in the drydock or yard. These shall be treated as part of the cost in manufacture or as part of the cost of preparation or fitting."

It is therefore clear that the wording of the directive influenced the draft text presented to and ultimately adopted by the 1974 Hamburg Conference so that in this respect no change in practice was envisaged in calculating the costs to which the deductions apply.

The text of the directive, including an addendum relating to the deductions to be applied to the cost of painting, is copied hereafter as an appendix.[8]

Drydock charges, moves for repairs and cleaning and painting of bottom

The concluding paragraphs of Rule XIII provide for the cost of these operations to be dealt with as follows:

7. AAA Advisory Committee Opinion, unnumbered, dated 27 February 1957.
8. Appendix 6, pp. 369–372.

- Drydock and slipway dues and costs of shifting the ship shall be allowed in full.
- The costs of cleaning, painting or coating of bottom shall not be allowed in general average unless the bottom has been painted or coated within the 12 months preceding the date of the general average act in which case one half of such costs shall be allowed.

It is submitted that the allowance for one half of the cost of cleaning and painting the bottom (subject to the proviso that the bottom was last painted within 12 months of the general average act) applies equally to cases where the vessel is drydocked for repair of sacrificial damage other than to her bottom, e.g. to her propeller, as it does to cases where the ship's bottom is damaged by the general average act, e.g. by a voluntary stranding.

In both cases where the allowance can be made (drydock charges etc. in full and cleaning and painting of bottom as to one half), the allowance provided for in Rule XIII is subject to division between sacrificial and accidental damage, and/or over the number of damages repaired in the drydock, in accordance with the relevant practice of adjusters.[9]

Credit for old materials

Although not referred to in Rule XIII, it is the universal practice of adjusters to show a credit against the cost of the supply of new parts for the value of the old parts so replaced which have been sold or taken into the repairers' stock with a corresponding reduction in the repair account.

However, there is a difference in practice between British and American adjusters in this respect, the British practice being to credit the value of the old material to the net figure after applying the "new for old" deduction, and the American practice being to credit the value of the old material to the gross cost of the new part. The consequence is that under the British practice the "new for old" deduction will be higher than under American practice, as the following example[10] will show:

Example

Cost of new bronze propeller:	£6,000
Credit for old bronze, as scrap:	1,500
Net cost:	£4,500

9. See commentary on practice, Rule XVIII, p. 244.

10. Based on the example given by Mr R. H. Arnold, Chairman's Address to the Association of Average Adjusters, 1963, pp. 5–6.

BRITISH PRACTICE

Cost of new propeller:	£6,000
Less one-third new for old:	2,000
	£4,000
Deduct credit for old bronze:	1,500
Allowance in general average:	£2,500

AMERICAN PRACTICE

Cost of new propeller:	£6,000
Credit for old bronze:	1,500
	£4,500
Less one-third new for old:	1,500
Allowance in general average:	£3,000

In the opinion of the author, the American practice achieves a fairer result.

RULE XIV

TEMPORARY REPAIRS

Where temporary repairs are effected to a ship at a port of loading, call or refuge, for the common safety, or of damage caused by general average sacrifice, the cost of such repairs shall be admitted as general average.

Where temporary repairs of accidental damage are effected in order to enable the adventure to be completed, the cost of such repairs shall be admitted as general average without regard to the saving, if any, to other interests, but only up to the saving in expense which would have been incurred and allowed in general average if such repairs had not been effected there.

No deductions "new for old" shall be made from the cost of temporary repairs allowable as general average.

EVOLUTION

In 1890 the following Rule was proposed and agreed to without discussion:

"No deductions 'new for old' shall be made from the cost of temporary repairs of damage allowable as general average."

Nothing was said as to the circumstances in which the cost of temporary repairs would be admissible in general average. This question would continue (until 1924) to be determined in accordance with the law and practice at the "place of adjustment".[1]

There was nothing revolutionary about the 1890 Rule. It was implicit that it applied only to the cost of temporary repairs effected to damage caused by a general average sacrifice.[2] Since, by definition, a temporary repair is one which does not confer any lasting benefit to the ship, it is quite clear that such a repair cannot bring with it any improvement in the value of the ship: hence there is no necessity to compensate for any alleged betterment by the provision of new material in place of old.

1. See Rule XVIII of York-Antwerp Rules 1890, omitted from 1924 onwards upon the introduction of Rule G. The text of this Rule is set out in Appendix 2 on p. 327.

2. See commentary below, observing that temporary repairs allowable in other circumstances are in the nature of expenditure, and not sacrifice.

In 1924 the occasion was taken to introduce an introductory paragraph setting out the circumstances in which the cost of temporary repairs would be allowed as general average. This paragraph read:

"Where temporary repairs are effected to a ship at a port of loading, call or refuge, for the common safety, or of damage caused by general average sacrifice, the cost of such repairs shall be admitted as general average; but where temporary repairs of accidental damage are effected merely to enable the adventure to be completed, the cost of such repairs shall be admitted as general average only up to the saving in expense which would have been incurred and allowed in general average had such repairs not been effected there."

The introduction of this paragraph into Rule XIV was intended to settle the debate as to the circumstances in which the cost of temporarily repairing accidental damage at the port of refuge should be allowed in general average. Was it to be on the ground that such repairs benefited the adventure by enabling it to be completed, or because by effecting such repairs general average expense was avoided?

Although the adopted solution preferred the thesis that the cost of temporary repairs to accidental damage should be allowed (if at all) as a substituted expense, there remained a good deal of uncertainty, particularly in the United Kingdom, as to whether the cost of the temporary repairs should be considered in relation only to the savings in general average, or whether all the savings, including the saving, if any, in repair charges, should be taken into account. The view was expressed that if only the savings to general average were taken into account, this Rule XIV would be inconsistent with the then Rule X(d). In order to bring British practice into line with that obtaining elsewhere, and for the avoidance of doubt, the Association of Average Adjusters passed a Uniformity Resolution in 1928 whereby the cost of temporary repairs to accidental damage, as referred to in Rule XIV, would be allowed in general average up to the saving occasioned to general average expenses, "without regard to the saving (if any) to other interests".

At the 1949 Amsterdam Conference these words were therefore added to the text of the Rule, and likewise to Rule F.

A further small amendment was made in 1974, when the word "merely" in the expression "merely to enable the adventure to be completed" was replaced by the words "in order". The intention of this amendment was to limit the admission in general average of temporary repairs to accidental damage to those cases where the temporary repairs had been effected with the object of saving general average expense.

In the course of the work done in preparation for the 1994 Sydney Conference, a great deal of thought was expended on the question whether to maintain the second paragraph dealing with the cost of temporary repairs of accidental damage, either in its existing form or amended, or at all. Added impetus was given to the debate by reason of its taking place contemporaneously with the passage through the English courts of the case of *The*

Bijela[3]—discussed in more detail later in this chapter. After extensive discussion in its Working Group B and International Sub-Committee, the AIDE General Assembly at Prague in September 1993 (while *The Bijela* was still under appeal to the House of Lords) passed a resolution that "the second paragraph of Rule XIV should continue to express the principle that the cost of temporary repairs to accidental damage should be allowed in general average up to the cost of the savings achieved in general average expenses which would have been incurred if permanent repairs had been undertaken". This was also the consensus at the CMI Sydney Conference in October 1994 (by which time the House of Lords had ruled in favour of the principle stated above), where a counter-proposal from the United States delegation to delete in toto the second paragraph of Rule XIV was defeated by a substantial majority. Result: no change in the wording of the Rule.

COMMENTARY

The Rule deals with the allowance for the cost of temporary repairs in three situations:

1. Temporary repairs for the common safety

The most frequently cited example is the fitting of a cement box in order to staunch a leakage, or the fitting of a patch over a more serious fracture in the shell plating. Such measures may be necessary for the common safety even though the vessel is in port at the time—see the examples given in the commentary on Rule X(b).[4]

It has been said that there is probably no necessity to refer in this Rule to temporary repairs for the common safety, since they are treated as general average in the practice of all maritime countries, and would in any event be allowable under the terms of Rule A. It is therefore to be assumed that the draftsman included such repairs, and also temporary repairs of general average sacrifice, for the sake of completeness, and this has a bearing upon the construction of Rule XIV as a whole.

The practice of the author is to treat the cost of temporary repairs for the common safety as a general average expenditure and not as a sacrifice, since the work done does not add any value to the ship.

3. *Marida Ltd.* v. *Oswal Steel (The Bijela)* (Com. Ct.) [1992] 1 Lloyd's Rep. 636; (C.A.) [1993] 1 Lloyd's Rep. 411; (H.L.) [1994] 2 Lloyd's Rep. 1.

4. Commentary on Rule X(b), pp. 159 *et seq.*

2. Temporary repairs of damage caused by general average sacrifice

If such repairs are effected at the port of refuge and are also necessary for the safe prosecution of the voyage, there may be dual grounds for their admission in general average. However, the terms of Rule XIV provide for the allowance of the cost of temporary repairs of sacrificial damage without any regard to savings.

Let us consider a case where a vessel's main engine has sustained damage by overheating in working in efforts to refloat. Clearly, the engine must be made workable in order to prosecute the remainder of the voyage in safety, and if the recommended permanent repair requires a number of new parts to be specifically ordered from the engine builders, the wages and maintenance of crew etc. during the extra period of detention whilst waiting for the new parts to be delivered would *prima facie* be allowable in the terms of Rule XI. However, it is the duty of the shipowner under the contract of affreightment to prosecute the voyage with reasonable despatch, and consequently if a temporary repair can be made which will satisfy classification requirements by, for example, machining and re-using some of the damaged parts, then the cost of this temporary repair will be allowed in general average without regard to the saving in detention expenses. Conversely, if the main engine had sustained a similar damage by accidental causes, and it was decided similarly to effect such temporary repairs, the case would come under the second paragraph of Rule XIV, and the cost of the temporary repairs would be allowable in general average only to the extent of the detention expenses saved.

Temporary repairs of sacrificial damage are however *not* allowable under this Rule XIV when they are effected after the end of the general average voyage. Once that voyage is completed, the shipowner is entitled to claim in general average the reasonable cost of repairs and replacements actually effected, in accordance with the provisions of Rules XVIII and XIII. It will then be for the average adjuster to consider whether the cost of any temporary repairs effected in these circumstances will form part of the reasonable cost of repairs.

In either case, the allowance will be treated as general average sacrifice and the cost of the temporary repairs will be included in the amount added to the damaged value of the vessel as "made good".

3. Temporary repairs of accidental damage effected in order to enable the adventure to be completed

At English common law and under the laws of the United States of America, it used to be considered that when a vessel was disabled at a port of refuge and could not be made fit to proceed on her voyage without effecting some temporary repair for that purpose, the cost of that temporary repair would be allowed in general average. The principle was that the cost of the temporary repair (which by definition was of no permanent value to the ship) conferred no benefit upon the shipowner and left him subject to the same expense in prosecuting the voyage and in ultimately effecting permanent repairs, as if the temporary repairs had never been made.[5] This, incidentally, is an example of the manner in which Anglo-Saxon jurisprudence preferred the "common benefit", rather than the "common safety" theory of general average.

As Buglass writes[6]:

> "In the United States, reasonable temporary repairs are treated as general average if they were necessary for the safe prosecution of the voyage, and it is immaterial whether or not permanent repairs could be effected at that time or place."[7]

Lowndes tells us that the practice in England, at least up to 1867, was to favour the treatment of the cost of temporary repairs as a substituted expense, saving the cost of cargo discharge and other expenses which would have been incurred if permanent repairs had been effected.[8] This theory received a profound jolt as a result of the decision in *Wilson* v. *Bank of Victoria*.[9]

In this case a sailing ship with an auxiliary engine, on a voyage from Australia to the United Kingdom, was dismasted as a result of hitting an iceberg, but managed to put into Rio de Janeiro with the assistance of her auxiliary engine. Repairs to her masts, spars and rigging, such as to enable her safely to proceed under sail, would have required the discharge, storing and reloading of the cargo, but instead, after effecting some temporary repairs, the shipowner decided that the vessel could complete the voyage under engine power only. Since the vessel's coals were virtually exhausted in bearing up for Rio, this involved the purchase of additional coals at Rio and at an intermediate port before arrival in the U.K. The claim before the court was for a general average contribution towards a part of the cost of these additional coals (as a substituted expense for the cost of discharging, storing and reloading the cargo), after giving credit for the estimated normal consumption and the contributions due from interests other than the cargo.

The court of Queen's Bench held that the claim was invalid, there being no principle tenable at law for an adjustment on the basis of substituted expenses, in the absence of custom or the insertion of an appropriate clause in the charterparty or bills of lading.

Although *Wilson*'s case is frequently cited in support of the proposition that the cost of temporary repairs of accidental damage at a port of refuge is not allowable in general average under English law, this was not part of the court's

5. See *Plummer* v. *Wildman* (1815) 3 M. & S. 482 *per* Lord Ellenborough. The decision was heavily criticised by Arnould, (2nd ed.), pp. 923–925, who remarked with uncharacteristic naiveté: "in practice it would obviously be very difficult to discover any kind of repairs which would not be of some benefit to the ship".

6. Buglass, *Marine Insurance & General Average in the United States*, (2nd ed.), p. 263.

7. See *Shoe* v. *Craig* 189 Fed. Rep. 227.

8. Lowndes (1st ed.), p. 149.

9. *Wilson* v. *Bank of Victoria* (1867) L.R. 2 Q.B. 203; 2 Mar. L.C. 449.

decision. In fact, the cost of the temporary repairs was not in dispute, and may well have formed part of the general average allowances, which were not contested.

Notwithstanding the disapproval of the principle of substituted expenses under English law in *Wilson*'s case, this was the route proposed by the Association of Average Adjusters for the proposed allowance of the cost of temporary repairs of accidental damage at the port of refuge. Although the wording is far from clear, the intention of the draftsman was to limit allowance under Rule XIV to those instances in which, by effecting temporary repairs, a saving of general average expenses has been achieved, and this intention was confirmed when the Rule was reconsidered by the British Maritime Law Association in the run-up to the 1949 Amsterdam Conference. The BMLA proposed an addition to the second paragraph to the effect there should be no allowance in general average for the cost of temporary repairs of accidental damage unless permanent repairs would have been practicable at the port of loading, call or refuge, and then only to the extent that such repairs were necessary to enable the adventure to be completed. This amendment was not incorporated into the 1950 Rule, and in the first edition of this book it was submitted that it was no longer open to contend that the second paragraph should be construed as if this restriction applied to it.

Furthermore, the 1949 Amsterdam Conference, as we have seen, approved the addition of a second paragraph in Rule X(a) under which the provisions of that Rule and Rule XI would be applied in the case of the vessel's removal to a second port or place to effect repairs when such repairs, i.e. those necessary for the safe prosecution of the voyage, could not be effected at the original port of refuge. In 1974 Rule X(a) was further amended so as to make it clear that the cost of such removal to a second port of refuge would include the cost of towage and temporary repairs effected for that purpose.

In the first edition of this book it was therefore submitted that these amendments had widened the circumstances in which the cost of temporary repairs of accidental damage may be allowed in general average. Since that time, however, the meaning and effect of the second paragraph of Rule XIV has been subject to a searching judicial scrutiny in the case of *The Bijela*.[10]

The case of The Bijela and afterwards

The facts of *The Bijela* case were straightforward. The vessel, a geared bulk carrier of 28,792 tons deadweight, loaded a full cargo of shredded scrap at

10. *Marida Ltd.* v. *Oswal Steel* (*The Bijela*) (Com. Ct.) [1992] 1 Lloyd's Rep. 636; (C.A.) [1993] 1 Lloyd's Rep. 411; (H.L.) [1994] 2 Lloyd's Rep. 1.

Providence, Rhode Island, under bills of lading dated 14 November 1985, for carriage to Kandla in India. Shortly after leaving Providence, the vessel went aground in Rhode Island Sound, causing substantial damage to her bottom plating and leakage into her double bottom tanks. In this damaged condition, she put into Jamestown as a port of refuge.

Following the survey, which established the serious nature of the damage, the ship's manager was faced with a difficult decision. To effect permanent repairs it would be necessary to put the vessel into a drydock, and for this purpose all the cargo would have to be discharged, either at Jamestown or at Providence. There was no drydock at Jamestown, the nearest drydocks with appropriate repair facilities being at either New York or Boston. On the assumption that it would be prudent to select New York as the repair port since the vessel could have proceeded there using the sheltered waters of Long Island Sound, it was accepted as a fact that if the vessel had discharged her cargo, proceeded to New York for repairs and, after repairs, returned to Rhode Island Sound and reloaded the cargo, the expenses of the removal and return passages and the cost of the cargo operations would have amounted to over US$535,000.

The alternative course of action was to effect temporary repairs at Jamestown, not merely by the underwater welding of doubling plates over the fractures in the bottom plating, but also repairing and concreting in way of the double bottom tanks, so as to make the vessel sufficiently fit to prosecute the remainder of the voyage. This was in fact the course which was taken. The cost of these temporary repairs was US$282,606. It was therefore evident that, leaving aside the cost of effecting the permanent repairs, the ship's manager achieved a substantial saving in cost by his decision to effect the temporary repairs.

In the Commercial Court, Hobhouse, J. held that the cost of the temporary repairs could not be admitted in general average, since the shipowner could not demonstrate that the expenses which had been saved (the cost of discharging and reloading cargo and the detention expenses for the additional period of time that would have been required in undertaking permanent repairs) would have been allowable as general average. The Judge's reasoning was that in the interpretation of Rules X(b) and XI(b) the repairs that would have been effected at New York *could not* have been necessary for the safe prosecution of the voyage, since the temporary repairs which were effected at Jamestown were all that were required for that purpose.

The decision caused some consternation among practitioners in the United Kingdom. The parties to the case had expected that they would obtain a decision on a simple point on the interpretation of Rule XIV, namely whether the cost of temporary repairs at a port of refuge would be admissible as a substituted expense not only when measured against the expenses which would have been incurred if it had been practicable to effect permanent repairs at that port (a point which the parties thought could not be disputed), but also when as a matter of fact it was not possible to effect permanent repairs at the port of refuge. Instead, the judgment cast doubt on the whole theory of substituted expenses as a basis for the allowance of temporary repairs of accidental damage at a port of refuge.

Pending appeal, the current practice in the United Kingdom was put on hold by the adoption of a Uniformity Resolution by members of the Association of Average Adjusters, supported by market underwriters, reading:

"York-Antwerp Rules 1974:
Application of Rule XIV.
That, in practice, in considering the saving in expense referred to in the second paragraph of Rule XIV of York-Antwerp Rules 1974, the determination as to whether permanent repairs would have been necessary for the safe prosecution of the voyage shall not be affected by the fact that temporary repairs were practicable."

The Court of Appeal, by a majority, upheld the decision for the reasons given by the judge in the Commercial Court, but two of the three judges opined that it was not necessary in the application of the second paragraph of Rule XIV that permanent repairs could have been carried out at the port where the temporary repairs were effected and consequently, if the shipowner could have shown that repairs in drydock in New York "were necessary for the safe prosecution of the voyage", it would have been quite appropriate to look to Rules X(a) and X(b) in order to ascertain what were the expenses saved to general average.

The case was further appealed to the House of Lords, whose judgment was delivered by Lord Lloyd of Berwick in April 1994. In a closely reasoned speech he disposed of all the contentious points and upheld the shipowner's claim, thus in effect restoring the validity of the second paragraph of Rule XIV. He said:

"The second paragaph of Rule XIV obliges us to suppose that the temporary repairs had not been effected at Jamestown. What then would have happened? The answer is simple. She would have gone into drydock in New York. Was the discharge of the cargo necessary to enable the damage to the ship to be repaired in drydock? The answer is clearly yes. Were those repairs necessary to enable the vessel to proceed safely from New York to India, always assuming that she had not already been repaired in Jamestown? The answer, again, is clearly yes. The assumption required by Rule XIV must be carried through when applying Rule X. It is not necessary to assume that the vessel *could not* have been repaired in Jamestown in order to give effect to the two rules. It is necessary only to assume that she was not so repaired, as Rule XIV requires. In this way effect can be given to the clear intention of the opening words of the second paragraph of Rule XIV, that the cost of temporary repairs of accidental damage are admissible in general average, subject only to the limit imposed by the second half of the paragraph."

In these circumstances, it does not appear to the author to be necessary to make any change to paragraphs (a) and (b), which follow in the same terms as they appeared in the first edition of this book:

(a) When repairs can be effected at the port of refuge

This is the situation contemplated by the 1924 draftsmen. It was envisaged that the shipowner would have an option either to effect permanent repairs which were necessary for the safe prosecution of the voyage or to effect a temporary repair which would be sufficient for this purpose, in which event he may claim in general average the cost of such temporary repairs up to the cost of the general average expenses saved, i.e. the difference between the extent of the general average allowances which would have been incurred if he had decided to effect permanent repairs at the port of refuge, and those which have been incurred (other than the cost of the temporary repairs themselves, of course).

Much argument has been expended on the question whether, and if so, to what extent the decision to effect temporary repairs at the port of refuge should have been motivated by the desire to save general average expense. It may be significant that Rule XIV does not say (as did the old Rule X(d), now abolished) that the purpose of the decision should be "in order to save expense". However, the purpose, or one of the purposes of effecting the temporary repairs must be the completion of the voyage: this was thought to be implied by the use of the word "merely" in the 1924 and 1950 texts—"where temporary repairs of accidental damage are effected *merely* to enable the adventure to be completed . . . ", but for the avoidance of doubt the text was altered in 1974 so that it read "where temporary repairs of accidental damage are effected in *order to* enable the adventure to be completed . . . ". The Rule recognises that purposes other than the completion of the voyage may be contemplated, e.g. a saving in the cost of permanent repairs, but provided that completion of the adventure is one of the purposes for effecting the temporary repairs, and that this results in the saving of general average expense, the fact that there is also a saving in the cost of permanent repairs, and a benefit to cargo interests in obtaining earlier delivery, is immaterial.

(b) When permanent repairs cannot be effected at the port of refuge

As we have seen, under Rule X(a) second paragraph, allowance is made in general average for the cost of temporary repairs effected at a port of refuge where permanent repairs cannot be carried out when they are undertaken to enable the vessel to be removed to another port at which she can carry out the repairs that are necessary for the safe prosecution of the voyage.

When the purpose of the temporary repairs is to enable the vessel to prosecute the remainder of the voyage in safety, it is submitted that the adjuster has to consider the options that were open to the shipowner at the time when the decision was taken to undertake the temporary repairs, and to calculate what alternative allowances would have been made in general average in those circumstances.

For example: A ship strikes a rock and sustains substantial damage to her forward bottom plating. She puts into port of refuge A, where she is surveyed. The findings are:

Permanent repairs require the vessel to be drydocked, for which purpose cargo will have to be discharged. There is no drydock large enough in port A, nor are there any storage facilities for cargo, but both are available at port B, to which the vessel could be removed under tug escort provided certain minimum temporary repairs are effected by way of fitting cement boxes and extra stiffening, at a cost, say, of £10,000. Such minimum temporary repairs would, however, be quite inadequate for the safe prosecution of the remainder of the voyage.

Alternatively, a complete false bow section could be manufactured and then secured over the damage by a team of underwater welders. This, the surveyors consider, would be strong enough to enable the vessel to proceed to destination without having to divert to port B for drydocking and permanent repairs. The cost of manufacturing the false bow and fitting it, say £100,000, would be less than the cost of removal to port B, discharging, storing and reloading cargo (say £150,000).

It is submitted that in principle the cost of temporary repairs effected by the fitting of a false bow, to enable the remainder of the voyage to be prosecuted in safety at a lesser cost to the general average contributors than would have been incurred if the vessel had taken the more conventional course of proceeding to a second port of refuge, should be allowed in general average.

The post-*Bijela* situation has recently been examined by an AIDE working group reporting to the XVIIth General Assembly at Rhodes, October 1995. In answer to the question "do you limit allowances under [the second paragaph of] Rule XIV to those cases where permanent repairs can be carried out at the port of refuge where the vessel is detained?" all respondents save one replied in the negative. The one dissentient qualified his reply "normally yes" by adding "but in some instances (port of refuge located in an area of high availability of repair yards) it can be taken into account the possibility of removal to a nearby port where permanent repairs can be effected more expeditiously (for instance immediate availability of drydock)".

The cost of temporary repairs of accidental damage allowable in general average is treated as general average expenditure.[11]

What are temporary repairs?

It will be appreciated from the foregoing that, although by definition temporary repairs are such that confer no lasting benefit to the ship, the extent of the temporary repairs may vary according to the purpose for which they are

11. See AAA Advisory Committee Opinion No. 6 dated 10 February 1942.

effected. Concern has therefore been expressed that there is a danger that allowance might be made under Rule XIV for the cost of a repair which, although described as temporary at the time it was effected, was afterwards accepted as being sufficient to enable the vessel to continue trading for a further period of time. At the 1949 Amsterdam Conference the French delegation proposed an addition to Rule XIV, which was not proceeded with, that if the vessel resumed her navigation and had not effected permanent repairs within a period of six months, the extent of the general average allowance should be reduced by 50 per cent. It is submitted that what is important is the intention at the time when the subject repairs are carried out, and the criterion of "temporariness" will be satisfied when the intention was merely to enable the adventure to be completed and not to put value back into the ship. In some cases the intention may be apparent from an examination of the repair account alone, and in others the average adjuster may need a good deal more in the way of circumstantial evidence, including the Classification Society's reports at the port of refuge and at the port where those repairs were subsequently examined.

As an example, when a vessel has sustained such damage to her working (manganese bronze) propeller as to require it to be replaced, the operation carried out at a port of refuge to fit her spare (cast iron) propeller would, in the absence of exceptional circumstances, be treated under British practice as a temporary repair under Rule XIV.[12]

Effect of the Rule Paramount

The substituted expense thesis is applied in the second paragraph of Rule XIV in a rather more restricted manner than in Rule F. Whereas Rule F applies to "any additional expense incurred in place of another expense which would have been allowable . . . ", the cost of temporary repairs of accidental damage effected in order to enable the adventure to be completed is allowable under Rule XIV only up to the saving in the allowances which would have been made if the temporary repairs had not been effected. Given this restricted alternative, we remind ourselves again of the shipowner's obligation, so well expressed by Kennedy J. in *Hansen* v. *Dunn*,[13] to repair the ship (if he can do so "without unreasonable sacrifice and within a reasonable time") and carry the goods to destination. The alternative course is restricted to the effecting of permanent repairs, either at the port of refuge or at some other convenient port. *Prima facie*, that course of action must be considered to be reasonable.

A similar approach was adopted by Mr D. J. Wilson in his response to the questionnaire put out by the AIDE working group referred to above. He said:

12. See AAA Advisory Committee Opinion No. 2 dated 13 December 1937.

13. *Hansen* v. *Dunn* (1906) 11 Com. Cas. 100; extract from Kennedy J.'s judgment copied above on pp. 87–88.

"On the rationale of Lord Lloyd in *The Bijela* case, when one is obliged by the wording of Rule XIV to ignore the course actually adopted of temporary repairs, the alternative course will generally become not only necessary, as required for the hypothetical allowance under Rules X(b) and XI(b) against which the cost of the temporary repairs will be set, but also *reasonable* as required by the Rule Paramount."

The question has also been considered recently by the AAA Advisory Committee in the context of a hypothetical case submitted to them under the York-Antwerp Rules 1994[14]:

> Facts. Whilst on a voyage from Europe to Singapore with cargo, a vessel strikes a submerged object and puts into Bombay with underwater damage and leakage. A drydock is available and permanent repairs could be undertaken at a cost of US$350,000. Other expenses which would be necessarily incurred:
>
> | | |
> |---|---|
> | Discharge, storage and reloading of cargo | US$200,000 |
> | Wages etc. of crew, fuel and port charges etc. for 60 days @ US$2,000 per day | US$120,000 |
>
> Instead, temporary repairs are effected afloat at a cost of US$50,000, occupying a period of 7 days only. After repair the ship proceeds to Singapore and having discharged her cargo is permanently repaired in 30 days at a cost of US$200,000.

The Committee was of the opinion that on the facts as stated it would be reasonable to allow the cost of the temporary repairs in general average in accordance with Rule XIV of YAR 1994, there having been a substantial saving in general average expenses which would otherwise have been incurred under Rules X and XI, *viz*:

Discharge, storage and reloading of cargo	US$200,000
Wages of crew etc. for the period of detention saved, 60–7 = 53 days @ US$2,000 per day	US$106,000
	US$306,000

On the aspect of the application of the Rule Paramount, the Committee concluded that: "the reasonable alternative [to effecting temporary repairs] can only mean the alternative which reasonable shipowners would adopt if temporary repairs at the port of refuge (or any port which could be substituted in accordance with Rule X) were not an available option, i.e. a course of action which, if adopted, would not be held to be in breach of contract". The committee then went on to say, rather cautiously: "However, if on the facts of the case, the shipowners would be entitled to abandon the voyage rather than

14. AAA Advisory Committee Opinion No. 46 dated 2 May 1995.

undertake the alternative course of action, then there is no reasonable alternative to temporary repairs at the port of refuge and the cost of these repairs cannot be allowed in general average".

In the opinion of the author, the last statement of the Advisory Committee is questionable. A shipowner is not in breach of the contract of carriage if he elects to repair his ship so as to enable the cargo to be carried to destination, even when the cost of those repairs is such as would have entitled him, had he so wished, to abandon the voyage on the ground that the ship was a constructive total loss in the commercial sense. Such cases have certainly occurred and, when they do, allowances are made in terms of Rules X and XI without objection. The only difficulty which has been experienced in such cases is as to the computation of the ship's contributory value—see the chapter on Rule XVII.[15]

Temporary repairs—when the cost also claimable upon hull underwriters

In some circumstances, the cost of temporary repairs may form part of the reasonable cost of repairing damage which is the subject of a claim upon hull underwriters. For example, there is a practice in the United Kingdom that underwriters will pay the cost of temporary repairs, "irrespective of whether there was any resultant saving in the total cost of repairs, in the case of:

(a) passenger liners running on advertised schedule, and
(b) cargo vessels maintaining a regular service in accordance with advertised sailing dates to which they adhere strictly or are committed."[16]

There is also a generally recognised practice that, when temporary repairs have been effected at the port at which the repair costs are expensive, so that permanent repairs can be effected at a cheaper port, hull underwriters will pay the cost of the temporary repairs plus the cost of the permanent repairs, but not exceeding the cost that would have been incurred in effecting permanent repairs at the first, more expensive, port.

However, the fact that the cost of temporary repairs could alternatively be recoverable under the vessel's hull insurances should not influence the average adjuster in deciding whether or not the cost of temporary repairs qualifies for allowance in general average.

15. See Rule XVII, section headed "Cost of repairs in excess of apparent value", *post*, p. 231 *et seq*.

16. The practice also applies to the cost of overtime on repairs. See correspondence exchanged with the Institute of London Underwriters in the book of AAA Advisory Committee Opinions, pp. 53–54.

RULE XV

LOSS OF FREIGHT

Loss of freight arising from damage to or loss of cargo shall be made good as general average, either when caused by a general average act, or when the damage to or loss of cargo is so made good.

Deduction shall be made from the amount of gross freight lost, of the charges which the owner thereof would have incurred to earn such freight, but has, in consequence of the sacrifice, not incurred.

EVOLUTION

This Rule had its origin as Rule XI approved at the 1864 York Conference, reading:

"In every case in which a sacrifice of cargo is made good as general average, the loss of freight, if any, which is caused by such loss of cargo, shall likewise be made good."

No change was made in 1877, but the wording was altered at the 1890 Liverpool Conference to read:

"Loss of freight arising from damage to or loss of cargo shall be made good as general average, either when caused by a general average act, or when the damage to or loss of cargo is so made good."

This amendment was made in order to remedy a defect in the Rule which had been exposed by the English law case of *Pirie* v. *Middle Dock Co.*[1] A cargo of coal was loaded on terms that the freight would be payable on right and true delivery at destination. During the voyage a fire occurred in the cargo and water was used to extinguish it. Survey of the cargo at the port of refuge revealed that the cargo was unfit to be carried on to destination by reason of the damage sustained through the application of water. The cargo was therefore sold and unexpectedly realised more than its f.o.b. value. Hence the cargo owner received his coal freight free, but having suffered no loss as a result of the general average act, there was nothing to be made good in general average for the cargo damage. The court held that under English law the

1. *Pirie* v. *Middle Dock Co.* (1881) 4 Asp. M.C. 388.

shipowner who had suffered a loss of his freight in consequence of the general average act was entitled to have this loss made good in general average.

Although the York-Antwerp Rules did not apply to this case, there was some concern that had they done so, the text of 1864 and 1877 might not have permitted the shipowner to recover his loss of freight: hence the 1890 amendment.

At the 1924 Stockholm Conference, the present second paragraph was added to the Rule at the suggestion of the Association of Average Adjusters, in similar terms to a Rule of Practice dating from 1894.[2]

The 1924 Conference also debated a proposal to add an additional paragraph providing for credit to be given against the allowance for loss of freight for any new freight (less expenses) earned by the shipowner having taken on new cargo to fill the space vacated by cargo lost through general average sacrifice. Although the delegates had no serious criticism to make of the principle contained in this resolution, it was not proceeded with on the ground that the matter was better left to the discretion of the average adjuster.

No change was made in the Rule in 1950, 1974 or 1994.

COMMENTARY

In the context of this Rule XV, "freight" means bill of lading or charterparty freight payable on right and true delivery of the cargo at destination. It has no application to pre-paid freight, or freight which is deemed to be earned "ship and/or cargo lost or not lost", the value of which, being at the risk of the concerned in cargo, is treated as part of the cargo value.

The Rule deals in terms only with loss of freight "arising from damage to or loss of cargo". However, this should not be construed restrictively: a loss of freight caused by a general average sacrifice of other property falls within Rule II[3] and in other cases regard may be had to the lettered Rules; Rule A as to admissions and Rule C as to the restrictions thereon. A loss of freight due to be earned on a subsequent voyage which is claimed on account of the inability of the vessel to meet her cancelling date by reason of general average detention on the current voyage would, for example, be excluded by Rule C.

Even when freight is payable on delivery, it is not every case of loss or damage to cargo that will result in a loss of freight. When chartered freight is payable as a lump sum or on intaken weights or quantity, a partial loss of cargo on the voyage will not, generally speaking, affect the shipowner's right to receive full freight. In much the same way, damage to cargo sustained on the voyage will not affect the shipowner's right to receive freight, unless:

2. AAA Rule of Practice F20, copied in Appendix 4, p. 359.
3. See example cited on p. 105–106.

— The damage received by the cargo causes it to lose its specie, i.e. when it ceases to be merchantable.
— When the damage is such that it is no longer fit, and cannot be made fit, for on-carriage.

Deduction for charges not incurred

Principle demands that the amount made good to the owner of the freight sacrificed should be confined to his actual loss, so that he should give credit against the gross amount that he expected to earn for the charges he would have incurred to earn it. In most instances, the only expense which the shipowner will have saved in the event of a partial loss of cargo will be the cost of discharging it at destination, as he will be obliged to pay the wages of crew and port charges for the remainder of the voyage in order to perform his contract to deliver the cargo which did not suffer any general average loss.

Credit for new freight

The principle contained in the resolution proposed, but not proceeded with, at Stockholm is clearly recognised in Anglo-Saxon jurisprudence, and it may be confidently stated that in practice whenever new freight has been earned by the carrier, whether shipowner or time charterer, loading new cargo in space which would not have been available but for a general average act, the carrier should give credit to the general average for the net additional freight he has earned, i.e. after any extra expense he has incurred to earn it.

This proposition is illustrated by the case of *The Rosamond*,[4] in which, following the jettison of a deck cargo of timber for the common safety, the vessel put into a port of refuge for repairs and thereafter secured a new deck cargo at an additional freight. By reason of the incorporation of Rule I of the York-Antwerp Rules 1890, the loss by jettison was not due to be made good in general average and, because the freight on it had been pre-paid, the shipowner had sustained no loss. The Court of Appeals came to the following conclusion:

> "If the net freight exceeds the general average expense, then there has in fact been no loss and no contribution is due from anyone; if the general average expense exceeds the amount of the net new freight, then only the amount of the excess should be apportioned among the contributing interests. We arrive at this result because the event causing the loss also enabled the ship to carry new cargo. Were it not for the event, such new cargo would not have been obtained. It is only right, we think, that the ship's profit be restricted to the amount of the excess of the net new freight over the general average expense."

4. *The Rosamond*, 1940 AMC 195.

The case has been criticised by Buglass[5] who pointed out that whereas the charterers had paid the original freight, it was the shipowner who filled up the space made vacant by the jettison and received the freight on the new cargo. Consequently, he said the case "should not be followed blindly".

5. Buglass, *Marine Insurance and General Average in the United States* (2nd ed.), p. 248.

RULE XVI

AMOUNT TO BE MADE GOOD FOR CARGO LOST OR DAMAGED BY SACRIFICE

The amount to be made good as general average for damage to or loss of cargo sacrificed shall be the loss which has been sustained thereby based on the value at the time of discharge, ascertained from the commercial invoice rendered to the receiver or if there is no such invoice from the shipped value. The value at the time of discharge shall include the cost of insurance and freight except insofar as such freight is at the risk of interests other than the cargo.

When cargo so damaged is sold and the amount of the damage has not been otherwise agreed, the loss to be made good in general average shall be the difference between the net proceeds of sale and the net sound value as computed in the first paragraph of this Rule.

EVOLUTION

This Rule was added at the 1877 Antwerp Conference, and for that reason was at one time called the Antwerp Rule. It said simply:

"The value to be allowed for goods sacrificed shall be that value which the owner would have received if such goods had not been sacrificed."

In 1890 the form of the words was recast to include a reference to the market value obtaining at the place where the adventure ended, *viz*:

"The amount to be made good as general average for damage or loss of goods sacrificed shall be the loss which the owner of the goods has sustained thereby, based on the market values at the date of the arrival of the vessel or at the termination of the adventure."

In 1924 the reference to the termination of the adventure was clarified by the addition of the words "where this ends at a place other than the original destination".

Between 1890 and 1974 the concept of market value at destination, or at the termination of the adventure, continued to govern both the calculation of the amount made good to cargo and its contributory value. However, when damaged goods were sold, there were three possible methods of calculating the extent of the allowance for made good, *viz*:

(a) the sound market value on arrival less proceeds of sale;

(b) the sound market value at the date of sale less proceeds, or
(c) to apply to the sound market value at the date of arrival the proportion of loss established by deducting the sale proceeds from the market value at the date of sale.

The 1924 Stockholm Conference approved method (c) above, and effect was given to this by the addition of a second paragraph reading:

"Where goods so damaged are sold after arrival, the loss to be made good in general average shall be calculated by applying to the sound value on the date of arrival of the vessel the percentage of loss resulting from a comparison of the proceeds with the sound value on date of sale."

This method of calculation did not commend itself to interests in the United States and, at least partly in deference to their objection, the method of calculation was revised at the 1949 Amsterdam Conference in favour of method (a). The Rule was therefore amended to this effect, and at the same time the date for the establishment of the market value was altered to the last day of discharging from the vessel, in order to reflect the practice that had grown up in this respect. The second paragraph of the 1950 Rule therefore read:

"Where the goods so damaged are sold and the amount of the damage has not been otherwise agreed, the loss to be made good in general average shall be the difference between the net proceeds of sale and the net sound value at the last day of discharge of the vessel or at the termination of the adventure where this ends at a place other than the original destination."

The Rule was again amended at Hamburg in 1974 in consequence of the decision taken at that time to substitute invoice values for market values as the basis both for the amounts to be made good to cargo and its contributory value.

COMMENTARY

Paragraph 1

In just the same way that the contributory value of cargo under Rule XVII "shall be the value at the time of discharge, ascertained from the commercial invoice rendered to the receiver or if there is no such invoice from the shipped value", so likewise the amount made good for loss or damage shall be "based on" such value. The expression "based on" was intended, *inter alia*, to support the practice, where the extent of general average damage is agreed as a percentage of value, of applying that percentage directly to the invoice value. However, other considerations may apply when the extent of the amount to be made good is to be computed in accordance with the second paragraph of the Rule, and/or when there is a prior termination of the adventure.

As to the effect generally of substituting invoice value for market value, see the practice notes which follow the commentary on Rule XVII.[1]

Difficulty has, however, been experienced in the interpretation of the words "value at the time of discharge". Such value expressly includes "the cost of insurance and freight except insofar as such freight is at the risk of interests other than the cargo". In practice, what has to be determined when the freight is at the carrier's risk is whether, but for the general average loss, the carrier would be entitled to a full freight or only to freight on the delivered quantity. This involves interpreting "at the time of discharge" as if it meant "on delivery of the cargo", and if the freight is then due and payable to the carrier in full, inclusive of the proportion attaching to the cargo lost or damaged by sacrifice, then that proportion was not at the carrier's risk and must therefore be included in the cargo value. This will be the case when the cargo arrives damaged, and also in the case of a partial loss of cargo when the charterparty provides for a lump sum freight or for freight to be payable on intaken quantity. On the other hand, when freight is payable on the delivered quantity, the receiver will not have to pay the freight in respect of any quantity lost on the voyage, and the amount made good for cargo lost by sacrifice will be calculated on its value excluding the freight element.

At the Sydney Conference in 1994, a determined effort was made by the British delegation to substitute "delivery under the contract of carriage" for "discharge" in both Rules XVI and XVII but, despite support from the AIDE and from the majority of delegations at the earlier meetings of the CMI Sub-Committee prior to Sydney, the proposal failed to attract a majority at the Conference itself.

A loss by sacrifice bears the risks of the voyager

This is an important factor to be taken into account in computing the amount to be made good for a loss of cargo by sacrifice. We begin with the principle that the owner of property sacrificed does not enjoy an *immediate* right to receive contributions to that loss from the other interests: his right is in fact *inchoate* and depends upon the safe completion of the adventure by the property which was saved by the sacrifice. This principle is also expressed in the statement that the values for contribution to any general average loss (expenditure as well as sacrifice) shall be taken at the time and place when and where the adventure ends—see Rule G.

The application of this principle affects the amount made good for sacrificial loss in two distinct ways:

1. *Post*, p. 234.

1. *The amount made good may not exceed the value which the goods would have had, if they had remained on board, taking the risks of the adventure.*

This applies both to prior damage which the goods may have sustained before they were sacrificed, and also to subsequent damage and/or charges to which the goods would have been subject if, instead of being sacrificed, they had remained on board until the completion of the adventure.

For example, suppose a ship carrying a cargo of wood goods including a deck load (carried in accordance with the custom of the trade) encounters a violent storm, and takes a heavy list. In order to avoid capsizing, a quantity of the deck load is jettisoned for the common safety. On arrival at destination the remainder of the deck load is discharged in a heavily wetted condition and with broken ends. In these circumstances the extent of the loss which has been sustained by jettison is limited to the value which the timber would have had if it had arrived in this damaged condition. This is calculated by applying to the invoice value the percentage of depreciation as suffered by the cargo which did arrive.

Let us extend our example. Supposing that the heavy list taken by the vessel caused the main engine to become inoperable, so that even after the jettison of part deck cargo to correct the list, the master needed to engage the services of a tug on "no cure—no pay" terms in order to tow the vessel into port. The property saved would thereupon become liable to pay the salvage reward, say at the rate of 10 per cent. on its salved value. The timber which was jettisoned would not, of course, be liable to pay anything to the salvor since it did not form part of the property salved but, on the principle which we have noted, the amount to be made good in general average for the loss by jettison would be reduced by 10 per cent. of its arrived value at destination as "hypothetical salvage". In the days when there was a need to prepare separate apportionments for salvage and general average, the correct result was achieved by reducing the amount made good for jettison by its proportion of hypothetical salvage.

Let us assume the figures are:

Ship value, in sound condition	£100,000
Less: damage	40,000
	£60,000
Under-deck cargo X, c.i.f. value	£30,000
Deck cargo Y (arrived damaged), c.i.f. value (extent of depreciation 20%)	£12,500
Deck cargo Z (jettisoned), c.i.f. value	£12,500
Salvage awarded	£10,000
General average expenditure	£7,500

Then, anticipating our comments on Rule XVII, the apportionments of salvage and general average would have proceeded as follows:

Salvage apportioned			
Ship		£60,000 pays	£6,000
Cargo X (delivered sound)		30,000 pays	3,000
Cargo Y c.i.f. value	£12,500		
Less: damage @ 20%	2,500		
		10,000 pays	1,000
		£100,000 pays	£10,000 or 10%

The amount made good for the jettison of cargo Z would be calculated thus:

C.i.f. value	£12,500
deduct: damage that would have been sustained @ 20%	2,500
	£10,000
Less: Hypothetical salvage @ 10%	1,000
Allowance in general average	£9,000

The total general average will consist of:

The amount admitted for jettison	£9,000
Shipowner's expenditure	7,500
Total general average	£16,500

General average apportioned			
Ship	£60,000		
Less: Salvage	6,000		
		£54,000 pays	£9,000
Cargo X	£30,000		
Less: Salvage	3,000		
		27,000 pays	4,500
Cargo Y	£10,000		
Less: Salvage	1,000		
		9,000 pays	1,500
Cargo Z			
Contributes on the amount made good		9,000 pays	1,500
		£99,000 pays	£16,500

The balance under this adjustment will be:

Shipowner pays:	Salvage		£6,000
	Proportion of general average		9,000
			£15,000
Shipowner receives:	Expenditure		7,500
	Net payment		£7,500
Cargo X pays:	Salvage	£3,000	
	Proportion of general average	4,500	
			7,500
Cargo Y pays:	Salvage	£1,000	
	Proportion of general average	1,500	
			2,500
			£17,500
Cargo Z receives:	Amount made good	£9,000	
	less: proportion of general average	1,500	
		£7,500	
Salvor receives:	his reward	10,000	
		£17,500	

Nowadays the practice is simpler. Since the amount paid in settlement of the salvage award forms a direct admission in general average by virtue of Rule VI, there is only one apportionment, and it is not necessary to deduct the hypothetical salvage from the amount made good, since that amount (in full) will be the basis on which the jettisoned cargo will contribute to all the losses, inclusive of the salvage reward, as the following figures demonstrate:

General average in accordance with York-Antwerp Rules 1994

Shipowner's expenditure		£7,500
Salvage award		10,000
Loss by jettison of deck cargo Z		
c.i.f. value	£12,500	
less: damage that would have been sustained @ 20%	2,500	
		10,000
		£27,500

Apportioned

Ship	£60,000 pays	£15,000
Cargo X	30,000 pays	7,500
Cargo Y	10,000 pays	2,500
Cargo Z		
Amount made good	10,000 pays	2,500
	£110,000 pays	£27,500

Balance		
Shipowner pays		£15,000
and receives his expenditure		7,500
pays on balance		£7,500
Cargo X pays		7,500
Cargo Y pays		2,500
		£17,500
Cargo Z receives amount made good	£10,000	
and pays contribution	2,500	
receives net	£7,500	
Salvor receives his award	10,000	
	£17,500	

2. *The amount made good for sacrificial loss or damage must also contribute to the general average.*

This rule is fundamental to the adjustment of general average, and it applies equally to sacrifices of ship, cargo, freight or any other interest. Were the rule not applied, the interest sacrificed would be better off than the interests saved. See further in the commentary on Rule XVII.[2]

Paragraph 2

This paragraph applies only when damaged cargo is sold and the extent of the damage has not been agreed by way of an allowance for depreciation. In practice, where goods have sustained damage by general average sacrifice and by other causes, and the damage as a whole makes them unacceptable to the receiver, the extent of the damage is ascertained by their sale, and the percentage allowances reported by the general average surveyor are then applied to the loss on sale.

Prior termination of the adventure[3]

In the 1890, 1924 and 1950 versions of the Rule, under which the amount to be allowed for sacrificial loss or damage was based upon the marked values, it was provided that in the event of a prior termination of the adventure, that would be the time and place for the assessment of such values. This was in accordance with the principle expressed since 1924 in Rule G that both general average loss and contribution shall be adjusted on the basis of values when and where the adventure ends. With the change in 1974 to invoice values as the basis for the amounts to be made good for sacrifice of cargo, the

2. *Post*, p. 230.
3. As to when there is a prior termination of the adventure, see the commentary on Rule G, *ante*, p. 87 *et seq*.

references to prior termination of the adventure in both paragraphs 1 and 2 were dropped, it being perceived by the draftsmen that, unlike market values, invoice values do not fluctuate from one place or time to another.

Since Rule XVI in its present form makes no reference to prior termination of the adventure, we have to distinguish two different situations which may follow an abandonment of the voyage or a termination of the adventure vis-à-vis the goods concerned:

— When there is no market for goods of that kind at the place where the adventure terminates, the loss which has been sustained by the sacrifice has to be ascertained by reference to the commercial invoice (Rule XVI) at the time of discharge; but where? The answer has to be found by applying the principle set out in Rule G, i.e. at the place where the adventure ends. *Prima facie* the goods have no value there, but a sound value can be deduced by deducting from their invoice value the cost of forwarding them to their original destination.[4]

— When, irrespective of market, the goods are sold in their damaged state, the positive provision contained in the second paragraph of Rule XVI applies, and the measure of the loss will be the difference between the invoice value and the net proceeds of sale (what in marine insurance terms would be called a "salvage loss").

4. See Buglass, *Marine Insurance and General Average in the United States* (2nd ed.), p. 278.

RULE XVII

CONTRIBUTORY VALUES

The contribution to a general average shall be made upon the actual net values of the property at the termination of the adventure except that the value of cargo shall be the value at the time of discharge, ascertained from the commercial invoice rendered to the receiver or if there is no such invoice from the shipped value. The value of the cargo shall include the cost of insurance and freight unless and insofar as such freight is at the risk of interests other than the cargo, deducting therefrom any loss or damage suffered by the cargo prior to or at the time of discharge. The value of the ship shall be assessed without taking into account the beneficial or detrimental effect of any demise or time charterparty to which the ship may be committed.

To these values shall be added the amount made good as general average for property sacrificed, if not already included, deduction being made from the freight and passage money at risk of such charges and crew's wages as would not have been incurred in earning the freight had the ship and cargo been totally lost at the date of the general average act and have not been allowed as general average; deduction being also made from the value of the property of all extra charges incurred in respect thereof subsequently to the general average act, except such charges as are allowed in general average or fall upon the ship by virtue of an award for special compensation under Article 14 of the International Convention on Salvage 1989 or under any other provision similar in substance.

In the circumstances envisaged in the third paragraph of Rule G, the cargo and other property shall contribute on the basis of its value upon delivery at original destination unless sold or otherwise disposed of short of that destination, and the ship shall contribute upon its actual net value at the time of completion of discharge of cargo.

Where cargo is sold short of destination, however, it shall contribute upon the actual net proceeds of sale, with the addition of any amount made good as general average.

Mails, passengers' luggage and personal effects and accompanied private motor vehicles shall not contribute in general average.

EVOLUTION

There were two Resolutions adopted at the 1860 Glasgow Conference which have a bearing on the development of the present Rule. They were:

"(9) That when the amount of expenses is less than the value of the property finally saved, the contributing values of ship, freight and cargo, ought to be their values to the owners of them respectively, at the termination of the adventure.

(11) That, in fixing the value of the freight, the wages and port charges up to the date of the general average act ought not to be deducted, and the wages and port charges after that date ought to be deducted from the gross freight at the risk of the shipowner."

Resolution (10) concerned the case of general average expenses in excess of the value of the property saved, but it was withdrawn at the 1864 York Conference and has not subsequently featured in the text of the York-Antwerp Rules.

The Rule which was approved at the 1864 York Conference read as follows:

"The contributions to a general average shall be made upon the actual values of the property at the termination of the adventure, to which shall be added the amount made good as general average for property sacrificed; deduction being made from the shipowner's freight and passage-money at risk of two-fifths of such freight, in lieu of crew's wages, port charges, and all other deductions; deduction being also made from the value of the property of all charges incurred in respect thereof subsequently to the arising of the claim to general average."

Several changes were made at the Conferences convened between 1877 and 1924, and these can be summarised as follows:

1877. There was a return to principle in the section dealing with the deduction to be made from shipowner's freight at risk, the new text in this respect reading:

" . . . deduction being made from the shipowner's freight and passage-money at risk, of such port charges and crew's wages as would not have been incurred had the ship and cargo been totally lost at the date of the general average act or sacrifice;"

1890. Words were added to make it clear that the deductions from shipowner's freight and passage money at risk, and also those made from the value of the property of all charges subsequent to the general average should not include any charges which had been allowed in general average. A new paragraph was added to exclude from contribution passengers' luggage and personal effects not shipped under bill of lading.

1924. A number of minor changes were made at the Stockholm Conference, the only one of any significance being the addition of the words "if not already included" after the reference to adding back the amount made good as general average for property sacrificed. The purpose of this amendment was to prevent the amount made good being added back twice, as had apparently occurred in the United States case of *The Strathdon*.[1]

1. *The Strathdon* (1899) 94 Fed. Rep. 206; (1900) 101 Fed. Rep. 600.

The successive texts approved by the Conferences in 1877, 1890, 1924 and 1950 are copied hereafter in Appendix 2.

The simplification of general average, both as regards the mechanics of adjustment and also in respect to procedure, was the chief challenge facing the delegates to the 1974 Hamburg Conference. In the realisation of these aims, the alterations made to Rule XVII for the assessment of contributory values played a large part. In short, these alterations were:

Cargo. Henceforth, the value of cargo would be assessed on the basis of invoice, rather than market value.

Ship. The value of the ship would be the "free" market value, without taking into account the beneficial or detrimental element by reason of the vessel being committed to any long-term charter.

Of these changes, that relating to the assessment of cargo values was the more significant, since in addition to simplifying the method of adjustment, it also cut out a great deal of the paper work that had previously been necessary in order to obtain satisfactory evidence of the market values at the ports of destination. Furthermore, as invoice values had been accepted for many years for the assessment of cargo values in cases of salvage, it became possible to avoid a good deal of duplication when the necessity arose for obtaining evidence of cargo value for salvage services as well as for general average contribution.

As a further towards simplification, the CMI International Sub-Committee, on the proposal of the British delegation, recommended at its meeting in December 1993 that the amount made good for loss or damage to cargo under Rule XVI and its contributory value by this Rule XVII should be assessed at the time of its delivery at destination under the contract of carriage, rather than at the time of its discharge ex ship. Unfortunately, for reasons which were not made entirely clear, this recommendation was not accepted at the 1994 Sydney Conference.

Changes were made in this Rule in 1994, however, as follows:

— a shipowner charged with an award for "special compensation" under Article 14 of the International Convention on Salvage 1989 (or any similar provision) will not be entitled to deduct the charge in determining the contributory value of the ship;

— a new paragraph has been added to the Rule setting out how the values will be assessed when cargo has been forwarded to destination in pursuance of the "Non-Separation" provisions contained in Rule G;

— mails and passengers' accompanied private motor vehicles have been added to the list of property exempted from contribution, and it will not matter whether they, or other exempted property, are shipped under bill of lading.

COMMENTARY

" . . . the actual net values of the property . . . "

In addition to ship, cargo and freight, each considered separately hereunder, the contributing interests to a general average will include, in principle, all physical property having a realisable value at the termination of the adventure. To this Rule there are several exceptions, for the most part based upon the aphorism of Benecke & Stevens[2] that "what pays no freight, pays no average". The notes that follow, however, are intended to provide guidance on a practical, rather than theoretical, basis:

- *Passengers' luggage and personal effects.* Passengers' cabin luggage has always been exempted from contribution, and this exemption was recognised and extended in 1890 to apply irrespective of where stowed, unless shipped under bill of lading. Since 1994, the exemption applies even if shipped as personal effects under a bill of lading, provided the owner is on board as a passenger.
- *Passengers' motor cars.* Unaccompanied motor cars shipped under bill of lading are certainly obliged to contribute, but the position in regard to accompanied passengers' cars on a ferry used to be uncertain. In the first place, it was unlikely that the terms on the passenger ticket obliged the passenger to pay according to York-Antwerp Rules; the cars were probably not insured for marine risks, and any attempt to obtain security from the passengers for the general average contributions due by their motor cars would almost certainly be counterproductive. In 1994, in the interest of utility, the Sydney Conference accepted a proposal to add passengers' accompanied private motor vehicles to the list of property exempted from contribution. Private motor vehicles shipped as cargo while their owners travel by air or on another ship would continue to be liable to contribute, as would commercial vehicles. Some delegates who objected to this proposal made the point that if a car ferry received salvage services, the salvor could not be expected to recognise this distinction when calling for salvage security, but the majority considered that this would be a special case falling outside the York-Antwerp Rules. In any event, it would be unlikely for the Rules to be incorporated in the terms of the passengers' tickets. In practice, most ferry operators are protected by a special clause in their hull insurances to absorb claims for general average and salvage up to a certain figure.

2. See Stevens, *Essay on Average* (4th ed.), 1822, p. 47.

— *Containers.* Containers are "property" and will contribute in general average as separate interests, the obligation to contribute being met either by the owners of the containers or under the terms of the agreement for their lease, which will also most certainly incorporate reference to the York-Antwerp Rules. Having regard to the number of containers carried by ships in liner service, the ascertainment of their individual values would be a daunting task, and the problem is usually solved in practice by reference to standard values for each type of container, as advised by the container operator or his insurers.[3]
— *Mails.* Although under the law of certain countries mails have been held liable to contribution in general average, they were in practice almost invariably exempted from contribution, even when carried under bills of lading. This exemption is now recognised in the fourth paragraph of Rule XVII of the YAR 1994.
— *Banknotes.* If shipped as a commercial consignment, e.g. from the country of manufacture to be put into circulation in the country of destination, banknotes will contribute (and be made good if sacrificed) on their intrinsic value, i.e. the cost of manufacture, and not their face value. As to banknotes in circulation, it has been suggested that if stolen by salvors, for example, they should be made good at their face value, but it is arguable whether banknotes in circulation constitute "property".
— *Munitions.* In time of war, munitions carried for the defence of a ship will almost certainly be the property of the government of the country concerned and *ipso facto* protected from civil claims. In the second world war the liability to contribute of munitions carried by allied ships was excluded under the terms of the government charterparties.
— *Trade samples.* It is usual for trade samples, even if carried under bill of lading, to be exempted from contribution.
— *Wireless and navigational equipment.* If owned by persons other than the shipowner, such equipment will be liable to contribute in general average as a separate interest. For many years this obligation was met by the principal wireless telegraph companies acceding to the York-Antwerp Rules, provided that the proportion of contribution attaching to their equipment exceeded a certain figure. However, the more

3. In the first edition of this book, reference was also made to a tariff issued by the Syndicat Français de l'Assurance Maritime et Transports and approved by the AIDE and IUMI. However, the tariff has not been revised since 1989, and the values set out in it must now (1995) be considered out of date.

modern practice is for such contribution to be met by the shipowner's hull insurance by virtue of a Leased Equipment Clause.

"To these values shall be added the amount made good as general average for property sacrificed, if not already included . . . "

Before looking at the method of assessing the values of the various types of property that comprise the contributing interests to a general average, we should recognise the fundamental principle that all property which is sacrificed has to be brought in to contribute on the amount which is made good in general average, in order to achieve parity of contribution with the interests that have been saved.

By way of illustration, let us consider a case of jettison with ultra-simple figures, where the values at risk are:

Ship	£3,000
Cargo X	£1,000
Cargo Y (jettisoned)	£1,000

If an apportionment were made over the values which arrived at destination, the result would be:

Ship	£3,000 pays	£750
Cargo X	£1,000 pays	£250
	£4,000 pays	£1,000

The effect of this apportionment would be to place cargo Y, receiving £1,000, in a better position than cargo X which, although it arrived safely, would have to pay £250 by way of contribution to the loss of cargo Y. Cargo Y would then be £250 better off.

This inequity is removed by the simple device of making cargo Y contribute on the value which it would have had on arrival, but for the sacrifice.

The figures will then be:

Ship	£3,000 pays	£600
Cargo X	£1,000 pays	£200
Cargo Y contributes on the amount made good	£1,000 pays	£200
	£5,000 pays	£1,000

Now cargo X and cargo Y are both put into the same position, namely of having to make a contribution of £200.

VALUATION

Ship

The ship will contribute to general average upon her "actual net value" at the termination of the adventure, that is to say, in her damaged condition if repairs have not been effected on the voyage. To the extent that repairs have been effected on the voyage to the damage that gave rise to the general average act, the cost of these repairs are to be deducted from the ship's arrived value as part of the "extra charges incurred in respect thereof". In Anglo-Saxon practice, the adjuster usually obtains an estimation of the ship's value at the end of the voyage, as in sound condition, from an expert ship valuer or appraiser, and when the damage has been repaired, either on the voyage or subsequently, the adjuster will deduct the physical cost of repairing the damage from the ship's sound value in order to arrive at her damaged value, or her actual value less "extra charges incurred", as the case may be. Under English practice, the average adjuster will restrict his calculation of the damage deductions to those physical repair costs that he would take into account in testing for an attainable particular average franchise, and not the wider list of deductions applied by solicitors to arrive at the net value of a ship for salvage purposes.

Cost of repairs in excess of apparent value

The practice of deducting the cost of repairs effected on the voyage from the vessel's market value at destination as "extra charges" achieves a fair and realistic figure in practically all cases, with one exception. This is when the cost of the repairs effected on the voyage exceeds the vessel's apparent value. By "apparent value" in this context we mean in either of the following situations:

- — When the cost of repairs exceeds the vessel's sound market value.
- — When the cost of repairs exceeds the difference between the vessel's market value when repaired and her scrap value.

As we shall see when we come to consider Rule XVIII,[4] the shipowner is entitled to claim in general average the reasonable cost of sacrificial damage repairs actually incurred on the voyage, and this factor points the way to the solution of this apparent problem.

Let us consider the following figures:

4. See commentary on Rule XVIII, *post*, p. 239.

Example

Market value of the ship in sound condition at destination	£200,000
Price which the ship, in damaged condition, would realise as scrap	£50,000
Cost of repairs effected on the voyage:	
Accidental damage . . .	£120,000
General average damage . . .	£60,000
	£180,000

It is apparent that if the total cost of repairs is deducted from the vessel's estimated market value, the resultant figure (£20,000) will be less than the vessel's scrap value of £50,000. On the other hand, if repairs had not been effected on the voyage, the starting point of our calculation would have been "the actual net value" of the vessel at the termination of the adventure, and this could not be less than the vessel's scrap value. This situation gave rise to some differences in practice but, so far as the United Kingdom is concerned, it is submitted that the correct solution was given by the Advisory Committee of the Association of Average Adjusters in 1982, to the effect that the net value of the vessel at destination should be based on the scrap value, to which would be added the amount made good in general average.[5] Applying this to the figures in our example, we would then have:

Scrap value	£50,000
Add: Made good in general average	£60,000
	£110,000

In the case submitted to them, the Advisory Committee assumed that the repairs were carried out after the termination of the voyage, but it is submitted that the same reasoning applies when the repairs are effected during the voyage. This has been the author's practice in several cases before and after 1982, and justification for it is readily available. If we start with the premise that the contributory value of the ship must be what she is worth *to the owner*,[6] we can see that here was a ship on which the owner was prepared to spend £180,000 on repairs and forego the prospect of a sale at £50,000.

The value of the ship to the owner was therefore:

5. AAA Advisory Committee Opinion No. 39 dated 15 March 1982.

6. *The Hohenzollern* [1906] P. 339; 10 Asp. M.C. 296; see also *"Liesbosch" Dredger* v. *Edison* [1933] A.C. 449 *per* Lord Wright.

Scrap value	£50,000
Add: Cost of repairs	£180,000
	£230,000
Deduct: Damage	£180,000
	£50,000
Add: Made good in general average	£60,000
	£110,000

Effect of ship being under long-term charter

In the English law of salvage, it has been held in the case of *The Castor*[7] that when the value of a ship is enhanced by reason of her being on a long-term fixture with an advantageous rate of freight or charter hire, the ship will be valued for the purpose of assessing the salvage reward at that enhanced value, and it is probably also the law that the depressing effect of disadvantageous charterparty will also be taken into account. Prior to the amendment of Rule XVII in 1974 it was the practice of some adjusters to follow this line of reasoning in assessing the contributory value of the ship for general average, but it is now specifically provided by Rule XVII that the beneficial or detrimental effect of the ship being subject to a demise or time charterparty will not be taken into account.

Effect of award against the shipowner for special compensation

As we have seen in the Chapter on Rule VI,[8] the International Convention on Salvage 1989—the effective parts of which have been incorporated into Lloyd's Form of Salvage Agreement[9]—has created a new form of compensation for salvors who go to the assistance of vessels which by themselves and/or their cargoes threaten damage to the environment. Article 14 provides that this special compensation is payable solely by the shipowner, but only in limited circumstances, that is to say, when there is a threat to the environment and, by reason of the damage sustained to or loss of the casualty, there is an insufficient fund to compensate the salvor by way of a "proper" salvage reward payable by the salved property under Article 13.

As agreed at the Paris Conference of 1990, paragraph (b) was added to Rule VI in order to ensure that if a shipowner had to pay special compensation as specified under Article 14, he would not be entitled to call upon other interests to contribute in general average to a charge that the Convention intended should remain his sole responsibility.

However, it was subsequently perceived that the existence of that responsibility might be construed as creating a charge upon the ship, in consequence

7. *The Castor* [1932] P. 142; 18 Asp. M.C. 312.
8. *Ante*, p. 122 *et seq.*
9. Copied herein as Appendix 5, p. 361.

of which the shipowner could claim to deduct the amount he had to pay as special compensation from the residual physical value of the ship in order to arrive at its contributory value under Rule XVII. This would clearly be inequitable, and consequently the opportunity was taken at Sydney to close the door to any such interpretation of the Rule, by adding as an exception to "all extra charges" deducted from the value of the property such charges as "fall upon the ship by virtue of an award for special compensation under Article 14 of the International Convention on Salvage 1989 or under any other provision similar in substance".

Cargo

Where the goods have been sold c.i.f. to the receiver, the value for contribution will *prima facie* be the amount of the c.i.f. invoice rendered to the receiver, unless under the terms of the bill of lading the freight was at carrier's risk.

When goods are sold c. & f. it will be necessary for the adjuster to ascertain from the receiver the amount of the insurance premium, if any, paid by him or on his behalf in respect of the consignment. If the goods were not insured, the cost of insurance drops out from the calculation, and the goods will contribute upon their c. & f. value, unless the freight was at carrier's risk.

To ascertain whether the freight was at carrier's risk it is necessary to look at the contract of carriage. Where the freight is stated to be pre-paid on shipment, or where the bill of lading stipulates a rate of freight which is deemed to be earned on shipment and payable "ship and/or cargo lost or not lost", the freight is treated as being at the risk of the merchant and is included in the cargo value. On the other hand, if the freight is stated to be payable "on right and true delivery" of the cargo and nothing is said as to its being earned at any earlier time, then the normal rule of law applies and the freight is at the risk of the carrier.

In the exceptional case where goods are shipped under bills of lading which reserve no freight, it will be necessary to look at the underlying arrangements for payment of the cost of carriage. In such a case it may be found that the ship has been time chartered by or on behalf of the shippers or receivers of the goods, and that the whole cost of the charter has been billed over to the receivers or has been settled directly by them as part of their cost of importation. When this is the case, the "value to the owner of the cargo" is the value on shipment, probably represented by the f.o.b. price, plus the cost of insurance, plus the whole cost of the charter, less the proportion of time charter hire and charges which would not have been payable "had the ship and cargo been totally lost at the date of the general average act". The figures given in the example below are based upon an actual case in the author's experience, as slightly simplified for the purpose of a report made to the AIDE.[10]

10. Report on "Contribution by time charter hire when no bill of lading freight provided for", submitted to the AIDE Council, September 1990.

Ship			
Value in damaged condition, plus made good in GA:			£336,500
Cargo			
Shipped value f.o.b. loading port		£186,250	
Time-charter hire, bunker fuel and other charges paid by cargo receivers in the purchase price		127,373	
Insurance premium		1,957	
		£315,580	
Less: Time-charter hire	£40,000		
and other charges which would not have been payable in the event of total loss:	10,000		
		50,000	
			265,580
Time charterers' bunkers remaining on board at completion of voyage:			920
Time-charter hire at shipowners' risk:		£40,000	
Less: crew's wages:		3,000	
			37,000
			£640,000

". . . value at the time of discharge . . ."

When, under the 1924 and 1950 texts, the values for contribution and the amounts made good for damage or loss of cargo were based on market values,[11] it was the practice to take the last day of discharging at each port of destination as the date for establishing the market value to be applied, thus assimilating the practice under Rule XVII with the text of Rule XVI. With the recasting of both these Rules in 1974, the assessment of the value has to be made "at the time of discharge", which on a strict interpretation would presumably mean the actual time when each particular consignment was lifted over the ship's rail. Furthermore, it is specifically provided that when the goods have suffered any damage or loss, the deduction shall be made from the invoice value of such damage or loss "suffered by the cargo prior to or at the time of discharge".

It is a matter for regret that neither at Hamburg in 1974 nor at Sydney in 1994 was the opportunity taken to effect a further simplification in the procedures necessary for the assessment of the contributory value of cargo, namely by stipulating for the extent of loss or damage to be ascertained at the time of delivery to the receiver, rather than discharge from the ship. It has to be borne in mind that containers and packages are not normally opened, nor are the contents examined, until they have arrived at receiver's premises.

11. See the evolution of Rule XVI, *ante*, p. 217.

Furthermore, there is sometimes a further extensive overland transit to be accomplished before the goods arrive at the receivers' premises, and when the containers or packages are opened there and damage is discovered, it may be entirely a matter of supposition whether the damage had been sustained during the sea voyage or the overland transit.

Taking this into account, the AIDE adopted the following Resolution in 1981:

"*Interpretation of Rules XVI and XVII of the York-Antwerp Rules 1974*

In the interests of commercial and practical expediency where cargo is destined for a place beyond the port at which it is discharged from the vessel involved in a general average, and when a literal interpretation of Rules XVI and XVII would create difficulties, expense or delay disproportionate to the amount of the general average, it will be appropriate for the average adjuster to interpret the words 'value at the time of discharge' in Rules XVI and XVII in practice to mean 'value at the time of delivery at final destination', except that loss or damage known to have occurred between the port of discharge and the final destination shall not be deducted to arrive at the contributory value."[12]

At Sydney in 1994 the British delegation proposed that Rules XVI and XVII be amended by substituting "at the time of delivery under the contract of carriage" in place of "at the time of discharge", but although this proposal had been recommended by the International Sub-Committee, it did not attract a majority of votes at the Conference. However, during the course of the debate it appeared that one aspect at least commanded general support, i.e. to accept for the purpose of Rule XVII the value of the c.i.f. invoice as at an inland destination without making any deduction for the value of the ultimate interior freight, unless of course that formed part of the frieght at risk of the carrier. Consequently, provided the freight due on a through bill of lading is prepaid and/or guaranteed on shipment, it can now be said to be the accepted practice to adopt in nearly all cases the arrived value of the goods at their inland destination except where the evidence shows that those goods have suffered loss or damage after discharge from the ship.[13]

Freight

As stated above, freight only contributes as a separate interest when it is at the risk of the carrier. Freight at the risk of cargo contributes as an element in the cargo value.

When freight or passage money at the risk of the carrier is assessed for contribution, deduction is made for crew's wages and contingent expenses which would not have been incurred if the ship and cargo had been totally lost

12. AIDE Resolution adopted by the XIth General Assembly, Hamburg, 1981, p. 74.

13. At the time of going to press, this subject was under examination by working groups appointed by the AAA and the AAA of the US.

at the time of the general average act. "Contingent expenses" cover such items as canal and port charges incurred to earn the freight subsequently to the general average act, and include the cost of discharging the cargo, where this expense is for the carrier's account under the terms of the charterparty or in accordance with the custom of the port of discharge. The calculation of crew's wages is to be made in accordance with the definition contained in Rule XI(c),[14] but the cost of maintenance is not included in the deduction to be made, on the assumption that the necessary provisions had already been purchased.

When a ship is carrying cargo loaded under bills of lading issued by time charterers, the question whether a contribution is payable by the voyage freight, whether provided for under a voyage charterparty entered into by the time charterers, or under bills of lading issued by them, is to be determined on the same principles as apply in the case of shipowners' voyage freight.

If the voyage freight is at time charterers' risk, it will contribute in the usual way, but the deductions for contingent expenses, in addition to port charges etc. payable by the time charterers and time charterers' bunkers purchased and consumed, will include the time charter hire, payable by the time charterers in order to earn the voyage freight, calculated from the termination of the general average act (e.g. on regaining position) until the discharge of the last parcel of cargo concerned in the general average. Where the time charterparty is silent on the subject, this element of the voyage freight represented by the time charter hire is at the risk of the shipowner, and will contribute separately, subject to deduction for crew's wages for the same period of time.

This will be shown in the adjustment on the following lines:

			Contributory values
Time charterers' voyage freight at risk		£5,000	
deduct: Contingent expenses	£500		
Time-charter hire	2,500		
		3,000	
			£2,000
Time-charter hire at shipowners' risk		£2,500	
deduct: Crew's wages		1,000	
			£1,500

On the other hand, if, as in the case of the Baltime form, the time charterparty provides: "Hire not to contribute to general average", the position is different. The effect of these words is *not* to remove time charter hire altogether as a contributing interest, since to have that effect words would

14. See commentary on Rule XI(c), *ante*, p. 182.

be needed in the contract of affreightment (whether voyage charterparty or bill of lading) to bind the cargo interests. Since the time charterparty is a document which can only affect the position of the parties to it, namely shipowner and time charterer, the provision that hire is "not to contribute to general average" has the effect of transferring the liability for the contribution attaching to time charter hire from the shipowner to the time charterer.

Assessment of values when cargo forwarded to destination

When cargo has been forwarded to destination from a port or place where the ship is "subject to average", i.e. in circumstances which would give rise to an allowance under Rules X and XI then, provided there has not been a termination of the adventure and cargo interests have been notified if practicable, the adventure is deemed to continue, notwithstanding that ship and cargo have physically separated. This is as provided in Rule G of the York-Antwerp Rules 1994, paragraphs 3 and 4 of which are based upon the forms of "Non-Separation" Agreements previously employed in these circumstances.[15] Under these forms it was provided that cargo and other property would contribute on the basis of their values at destination (unless sold or disposed of short of destination), whereas the ship would contribute upon her actual net value at the time and place where she was when she completed discharging.

These provisions as to valuation when cargo is forwarded to destination in performance of the contract of carriage have also now been incorporated in the 1994 Rules, but because the time and place for the valuation of cargo (delivery at original destination) is necessarily different from what it would have been if carried on by the original carrying vessel, the drafting committee at Sydney recommended that the valuation provisions should be transferred to Rule XVII in order to protect them against any attack based upon the Rule of Interpretation. It is to be noted that, following the terms of the "Non-Separation" Agreements on which the wording is based, this third paragraph of XVII provides for the valuation of cargo and other property "upon delivery" at destination rather than by reference to discharge from the forwarding vessel or vessels; the reason being to assimilate cases of forwarding, whether by waterborne or overland conveyances.

15. See commentary on Rule G, the "Non-Separation Clauses", *ante*, p. 93 *et seq*.

RULE XVIII

DAMAGE TO SHIP

The amount to be allowed as general average for damage or loss to the ship, her machinery and/or gear caused by a general average act shall be as follows:

(a) When repaired or replaced,
The actual reasonable cost of repairing or replacing such damage or loss, subject to deduction in accordance with Rule XIII;
(b) When not repaired or replaced,
The reasonable depreciation arising from such damage or loss, but not exceeding the estimated cost of repairs. But where the ship is an actual total loss or when the cost of repairs of the damage would exceed the value of the ship when repaired, the amount to be allowed as general average shall be the difference between the estimated sound value of the ship after deducting therefrom the estimated cost of repairing damage which is not general average and the value of the ship in her damaged state which may be measured by the net proceeds of sale, if any.

EVOLUTION

This Rule was introduced in 1924 as part of the process of adding flesh to the bare bones of the 1890 Rules, and apart from a small drafting amendment the text remained unaltered in 1950. It then read:

"RULE XVIII. Damage to ship

The amount to be allowed as general average for damage or loss to the ship, her machinery and/or gear when repaired or replaced shall be the actual reasonable cost of repairing or replacing such damage or loss, subject to deduction in accordance with Rule XIII. When not repaired, the reasonable depreciation shall be allowed, not exceeding the estimated cost of repairs.
Where there is an actual or constructive total loss of the ship the amount to be allowed as general average for damage or loss to the ship caused by a general average act shall be the estimated sound value of the ship after deducting therefrom the estimated cost of repairing damage which is not general average and the proceeds of sale, if any."

The main reason for the introduction of this Rule was to promote uniformity of practice in the assessment of the amounts to be made good for sacrifice of ship, since in some countries in continental Europe it had previously been the practice to allow a figure based upon a surveyor's report irrespective of the actual cost of repairs. In general, the application of the first paragraph gave rise to no problems in practice, but it became apparent that there were differences in practice when damage repairs had in fact been effected, but at such a cost as might lead the adjuster to consider that the vessel had in fact been a constructive total loss. This problem was seen as having a close connection with the question of how, in these circumstances, to establish the contributory value of the ship. This was discussed in the commentary on Rule XVII, when our illustrative figures were:

Example 1

Sound value of ship	£200,000
Price which the ship, in damaged condition, would realise as scrap	50,000
Difference	£150,000
Cost of repairs to accidental damage	£120,000
Cost of repairs to general average damage	60,000
Total cost of repairs	£180,000

In these circumstances the questions considered in anticipation of the Hamburg Conference of 1974 were:

— What was meant by "constructive total loss"? In our example, it will be seen that if the value of the wreck were taken into account, the ship could be considered a constructive total loss in the commercial sense, whereas if one applied the definition of a constructive total loss in the (U.K.) Marine Insurance Act,[1] the ship would not be a constructive total loss.

— If the shipowner decides to effect repairs, notwithstanding that the figures would show her to have been a constructive total loss, will the amount to be allowed in general average be the cost of repairs effected, less any Rule XIII deductions, under the first paragraph of the Rule, or was the second paragraph to apply?

The majority of average adjusters were of the opinion that when the shipowner had decided to effect repairs, he was entitled to claim for the reasonable cost he had expended in the repair of sacrificial damage, and this view was endorsed by a working group of AIDE, which recommended that an amendment should be introduced in Rule XVIII to this effect, and also to clarify what was meant by the expression "constructive total loss". These

1. Marine Insurance Act 1906, s. 60(2): "In particular there is a constructive total loss—(ii) In the case of damage to a ship, where she is so damaged by a peril insured against that the cost of repairing the damage would exceed the value of the ship when repaired."

recommendations were accepted at the 1974 Hamburg Conference, with consequent changes to the text of the Rule.

No change was made in 1994, although alternative texts had been prepared and circulated with the object of rectifying what critics of the Rule continued to view as unfair in its application.

COMMENTARY

The Rule closely follows English law as to the measure of indemnity payable by insurers when a ship has sustained damage resulting from insured perils.[2]

The second paragraph is also closely modelled on English law, as laid down in the case of *Henderson* v. *Shankland*.[3] In that case a sailing ship encountered a violent storm and was flung onto her beam ends. The mainmast and foremast were cut away for the common safety and she was then towed into Calcutta, where it was established that the cost of repairing her would exceed her value when repaired. An adjustment was prepared in which the allowance for general average damage was arrived at by deducting the proceeds of sale from the ship's sound value in order to ascertain the extent of depreciation, and then apportioning this figure over the respective estimated costs of general and particular average repairs. This method was objected to by cargo interests, and in the legal proceedings which followed it was decided by the Court of Appeal that the correct method of ascertaining what the shipowner had lost by the sacrifice was to deduct the estimated cost of the particular average repairs from the sound value, and then deduct from that figure the proceeds of sale.

If we make a slight alteration in our example figures, so that the estimated cost of repairs (accidental damage £145,000 plus sacrificial damage £60,000) exceeds the value of the ship when repaired, we can illustrate the effect of applying the *Henderson* v. *Shankland* principle, as follows:

2. Marine Insurance Act, s. 69, which reads:

"69. Where a ship is damaged, but is not totally lost, the measure of indemnity, subject to any express provision in the policy, is as follows:

(1) Where the ship has been repaired, the assured is entitled to the reasonable cost of the repairs, less the customary deductions, but not exceeding the sum insured in respect of any one casualty:

(2) Where the ship has been only partially repaired, the assured is entitled to the reasonable cost of such repairs, computed as above, and also to be indemnified for the reasonable depreciation, if any, arising from the unrepaired damage, provided that the aggregate amount shall not exceed the cost of repairing the whole damage, computed as above:

(3) Where the ship has not been repaired, and has not been sold in her damaged state during the risk, the assured is entitled to be indemnified for the reasonable depreciation arising from the unrepaired damage, but not exceeding the reasonable cost of repairing such damage, computed as above."

3. *Henderson* v. *Shankland* [1896] 1 Q.B. 525; 1 Com. Cas. 252, 333; 9 Asp. M.C. 354.

Example 2

Sound value	£200,000
Less estimated cost of accidental damage repairs	145,000
Difference	£55,000
Deduct proceeds of sale of wreck	50,000
Allowance in general average	£5,000

This method of adjustment has been heavily criticised in some quarters as producing a result which is unfair to the shipowner and inconsistent with the usual method adopted by adjusters in cases where the extent of depreciation is not so severe as to render the ship either a constructive total loss (i.e. when the cost of damage repairs exceeds the sound value) or a "commercial" total loss (i.e. when the cost of damage repairs exceeds the difference between the sound value and the proceeds of the wreck). An alternative text for paragraph (b) intended to meet this line of criticism was recommended by the Prague General Assembly of AIDE in September 1993.[4] It read:

"(b) When not repaired or replaced,
The reasonable depreciation arising from such damage or loss, but not exceeding the estimated cost of repairs. But when the ship has sustained both sacrificial and accidental damage, the amount to be allowed as general average, irrespective of the fact that the estimated cost of repairs may exceed the value of the ship when repaired, shall be ascertained by apportioning the extent of the depreciation suffered by the ship over the estimated cost of repairing the sacrificial and accidental damage."

This was not put forward as a substantive proposal at the 1994 Sydney Conference, and consequently was not debated in that forum.

Because these two methods of adjustment, the one following the rule in *Henderson* v. *Shankland* and the other applying a system of apportionment, are totally at variance with each other, one should not expect to find uniformity of practice in the "grey area" where the ship is not a constructive total loss (the cost of repairs exceeding the sound value), but may be a "commercial" total loss in that the cost of repairs exceeds the difference between the ship's sound and scrap values.

Let us consider again the figures given in Example 1, but assume that repairs have not been effected and the ship has been sold for demolition:

Ship's sound value	£200,000
Proceeds of sale of the wreck	50,000
Depreciation established by sale	£150,000
Estimated cost of accidental damage repairs	£120,000
Estimated cost of sacrificial damage repairs	60,000
Total estimated repair cost	£180,000

4. See the AIDE Report, 1993, p. 55.

Since the ship is not an actual total loss, nor does the cost of damage repairs exceed the ship's value when repaired, it is not necessary in terms of Rule XVIII to apply the *Henderson* v. *Shankland* principle, and an adjustment based upon an apportionment of the extent of depreciation established by the sale of the ship, *viz*. £150,000, would look like this:

Estimated cost of repairing accidental damage	£120,000 in proportion	£100,000
Estimated cost of repairing sacrificial damage	60,000	50,000
	£180,000 in proportion	£150,000
Allowance in general average		£50,000

On the other hand, advocates of the *Henderson* v. *Shankland* principle[5] would argue that the allowance made in general average should be limited as follows:

Sound value of ship		£200,000
Deduct: Estimated cost of repairing accidental damage	£120,000	
Proceeds of sale of wreck	50,000	
		170,000
Allowance in general average		£30,000

A less serious, but not less valid, objection was raised by the Danish delegation at the 1949 Amsterdam Conference. Their criticism was that application of the formula does not make it possible to make good such sacrifices as have actually reduced the proceeds of the wreck. They instanced a case where the cost of repairing accidental damage plus the proceeds of the wreck exceeded the ship's sound value by £1,000. But, they said, suppose that an anchor and a boat had been sacrificed, which if saved could have sold for £100. Thus, although it could be demonstrated that the sacrifice had indeed diminished the proceeds to that extent, the loss was precluded from allowance by the application of the *Henderson* v. *Shankland* formula.

Although the figures in the Danish example do not, owing to the 1974 amendment, have the result of excluding the £100 sacrificial loss under the present text, the anomaly remains. The AIDE has suggested that the addition of the following wording at the end of present paragraph (b) would remedy the position:

"When the application of this formula would produce no allowance in general average, but the net proceeds of sale, if any, have been reduced by reason of the general average

5. See Lowndes & Rudolf (11th ed.), sect. 18.17.

act, there shall be allowed the difference between such net proceeds of sale and the sum the ship would have realised but for the sacrifice."

PRACTICE

The reasonable cost of repairs

It is submitted that, for the sake of consistency, the adjuster should be guided by the same criteria as apply when he is considering the reasonable cost of repairs as the measure of indemnity for a claim under a vessel's hull insurances. When, by reason of both accidental and sacrificial damage sustained on the voyage, the vessel has to enter a port of refuge in order to effect repairs necessary for the safe prosecution of the voyage, it is the practice to allow the actual repair costs at that port, even though such costs may be exorbitant in relation to the cost of repairs elsewhere.

For repairs which can be deferred, it was sometimes thought prior to the introduction of Rule XVIII that the cost of sacrificial damage repairs should be estimated as at the prices obtaining at the time and place when and where the adventure ended. However, the port of destination is not necessarily the most convenient and economical place at which to effect repairs, and consequently the present practice is to allow the cost at the time and place reasonably selected for the execution of the repair. When the damage does not affect the vessel's seaworthiness, the first reasonable occasion for effecting such repairs is likely to be at the next routine drydocking or overhaul of the ship. In the event of deferment of the outstanding repair beyond this time, the adjuster should take care to check whether the cost incurred has been increased by inflation, and if it has and the extent of deferment was unreasonable, the adjuster should limit his allowance to the cost that would have been incurred if the repair had been effected at the first reasonable opportunity.

The cost of drydocking and other common charges

When a ship is drydocked as an immediate consequence of the casualty in order to repair both accidental and sacrificial damage, it is the common practice of adjusters to divide the cost of drydocking the ship and other common charges in moieties, i.e. 50 per cent. to the accidental damage repair and 50 per cent. to the sacrificial damage repair. However, there are variations in practice as to the division of time-based charges, the practice in France and Germany in this respect being different from that which is applied in most other countries. The differences in practice are even more noticeable when it comes to dividing drydock dues and other common charges incurred for the repair of sacrificial damage concurrently with the repair of damages sustained in a number of different accidents, as well as work undertaken for the shipowners' account. This subject was examined in detail by a working group of AIDE,[6] which concluded rather lamely that although it might be considered desirable in theory to make some effort to achieve uniformity of practice in this respect, the differences in practice, in terms of their monetary effect, did not really justify the effort that would be involved.

The reasonable depreciation arising from unrepaired damage

This is the basis of allowance for unrepaired sacrificial damage. In practice, if a shipowner intends to effect his repairs within a reasonable time, he will probably defer submitting his claim until he is in a position to provide the appropriate repair accounts and reports of survey in justification of his claim for the reasonable cost of repairs. If he does not do this, he is likely to claim for the reasonable depreciation in the value of the vessel arising out of the fact that sacrificial damage remains unrepaired. It is a question of fact in each case whether, and to what extent, a ship has been depreciated in value in consequence of her carrying unrepaired damage, particularly if it does not affect seaworthiness. An old ship with unrepaired shell plating damage, say caused by contact with a salving tug, may not suffer any depreciation in her value unless a shipowner acting reasonably, and having regard to the market and the age of the ship, would cause the damage to be repaired at some time during her expected trading life.

In most cases the average adjuster can rely upon the evidence of his shipowner client as to his intentions in this respect, but in case such evidence is not available, or cannot be relied upon, the adjuster will have to consider objectively the question whether a willing buyer wishing to employ the ship in the same trade would be likely to mark down his offer on account of the existence of the unrepaired damage.

Of course, if the ship is sold in her damaged condition shortly after the casualty that gave rise to the general average, the depreciation in value will be measured by the loss on sale, i.e. the difference between her value if repaired and the net proceeds of sale.

In either case, having measured the depreciation in value, the adjuster will need to compare this figure with the estimated cost of repairs, will usually have been established by a contemporaneous survey. If the adjuster does not have this information, he will have to do the best he can by taking advice from an independent surveyor. In the unusual (but not impossible) case of the depreciation exceeding the estimated cost of repairs, it will be the latter which will be allowable. More usually, the estimated cost of repairs will exceed the figure for depreciation, and when the unrepaired damage in existence had been caused by accident and sacrifice, the usual practice of adjusters is to

6. Report of AIDE working group, Rule XVIII, presented to the XVth General Assembly, York, 1989.

apportion the figure for depreciation over the respective cost estimates for both accidental and sacrificial damage repairs, *viz*:

Example 3

Sound value of ship			£200,000
Sold in damaged condition for			140,000
Extent of depreciation established by the sale			£60,000
Apportioned			
Estimated cost of accidental damage repairs	£75,000	in proportion	£45,000
Estimated cost of sacrificial damage repairs	25,000	in proportion	15,000
	£100,000	in proportion	£60,000
Allowance in general average			£15,000

RULE XIX

UNDECLARED OR WRONGFULLY DECLARED CARGO

Damage or loss caused to goods loaded without the knowledge of the shipowner or his agent or to goods wilfully misdescribed at time of shipment shall not be allowed as general average, but such goods shall remain liable to contribute, if saved.

Damage or loss caused to goods which have been wrongfully declared on shipment at a value which is lower than their real value shall be contributed for at the declared value, but such goods shall contribute upon their actual value.

HISTORY

The purpose of the Rule is to prevent a fraudulent shipper of goods gaining at the expense of honest contributors in general average. There is no known English authority on the subject, although Arnould stated that there can be no claim to contribution in the case of a jettison of goods for which there is no bill of lading.[1] However, in so saying, he was probably relying upon statements in the commercial codes of civil law countries.

No amendments to the Rule, nor objections to it, have been made since its introduction in 1924.

COMMENTARY

The first paragraph precludes allowance in general average for loss or damage caused to two categories of goods which are wrongfully loaded. It does not have any application to property, other than goods, which are quite properly shipped on board without a bill of lading. The two categories of goods intended to be caught by the Rule are:

- goods loaded without the knowledge of the shipowner or his agent: this appears to accord with the continental practice of excluding any claim in general average in respect of goods which do not appear on the ship's manifest or for which no bill of lading has been issued.

1. Arnould (2nd ed.), p. 904.

— goods wilfully misdescribed at the time of shipment. A not too fanciful example would be guns and other small arms shipped as "vacuum cleaner parts".

The second paragraph, which exacts a lesser penalty, is designed to catch an owner of goods of high value, who has wrongfully declared them to the ship's agent at a lower value in order to gain the benefit of a lower rate of freight. If subject to general average loss or damage, the amount made good will be reduced *pro rata* to the amount declared, whereas if called upon to pay general average contribution, such goods will be assessed for contribution at their actual invoice value.

The Rule is hardly ever invoked, but in those limited cases where it will apply, its effect is to make the punishment fit the crime.

RULE XX

PROVISION OF FUNDS

A commission of 2 per cent. on general average disbursements, other than the wages and maintenance of master, officers and crew and fuel and stores not replaced during the voyage, shall be allowed in general average.

The capital loss sustained by the owners of goods sold for the purpose of raising funds to defray general average disbursements shall be allowed in general average.

The cost of insuring general average disbursements shall also be admitted in general average.

INTRODUCTION

The law maritime has always recognised the obligation of co-adventurers to furnish funds in the event of an emergency. Lowndes tells us, on the authority of the *Consolado del Mare* that "if the merchants have money, and if they are in a place where the master has need of supply or things necessary for the ship, the merchant must lend it to him", subject to the agreement of the co-adventurers. However, if funds were available from an outside source, the merchants were not obliged to lend their money to the master, though they might do so if they thought fit.

When the merchants ceased to travel with the ship, their authority became invested in the master who, in case of necessity, was empowered to employ the following extraordinary means to raise funds, but only after all ordinary efforts had failed. In ascending order of extremity, the master might raise funds:

(a) on the security of the ship and pending freight, by way of a bottomry bond;
(b) on the security of ship, freight and cargo by way of a *respondentia* bond;
(c) as a last resort, by selling a part of the cargo.

In so doing, the master is said to be acting as an "agent of necessity", but for such agency to be recognised by English law, it is essential that the master should have attempted to obtain funds or direct instructions from the shipowner and, in the case of sale of cargo, to have attempted to obtain the express authority of the cargo owner.[1]

Bottomry and *respondentia* bonds were forms whereby the property was hypothecated to the lender on terms that the loan would be repayable within a short time (usually three days) after the arrival of ship and cargo at destination. If the ship and cargo failed to arrive safely, nothing was repayable. The lender had an insurable interest in the amount which he had advanced, and the premium chargeable on the bottomry or *respondentia* bond could be expected to be fairly high, as it would comprise both the lender's commission and the cost of insuring the loan for the remainder of the voyage.

Since the obligation to repay the loan formed a charge on the property at destination, it can be seen that when and in so far as the loan was necessary to defray general average disbursements, the charge on the property was akin to a sacrifice of part of its value. Hence, the bottomry or *respondentia* premium, and the loss of sale on cargo was allowable in general average to the extent that the loan had been used to pay for general average disbursements.

With better communications, and more efficient banking methods, these extreme methods of raising funds are now all but obsolete.

In the everyday case of sending funds to a foreign port to pay for disbursements, a shipowner has always been entitled to claim the bank charges he has incurred as part of the cost of remitting those funds, and when disbursements have been paid by a time charterer and debited to the shipowner subsequently, it is customary for the time charterer to charge a disbursing commission, usually $2\frac{1}{2}$ per cent., on the amount of the disbursements which are for the shipowner's account. In practice, these commissions have always been reflected in the allowances made in a general average adjustment, but as for any commission to be credited to a shipowner in recompense for his time and trouble, there was a difference in practice between the United Kingdom and other countries. Such commission was allowed in the United States at $2\frac{1}{2}$ per cent., and at various rates in European countries, whereas in the United Kingdom no such allowance was made.[2]

EVOLUTION

Rule XX was therefore put together at the time of the 1924 revision of the York-Antwerp Rules in order to bring uniformity into the matter of the

1. See Carver, *Carriage by Sea* (13th ed.), sect. 1231 and cases there cited.
2. See Rules of Practice A2 and A3 of the AAA:

A2. "That, in practice, interest and commission for advancing funds are only allowable in average when, proper and necessary steps having been taken to make a collection on account, an out-of-pocket expense for interest and/or commission for advancing funds is reasonably incurred."

A3. "That, in practice, neither commission (excepting bank commission) nor any charge by way of agency or remuneration for trouble is allowed to the shipowner in average, except in respect of services rendered on behalf of cargo when such services are not involved in the contract of affreightment."

commission allowable to shipowners, or other parties to the adventure, for advancing money, and at the same time make provision for the exceptional methods of obtaining funds abroad, to which we have already alluded. In 1924 the Rule was numbered XXI and read as follows:

> "*Provision of funds*
>
> A commission of 2% on general average disbursements shall be allowed in general average, but when the funds are not provided by any of the contributing interests, the necessary cost of obtaining the funds required by means of a bottomry bond or otherwise, or the loss sustained by owners of goods sold for the purpose, shall be allowed in general average.
>
> The cost of insuring the money advanced to pay for general average disbursements shall also be allowed in general average."

At the 1949 Amsterdam Conference it was considered by some that the rate of 2 per cent. was overly generous, and the Conference accepted an amendment proposed by the United States which had the effect of excluding commission on allowances made in the adjustment for wages and maintenance of crew and for fuel and stores not replaced during the voyage.

There was no change in 1974.

In the run-up to the 1994 Conference the view was expressed that the exclusion of commission on the wages and maintenance of crew and fuel and stores not replaced during the voyage was really not justified, since the shipowner claiming the allowance for commission would have funded these expenses, and to the extent that they were admissible in general average by virtue of Rules X and XI, he (the shipowner) was entitled to a commission for advancing the funds. The BMLA adopted this argument, which was rather surprisingly supported by the United States, but by the time this proposal to delete the words "other than the wages and maintenance of the master, officers and crew and fuel and stores not replaced during the voyage" came to be considered at the Sydney Conference, it became a victim of the cross-fire of criticism aimed by UNCTAD and IUMI at the alleged tendency "to enlarge the scope of general average". The proposal was accordingly withdrawn.

On the other hand, other proposals of a less contentious nature, also moved by the British delegation, were approved by the Conference without objection. They were:

- — to delete the words: "but when the funds are not provided by any of the contributing interests, the necessary cost of obtaining the funds required by means of a bottomry bond or otherwise . . . shall be allowed in general average";
- — to maintain, in more straightforward language, the allowance for "the capital loss sustained by the owners of goods sold for the purpose of raising funds to defraud general average disbursements";
- — to simplify the reference to the cost of insuring general average disbursements.

COMMENTARY

Paragraph 1

The allowance is made at a flat rate of 2 per cent. on the moneys actually disbursed by the parties to the adventure for general average purposes. The word used is "disbursements", which appears in all three paragraphs of the Rule, and has the same meaning throughout. The expression "disbursements" is wider than "expenditure", since it covers any sums paid on account of the general average, including repairs to the ship and the cost of reconditioning cargo, both of which are in the nature of general average sacrifice. Furthermore, no distinction is made between payments which are made whilst the voyage is in progress, e.g. to defray expenses at a port of refuge, and payments made afterwards, e.g. the cost of repairing sacrificial damage to ship after the voyage has been completed.

The exclusion of commission on the wages and maintenance of master, officers and crew and fuel and stores not replaced during the voyage, thought by many to be unfair, can be justified on the grounds that these are in the nature of enhanced voyage expenses to which the shipowner is committed before the occurrence of the general average act. In particular, an allowance in general average for the cost of replacing fuel and stores which were on board at the time of the general average act would not necessarily involve an outlay of money during the voyage. Following this line of reasoning, when the ship has bunkered during the voyage subsequently to the general average act, the practice is to allow commission on the cost of the bunkers so purchased only to the extent that the general average allowance qualifies as "expenditure".

Amounts paid by the parties to the adventure in settlement of salvage under contract, e.g. under Lloyd's Form, were, under British practice, treated as general average disbursements under a Rule of Practice dating from 1927, even before the inclusion of Rule VI in the York-Antwerp Rules 1974. This was done in order to achieve parity of treatment when the amount of the salvage reward was payable by the parties in different proportions from those which were established under the general average adjustment. In practice, the amounts payable to the salvors are frequently advanced directly by hull and cargo underwriters, and in such circumstances it is British practice to credit the 2 per cent. commission directly to the underwriters in this respect. This is based upon Rule of Practice C2 of the Association of Average Adjusters,[3] which provides that the commission of 2 per cent. "shall be credited in full to the party who has authorised the expenditure and is liable for payment, except that where the funds for payment are provided in the first instance in whole or in part from the deposit funds, or by other parties to the adventure, or by underwriters, the commission on such advances shall be credited to the

3. See Appendix 4, p. 354.

deposit funds or to the parties or underwriters providing the funds for payment".

Paragraph 2—Cargo sold to raise funds

This provision now stands on its own. It used to be situated in the rather clumsily drafted first paragraph, associated by propinquity with the cost of raising funds by means of a bottomry bond "or otherwise". The 1994 amendment has swept away the archaic and obscure wording.

Gone are the references to the provision of funds from outside "the contributing interests", whether by means of a bottomry bond or otherwise. In the unlikely event that the master of a ship has to resort to such methods, the cost of obtaining the funds will fall to be dealt with in accordance with the law governing the adjustment. If a shipowner has to borrow money from bankers, and the rates are exorbitant, he cannot now contend that this Rule XX entitles him to charge the general average with the cost of the loan. It was a doubtful claim, even before the 1994 amendment; now he will have to be satisfied with the flat 2 per cent. provided for in paragraph 1.

On the other hand, the admission in general average of the loss on sale of cargo to raise money in order to pay for general average disbursements has been retained in clear terms. However, it must be emphasised yet again that this means of obtaining funds may be employed only as an absolutely last resort, and after seeking the cargo owner's authority when all other methods have been exhausted. The "capital loss sustained by the owner of the goods" means the amount he has suffered financially by the transaction, i.e. the difference between the value of the goods to him (not necessarily the c.i.f. value) and the balance of the proceeds of sale (if any) after and to the extent that they have been used to pay the general average disbursements. The goods owner will also be entitled to receive his 2 per cent. commission on this amount, as provided for in paragraph 1.

Paragraph 3—Insurance of general average disbursements

The occasion for this insurance arises when a shipowner (or some other party who may be called upon to provide the finance) finds himself obliged to pay for general average disbursements or incurs a liability to salvors or other contractors in regard to expenses which will ultimately form the subject of a general average contribution from the other parties to the adventure.

In placing the insurance, the shipowner (or other financier of the maritime adventure) may well have two separate objects in view. His initial object will be:

(a) to protect himself against the risk that, between the time that he has incurred the liability to pay and the time that he can enforce his right to receive the contributions contingently due from the other parties to the common maritime adventure, the property liable to make such contributions may become a total loss or suffer such reduction in value that the fund available to pay those contributions will be insufficient to reimburse him for their proportion of the expenses and liabilities for which he has assumed responsibility.

Additionally the shipowner and his advisers may have in mind a further object, *viz*:

(b) to protect all the parties to the common maritime adventure (including himself) against the risk that, by reason of an event occurring after he has incurred such liability and before the contribution of all parties will be assessed, the basis of the contribution will be altered in such a way as to vary the incidence of liability to contribute to those expenses, thus placing an additional burden upon some of the contributing interests.

There are various forms for this type of insurance. The forms in use in the United Kingdom are designated the Average Disbursements Clauses (A) and (B), which were introduced in 1987. The (B) Clauses cover the risks of total loss of the contributing interests or their insufficiency to pay the contribution due (i.e. the cover described in paragraph (a) above), whereas the (A) Clauses provide the additional cover referred to in paragraph (b) above. For additional information on the subject, the reader is referred to the booklet entitled *The Insurance of Average Disbursements*, published by Lloyd's of London Press in 1987.[4]

The usual practice is that the shipowner, in consultation with his average adjuster, makes an estimation of the likely amount of his disbursements, including any bail for salvage, as soon as the ship has arrived at the port of refuge, and requests that an insurance be opened for this amount at the inception of the risk. Subsequently, when the insurable value can be finally ascertained, the insurance is closed for the total of the disbursements, costs and charges which were at risk, including the cost of the premium thereon, and a *pro rata* additional or return of premium is settled. The amount of the finally agreed premium is the figure which is entered in the general average adjustment as the cost of insuring the disbursements.

4. Also published in [1987] 4 L.M.C.L.Q. 443.

RULE XXI

INTEREST ON LOSSES MADE GOOD IN GENERAL AVERAGE

Interest shall be allowed on expenditure, sacrifices and allowances in general average at the rate of 7 per cent. per annum, until three months after the date of issue of the general average adjustment, due allowance being made for any payment on account by the contributory interests or from the general average deposit fund.

EVOLUTION

The Rule was proposed by the Association of Average Adjusters in 1924 in order to remedy the apparent gap in English law and practice, which was that neither commission nor interest would be allowed to the shipowner in average unless, having taken some steps to obtain a collection of account, "an out-of-pocket expense for interest and/or commission for advancing funds is reasonably incurred".[1] The text of the Rule agreed by the 1924 Stockholm Conference, then numbered XXII, read as follows:

"*Interest on losses made good in general average*

Interest shall be allowed on expenditure, sacrifices and allowances charged to general average at the legal rate per annum prevailing at the final port of destination at which the adventure ends, or where there is no recognised legal rate, at the rate of 5% per annum until the date of the general average statement, due allowance being made for any interim reimbursement from the contributory interests or from the general average deposit fund."

The reference to the "legal rate" of interest suggests that the draft may have been based upon United States practice to allow interest at the legal rate prevailing at the place of adjustment.[2]

The concept of the "legal rate" was, however, very difficult to apply in practice, particularly when the voyage ended in a country subject to fluctuating rates of interest, and consequently at the 1949 Conference in Amsterdam

1. See Rule of Practice A2 of the AAA, referred to above, in the commentary on Rule XX, p. 250, fn. 2. This Rule of Practice was passed in 1878, but in practice was treated as restrictive, rather than permissive.
2. See *Sims* v. *Willing* (1822) 8 Serg. & R. 103.

the reference to the legal rate prevailing at the port of destination was omitted from the Rule, and a standard rate of interest at 5 per cent. was adopted.

At the 1974 Hamburg Conference the standard rate of interest was increased from 5 to 7 per cent.

In the run-up to the 1994 Sydney Conference there were two separate but similarly motivated proposals—one from the BMLA and the other recommended by the AIDE—to insert into Rule XXI new provisions to regulate the selection of the currency in which the adjustment should be prepared and the calculation of currency conversion. In the event, neither of these proposals was adopted by the Conference, but in view of the importance of the subject, they are both reported upon later in this Chapter.[3]

One alteration of importance was, however, made at Sydney, namely to extend the period of time for which interest is calculated until three months after the date of issue of the adjustment.

COMMENTARY

Unlike the allowance for commission under Rule XX, the allowance of interest is made on all items of "expenditure, sacrifices and allowances charged to general average", and not merely on disbursements. Hence, allowances for loss or damage to cargo (other than for reconditioning expenses paid as a disbursement), and for the depreciation arising from unrepaired sacrificial damage to ship, while not earning commission under Rule XX, will carry a right to interest under Rule XXI.

No allowance for interest should however be made for accounts remaining unpaid at the date of the adjustment.

When do the allowances for interest begin?

Because the allowances for interest have to be calculated separately for each item in the adjustment, a consistent practice has emerged for the ascertainment of the date on which interest will commence to run, *viz*:

(a) Disbursements. Items of general average expenditure, and repair or reconditioning costs actually paid—the date of payment.
(b) Allowances for the wages and maintenance of crew—on the last day of each month for which allowance is made.
(c) Allowances for loss or damage to cargo (other than reconditioning

3. *Post*, p. 259.

charges actually paid)—on the last day of discharging at the port of discharge of the cargo concerned.

(d) Allowances for depreciation arising from unrepaired damage to ship—on the last day of discharging at the final port of discharge.

One reason for the emergence of this practice is that when an adjustment has to be prepared in a currency other than that in which the majority of the accounts are rendered, it is necessary to itemise carefully the dates upon which each account was paid or on which the allowance for any unpaid items accrued, in order to establish the rate of exchange ruling on each date.

When do the allowances for interest cease?

According to the English text until amended in 1994, the allowances ceased on the date of the general average statement. While this accorded with English practice, it did not reflect the practice (apart from the York-Antwerp Rules) in the United States, where interest is normally calculated up to the assumed date of settlement under the adjustment—a period of two or three months being usually estimated for this purpose. Under the French text until 1994, interest was to be calculated " . . . jusqu'à la date du règlement". The Association des Dispacheurs Françaises interpreted the word "règlement" in its sense as "settlement", but were more modest in their estimation of the time for settlement, customarily taken as being one month after the issue of the adjustment.

The wording of the Rule until 1994 placed a considerable restraint upon average adjusters practising in those countries where it has been considered equitable to allow interest to run until the estimated date of settlement. The matter was considered by an AIDE working group and, upon presentation of their report to the XIIth General Assembly at Copenhagen in 1983, a Resolution was passed, reading:

"The allowance of interest after the date of issue of the general average settlement can only be justified when made in accordance with the law or practice obtaining at the place where the adjustment is drawn up."[4]

Now, as decided at the Sydney Conference, it has been agreed that interest should continue to run until three months after the date of issue of the adjustment, that being considered to be a reasonable period of time for debtor interests to examine the adjustment and put in hand arrangements for payment of their contributions.

4. See report of the working group on Rule XXI, presented to the XIIth General Assembly of AIDE at Copenhagen, 1983, p. 44.

Payments "on account"

The Rule provides that due allowance shall be made for settlements on account by any of the contributory interests or from the general average deposit fund. This, of course, reflects the equitable principle that the claimant should receive interest only to the extent that he is out of pocket for the amount of his claim, and that the party or parties advancing their settlements should receive the benefit of a rebate for early settlement. Although there are different ways in which the calculations can be made, it is Anglo-American practice to calculate in the adjustment the full allowances for interest as if no interim settlement had been made and bring this figure into the apportionment as part of the total of the general average allowances; thereafter in the balances for each contributor to credit the parties making the interim payment with the amounts which they have advanced together with interest from the time of their advances until the date of the adjustment, debiting the corresponding figures to the party or parties receiving the interim payment. The following figures may help to make the position clear:

Shipowner's expenditure		£10,000
Rule XXI allowance for interest—2 years @ 7%		1,400
		£11,400
Sacrifice of cargo A	£4,000	
Rule XXI allowance for interest—2 years @ 7%	560	
		4,560
Total allowances in general average		£15,960

Cargo B, after 1 year, advances in accordance with the adjuster's certificate:

in respect of shipowner's expenditure	£6,000
in respect of sacrifice of cargo A	2,000
	£8,000

The general average adjustment will show:

Total general average as above:			£15,960
Apportioned			
Ship, value		£100,000 pays	£2,280
Cargo A. Arrived value	£96,000		
add: made good	4,000		
		100,000 pays	2,280
Cargo B. Value		500,000 pays	11,400
		£700,000 pays	£15,960

Balances			
Shipowner receives:			
Allowances inclusive of interest			£11,400
deduct: received on account		£6,000	
interest attaching thereto—1 year @ 7%		420	
			6,420
			£4,980
and pays general average contribution			2,280
receives on balance			£2,700
Cargo A receives:			
Amount made good including interest		£4,560	
deduct: received on account	£2,000		
interest attaching thereto—1 year @ 7%	140		
		2,140	
		£2,420	
and pays general average contribution		2,280	
receives on balance			140
			£2,840
Cargo B pays:			
General average contribution		£11,400	
less: advanced on account	£8,000		
credit for interest thereon—1 year @ 7%	560		
		8,560	
pays on balance		£2,840	

Currency of adjustment and rates of exchange

Although the delegates at the Sydney Conference were not able to bring themselves to approve a text to be incorporated in the scheme of the Rules to regulate the interconnected questions of the currency in which an adjustment should be prepared and the rates of exchange to be employed in converting allowances in other currencies into the currency of the adjustment, these subjects had been widely researched within both AIDE and CMI in the run-up to the Conference; indeed, these topics had been placed first on the list of questions asked of national Maritime Law Associations in part B of the questionnaire despatched by the chairman of the CMI International Sub-Committee in 1991.

In order to appreciate the desirability of establishing some international rule on these related subjects—or at least some internationally accepted practice—it is perhaps useful to observe how both jurisprudence and the practice of adjusters have changed under the influence of commercial and economic considerations:

Anglo-American Jurisprudence up to the 1960s

The general average adjustment should be prepared in the national currency of the port of destination. In broad terms, the rate for exchanging general average admissions into the currency of adjustment should be that ruling at the time of the loss, and not that at the time of preparing the adjustment. The cases in which these general principles were expressed were:

— in England, *Noreuro Traders Ltd.* v. *Hardy*[5] and *Chandris* v. *Argo Insurance Co. Ltd.*[6]
— in United States, *The Arkansas.*[7]

Under the commercial influences operating in the 1960s and 1970s

In some instances bills of lading and charterparties would stipulate for any case of general average to be adjusted in a specified currency—frequently, but not always, United States dollars. For this purpose it became the accepted practice of adjusters to exchange the contributory values and amounts made good for general average sacrifice (other than disbursements) into the specified currency at the rate of exchange prevailing at the termination of the adventure, and for disbursements to be exchanged at the rate prevailing when payment had been made. Influenced by these tendencies, an AIDE working group drafted two alternative recommended clauses dealing with the currency of adjustment and rates of exchange, and included them in a booklet of recommended clauses for insertion in bills of lading and charterparties published in 1981.[8]

Changes in the law in the 1980s and thereafter

Rather belatedly the world's legal systems came to recognise that the majority of international trade was financed not so much by transactions in domestic currencies, but in a relatively few stable currencies which were readily convertible. So far as English law is concerned, the breakthrough came with the case of *Miliangos* v. *George Frank (Textiles)*[9] in which the English courts were prepared for the first time to give judgment in a currency other than sterling. From there it was a short step to the recognition of international currencies in shipping transactions. See *The Despina R and the Folias.*[10]

5. *Noreuro Traders Ltd.* v. *Hardy* (1923) 16 Ll.L.Rep. 319.
6. *Chandris* v. *Argo Insurance Ltd.* [1963] 2 Lloyd's Rep. 65.
7. *Det Forenede Dampskibsselskab* v. *Insurance Co. of North America (The Arkansas)*, 1929 AMC 581.
8. See report of AIDE working group on General Average clauses presented to the Xth General Assembly at Cambridge 1979.
9. *Miliangos* v. *George Frank (Textiles) Ltd.* (H.L.) [1976] 1 Lloyd's Rep. 201.
10. The *Despina R and The Folias* (consolidated in H.L.) [1979] 1 Lloyd's Rep. 1.

The rationale now developed from these cases was that, irrespective of the nature of the transaction, a plaintiff was entitled to judgment in the currency in which he had "felt his loss", i.e. the currency in which he maintained his accounts.

The practice of adjusters has followed these developments fairly closely and can now be said to be reasonably well settled, but difficulties continue to arise when, in addition to the shipowner's claim in the currency in which he keeps his accounts, there are also a number of cargo claims in a different currency or currencies.

When this is the case, and unless a specific currency has been selected for the adjustment by the terms of the bill of lading or charterparty, the adjuster has to do his best to solve the problem in one of the following ways:

1. To select a common currency for the establishment of the contributory values and use this as the basis for apportioning each of the various claims in the currencies in which they have been established. So far so good, but the system becomes complicated after the apportionment of the total of the admissions in each currency, at which stage the debit and credit currencies in each currency have to be assembled and set off at the rates of exchange ruling at the time of adjustment. Although theoretically fair and equitable, this system adds to the complexities of the final stages of adjustment as well as in the settlements to be made thereunder.
2. To select a "currency of convenience", taking into consideration the currencies in which the major claimants keep their accounts, and considering which of them has remained, and is likely to continue to remain, relatively stable vis-à-vis the others. In extreme cases, it may be prudent for the adjuster to seek the agreement of the claimants to the currency proposed for the adjustment.

The conundrum—how to avoid the effect of currency variations—has exercised the minds of average adjusters for as long as the author can remember. Since no-one can predict how the value of different currencies will move between the date of incurring the expense or suffering the sacrifice and the date when the adjustment will be issued, the nearest one can get to a solution in practice is to select for the adjustment a currency offering the best chance of stability or, better still, a worldwide index to which all national currencies are related. This approach was considered very seriously during the run-up to the Sydney Conference, and was expressed in two different ways, the Americans canvassing the extended use of clauses in bills of lading and charterparties stipulating for adjustment in United States currency, and the BMLA proposing formally the introduction of a new paragraph into Rule XXI in the following terms:

"Unless the parties have agreed that the adjustment shall be prepared in a specific currency, the adjustment shall be prepared in Special Drawing Rights (SDRs). For this purpose the contributory values and the amounts made good for general average sacrifice (other than disbursements) shall be converted into SDRs or the specified currency at the rate of exchange prevailing at the termination of the adventure, and disbursements shall be so converted at the rate of exchange prevailing on the dates when payment was made. The final balances so calculated shall be paid to the creditors in the currency of their choice at the rate of exchange prevailing on the date of settlement. Where no official SDR exchange rate is quoted for any currency, conversion to and from SDRs shall be made by reference to United States dollars."

The BMLA proposal excited a good deal of interest when it was discussed at working meetings of the International Sub-Committees of CMI and AIDE. The latter, being particularly concerned at the mechanics of adjustment, appointed two members of its working group G (Mr Gerritzen and Mr Hebditch) to investigate what practical problems there might be in ascertaining the information necessary for the preparation of an average adjustment, and to provide guidance as to the easiest way of obtaining this information. The results of their research were incorporated in the AIDE Report.[11] They concluded that there was no problem: the current rates of exchange for SDRs are widely available in the international and national financial press; rates of exchange for SDRs of an older date could always be obtained at the central bank of the country where the average adjuster is resident. Notwithstanding this endorsement, the AIDE recommendation, approved at its General Assembly in Prague in September 1993, was that, in the absence of agreement by the parties, the average adjuster should have a discretion to select an appropriate currency. The AIDE recommended text for insertion into Rule XXI was:

"Unless the parties have agreed that the adjustment shall be prepared in a specific currency, the adjustment shall be prepared in such currency or currencies as may be equitable in the interests of the parties, having regard to the currencies in which the major claimants in general average have sustained financial loss.

For this purpose the contributory values and the amounts made good for general average sacrifice (other than disbursements) shall be converted into the currency of the adjustment at the rate of exchange prevailing on the last day of discharge at the final port of destination, or at the termination of the adventure when this occurs at a port or place other than the final port of destination, and disbursements shall be so converted at the rate of exchange prevailing on the dates when payment was made."

At the Sydney Conference both these projected solutions found enthusiastic advocates as well as fierce critics. The Brazilian delegation, as representing a country which has suffered severe devaluations in its currency in past years, was particularly strong in its support for the SDR solution, but in the voting neither proposal was able to command the required majority.

We conclude therefore that although both questions—the selection of an appropriate currency of the adjustment and the mechanics for converting into that currency the admissions in general average of claims presented in other

11. The AIDE Report of 30 July 1993 at pp. 60–61.

currencies—have to be solved without guidance from the York-Antwerp Rules, the debates have at least demonstrated a general desire that these problems should be addressed in a pragmatic manner. Thus, in the author's submission:

— the problem as to the selection of the currency of the adjustment can be avoided by the inclusion in the general average clauses contained in bills of lading and charterparties of a stipulation that the adjustment will be prepared in a specified currency;
— absent such provision in the general average clause in the document governing the contract of carriage, objection should not be taken to an adjustment dealing only with a claim submitted for sacrifices of ship and/or expenses incurred by the shipowner if it is prepared in the currency in which the shipowner keeps his accounts; but when there are substantial cargo claims in other currencies the adjuster will have to exercise his discretion, subject to any law and practice governing the adjustment, to find a solution which will maintain an equitable balance between the interests of the parties;
— in adjustments which are prepared in a single currency, there is a widely accepted practice (as incorporated in both the BMLA and AIDE proposals referred to above) as to the dates to be taken for the ascertainment of the rates of exchange to be adopted for the purpose of the adjustment.

RULE XXII

TREATMENT OF CASH DEPOSITS

Where cash deposits have been collected in respect of cargo's liability for general average, salvage or special charges, such deposits shall be paid without any delay into a special account in the joint names of a representative nominated on behalf of the shipowner and a representative nominated on behalf of the depositors in a bank to be approved by both. The sum so deposited, together with accrued interest, if any, shall be held as security for payment to the parties entitled thereto of the general average, salvage or special charges payable by cargo in respect to which the deposits have been collected. Payments on account or refunds of deposits may be made if certified to in writing by the average adjuster. Such deposits and payments or refunds shall be without prejudice to the ultimate liability of the parties.

INTRODUCTION

The collection of cash deposits is but one of the means whereby security may be provided by the concerned in cargo for their eventual payment of general average contribution. In most jurisdictions a shipowner is invested with a possessory lien over the cargo on board the ship for unpaid freight and for general average. On delivery of the cargo to the consignee, the shipowner loses his right of lien but may demand alternative security for the general average in return for so doing. The nature of such alternative security that may be demanded is not governed by the York-Antwerp Rules, and varies from case to case. Although there is no uniformity in this respect, such alternative security will normally consist of an average bond or other undertaking signed by the receiver of the cargo, supported by one of the following:

- — a guarantee furnished by the cargo underwriters, or
- — a bank guarantee, or
- — a cash deposit.[1]

Where there has been a sacrifice of cargo, a shipowner is obliged under English law to collect general average security from the other cargo interests in

1. For a concise account of the normal procedure for collecting general average security, and for the forms customarily employed for the purpose, see Hudson & Allen, *Marine Claims Handbook* (4th ed.), pp. 13–15 and 76–80.

order to protect the position of the party whose goods have been sacrificed.[2] In cases where the general average consists of the shipowner's sacrifices and/or expenditure, he is at liberty to decide whether or not to take security for his own protection, and the form of such security is also within his own discretion, provided that it is reasonable in all the circumstances. The question as to what security is reasonable will be decided in accordance with the law prevailing at the place where security is demanded. In England a form of average bond which purported to make the average adjuster an arbitrator has been held to be unreasonable.[3]

It is usual for liner bills of lading, particularly for lines trading to a number of different countries whose domestic law may be rudimentary or uncertain, to include a clause to reinforce the shipowner's right to take general average security, and particularly to collect general average deposits.

EVOLUTION

The Rule was introduced in 1924 in order to regulate the treatment of cash deposits from the time they were collected until the time of settlement under the adjustment. Prior thereto, there was a great deal of variation in practice in the way in which general average deposits were handled, and it was apparent that in quite a number of cases the depositors were not accorded fair treatment.[4] The Association of Average Adjusters therefore proposed a new Rule designed to protect the rights of depositors as far as possible, in particular by requiring that deposits should be paid into a special account, earning interest whenever possible, in the joint names of two trustees. This Rule, which was numbered XXIII, read:

"*Treatment of Cash Deposits*

Where cash deposits have been collected in respect of cargo's liability for general average, salvage or special charges, such deposits shall be paid into a special account, earning interest where possible, in the joint names of two trustees (one to be nominated on behalf of the shipowner and the other on behalf of the depositors) in a bank to be approved by such trustees. The sum so deposited, together with accrued interest, if any, shall be held as security for and upon trust for payment to the parties entitled thereto of the general average, salvage or special charges payable by the cargo in respect of which the deposits have been collected. The trustees shall have power to make payments on account or refunds of deposits which may be certified to in writing by the average adjuster. Such deposits and payments or refunds shall be without prejudice to the ultimate liability of the parties."

2. *Crooks* v. *Allan* (1879) 5 Q.B.D. 38; 4 Asp. M.C. 216.

3. *Huth* v. *Lamport* (1886) 16 Q.B.D. 442, 735; 5 Asp. M.C. 543, 593.

4. See article entitled "General Average: Treatment of Deposits", published in *Lloyd's List and Shipping Gazette*, 27 and 28 March 1922, giving details of the practice followed in the United Kingdom, most countries of Europe, United States, Argentina and Japan.

The application of this Rule did not accord with the practice in the United States, where it was customary for general average deposits to be handled by the average adjuster in a single-name account, and consequently it became usual for bills of lading issued by American shipowners to exclude the application of the Rule. At the 1949 Amsterdam Conference, the United States representatives stated that they were concerned that the 1924 Rule might offend against the anti-trust laws in some of the States of the U.S.A., and in consequence the text of the Rule was amended by deleting the word "trustees" and all references to the creation of a trust.

The text agreed in 1950 was approved again in 1974 and 1994 without amendment.

COMMENTARY

It cannot be said that the Rule is uniformly applied in practice. In the first place, despite the acceptance of the 1950 text by the United States Maritime Law Association, and the absence of any proposal from the United States to vary it, the practice of average adjusters in the United States remains much the same as it was, namely to place general average deposits in a "special account" (though not necessarily a separate account for each case) in the single name of the average adjuster. The reason for ignoring the dual representative provision has nothing to do with anti-trust laws; rather it is due to the reluctance of the U.S. banking system to cater for, or to offer reasonable terms for, joint-name accounts.

In the case of *The Motomar*[5] it was held in the District Court that a person who places funds in a "special deposit" to be held there for disbursement to others has created a trust; that this was equivalent to a bailment of the money and is not converted into a loan unless the person holding the funds uses them for his own purposes; consequently, by creating the deposit and making it available where and in the form it was collected, the trustee has fulfilled his obligation. The decision was upheld in the Court of Appeals (Second Circuit) and is considered to support the practice of adjusters, since although Rule XXII requires a dual representative account, the creation of a special account by one party would not be considered to be prejudicial to the other unless he suffered some financial loss as a result.

In the United Kingdom, unless the depositor, or a cargo insurer who has refunded the deposit, nominates a representative, it is frequently the average adjuster who acts in this respect and consults the shipowner or his agent in regard to the selection of the bank in which the deposits are to be lodged and the arrangements to be made whereby, whenever possible, interest is to be earned thereon. However, when the deposits are taken and retained in a

5. *St. Paul Fire & Marine Insurance Co.* v. *S.S. Motomar* (1954) 211 Fed. Rep. 690.

country where the average adjuster has no office or representation, it is customary for the ship's agents to be the shipowner's representative and for Lloyd's agents to be invited to act as the representative of the depositors. Lloyd's agents, when so acting, are entitled to charge a fee for this service.

In European countries, it is likewise recognised that the average adjuster has an obligation to use his influence to ensure as far as possible that the deposit funds are well looked after and that the interests of the depositors, as well as those of the shipowners, are protected. The AIDE have considered the question of the average adjuster's responsibilities in this connection at their General Assemblies in 1975, 1977 and 1985, and have adopted a set of recommendations in this respect, which are of considerable importance.[6]

From time to time concern has been expressed, both as to the legal rights of the depositors and as to the protection of the adjustment creditors, when deposits have been taken in a currency which may be subject to fluctuation in value between the time the deposits are taken and the time settlements are made under the adjustment. In 1933, the International Union of Marine Insurance adopted a Resolution favouring the conversion of such deposits into the currency of the average adjustment.[7] This was soon recognised as being too sweeping, and is no longer accepted as a guide to practice. As a general rule it is now considered more prudent to retain the deposits in the currency in which they were originally lodged. However, in the author's experience, this can lead to practical difficulties in large general average cases where deposits have been tendered in several different currencies, and it is submitted that neither the shipowner nor the average adjuster could be faulted in the exercise of their best endeavours to care for the general average deposits if, as recommended in the AIDE Resolution referred to, they "have regard to the relative stability of the currency in which the deposit funds were originally lodged and any advantage which might be gained by re-investing the funds in any available stronger currency".

6. These recommendations, adopted by Resolution of the XIIIth General Assembly, Venice, 1985, are set out hereafter as Appendix 7 on pp. 373–374.

7. The "Montreux Resolution", which read:

"The members of the International Union of Marine Insurance, in general meeting assembled, express the view that shipowners, or the average adjusters, on receipt of deposits should convert such deposits into the currency of the average statement without undue delay and also state on the average receipt the rate of exchange of these deposits, and the currency in which the statement will be drawn up."

APPENDIX 1

THE YORK-ANTWERP RULES 1994
CONTRASTED WITH THE YORK-ANTWERP RULES 1974, AS AMENDED 1990

YORK-ANTWERP RULES 1974, as amended 1990	YORK-ANTWERP RULES 1994 (*New material in italics*)
RULE OF INTERPRETATION	
In the adjustment of general average the following lettered and numbered Rules shall apply to the exclusion of any Law and Practice inconsistent therewith.	In the adjustment of general average the following Rules shall apply to the exclusion of any Law and Practice inconsistent therewith.
Except as provided by the numbered Rules, general average shall be adjusted according to the lettered Rules.	Except as provided by the *Rule Paramount and the* numbered Rules, general average shall be adjusted according to the lettered Rules.
	RULE PARAMOUNT
	In no case shall there be any allowance for sacrifice or expenditure unless reasonably made or incurred.
RULE A	
There is a general average act when, and only when, any extraordinary sacrifice or expenditure is intentionally and reasonably made or incurred for the common safety for the purpose of preserving from peril the property involved in a common maritime adventure.	There is a general average act when, and only when, any extraordinary sacrifice or expenditure is intentionally and reasonably made or incurred for the common safety for the purpose of preserving from peril the property involved in a common maritime adventure.

Rule A—cont.

General average sacrifices and *expenditures* shall be borne by the different contributing interests on the basis hereinafter provided.

RULE B

General average sacrifices and expenses shall be borne by the different contributing interests on the basis hereinafter provided.

There is a common maritime adventure when one or more vessels are towing or pushing another vessel or vessels, provided that they are all involved in commercial activities and not in a salvage operation.

When measures are taken to preserve the vessels and their cargoes, if any, from a common peril, these Rules shall apply.

A vessel is not in common peril with another vessel or vessels if by simply disconnecting from the other vessel or vessels she is in safety; but if the disconnection is itself a general average act the common maritime adventure continues.

RULE C

Only such losses, damages or expenses which are the direct consequence of the general average act shall be allowed as general average.

Only such losses, damages or expenses which are the direct consequence of the general average act shall be allowed as general average.

In no case shall there be any allowance in general average for losses, damages or expenses incurred in respect of damage to the environment or in consequence of the escape or release of pollutant substances from the property involved in the common maritime adventure.

Loss or damage sustained by the ship or cargo through delay, whether on the voyage or subsequently, such as demurrage, and any indirect loss whatsoever, such as loss of market, shall not be admitted as general average.

Demurrage, loss of market, and any loss or damage sustained or expense incurred by reason of delay, whether on the voyage or subsequently, and any indirect loss whatsoever, shall not be admitted as general average.

RULE D

Rights to contribution in general average shall not be affected, though the event which gave rise to the sacrifice or expenditure may have been due to the fault of one of the parties to the adventure; but this shall not prejudice any remedies or defences which may be open against or to that party in respect of such fault.	Rights to contribution in general average shall not be affected, though the event which gave rise to the sacrifice or expenditure may have been due to the fault of one of the parties to the adventure; but this shall not prejudice any remedies or defences which may be open against or to that party in respect of such fault.

RULE E

The onus of proof is upon the party claiming in general average to show that the loss or expense claimed is properly allowable as general average.	The onus of proof is upon the party claiming in general average to show that the loss or expense claimed is properly allowable as general average. *All parties claiming in general average shall give notice in writing to the average adjuster of the loss or expense in respect of which they claim contribution within 12 months of the date of the termination of the common maritime adventure.* *Failing such notification, or if within 12 months of a request for the same any of the parties shall fail to supply evidence in support of a notified claim, or particulars of value in respect of a contributory interest, the average adjuster shall be at liberty to estimate the extent of the allowance or the contributory value on the basis of the information available to him, which estimate may be challenged only on the ground that it is manifestly incorrect.*

RULE F

Any extra expense incurred in place of another expense which would have	Any *additional* expense incurred in place of another expense which

Rule F—cont.

been allowable as general average shall be deemed to be general average and so allowed without regard to the saving, if any, to other interests, but only up to the amount of the general average expense avoided.

would have been allowable as general average shall be deemed to be general average and so allowed without regard to the saving, if any, to other interests, but only up to the amount of the general average expense avoided.

RULE G

General average shall be adjusted as regards both loss and contribution upon the basis of values at the time and place when and where the adventure ends.

This rule shall not affect the determination of the place at which the average statement is to be made up.

General average shall be adjusted as regards both loss and contribution upon the basis of values at the time and place when and where the adventure ends.

This rule shall not affect the determination of the place at which the average statement is to be made up.

When a ship is at any port or place in circumstances which would give rise to an allowance in general average under the provisions of Rules X and XI, and the cargo or part thereof is forwarded to destination by other means, rights and liabilities in general average shall, subject to cargo interests being notified if practicable, remain as nearly as possible the same as they would have been in the absence of such forwarding, as if the adventure had continued in the original ship for so long as justifiable under the contract of affreightment and the applicable law.

The proportion attaching to cargo of the allowances made in general average by reason of applying the third paragraph of this Rule shall not exceed the cost which would have been borne by the owners of cargo if the cargo had been forwarded at their expense.

RULE I

JETTISON OF CARGO

No jettison of cargo shall be made good as general average, unless such cargo is carried in accordance with the recognised custom of the trade.	No jettison of cargo shall be made good as general average, unless such cargo is carried in accordance with the recognised custom of the trade.

RULE II

DAMAGE BY JETTISON AND SACRIFICE FOR THE COMMON SAFETY	*LOSS OR DAMAGE BY SACRIFICES FOR THE COMMON SAFETY*
Damage done to a ship and cargo, or either of them, by or in consequence of a sacrifice made for the common safety, and by water which goes down a ship's hatches opened or other opening made for the purpose of making a jettison for the common safety, shall be made good as general average.	*Loss of or damage to the property involved in the common maritime adventure* by or in consequence of a sacrifice made for the common safety, and by water which goes down a ship's hatches opened or other opening made for the purpose of making a jettison for the common safety, shall be made good as general average.

RULE III

EXTINGUISHING FIRE ON SHIPBOARD

Damage done to a ship and cargo, or either of them, by water or otherwise, including damage by beaching or scuttling a burning ship, in extinguishing a fire on board the ship, shall be made good as general average; except that no compensation shall be made for damage by smoke or heat however caused.	Damage done to a ship and cargo, or either of them, by water or otherwise, including damage by beaching or scuttling a burning ship, in extinguishing a fire on board the ship, shall be made good as general average; except that no compensation shall be made for damage by smoke however caused *or by heat of the fire*.

RULE IV

CUTTING AWAY WRECK

Loss or damage sustained by cutting away wreck or parts of the ship which have been previously carried away or are effectively lost by accident shall not be made good as general average.	Loss or damage sustained by cutting away wreck or parts of the ship which have been previously carried away or are effectively lost by accident shall not be made good as general average.

RULE V

VOLUNTARY STRANDING

When a ship is intentionally run on shore for the common safety, whether or not she might have been driven on shore, the consequent loss or damage shall be allowed in general average.

When a ship is intentionally run on shore for the common safety, whether or not she might have been driven on shore, the consequent loss or damage *to the property involved in the common maritime adventure* shall be allowed in general average.

RULE VI

SALVAGE REMUNERATION

(a) Expenditure incurred by the parties to the adventure in the nature of salvage, whether under contract or otherwise, shall be allowed in general average provided that the salvage operations were carried out for the purpose of preserving from peril the property involved in the common maritime adventure.

Expenditure allowed in general average shall include any salvage remuneration in which the skill and efforts of the salvors in preventing or minimizing damage to the environment such as is referred to in Article 13 paragraph 1(b) of the International Convention on Salvage, 1989 have been taken into account.

(b) Special compensation payable to a salvor by the shipowner under Article 14 of the said Convention to the extent specified in paragraph 4 of that Article or under any other provision similar in substance shall not be allowed in general average.

(a) Expenditure incurred by the parties to the adventure in the nature of salvage, whether under contract or otherwise, shall be allowed in general average provided that the salvage operations were carried out for the purpose of preserving from peril the property involved in the common maritime adventure.

Expenditure allowed in general average shall include any salvage remuneration in which the skill and efforts of the salvors in preventing or minimizing damage to the environment such as is referred to in Article 13 paragraph 1(b) of the International Convention on Salvage, 1989 have been taken into account.

(b) Special compensation payable to a salvor by the shipowner under Article 14 of the said Convention to the extent specified in paragraph 4 of that Article or under any other provision similar in substance shall not be allowed in general average.

RULE VII

DAMAGE TO MACHINERY AND BOILERS

Damage caused to any machinery and boilers of a ship which is ashore and in a position of peril, in endeavouring to refloat, shall be allowed in general average when shown to have arisen from an actual intention to float the ship for the common safety at the risk of such damage; but where a ship is afloat no loss or damage caused by working the propelling machinery and boilers shall in any circumstances be made good as general average.

Damage caused to any machinery and boilers of a ship which is ashore and in a position of peril, in endeavouring to refloat, shall be allowed in general average when shown to have arisen from an actual intention to float the ship for the common safety at the risk of such damage; but where a ship is afloat no loss or damage caused by working the propelling machinery and boilers shall in any circumstances be made good as general average.

RULE VIII

EXPENSES LIGHTENING A SHIP WHEN ASHORE, AND CONSEQUENT DAMAGE

When a ship is ashore and cargo and ship's fuel and stores or any of them are discharged as a general average act, the extra cost of lightening, lighter hire and reshipping (if incurred), and the loss or damage sustained thereby, shall be admitted as general average.

When a ship is ashore and cargo and ship's fuel and stores or any of them are discharged as a general average act, the extra cost of lightening, lighter hire and reshipping (if incurred), *and any loss or damage to the property involved in the common maritime adventure in consequence thereof*, shall be admitted as general average.

RULE IX

SHIP'S MATERIALS AND STORES BURNT FOR FUEL

Ship's materials and stores, or any of them, necessarily burnt for fuel for the common safety at a time of peril, shall be admitted as general average, when and only when an ample supply

CARGO, SHIP'S MATERIALS AND STORES FOR FUEL

Cargo, ship's materials and stores, or any of them, necessarily *used* for fuel for the common safety at a time of peril shall be admitted as general average, *but when such an allowance is*

Rule IX—cont.

of fuel had been provided; but the estimated quantity of fuel that would have been consumed, calculated at the price current at the ship's last port of departure at the date of her leaving, shall be credited to the general average.

made for the cost of ship's materials and stores the general average shall be credited with the estimated cost of the fuel which would otherwise have been consumed in prosecuting the intended voyage.

RULE X

EXPENSES AT PORT OF REFUGE, ETC.

(a) When a ship shall have entered a port or place of refuge, or shall have returned to her port or place of loading in consequence of accident, sacrifice or other extraordinary circumstances, which render that necessary for the common safety, the expenses of entering such port or place shall be admitted as general average; and when she shall have sailed thence with her original cargo, or a part of it, the corresponding expenses of leaving such port or place consequent upon such entry or return shall likewise be admitted as general average.

When a ship is at any port or place of refuge and is necessarily removed to another port or place because repairs cannot be carried out in the first port or place, the provisions of this Rule shall be applied to the second port or place as if it were a port or place of refuge and the cost of such removal including temporary repairs and towage shall be admitted as general average. The provisions of Rule XI shall be applied to the prolongation of the voyage occasioned by such removal.

(b) The cost of handling on board or discharging cargo, fuel or stores whether at a port or place of loading,

(a) When a ship shall have entered a port or place of refuge or shall have returned to her port or place of loading in consequence of accident, sacrifice or other extraordinary circumstances which render that necessary for the common safety, the expenses of entering such port or place shall be admitted as general average; and when she shall have sailed thence with her original cargo, or a part of it, the corresponding expenses of leaving such port or place consequent upon such entry or return shall likewise be admitted as general average.

When a ship is at any port or place of refuge and is necessarily removed to another port or place because repairs cannot be carried out in the first port or place, the provisions of this Rule shall be applied to the second port or place as if it were a port or place of refuge and the cost of such removal including temporary repairs and towage shall be admitted as general average. The provisions of Rule XI shall be applied to the prolongation of the voyage occasioned by such removal.

(b) The cost of handling on board or discharging cargo, fuel or stores whether at a port or place of loading,

Rule X—cont.

call or refuge, shall be admitted as general average, when the handling or discharge was necessary for the common safety or to enable damage to the ship caused by sacrifice or accident to be repaired, if the repairs were necessary for the safe prosecution of the voyage, except in cases where the damage to the ship is discovered at a port or place of loading or call without any accident or other extraordinary circumstance connected with such damage having taken place during the voyage.	call or refuge, shall be admitted as general average, when the handling or discharge was necessary for the common safety or to enable damage to the ship caused by sacrifice or accident to be repaired, if the repairs were necessary for the safe prosecution of the voyage, except in cases where the damage to the ship is discovered at a port or place of loading or call without any accident or other extraordinary circumstance connected with such damage having taken place during the voyage.
The cost of handling on board or discharging cargo, fuel or stores shall not be admissible as general average when incurred solely for the purpose of restowage due to shifting during the voyage, unless such restowage is necessary for the common safety.	The cost of handling on board or discharging cargo, fuel or stores shall not be admissible as general average when incurred solely for the purpose of restowage due to shifting during the voyage, unless such restowage is necessary for the common safety.
(c) Whenever the cost of handling or discharging cargo, fuel or stores is admissible as general average, the costs of storage, including insurance if reasonably incurred, reloading and stowing of such cargo, fuel or stores shall likewise be admitted as general average.	(c) Whenever the cost of handling or discharging cargo, fuel or stores is admissible as general average, the costs of storage, including insurance if reasonably incurred, reloading and stowing of such cargo, fuel or stores shall likewise be admitted as general average. *The provisions of Rule XI shall be applied to the extra period of detention occasioned by such reloading or restowing.*
But when the ship is condemned or does not proceed on her original voyage, storage expenses shall be admitted as general average only up to the date of the ship's condemnation or of the abandonment of the voyage or up to the date of completion of discharge of cargo if the condemnation or abandonment takes place before that date.	But when the ship is condemned or does not proceed on her original voyage, storage expenses shall be admitted as general average only up to the date of the ship's condemnation or of the abandonment of the voyage or up to the date of completion of discharge of cargo if the condemnation or abandonment takes place before that date.

RULE XI

WAGES AND MAINTENANCE OF CREW AND OTHER EXPENSES BEARING UP FOR AND IN A PORT OF REFUGE, ETC.

(a) Wages and maintenance of master, officers and crew reasonably incurred and fuel and stores consumed during the prolongation of the voyage occasioned by a ship entering a port or place of refuge or returning to her port or place of loading shall be admitted as general average when the expenses of entering such port or place are allowable in general average in accordance with Rule X(a).

(b) When a ship shall have entered or been detained in any port or place in consequence of accident, sacrifice or other extraordinary circumstances which render that necessary for the common safety, or to enable damage to the ship caused by sacrifice or accident to be repaired, if the repairs were necessary for the safe prosecution of the voyage, the wages and maintenance of the master, officers and crew reasonably incurred during the extra period of detention in such port or place until the ship shall or should have been made ready to proceed upon her voyage, shall be admitted in general average.

Provided that when damage to the ship is discovered at a port or place of loading or call without any accident or other extraordinary circumstance connnected with such damage having taken place during the voyage, then the wages and maintenance of master, officers and crew and fuel and stores consumed during the extra detention for repairs to damages so discovered shall not be admissible as

(a) Wages and maintenance of master, officers and crew reasonably incurred and fuel and stores consumed during the prolongation of the voyage occasioned by a ship entering a port or place of refuge or returning to her port or place of loading shall be admitted as general average when the expenses of entering such port or place are allowable in general average in accordance with Rule X(a).

(b) When a ship shall have entered or been detained in any port or place in consequence of accident, sacrifice or other extraordinary circumstances which render that necessary for the common safety, or to enable damage to the ship caused by sacrifice or accident to be repaired, if the repairs were necessary for the safe prosecution of the voyage, the wages and maintenance of the master, officers and crew reasonably incurred during the extra period of detention in such port or place until the ship shall or should have been made ready to proceed upon her voyage, shall be admitted in general average.

Fuel and stores consumed during the extra period of detention shall be admitted as general average, except such fuel and stores as are consumed in effecting repairs not allowable in general average.

Rule XI—cont.

general average, even if the repairs are necessary for the safe prosecution of the voyage.	
When the ship is condemned or does not proceed on her original voyage, wages and maintenance of the master, officers and crew and fuel and stores consumed shall be admitted as general average only up to the date of the ship's condemnation or of the abandonment of the voyage or up to the date of completion of discharge of cargo if the condemnation or abandonment takes place before that date.	Port charges incurred during the extra period of detention shall likewise be admitted as general average except such charges as are incurred solely by reason of repairs not allowable in general average.
Fuel and stores consumed during the extra period of detention shall be admitted as general average, except such fuel and stores as are consumed in effecting repairs not allowable in general average.	Provided that when damage to the ship is discovered at a port or place of loading or call without any accident or other extraordinary circumstance connected with such damage having taken place during the voyage, then the wages and maintenance of master, officers and crew and fuel and stores consumed *and port charges incurred* during the extra detention for repairs to damages so discovered shall not be admissible as general average, even if the repairs are necessary for the safe prosecution of the voyage.
Port charges incurred during the extra period of detention shall likewise be admitted as general average except such charges as are incurred solely by reason of repairs not allowable in general average.	When the ship is condemned or does not proceed on her original voyage, the wages and maintenance of the master, officers and crew and fuel and stores consumed and *port charges* shall be admitted as general average only up to the date of the ship's condemnation or of the abandonment of the voyage or up to the date of completion of discharge of cargo if the condemnation or abandonment takes place before that date.

Rule XI—cont.

(c) For the purpose of this and the other Rules wages shall include all payments made to or for the benefit of the master, officers and crew, whether such payments be imposed by law upon the shipowners or be made under the terms or articles of employment.

(d) When overtime is paid to the master, officers or crew for maintenance of the ship or repairs, the cost of which is not allowable in general average, such overtime shall be allowed in general average only up to the saving in expense which would have been incurred and admitted as general average, had such overtime not been incurred.

(c) For the purpose of this and the other Rules wages shall include all payments made to or for the benefit of the master, officers and crew, whether such payments be imposed by law upon the shipowners or be made under the terms or articles of employment.

(d) *The cost of measures undertaken to prevent or minimise damage to the environment shall be allowed in general average when incurred in any or all of the following circumstances:*

(i) *as part of an operation performed for the common safety which, had it been undertaken by a party outside the common maritime adventure, would have entitled such party to a salvage reward;*

(ii) *as a condition of entry into or departure from any port or place in the circumstances prescribed in Rule X(a);*

(iii) *as a condition of remaining at any port or place in the circumstances prescribed in Rule XI(b), provided that when there is an actual escape or release of pollutant substances the cost of any additional measures required on that account to prevent or minimise pollution or environmental damage shall not be allowed as general average;*

(iv) *necessarily in connection with the discharging, storing or reloading of cargo whenever the cost of those operations is admissible as general average.*

RULE XII

DAMAGE TO CARGO IN DISCHARGING, ETC.

Damage to or loss of cargo, fuel or stores caused in the act of handling, discharging, storing, reloading and

Damage to or loss of cargo, fuel or stores *sustained in consequence of their* handling, discharging, storing,

Rule XII—cont.

stowing shall be made good as general average, when and only when the cost of those measures respectively is admitted as general average.

reloading and stowing shall be made good as general average, when and only when the cost of those measures respectively is admitted as general average.

RULE XIII

DEDUCTIONS FROM COST OF REPAIRS

Repairs to be allowed in general average shall not be subject to deductions in respect of "new for old" where old material or parts are replaced by new unless the ship is over fifteen years old in which case there shall be a deduction of one third. The deductions shall be regulated by the age of the ship from 31 December of the year of completion of construction to the date of the general average act, except for insulation, life and similar boats, communications and navigational apparatus and equipment, machinery and boilers for which the deductions shall be regulated by the age of the particular parts to which they apply.

The deductions shall be made only from the cost of the new material or parts when finished and ready to be installed in the ship.

No deduction shall be made in respect of provisions, stores, anchors and chain cables.

Drydock and slipway dues and costs of shifting the ship shall be allowed in full.

The costs of cleaning, painting or coating of bottom shall not be allowed in general average unless the bottom has been painted or coated within the twelve months preceding the date of the general average act in which case one half of such costs shall be allowed.

Repairs to be allowed in general average shall not be subject to deductions in respect of "new for old" where old material or parts are replaced by new unless the ship is over fifteen years old in which case there shall be a deduction of one third. The deductions shall be regulated by the age of the ship from 31 December of the year of completion of construction to the date of the general average act, except for insulation, life and similar boats, communications and navigational apparatus and equipment, machinery and boilers for which the deductions shall be regulated by the age of the particular parts to which they apply.

The deductions shall be made only from the cost of the new material or parts when finished and ready to be installed in the ship.

No deduction shall be made in respect of provisions, stores, anchors and chain cables.

Drydock and slipway dues and costs of shifting the ship shall be allowed in full.

The costs of cleaning, painting or coating of bottom shall not be allowed in general average unless the bottom has been painted or coated within the twelve months preceding the date of the general average act in which case one half of such costs shall be allowed.

RULE XIV

TEMPORARY REPAIRS

Where temporary repairs are effected to a ship at a port of loading, call or refuge, for the common safety, or of damage caused by general average sacrifice, the cost of such repairs shall be admitted as general average.

Where temporary repairs of accidental damage are effected in order to enable the adventure to be completed, the cost of such repairs shall be admitted as general average without regard to the saving, if any, to other interests, but only up to the saving in expense which would have been incurred and allowed in general average if such repairs had not been effected there.

No deductions "new for old" shall be made from the cost of temporary repairs allowable as general average.

Where temporary repairs are effected to a ship at a port of loading, call or refuge, for the common safety, or of damage caused by general average sacrifice, the cost of such repairs shall be admitted as general average.

Where temporary repairs of accidental damage are effected in order to enable the adventure to be completed, the cost of such repairs shall be admitted as general average without regard to the saving, if any, to other interests, but only up to the saving in expense which would have been incurred and allowed in general average if such repairs had not been effected there.

No deductions "new for old" shall be made from the cost of temporary repairs allowable as general average.

RULE XV

LOSS OF FREIGHT

Loss of freight arising from damage to or loss of cargo shall be made good as general average, either when caused by a general average act, or when the damage to or loss of cargo is so made good.

Deduction shall be made from the amount of gross freight lost, of the charges which the owner thereof would have incurred to earn such freight, but has, in consequence of the sacrifice, not incurred.

Loss of freight arising from damage to or loss of cargo shall be made good as general average, either when caused by a general average act, or when the damage to or loss of cargo is so made good.

Deduction shall be made from the amount of gross freight lost, of the charges which the owner thereof would have incurred to earn such freight, but has, in consequence of the sacrifice, not incurred.

RULE XVI

AMOUNT TO BE MADE GOOD FOR CARGO LOST OR DAMAGED BY SACRIFICE

The amount to be made good as general average for damage to or loss of cargo sacrificed shall be the loss which has been sustained thereby based on the value at the time of discharge, ascertained from the commercial invoice rendered to the receiver or if there is no such invoice from the shipped value. The value at the time of discharge shall include the cost of insurance and freight except insofar as such freight is at the risk of interests other than the cargo.

When cargo so damaged is sold and the amount of the damage has not been otherwise agreed, the loss to be made good in general average shall be the difference between the net proceeds of sale and the net sound value as computed in the first paragraph of this Rule.

The amount to be made good as general average for damage to or loss of cargo sacrificed shall be the loss which has been sustained thereby based on the value at the time of discharge, ascertained from the commercial invoice rendered to the receiver or if there is no such invoice from the shipped value. The value at the time of discharge shall include the cost of insurance and freight except insofar as such freight is at the risk of interests other than the cargo.

When cargo so damaged is sold and the amount of the damage has not been otherwise agreed, the loss to be made good in general average shall be the difference between the net proceeds of sale and the net sound value as computed in the first paragraph of this Rule.

RULE XVII

CONTRIBUTORY VALUES

The contribution to a general average shall be made upon the actual net values of the property at the termination of the adventure except that the value of cargo shall be the value at the time of discharge, ascertained from the commercial invoice rendered to the receiver or if there is no such invoice from the shipped value. The value of the cargo shall include the cost of insurance and freight unless and insofar as such freight is at the risk of interests other than the cargo,

The contribution to a general average shall be made upon the actual net values of the property at the termination of the adventure except that the value of cargo shall be the value at the time of discharge, ascertained from the commercial invoice rendered to the receiver or if there is no such invoice from the shipped value. The value of the cargo shall include the cost of insurance and freight unless and insofar as such freight is at the risk of interests other than the cargo,

Rule XVII—cont.

deducting therefrom any loss or damage suffered by the cargo prior to or at the time of discharge. The value of the ship shall be assessed without taking into account the beneficial or detrimental effect of any demise or time charterparty to which the ship may be committed.

To these values shall be added the amount made good as general average for property sacrificed, if not already included, deduction being made from the freight and passage money at risk of such charges and crew's wages as would not have been incurred in earning the freight had the ship and cargo been totally lost at the date of the general average act and have not been allowed as general average; deduction being also made from the value of the property of all extra charges incurred in respect thereof subsequently to the general average act, except such charges as are allowed in general average.

deducting therefrom any loss or damage suffered by the cargo prior to or at the time of discharge. The value of the ship shall be assessed without taking into account the beneficial or detrimental effect of any demise or time charterparty to which the ship may be committed.

To these values shall be added the amount made good as general average for property sacrificed, if not already included, deduction being made from the freight and passage money at risk of such charges and crew's wages as would not have been incurred in earning the freight had the ship and cargo been totally lost at the date of the general average act and have not been allowed as general average; deduction being also made from the value of the property of all extra charges incurred in respect thereof subsequently to the general average act, except such charges as are allowed in general average *or fall upon the ship by virtue of an award for special compensation under Article 14 of the International Convention on Salvage, 1989 or under any other provision similar in substance.*

In the circumstances envisaged in the third paragraph of Rule G, the cargo and other property shall contribute on the basis of its value upon delivery at original destination unless sold or otherwise disposed of short of that destination, and the ship shall contribute upon its actual net value at the time of completion of discharge of cargo.

Rule XVII—cont.

Where cargo is sold short of destination, however, it shall contribute upon the actual net proceeds of sale, with the addition of any amount made good as general average.

Passengers' luggage and personal effects not shipped under bill of lading shall not contribute in general average.

Where cargo is sold short of destination, however, it shall contribute upon the actual net proceeds of sale, with the addition of any amount made good as general average.

Mails, passengers' luggage, personal effects and accompanied private motor vehicles shall not contribute in general average.

RULE XVIII

DAMAGE TO SHIP

The amount to be allowed as general average for damage or loss to the ship, her machinery and/or gear caused by a general average act shall be as follows:

(a) When repaired or replaced,

The actual reasonable cost of repairing or replacing such damage or loss, subject to deductions in accordance with Rule XIII;

(b) When not repaired or replaced,

The reasonable depreciation arising from such damage or loss, but not exceeding the estimated cost of repairs. But where the ship is an actual total loss or when the cost of repairs of the damage would exceed the value of the ship when repaired, the amount to be allowed as general average shall be the difference between the estimated sound value of the ship after deducting therefrom the estimated cost of repairing damage which is not general average and the value of the ship in her damaged state which may be measured by the net proceeds of sale, if any.

The amount to be allowed as general average for damage or loss to the ship, her machinery and/or gear caused by a general average act shall be as follows:

(a) When repaired or replaced,

The actual reasonable cost of repairing or replacing such damage or loss, subject to deductions in accordance with Rule XIII;

(b) When not repaired or replaced,

The reasonable depreciation arising from such damage or loss, but not exceeding the estimated cost of repairs. But where the ship is an actual total loss or when the cost of repairs of the damage would exceed the value of the ship when repaired, the amount to be allowed as general average shall be the difference between the estimated sound value of the ship after deducting therefrom the estimated cost of repairing damage which is not general average and the value of the ship in her damaged state which may be measured by the net proceeds of sale, if any.

RULE XIX

UNDECLARED OR WRONGFULLY DECLARED CARGO

Damage or loss caused to goods loaded without the knowledge of the shipowner or his agent or to goods wilfully misdescribed at time of shipment shall not be allowed as general average, but such goods shall remain liable to contribute, if saved.	Damage or loss caused to goods loaded without the knowledge of the shipowner or his agent or to goods wilfully misdescribed at time of shipment shall not be allowed as general average, but such goods shall remain liable to contribute, if saved.
Damage or loss caused to goods which have been wrongfully declared on shipment at a value which is lower than their real value shall be contributed for at the declared value, but such goods shall contribute upon their actual value.	Damage or loss caused to goods which have been wrongfully declared on shipment at a value which is lower than their real value shall be contributed for at the declared value, but such goods shall contribute upon their actual value.

RULE XX

PROVISION OF FUNDS

A commission of 2 per cent. on general average disbursements, other than the wages and maintenance of master, officers and crew and fuel and stores not replaced during the voyage, shall be allowed in general average, but when the funds are not provided by any of the contributing interests, the necessary cost of obtaining the funds required by means of a bottomry bond or otherwise, or the loss sustained by owners of goods sold for the purpose, shall be allowed in general average.	A commission of 2 per cent. on general average disbursements, other than the wages and maintenance of master, officers and crew and fuel and stores not replaced during the voyage, shall be allowed in general average. *The capital loss sustained by the owners of goods sold for the purpose of raising funds to defray general average disbursements shall be allowed in general average.*
The cost of insuring money advanced to pay for general average disbursements shall also be allowed in general average.	The cost of insuring general average disbursements shall also be admitted in general average.

RULE XXI

INTEREST ON LOSSES MADE GOOD IN GENERAL AVERAGE

Interest shall be allowed on expenditure, sacrifices and allowances charged to general average at the rate of 7 per cent. per annum, until the date of the general average statement, due allowance being made for any interim reimbursement from the contributory interests or from the general average deposit fund.

Interest shall be allowed on expenditure, sacrifices and allowances in general average at the rate of 7 per cent. per annum, until *three months after* the date of *issue of* the general average adjustment, due allowance being made for *any payment on account by* the contributory interests or from the general average deposit fund.

RULE XXII

TREATMENT OF CASH DEPOSITS

Where cash desposits have been collected in respect of cargo's liability for general average, salvage or special charges, such deposits shall be paid without any delay into a special account in the joint names of a representative nominated on behalf of the shipowner and a representative nominated on behalf of the depositors in a bank to be approved by both. The sum so deposited, together with accrued interest, if any, shall be held as security for payment to the parties entitled thereto of the general average, salvage or special charges payable by cargo in respect to which the deposits have been collected. Payments on account or refunds of deposits may be made if certified to in writing by the average adjuster. Such deposits and payments or refunds shall be without prejudice to the ultimate liability of the parties.

Where cash deposits have been collected in respect of cargo's liability for general average, salvage or special charges, such deposits shall be paid without any delay into a special account in the joint names of a representative nominated on behalf of the shipowner and a representative nominated on behalf of the depositors in a bank to be approved by both. The sum so deposited, together with accrued interest, if any, shall be held as security for payment to the parties entitled thereto of the general average, salvage or special charges payable by cargo in respect to which the desposits have been collected. Payments on account or refunds of deposits may be made if certified to in writing by the average adjuster. Such deposits and payments or refunds shall be without prejudice to the ultimate liability of the parties.

APPENDIX 2

COMPARATIVE TEXTS
YORK RULES 1864
TO
YORK-ANTWERP RULES 1974, AS AMENDED 1990

RULE OF INTERPRETATION

York-Antwerp Rules 1950

In the adjustment of general average the following lettered and numbered Rules shall apply to the exclusion of any Law and Practice inconsistent therewith.

Except as provided by the numbered Rules, general average shall be adjusted according to the lettered Rules.

York-Antwerp Rules 1974

No change.

RULE A

York-Antwerp Rules 1924

There is a general average act when, and only when, any extraordinary sacrifice or expenditure is intentionally and reasonably made or incurred for the common safety for the purpose of preserving from peril the property involved in a common maritime adventure.

York-Antwerp Rules 1950

No change.

York-Antwerp Rules 1974

No change.

RULE B

York-Antwerp Rules 1924

General average sacrifices and expenses shall be borne by the different contributing interests on the basis hereinafter provided.

Rule B—cont.

York-Antwerp Rules 1950 No change.

York-Antwerp Rules 1974 No change.

RULE C

York-Antwerp Rules 1924 Only such damages, losses or expenses which are the direct consequence of the General Average Act shall be allowed as general average.

Damage or loss sustained by the ship or cargo through delay on the voyage, and indirect loss from the same cause, such as demurrage and loss of market, shall not be admitted as general average.

York-Antwerp Rules 1950 Only such losses, damages or expenses which are the direct consequence of the general average act shall be allowed as general average.

Loss or damage sustained by the ship or cargo through delay, whether on the voyage or subsequently, such as demurrage, and any indirect loss whatsoever, such as loss of market, shall not be admitted as general average.

York-Antwerp Rules 1974 No change.

RULE D

York-Antwerp Rules 1924 Rights to contribution in general average shall not be affected, though the event which gave rise to the sacrifice or expenditure may have been due to the fault of one of the parties to the adventure; but this shall not prejudice any remedies which may be open against that party for such fault.

York-Antwerp Rules 1950 No change.

Rule D—cont.

York-Antwerp Rules 1974	Rights to contribution in general average shall not be affected, though the event which gave rise to the sacrifice or expenditure may have been due to the fault of one of the parties to the adventure, but this shall not prejudice any remedies or defences which may be open against or to that party in respect of such fault.

RULE E

York-Antwerp Rules 1924	The onus of proof is upon the party claiming in general average to show that the loss or expense claimed is properly allowable as general average.
York-Antwerp Rules 1950	No change.
York-Antwerp Rules 1974	No change.

RULE F

York-Antwerp Rules 1924	Any extra expense incurred in place of another expense which would have been allowable as general average, shall be deemed to be general average, and so allowed, but only up to the amount of the general average expense avoided.
York-Antwerp Rules 1950	Any extra expense incurred in place of another expense which would have been allowable as general average shall be deemed to be general average and so allowed without regard to the saving, if any, to other interests, but only up to the amount of the general average expense avoided.
York-Antwerp Rules 1974	No change.

RULE G

York-Antwerp Rules 1924	General average shall be adjusted as regards both loss and contribution upon the basis of values at the time and place when and where the adventure ends. This rule shall not affect the determination of the place at which the average statement is to be made up.
York-Antwerp Rules 1950	No change.
York-Antwerp Rules 1974	No change.

RULE I

JETTISON OF DECK CARGO

York Rules 1864	A jettison of timber or deals, or any other description of wood cargo, carried on the deck of a ship in pursuance of a general custom of the trade in which the ship is then engaged, shall be made good as general average, in like manner as if such cargo had been jettisoned from below deck. No jettison of deck cargo, other than timber or deals, or other wood cargo, so carried as aforesaid, shall be made good as general average. Every structure not built in with the frame of the vessel shall be considered to be a part of the deck of the vessel.
York & Antwerp Rules 1877	No jettison of deck cargo shall be made good as general average. Every structure not built in with the frame of the vessel shall be considered to be a part of the deck of the vessel.
York-Antwerp Rules 1890	No change.

Rule I—cont.

JETTISON OF CARGO

York-Antwerp Rules 1924	No jettison of cargo shall be made good as general average, unless such cargo is carried in accordance with the recognised custom of the trade.
York-Antwerp Rules 1950	No change.
York-Antwerp Rules 1974	No change.

RULE II

DAMAGE BY JETTISON

York Rules 1864	Damage done to goods or merchandise by water which unavoidably goes down a ship's hatches opened, or other opening made, for the purpose of making a jettison shall be made good as general average, in case the loss by jettison is so made good. Damage done by breakage or chafing, or otherwise from derangement of stowage consequent upon a jettison, shall be made good as general average.
York & Antwerp Rules 1877	Damage done to goods or merchandise by water which unavoidably goes down a ship's hatches opened, or other opening made, for the purpose of making a jettison, shall be made good as general average, in case the loss by jettison is so made good. Damage done by breakage and chafing, or otherwise from derangement of stowage consequent upon a jettison, shall be made good as general average, in case the loss by jettison is so made good.

Rule II—cont.

DAMAGE BY JETTISON AND SACRIFICE FOR THE COMMON SAFETY

York-Antwerp Rules 1890	Damage done to a ship and cargo, or either of them, by or in consequence of a sacrifice made for the common safety, and by water which goes down a ship's hatches opened or other opening made for the purpose of making a jettison for the common safety, shall be made good as general average.
York-Antwerp Rules 1924	No change.
York-Antwerp Rules 1950	No change.
York-Antwerp Rules 1974	No change.

RULE III

EXTINGUISHING FIRE ON SHIPBOARD

York Rules 1864	Damage done to a ship and cargo, or either of them, by water or otherwise, in extinguishing a fire on board the ship, shall be general average.
York & Antwerp Rules 1877	Damage done to a ship and cargo, or either of them by water or otherwise, in extinguishing a fire on board the ship, shall be general average; except that no compensation be made for damage done by water to packages which have been on fire.
York-Antwerp Rules 1890	Damage done to a ship and cargo, or either of them, by water or otherwise, including damage by beaching or scuttling a burning ship, in extinguishing a fire on board the ship, shall be made good as general average; except that no compensation shall be made for damage to such portions of the ship and bulk cargo, or to such separate packages of cargo, as have been on fire.
York-Antwerp Rules 1924	No change.

Rule III—cont.

York-Antwerp Rules 1950	No change.
York-Antwerp Rules 1974	Damage done to a ship and cargo, or either of them, by water or otherwise, including damage by beaching or scuttling a burning ship, in extinguishing a fire on board the ship, shall be made good as general average; except that no compensation shall be made for damage by smoke or heat however caused.

RULE IV

CUTTING AWAY WRECK

York Rules 1864	Loss or damage caused by cutting away the wreck or remains of spars or of other things which have previously been carried away by sea-peril, shall not be made good as general average.
York & Antwerp Rules 1877	No change.
York-Antwerp Rules 1890	No change.
York-Antwerp Rules 1924	No change.
York-Antwerp Rules 1950	No change.
York-Antwerp Rules 1974	Loss or damage sustained by cutting away wreck or parts of the ship which have been previously carried away or are effectively lost by accident shall not be made good as general average.

RULE V

VOLUNTARY STRANDING

York Rules 1864	When a ship is intentionally run on shore because she is sinking or driving on shore or rocks, no damage caused to the ship, the cargo and the freight, or any or either of them, by such intentional running on shore, shall be made good as general average.

Rule V—cont.

York & Antwerp Rules 1877

No change.

York-Antwerp Rules 1890

When a ship is intentionally run on shore, and the circumstances are such that if that course were not adopted, she would inevitably sink or drive on shore or on rocks, no loss or damage caused to the ship, cargo and freight, or any of them by such intentional running on shore shall be made good as general average. But in all other cases where a ship is intentionally run on shore for the common safety, the consequent loss or damage shall be allowed as general average.

York-Antwerp Rules 1924

No change.

York-Antwerp Rules 1950

When a ship is intentionally run on shore, and the circumstances are such that if that course were not adopted she would inevitably drive on shore or on rocks, no loss or damage caused to the ship, cargo and freight or any of them by such intentional running on shore shall be made good as general average, but loss or damage incurred in refloating such a ship shall be allowed as general average.
In all other cases where a ship is intentionally run on shore for the common safety, the consequent loss or damage shall be allowed as general average.

York-Antwerp Rules 1974

When a ship is intentionally run on shore for the common safety, whether or not she might have been driven on shore, the consequent loss or damage shall be allowed in general average.

RULE VI

CARRYING A PRESS OF SAIL

York Rules 1864

Damage occasioned to a ship or cargo by carrying a press of sail shall not be made good as general average.

Rule VI—cont.

York & Antwerp Rules 1877	No change.

CARRYING PRESS OF SAIL—DAMAGE TO OR LOSS OF SAILS

York-Antwerp Rules 1890	Damage to or loss of sails and spars, or either of them, caused by forcing a ship off the ground or by driving her higher up the ground, for the common safety, shall be made good as general average; but where a ship is afloat, no loss or damage caused to the ship, cargo and freight, or any of them, by carrying a press of sail, shall be made good as general average.
York-Antwerp Rules 1924	No change.
York-Antwerp Rules 1950	No change.

SALVAGE REMUNERATION

York-Antwerp Rules 1974	Expenditure incurred by the parties to the adventure on account of salvage, whether under contract or otherwise, shall be allowed in general average to the extent that the salvage operations were undertaken for the purpose of preserving from peril the property involved in the common maritime adventure.

SALVAGE

York-Antwerp Rules 1974 (as amended 1990)	(a) Expenditure incurred by the parties to the adventure in the nature of salvage, whether under contract or otherwise, shall be allowed in general average provided that the salvage operations were carried out for the purpose of preserving from peril the property involved in the common maritime adventure. Expenditure allowed in general average shall include any salvage remuneration in which the skill and efforts of the salvors

Rule VI—cont.

in preventing or minimizing damage to the environment such as is referred to in Art. 13 paragraph 1(b) of the International Convention on Salvage, 1989 have been taken into account.

(b) Special compensation payable to a salvor by the shipowner under Art. 14 of the said Convention to the extent specified in paragraph 4 of that Article or under any other provision similar in substance shall not be allowed in general average.

RULE VII

DAMAGE TO ENGINES IN REFLOATING A SHIP

York-Antwerp Rules 1890

Damage caused to machinery and boilers of a ship, which is ashore and in a position of peril, in endeavouring to refloat, shall be allowed in general average, when shown to have arisen from an actual intention to float the ship for the common safety at the risk of such damage.

York-Antwerp Rules 1924

Damage caused to machinery and boilers of a ship, which is ashore and in a position of peril, in endeavouring to refloat, shall be allowed in general average, when shown to have arisen from an actual intention to float the ship for the common safety at the risk of such damage; but where a ship is afloat no loss or damage caused by working the machinery and boilers shall be made good as general average.

DAMAGE TO MACHINERY AND BOILERS

York-Antwerp Rules 1950

Damage caused to machinery and boilers of a ship which is ashore and in a position of peril, in endeavouring to refloat, shall

Rule VII—cont.

be allowed in general average when shown to have arisen from an actual intention to float the ship for the common safety at the risk of such damage; but where a ship is afloat no loss or damage caused by working the machinery and boilers, including loss or damage due to compounding of engines or such measures, shall in any circumstances be made good as general average.

York-Antwerp Rules 1974

Damage caused to any machinery and boilers of a ship which is ashore and in a position of peril, in endeavouring to refloat, shall be allowed in general average when shown to have arisen from an actual intention to float the ship for the common safety at the risk of such damage; but where a ship is afloat no loss or damage caused by working the propelling machinery and boilers shall in any circumstances be made good as general average.

RULE VIII

EXPENSES AND LIGHTENING A SHIP WHEN ASHORE, AND CONSEQUENT DAMAGE

York-Antwerp Rules 1890

When a ship is ashore and, in order to float her, cargo, bunker coals and ship's stores, or any of them are discharged, the extra cost of lightening, lighter hire and re-shipping (if incurred), and the loss or damage sustained thereby, shall be admitted as general average.

York-Antwerp Rules 1924

When a ship is ashore and cargo and ship's fuel and stores or any of them are discharged as a general average act, the extra cost of lightening, lighter hire and re-shipping (if incurred), and the loss or damage sustained thereby, shall be admitted as general average.

Rule VIII—cont.

York-Antwerp Rules 1950 No change.

York-Antwerp Rules 1974 No change.

RULE IX

CARGO, SHIP'S MATERIALS AND STORES BURNT FOR FUEL

York Rules 1890 Cargo, ship's materials and stores, or any of them, necessarily burnt for fuel for the common safety at a time of peril, shall be admitted as general average, when and only when an ample supply of fuel had been provided; but the estimated quantity of coals that would have been consumed, calculated at the price current at the ship's last port of departure at the date of her leaving shall be charged to the shipowner and credited to the general average.

SHIP'S MATERIALS AND STORES BURNT FOR FUEL

York-Antwerp Rules 1924 Ship's materials and stores, or any of them, necessarily burnt for fuel for the common safety at a time of peril, shall be admitted as general average, when and only when an ample supply of fuel had been provided; but the estimated quantity of fuel that would have been consumed, calculated at the price current at the ship's last port of departure at the date of her leaving, shall be credited to the general average.

York-Antwerp Rules 1950 No change.

York-Antwerp Rules 1974 No change.

RULE X (VII*)

PORT OF REFUGE EXPENSES

York Rules 1864 (Rule VII)

When a ship shall have entered a port of refuge under such circumstances that the expenses of entering the port are admissible as general average, and when she shall have sailed thence with her original cargo or a part of it, the corresponding expenses of leaving such port shall likewise be so admitted as general average; and whenever the cost of discharging cargo at such port is admissible as general average, the cost of reloading and stowing such cargo on board the said ship, together with all storage charges on such cargo, shall likewise be so admitted. Except that any portion of the cargo left at such port of refuge, on account of its being unfit to be carried forward, or on account of the unfitness or inability of the ship to carry it, shall not be called on to contribute to such general average.

York & Antwerp Rules 1877 (Rule VII)

When a ship shall have entered a port of refuge under such circumstances that the expenses of entering the port are admissible as general average, and when she shall have sailed thence with her original cargo or a part of it, the corresponding expenses of leaving such port shall likewise be admitted as general average; and, whenever the cost of discharging cargo at such port is admissible as general average, the cost of reloading and stowing such cargo on board the said ship, together with all storage charges on such cargo, shall likewise be so admitted.

* So numbered in the Rules of 1864 and 1877. Re-numbered in 1890.

RULE X(a)

York-Antwerp Rules 1890

When a ship shall have entered a port or place of refuge, or shall have returned to her port or place of loading, in consequence of accident, sacrifice, or other extraordinary circumstances which render that necessary for the common safety, the expenses of entering such port or place shall be admitted as general average; and when she shall have sailed thence with her original cargo, or a part of it, the corresponding expenses of leaving such port or place, consequent upon such entry or return, shall likewise be admitted as general average.

York-Antwerp Rules 1924

No change.

EXPENSES AT PORT OF REFUGE, ETC.

York-Antwerp Rules 1950

When a ship shall have entered a port or place of refuge, or shall have returned to her port or place of loading in consequence of accident, sacrifice or other extraordinary circumstances, which render that necessary for the common safety, the expenses of entering such port or place shall be admitted as general average; and when she shall have sailed thence with her original cargo, or a part of it, the corresponding expenses of leaving such port or place consequent upon such entry or return shall likewise be admitted as general average.

When a ship is at any port or place of refuge and is necessarily removed to another port or place because repairs cannot be carried out in the first port or place, the provisions of this Rule shall be applied to the second port or place as if it were a port or place of refuge. The provisions of Rule XI shall be applied to the prolongation of the voyage occasioned by such removal.

Rule X(a)—cont.

York-Antwerp Rules 1974

When a ship shall have entered a port or place of refuge, or shall have returned to her port or place of loading in consequence of accident, sacrifice or other extraordinary circumstances, which render that necessary for the common safety, the expenses of entering such port or place shall be admitted as general average; and when she shall have sailed thence with her original cargo, or a part of it, the corresponding expenses of leaving such port or place consequent upon such entry or return shall likewise be admitted as general average.

When a ship is at any port or place of refuge and is necessarily removed to another port or place because repairs cannot be carried out in the first port or place, the provisions of this Rule shall be applied to the second port or place as if it were a port or place of refuge and the cost of such removal including temporary repairs and towage shall be admitted as general average. The provisions of Rule XI shall be applied to the prolongation of the voyage occasioned by such removal.

RULE X(b)

York-Antwerp Rules 1890

The cost of discharging cargo from a ship, whether at a port or place of loading, call or refuge, shall be admitted as general average, when the discharge was necessary for the common safety or to enable damage to the ship, caused by sacrifice or accident during the voyage, to be repaired, if the repairs were necessary for the safe prosecution of the voyage.

York-Antwerp Rules 1924

The cost of handling on board or discharging cargo, fuel or stores, whether at a port or place of loading, call or refuge,

Rule X(b)—cont.

shall be admitted as general average when the handling or discharge was necessary for the common safety or to enable damage to the ship caused by sacrifice or accident to be repaired, if the repairs were necessary for the safe prosecution of the voyage.

York-Antwerp Rules 1950

No change.

York-Antwerp Rules 1974

The cost of handling on board or discharging cargo, fuel or stores whether at a port or place of loading, call or refuge, shall be admitted as general average, when the handling or discharge was necessary for the common safety or to enable damage to the ship caused by sacrifice or accident to be repaired, if the repairs were necessary for the safe prosecution of the voyage, except in cases where the damage to the ship is discovered at a port or place of loading or call without any accident or other extraordinary circumstances connected with such damage having taken place during the voyage.

The cost of handling on board or discharging cargo, fuel or stores shall not be admissible as general average when incurred solely for the purpose of restowage due to shifting during the voyage, unless such restowage is necessary for the common safety.

RULE X(c)

York-Antwerp Rules 1890

Whenever the cost of discharging cargo from a ship is admissible as general average, the cost of reloading and storing such cargo on board the said ship, together with all storage charges on such cargo, shall likewise be so admitted. But when the ship is condemned or does not

Rule X(c)—cont.

proceed on her original voyage, no storage expenses incurred after the date of the ship's condemnation or of the abandonment of the voyage shall be admitted as general average.

York-Antwerp Rules 1924

Whenever the cost of handling or discharging cargo, fuel or stores is admissible as general average, the cost of reloading and stowing such cargo, fuel or stores on board the ship, together with all storage charges (including fire insurance, if incurred) on such cargo, fuel or stores, shall likewise be so admitted. But when the ship is condemned or does not proceed on her original voyage, no storage expenses incurred after the date of the ship's condemnation or of the abandonment of the voyage shall be admitted as general average. In the event of the condemnation of the ship or the abandonment of the voyage before completion of discharge of cargo, storage expenses, as above, shall be admitted as general average up to date of completion of discharge.

York-Antwerp Rules 1950

Whenever the cost of handling or discharging cargo, fuel or stores is admissible as general average, the cost of reloading and stowing such cargo, fuel or stores on board the ship, together with all storage charges (including insurance, if reasonably incurred) on such cargo, fuel or stores, shall likewise be so admitted. But when the ship is condemned or does not proceed on her original voyage, no storage expenses incurred after the date of the ship's condemnation or of the abandonment of the voyage shall be admitted as general average. In the event of the condemnation of the ship or the abandonment of the voyage before completion of discharge of cargo, storage expenses, as

Rule X(c)—cont.

above, shall be admitted as general average up to the date of completion of discharge.

York-Antwerp Rules 1974

Whenever the cost of handling or discharging cargo, fuel or stores is admissible as general average, the costs of storage, including insurance if reasonably incurred, reloading and stowing of such cargo, fuel or stores shall likewise be admitted as general average.

But when the ship is condemned or does not proceed on her original voyage, storage expenses shall be admitted as general average only up to the date of the ship's condemnation or of the abandonment of the voyage or up to the date of completion of discharge of cargo if the condemnation or abandonment takes place before that date.

RULE X(d)

York-Antwerp Rules 1890

If a ship under average be in a port or place at which it is practicable to repair her, so as to enable her to carry on the whole cargo, and if, in order to save expenses, either she is towed thence to some other port or place of repair or to her destination, or the cargo or a portion of it is transhipped by another ship, or otherwise forwarded, then the extra cost of such towage, transhipment, and forwarding, or any of them (up to the amount of the extra expense saved) shall be payable by the several parties to the adventure in proportion to the extraordinary expense saved.

York-Antwerp Rules 1924

No change.

York-Antwerp Rules 1950

If a ship under average be in a port or place at which it is practicable to repair

Rule X(d)—cont.

her, so as to enable her to carry on the whole cargo, and if, in order to save expense, either she is towed thence to some other port or place of repair or to her destination, or the cargo or a portion of it is transhipped by another ship, or otherwise forwarded, then the extra cost of such towage, transhipment and forwarding, or any of them (up to the amount of the extra expense saved) shall be payable by the several parties to the adventure in proportion to the extraordinary expense saved.

York-Antwerp Rules 1974 has been deleted.

All "substituted expenses" will now be subject to the same treatment, namely that provided by Rule F.

RULE XI (RULE VIII*)

WAGES AND MAINTENANCE OF CREW IN PORT OF REFUGE

York Rules 1864 (Rule VIII)

When a ship shall have entered a port of refuge under the circumstances defined in Rule VII, the wages and cost of maintenance of the master and mariners, from the time of entering such port until the ship shall have been made ready to proceed upon her voyage, shall be made good as general average. Except that any portion of the cargo left at such port of refuge on account of its being unfit to be carried forward, or on account of the unfitness or inability of the ship to carry it, shall not be called on to contribute to such general average.

York & Antwerp Rules 1877 (Rule VIII)

When a ship shall have entered a port of refuge under the circumstances defined in Rule VII, the wages and cost of maintenance of the master and mariners, from

* So numbered in the Rules of 1864 and 1877. Re-numbered in 1890.

Rule XI—cont.

the time of entering such port until the ship shall have been made ready to proceed upon her voyage, shall be made good as general average.

York-Antwerp Rules 1890

When a ship shall have entered or been detained in any port or place under the circumstances, or for the purposes of the repairs, mentioned in Rule X, the wages, payable to the master, officers and crew together with the cost of maintenance of the same, during the extra period of detention in such port or place until the ship shall or should have been made ready to proceed upon her voyage, shall be admitted as general average. But when the ship is condemned or does not proceed on her original voyage, the wages and maintenance of the master, officers and crew, incurred after the date of the ship's condemnation or of the abandonment of the voyage, shall not be admitted as general average.

York-Antwerp Rules 1924

When a ship shall have entered or been detained in any port or place under the circumstances, or for the purposes of repairs mentioned in Rule X, the wages payable to the master, officers and crew, together with the cost of maintenance of the same, during the extra period of detention in such port or place until the ship shall or should have been made ready to proceed upon her voyage, shall be admitted as general average. But when the ship is condemned or does not proceed on her original voyage, the wages and maintenance of the master, officers and crew, incurred after the date of the ship's condemnation or of the abandonment of the voyage, shall not be admitted as general average. In the event of the condemnation of the ship or the abandonment of the voyage before completion

Rule XI—cont.

of discharge of cargo, wages and maintenance of crew, as above, shall be admitted as general average up to the date of completion of discharge.

WAGES AND MAINTENANCE OF CREW AND OTHER EXPENSES BEARING UP FOR AND IN A PORT OF REFUGE, ETC.

York-Antwerp Rules 1950

(a) Wages and maintenance of master, officers and crew reasonably incurred and fuel and stores consumed during the prolongation of the voyage occasioned by a ship entering a port or place of refuge or returning to her port or place of loading shall be admitted as general average when the expenses of entering such port or place are allowable in general average in accordance with Rule X(a).

York-Antwerp Rules 1974

No change.

York-Antwerp Rules 1950

(b) When a ship shall have entered or been detained in any port or place in consequence of accident, sacrifice or other extraordinary circumstances which render that necessary for the common safety, or to enable damage to the ship caused by sacrifice or accident to be repaired, if the repairs were necessary for the safe prosecution of the voyage, the wages and maintenance of the master, officers and crew reasonably incurred during the extra period of detention in such port or place until the ship shall or should have been made ready to proceed upon her voyage, shall be admitted in general average. When the ship is condemned or does not proceed on her original voyage, the extra period of detention shall be deemed not to extend beyond the date of the ship's condemnation or of the abandonment of the voyage or, if discharge of cargo is not then completed, beyond the date of completion of discharge.

Rule XI—cont.

Fuel and stores consumed during the extra period of detention shall be admitted as general average, except such fuel and stores as are consumed in effecting repairs not allowable in general average.

Port charges incurred during the extra period of detention shall likewise be admitted as general average except such charges as are incurred solely by reason of repairs not allowable in general average.

York-Antwerp Rules 1974

(b) When a ship shall have entered or been detained in any port or place in consequence of accident, sacrifice or other extraordinary circumstances which render that necessary for the common safety, or to enable damage to the ship caused by sacrifice or accident to be repaired, if the repairs were necessary for the safe prosecution of the voyage, the wages and maintenance of the master, officers and crew reasonably incurred during the extra period of detention in such port or place until the ship shall or should have been made ready to proceed upon her voyage, shall be admitted in general average.

Provided that when damage to the ship is discovered at a port or place of loading or call without any accident or other extraordinary circumstance connected with such damage having taken place during the voyage, then the wages and maintenance of master, officers and crew and fuel and stores consumed during the extra detention for repairs to damages so discovered shall not be admissible as general average, even if the repairs are necessary for the safe prosecution of the voyage.

Rule XI—cont.

When the ship is condemned or does not proceed on her original voyage, wages and maintenance of the master, officers and crew and fuel and stores consumed shall be admitted as general average only up to the date of the ship's condemnation or of the abandonment of the voyage or up to the date of completion of discharge of cargo if the condemnation or abandonment takes place before that date.

Fuel and stores consumed during the extra period of detention shall be admitted as general average, except such fuel and stores as are consumed in effecting repairs not allowable in general average.

Port charges incurred during the extra period of detention shall likewise be admitted as general average except such charges as are incurred solely by reason of repairs not allowable in general average.

York-Antwerp Rules 1950

(c) For the purpose of this and the other Rules wages shall include all payments made to or for the benefit of the master, officers and crew, whether such payments be imposed by law upon the shipowners or be made under the terms or articles of employment.

York-Antwerp Rules 1974

No change.

York-Antwerp Rules 1950

(d) When overtime is paid to the master, officers or crew for maintenance of the ship or repairs, the cost of which is not allowable in general average, such overtime shall be allowed in general average only up to the saving in expense which would have been incurred and admitted as general average, had such overtime not been incurred.

York-Antwerp Rules 1974

No change.

RULE XII (IX*)

DAMAGE TO CARGO IN DISCHARGING

York Rules 1864 (Rule IX)	Damage done to cargo by discharging it at a port of refuge shall not be admissible as general average in case such cargo shall have been discharged at the place and in the manner customary at that port with ships not in distress.
York & Antwerp Rules 1877 (Rule IX)	No change.
York-Antwerp Rules 1890	Damage done to or loss of cargo necessarily caused in the act of discharging, storing, reloading and stowing, shall be made good as general average when and only when the cost of those measures respectively is admitted as general average.
York-Antwerp Rules 1924	Damage to or loss of cargo, fuel or stores caused in the act of handling, discharging, storing, reloading and stowing shall be made good as general average, when and only when the cost of those measures respectively is admitted as general average.
York-Antwerp Rules 1950	No change.
York-Antwerp Rules 1974	No change.

RULE XIII

DEDUCTIONS FROM COST OF REPAIRS

York-Antwerp Rules 1890

A. Up to 1 year old
All repairs to be allowed in full, except painting or coating of bottom, from which one-third is to be deducted.

B. Between 1 and 3 years
One-third to be deducted off repairs to and renewal of woodwork of hull, masts and spars, furniture, upholstery, crockery, metal- and glassware, also sails, rig-

* So numbered in the Rules of 1864 and 1877. Re-numbered in 1890.

Rule XIII—cont.

ging, ropes, sheets and hawsers (other than wire and chain), awnings, covers and painting.

One-sixth to be deducted off wire rigging, wire ropes and wire hawsers, chain cables and chains, donkey engines, steam winches and connections, steam cranes and connections; other repairs in full.

C. Between 3 and 6 years
Deductions as above under Clause B, except that one-sixth be deducted off ironwork of masts and spars, and machinery (inclusive of boilers and their mountings).

D. Between 6 and 10 years
Deductions as above under Clause C, except that one-third be deducted off ironwork of masts and spars, repairs to and renewal of all machinery (inclusive of boilers and their mountings), and all hawsers, ropes, sheets and rigging.

E. Between 10 and 15 years
One third to be deducted off all repairs and renewals, except ironwork of hull and cementing and chain cables, from which one-sixth to be deducted. Anchors to be allowed in full.

F. Over 15 years
One-third to be deducted off all repairs and renewals. Anchors to be allowed in full. One-sixth to be deducted off chain cables.

G. Generally
The deductions (except as to provisions and stores, machinery and boilers) to be regulated by the age of the ship, and not the age of the particular part of her to which they apply. No painting bottom to be allowed if the bottom has not been painted within six months previous to the date of accident. No deduction to be

Rule XIII—cont.

made in respect of old material which is repaired without being replaced by new, and provisions and stores which have not been in use.

In the case of wooden or composite ships:

When a ship is under one year old from date of original register, at the time of accident, no deduction new for old shall be made. After that period a deduction of one-third shall be made, with the following exceptions:

Anchors shall be allowed in full.

Chain cables shall be subject to a deduction of one-sixth only.

No deduction shall be made in respect of provisions and stores which had not been in use.

Metal sheathing shall be dealt with, by allowing in full the cost of a weight equal to the gross weight of the metal sheathing stripped off, minus the proceeds of the old metal. Nails, felt, and labour metalling are subject to a deduction of one-third.

In the case of ships generally:

In the case of all ships, the expense of straightening bent ironwork, including labour of taking out and replacing it, shall be allowed in full.

Graving dock dues, including expenses of removals, cartages, use of shears, stages, and graving dock materials, shall be allowed in full.

York-Antwerp Rules 1924

In adjusting claims for general average, repairs to be allowed in general average shall be subject to the following deductions in respect of "new for old", viz:

In the case of iron or steel ships, from date of original register to the date of accident:

Rule XIII—cont.

A. Up to 1 year old
All repairs to be allowed in full, except painting or coating of bottom, from which one-third is to be deducted.

B. Between 1 and 3 years
One third to be deducted off repairs to and renewals of woodwork of hull, masts and spars, furniture, upholstery, crockery, metal- and glassware, also sails, rigging, ropes, sheets and hawsers (other than wire and chain), awnings, covers and painting.

One-sixth to be deducted off wire rigging, wire ropes and wire hawsers, wireless apparatus, chain cables and chains, insulation, donkey engines, steam steering gear and connections, steam winches and connections, steam cranes and connections and electrical machinery; other repairs in full.

C. Between 3 and 6 years
Deductions as above under Clause B, except that one-third be deducted off insulation, and one-sixth be deducted off ironwork of masts and spars, and all machinery (inclusive of boilers and their mountings).

D. Between 6 and 10 years
Deductions as above under Clause C, except that one-third be deducted off ironwork of masts and spars, donkey engines, steam steering gear, winches, cranes and connections, repairs to and renewal of all machinery (inclusive of boilers and their mountings), wireless apparatus and all hawsers, ropes, sheets and rigging.

E. Between 10 and 15 years
One-third to be deducted off all repairs and renewals except ironwork of hull and

Rule XIII—cont.

cementing and chain cables, from which one-sixth to be deducted. Anchors to be allowed in full.

F. Over 15 years
One-third to be deducted off all repairs and renewals. Anchors to be allowed in full. One-sixth to be deducted off chain cables.

G. Generally
The deductions (except as to provisions and stores, insulation, wireless apparatus, machinery and boilers) to be regulated by the age of the ship, and not the age of the particular part of her to which they apply. No painting bottom to be allowed if the bottom has not been painted within six months previous to the date of the accident. No deduction to be made in respect of old material which is repaired, without being replaced by new, and provisions, stores and gear which have not been in use.

In the case of wooden or composite ships:
When a ship is under one year old from date of original register, at the time of accident, no deduction new for old shall be made. After that period a deduction of one-third shall be made, with the following exceptions:

Anchors shall be allowed in full.

Chain cables shall be subject to a deduction of one-sixth only.

No deduction shall be made in respect of provisions and stores which had not been in use.

Metal sheathing shall be dealt with, by allowing in full the cost of a weight equal to the gross weight of metal sheathing stripped off, minus the proceeds of the old metal. Nails, felt, and

Rule XIII—cont.

labour metalling are subject to a deduction of one-third.

York-Antwerp Rules 1950

In adjusting claims for general average, repairs to be allowed in general average shall be subject to deductions in respect of "new for old" according to the following rules, where old material or parts are replaced by new.

The deductions to be regulated by the age of the ship from date of original register to the date of accident, except for provisions and stores, insulation, life- and similar boats, gyro compass equipment, wireless, direction finding, echo sounding and similar apparatus, machinery and boilers for which the deductions shall be regulated by the age of the particular parts to which they apply.

No deduction to be made in respect of provisions, stores and gear which have not been in use.

The deductions shall be made from the cost of new materials or parts, including labour and establishment charges, but excluding cost of opening up.

Drydock and slipway dues and cost of shifting the ship shall be allowed in full.

No cleaning and painting of bottom to be allowed, if the bottom has not been painted within six months previous to the date of the accident.

A. Up to 1 year old
All repairs to be allowed in full, except scaling and cleaning and painting or coating of bottom, from which one-third is to be deducted.

B. Between 1 and 3 years old.
Deduction off scaling, cleaning and painting bottom as above under Clause A.

Rule XIII—cont.

One-third to be deducted off sails, rigging, ropes, sheets and hawsers (other than wire and chain), awnings, covers, provisions and stores and painting.

One-sixth to be deducted off woodwork of hull, including hold ceiling, wooden masts, spars and boats, furniture, upholstery, crockery, metal- and glass-ware, wire rigging, wire ropes and wire hawsers, gyro compass equipment, wireless, direction finding, echo sounding and similar apparatus, chain cables and chains, insulation, auxiliary machinery, steering gear and connections, winches and cranes and connections and electrical machinery and connections other than electric propelling machinery; other repairs to be allowed in full.

Metal sheathing for wooden or composite ships shall be dealt with by allowing in full the cost of a weight equal to the gross weight of metal sheathing stripped off, minus the proceeds of the old metal. Nails, felt and labour metalling are subject to a deduction of one-third.

C. Between 3 and 6 years
Deductions as above under Clause B, except that one-third to be deducted off woodwork of hull including hold ceiling, wooden masts, spars and boats, furniture, upholstery, and one-sixth be deducted off iron work of masts and spars and all machinery (inclusive of boilers and their mountings).

D. Between 6 and 10 years
Deductions as above under Clause C, except that one-third be deducted off all rigging, ropes, sheets and hawsers, ironwork of masts and spars, gyro compass equipment, wireless, direction finding, echo sounding and similar apparatus, insulation, auxiliary machinery, steering

Rule XIII—cont.

gear, winches, cranes and connections and all other machinery (inclusive of boilers and their mountings).

E. Between 10 and 15 years
One-third to be deducted off all renewals, except ironwork of hull and cementing and chain cables, from which one-sixth to be deducted, and anchors, which are allowed in full.

F. Over 15 years
One-third, to be deducted off all renewals, except chain cables, from which one-sixth to be deducted, and anchors, which are allowed in full.

York-Antwerp Rules 1974

Repairs to be allowed in general average shall not be subject to deductions in respect of "new for old" where old material or parts are replaced by new unless the ship is over fifteen years old in which case there shall be a deduction of one third. The deductions shall be regulated by the age of the ship from the 31st December of the year of completion of construction to the date of the general average act, except for insulation, life and similar boats, communications and navigational apparatus and equipment, machinery and boilers for which the deductions shall be regulated by the age of the particular parts to which they apply.

The deductions shall be made only from the cost of the new materials or parts when finished and ready to be installed in the ship.

No deduction shall be made in respect of provisions, stores, anchors and chain cables.

Drydock and slipway dues and costs of shifting the ship shall be allowed in full.

The costs of cleaning, painting or coating of bottom shall not be allowed

Rule XIII—cont.

in general average unless the bottom has been painted or coated within the twelve months preceding the date of the general average act in which case one half of such costs shall be allowed.

RULE XIV

TEMPORARY REPAIRS

York-Antwerp Rules 1890

No deductions "new for old" shall be made from the cost of temporary repairs of damage allowable as general average.

York-Antwerp Rules 1924

Where temporary repairs are effected to a ship at a port of loading, call or refuge, for the common safety, or of damage caused by general average sacrifice, the cost of such repairs shall be admitted as general average; but where temporary repairs of accidental damage are effected merely to enable the adventure to be completed, the cost of such repairs shall be admitted as general average only up to the saving in expense which would have been incurred and allowed in general average had such repairs not been effected there.

No deductions "new for old" shall be made from the cost of temporary repairs allowable as general average.

York-Antwerp Rules 1950

Where temporary repairs are effected to a ship at a port of loading, call or refuge, for the common safety, or of damage caused by general average sacrifice, the cost of such repairs shall be admitted as general average.

Where temporary repairs of accidental damage are effected merely to enable the adventure to be completed, the cost of such repairs shall be admitted as general average without regard to the saving, if any, to other interests, but only up to the

Rule XIV—cont.

saving in expense which would have been incurred and allowed in general average if such repairs had not been effected there.

No deductions "new for old" shall be made from the cost of temporary repairs allowable as general average.

York-Antwerp Rules 1974

Where temporary repairs are effected to a ship at a port of loading, call or refuge, for the common safety, or of damage caused by general average sacrifice, the cost of such repairs shall be admitted as general average.

Where temporary repairs of accidental damage are effected in order to enable the adventure to be completed, the cost of such repairs shall be admitted as general average without regard to the saving, if any, to other interests, but only up to the saving in expense which would have been incurred and allowed in general average if such repairs had not been effected there.

No deductions "new for old" shall be made from the cost of temporary repairs allowable as general average.

RULE XV (XI*)

LOSS OF FREIGHT

York Rules 1864 (Rule XI)

In every case in which a sacrifice of cargo is made good as general average, the loss of freight, if any, which is caused by such loss of cargo, shall likewise be so made good.

York & Antwerp Rules 1877 (Rule XI)

No change.

York-Antwerp Rules 1890

Loss of freight arising from damage to or loss of cargo shall be made good as gen-

* So numbered in the Rules of 1864 and 1877. Re-numbered in 1890.

Rule XV—cont.

eral average, either when caused by a general average act, or when the damage to or loss of cargo is so made good.

York-Antwerp Rules 1924

Loss of freight arising from damage to or loss of cargo shall be made good as general average, either when caused by a general average act, or when the damage to or loss of cargo is so made good.

Deduction shall be made from the amount of gross freight lost, of the charges which the owner thereof would have incurred to earn such freight, but has, in consequence of the sacrifice, not incurred.

York-Antwerp Rules 1950

No change.

York-Antwerp Rules 1974

No change.

RULE XVI (XII*)

AMOUNT TO BE MADE GOOD FOR CARGO

York & Antwerp Rules 1877 (Rule XII)

The value to be allowed for goods sacrificed shall be that value which the owner would have received if such goods had not been sacrificed.

AMOUNT TO BE MADE GOOD FOR CARGO LOST OR DAMAGED BY SACRIFICE

York-Antwerp Rules 1890

The amount to be made good as general average for damage or loss of goods sacrificed shall be the loss which the owner of the goods has sustained thereby, based on the market values at the date of the arrival of the vessel or at the termination of the adventure.

York-Antwerp Rules 1924

The amount to be made good as general average for damage to or loss of goods sacrificed shall be the loss which the

* So numbered in the 1877 Rules. Re-numbered in 1890.

Rule XVI—cont.

owner of the goods has sustained thereby, based on the market values at the date of the arrival of the vessel or at the termination of the adventure where this ends at a place other than the original destination.

Where goods so damaged are sold after arrival, the loss to be made good in general average shall be calculated by applying to the sound value on the date of arrival of the vessel the percentage of loss resulting from a comparison of the proceeds with the sound value on date of sale.

York-Antwerp Rules 1950

The amount to be made good as general average for damage to or loss of goods sacrificed shall be the loss which the owner of the goods has sustained thereby, based on the market values at the last day of discharge of the vessel or at the termination of the adventure where this ends at a place other than the original destination.

Where goods so damaged are sold and the amount of the damage has not been otherwise agreed, the loss to be made good in general average shall be the difference between the net proceeds of sale and the net sound value at the last day of discharge of the vessel or at the termination of the adventure where this ends at a place other than the original destination.

York-Antwerp Rules 1974

The amount to be made good as general average for damage to or loss of cargo sacrificed shall be the loss which has been sustained thereby, based on the value at the time of discharge, ascertained from the commercial invoice rendered to the receiver or if there is no such invoice from the shipped value. The value at the time of discharge shall include the cost of insurance and freight except insofar as such freight is at the risk of interests other than the cargo.

Rule XVI—cont.

When cargo so damaged is sold and the amount of the damage has not been otherwise agreed, the loss to be made good in general average shall be the difference between the net proceeds of sale and the net sound value as computed in the first paragraph of this Rule.

RULE XVII (X*)

CONTRIBUTORY VALUES

York Rules 1864 (Rule X)

The contributions to a general average shall be made upon the actual values of the property at the termination of the adventure, to which shall be added the amount made good as general average for property sacrificed; deduction being made from the shipowner's freight and passage-money at risk of two-fifths of such freight, in lieu of crew's wages, port charges, and all other deductions; deduction being also made from the value of the property of all charges incurred in respect thereof subsequently to the arising of the claim to general average.

York & Antwerp Rules 1877 (Rule X)

The contribution to a general average shall be made upon the actual values of the property at the termination of the adventure, to which shall be added the amount made good as general average for property sacrificed; deduction being made from the shipowner's freight and passage-money at risk, of such port charges and crew's wages as would not have been incurred had the ship and cargo been totally lost at the date of the general average act or sacrifice; deduction being also made from the value of the property of all charges incurred in respect thereof subsequently to the arising of the claim to general average.

* So numbered in the Rules of 1864 and 1877. Re-numbered in 1890.

Rule XVII—cont.

York-Antwerp Rules 1890

The contribution to a general average shall be made upon the actual values of the property at the termination of the adventure, to which shall be added the amount made good as general average for property sacrificed; deduction being made from the shipowner's freight and passage-money at risk, of such port charges and crew's wages as would not have been incurred had the ship and cargo been totally lost at the date of the general average act or sacrifice, and have not been allowed as general average; deduction being also made from the value of the property of all charges incurred in respect thereof subsequently to the general average act, except such charges as are allowed in general average.

Passengers' luggage and personal effects, not shipped under bill of lading, shall not contribute to general average.

York-Antwerp Rules 1924

The contribution to a general average shall be made upon the actual net values of the property at the termination of the adventure, to which values shall be added the amount made good as general average for property sacrificed, if not already included, deduction being made from the shipowner's freight and passage-money at risk, of such charges and crew's wages as would not have been incurred in earning the freight had the ship and cargo been totally lost at the date of the general average act and have not been allowed as general average; deduction being also made from the value of the property, of all charges incurred in respect thereof subsequently to the general average act, except such charges as are allowed in general average.

Passengers' luggage and personal effects not shipped under bill of lading shall not contribute in general average.

Rule XVII—cont.

York-Antwerp Rules 1950

No change.

York-Antwerp Rules 1974

The contribution to a general average shall be made upon the actual net values of the property at the termination of the adventure except that the value of cargo shall be the value at the time of discharge, ascertained from the commercial invoice rendered to the receiver or if there is no such invoice from the shipped value. The value of the cargo shall include the cost of insurance and freight unless and insofar as such freight is at the risk of interests other than the cargo, deducting therefrom any loss or damage suffered by the cargo prior to or at the time of discharge. The value of the ship shall be assessed without taking into account the beneficial or detrimental effect of any demise or time charterparty to which the ship may be committed.

To these values shall be added the amount made good as general average for property sacrificed, if not already included, deduction being made from the freight and passage money at risk of such charges and crew's wages as would not have been incurred in earning the freight had the ship and cargo been totally lost at the date of the general average act and have not been allowed as general average; deduction being also made from the value of the property of all extra charges incurred in respect thereof subsequently to the general average act, except such charges as are allowed in general average.

Where cargo is sold short of destination, however, it shall contribute upon the actual net proceeds of sale, with the addition of any amount made good as general average.

Passengers' luggage and personal effects not shipped under bill of lading shall not contribute in general average.

RULE XVIII

ADJUSTMENT

York-Antwerp Rules 1890

Except as provided in the foregoing rules, the adjustment shall be drawn up in accordance with the law and practice that would have governed the adjustment had the contract of affreightment not contained a clause to pay general average according to these rules.

York-Antwerp Rules 1950 and subsequently

See Rule of Interpretation.

RULE XVIII

DAMAGE TO SHIP

York-Antwerp Rules 1924

The amount to be allowed as general average for damage or loss to the ship, her machinery and/or gear when repaired or replaced shall be the actual reasonable cost of repairing or replacing such damage or loss, deductions being made as above (Rule XIII) when old material is replaced by new. When not repaired, the reasonable depreciation shall be allowed, not exceeding the estimated cost of repairs.

Where there is an actual or constructive total loss of the ship the amount to be allowed as general average for damage or loss to the ship caused by a general average act shall be the estimated sound value of the ship after deducting therefrom the estimated cost of repairing damage which is not general average and the proceeds of sale, if any.

York-Antwerp Rules 1950

The amount to be allowed as general average for damage or loss to the ship, her machinery and/or gear when repaired or

Rule XVIII—cont.

replaced shall be the actual reasonable cost of repairing or replacing such damage or loss, subject to deduction in accordance with Rule XIII. When not repaired, the reasonable depreciation shall be allowed, not exceeding the estimated cost of repairs.

Where there is an actual or constructive total loss of the ship the amount to be allowed as general average for damage or loss to the ship caused by a general average act shall be the estimated sound value of the ship after deducting therefrom the estimated cost of repairing damage which is not general average and the proceeds of sale, if any.

York-Antwerp Rules 1974

The amount to be allowed as general average for damage or loss to the ship, her machinery and/or gear caused by a general average act shall be as follows:

(a) When repaired or replaced. The actual reasonable cost of repairing or replacing such damage or loss, subject to deductions in accordance with Rule XIII;

(b) When not repaired or replaced. The reasonable depreciation arising from such damage or loss, but not exceeding the estimated cost of repairs. But where the ship is an actual total loss or when the cost of repairs of the damage would exceed the value of the ship when repaired, the amount to be allowed as general average shall be the difference between the estimated sound value of the ship after deducting therefrom the estimated cost of repairing damage which is not general average and the value of the ship in her damaged state which may be measured by the net proceeds of sale, if any.

RULE XIX

UNDECLARED OR WRONGLY DECLARED CARGO

York-Antwerp Rules 1924

Damage or loss caused to goods loaded without the knowledge of the shipowner or his agent or to goods wilfully misdescribed at time of shipment shall not be allowed as general average, but such goods shall remain liable to contribute, if saved.

Damage or loss caused to goods which have been wrongfully declared on shipment at a value which is lower than their real value shall be contributed for at the declared value, but such goods shall contribute upon their actual value.

York-Antwerp Rules 1950

No change.

York-Antwerp Rules 1974

No change.

RULE XX

EXPENSES BEARING UP FOR PORT, ETC.

York-Antwerp Rules 1924

Fuel and stores consumed, and wages and maintenance of master, officers and crew incurred, during the prolongation of the voyage occasioned by a ship entering a port or place of refuge or returning to her port or place of loading shall be admitted as general average when the expenses of entering such port or place are allowable in general average in accordance with Rule X(a).

Fuel and stores consumed during extra detention in a port or place of loading, call or refuge shall also be allowed in general average for the period during which wages and maintenance of master, officers and crew are allowed in terms of

Rule XX—cont.

Rule XI, except such fuel and stores as are consumed in effecting repairs not allowable in general average.

(*The corresponding provisions are now to be found in Rule XI.*)

RULE XX (XXI*)

PROVISION OF FUNDS

York-Antwerp Rules 1924 (Rule XXI)

A commission of 2 per cent. on general average disbursements shall be allowed in general average, but when the funds are not provided by any of the contributing interests, the necessary cost of obtaining the funds required by means of a bottomry bond or otherwise, or the loss sustained by owners of goods sold for the purpose, shall be allowed in general average.

The cost of insuring money advanced to pay for general average disbursements shall also be allowed in general average.

York-Antwerp Rules 1950

A commission of 2 per cent. on general average disbursements, other than the wages and maintenance of master, officers and crew and fuel and stores not replaced during the voyage, shall be allowed in general average, but when the funds are not provided by any of the contributing interests, the necessary cost of obtaining the funds required by means of a bottomry bond or otherwise, or the loss sustained by owners of goods sold for the purpose, shall be allowed in general average.

The cost of insuring money advanced to pay for general average disbursements shall also be allowed in general average.

York-Antwerp Rules 1974

No change.

* So numbered in the Rules of 1924.

RULE XXI (XXII*)

INTEREST ON LOSSES MADE GOOD IN GENERAL AVERAGE

York-Antwerp Rules 1924 (Rule XXII)

Interest shall be allowed on expenditure, sacrifices and allowances charged to general average at the legal rate per annum prevailing at the final port of destination at which the adventure ends, or where there is no recognised legal rate, at the rate of 5 per cent. per annum, until the date of the general average statement, due allowance being made for any interim reimbursement from the contributory interests or from the general average deposit fund.

York-Antwerp Rules 1950

Interest shall be allowed on expenditure, sacrifices and allowances charged to general average at the rate of 5 per cent. per annum, until the date of the general average statement, due allowance being made for any interim reimbursement from the contributory interests or from the general average deposit fund.

York-Antwerp Rules 1974

Interest shall be allowed on expenditure, sacrifices and allowances charged to general average at the rate of 7 per cent. per annum, until the date of the general average statement, due allowance being made for any interim reimbursement from the contributory interests or from the general average deposit fund.

* So numbered prior to 1950.

RULE XXII (XXIII*)

TREATMENT OF CASH DEPOSITS

York-Antwerp Rules 1924 (Rule XXIII)

Where cash deposits have been collected in respect of cargo's liability for general average, salvage or special charges, such deposits shall be paid into a special account, earning interest where possible, in the joint names of two trustees (one to be nominated on behalf of the shipowner and the other on behalf of the depositors) in a bank to be approved by such trustees. The sum so deposited, together with accrued interest, if any, shall be held as security for and upon trust for payment to the parties entitled thereto of the general average, salvage or special charges payable by the cargo in respect of which the deposits have been collected. The trustees shall have power to make payments on account or refunds of deposits which may be certified to in writing by the average adjuster. Such deposits and payments or refunds shall be without prejudice to the ultimate liability of the parties.

York-Antwerp Rules 1950

Where cash deposits have been collected in respect of cargo's liability for general average, salvage or special charges, such deposits shall be paid without any delay into a special account in the joint names of a representative nominated on behalf of the shipowner and a representative nominated on behalf of the depositors in a bank to be approved by both. The sum so deposited, together with accrued interest, if any, shall be held as security for payment to the parties entitled thereto of the general average, salvage or special charges payable by cargo in respect to which the

* So numbered prior to 1950.

Rule XXII—cont.

deposits have been collected. Payments on account or refunds of deposits may be made, if certified to in writing by the average adjuster. Such deposits and payments or refunds shall be without prejudice to the ultimate liability of the parties.

York-Antwerp Rules 1974 No change.

APPENDIX 3

FRENCH TEXT OF THE YORK-ANTWERP RULES 1994

VERSION FRANÇAISE DES REGLES D'YORK ET D'ANVERS 1994*

Règle d'interpretation

Dans le règlement d'avaries communes, les Règles suivantes doivent s'appliquer à l'exclusion de toute loi et pratique incompatibles avec elles.

A l'exception de ce qui est prévu par la Règle "Paramount" et les Règles numérotées, l'avarie commune doit être réglée conformément aux Règles précédées de lettres.

Règle "Paramount"

Une admission en avarie commune ne pourra être en aucun cas prononcée pour un sacrifice ou une dépense qui n'aurait pas été raisonnablement consenti.

Règle A

Il y a acte d'avarie commune quand, et seulement quand, intentionnellement et raisonnablement, un sacrifice extraordinaire est fait ou une dépense extraordinaire encourue pour le salut commun, dans le but de préserver d'un péril les propriétés engagées dans une aventure maritime commune.

Les sacrifices et dépenses d'avarie commune seront supportés par les divers intérêts appelés à contribuer sur les bases déterminées ci-après.

Règle B

Il y a aventure maritime commune lorsqu'un ou plusiers navires remorquent ou poussent un ou plusiers autres navires, pourvu que tous soient

* Version française établie par l'Association Française du Droit Maritime.

engagés dans des activités commerciales et non dans une opération d'assistance.

Lorsque des mesures seront prises pour préserver les navires et leurs éventuelles cargaisons d'un péril commun, les Régles seront applicables.

Un navire n'est pas en situation de péril commun avec un ou plusiers autres navires s'il lui suffit de s'en détacher pour se trouver en sécurité; mais si le fait de s'en détacher est lui-même constitutif d'un acte d'avarie commune, l'aventure maritime commune n'est pas pour autant interrompue.

Règle C

Seuls les pertes, dommages ou dépenses qui sont la conséquence directe de l'acte d'avarie commune seront admis en avarie commune.

Une admission en avarie commune ne pourra être en aucun cas prononcée pour des dommages, pertes ou dépenses encourus au titre de dommages à l'environnement ou consécutivement à des fuites ou rejets de substances polluantes émanant des propriétés engagées dans l'aventure maritime commune.

Chômage, différence de cours, et toute perte ou dommage subi ou dépense encourue par suite du retard, soit au cours du voyage, soit postérieurement, de même que toute perte indirecte quelconque, ne seront pas admis en avarie commune.

Règle D

Lorsque l'événement qui a donné lieu au sacrifice ou à la dépense aura été la conséquence d'une faute commise par l'une des parties engagées dans l'aventure, il n'y aura pas moins lieu à contribution, mais sans préjudice des recours ou des défenses pouvant concerner cette partie à raison d'une telle faute.

Règle E

La preuve qu'une perte ou une dépense doit effectivement être admise en avarie commune incombe à celui qui réclame cette admission.

Les parties qui entendent présenter réclamation au titre de l'avarie commune doivent notifier par écrit au dispacheur, dans les 12 mois de la date à laquelle a pris fin l'aventure maritime commune, la perte ou la dépense pour laquelle elles réclament contribution.

A défaut d'une telle notification, ou encore à défaut, pour l'une quelconque des parties, de fournir dans les 12 mois de la date à laquelle la demande lui en est faite, les justificatifs de sa réclamation ou les précisions relatives à la valeur d'un intérêt appelé à contribuer, le dispacheur sera autorisé à estimer le montant de l'admission ou de la valeur contributive sur la base des informations dont il dispose, son estimation ne pouvant être dès lors contestée qu'en cas d'erreur manifeste.

Règle F

Toute dépense supplementaire encourue en substitution d'une autre dépense qui aurait été admissible en avarie commune sera réputée elle-même avarie commune et admise à ce titre, sans égard à l'économie éventuellement réalisée par d'autres intérêts, mais seulement jusqu'à concurrence du montant de la dépense d'avarie commune ainsi évitée.

Règle G

Le règlement des avaries communes doit être établi, tant pour l'estimation des pertes que pour la contribution, sur la base des valeurs au moment et au lieu où se termine l'aventure.

Cette règle est sans influence sur la détermination du lieu où le règlement doit être établi.

Quand un navire se trouve en quelque port ou lieu que ce soit, dans des circonstances qui seraient susceptibles de donner lieu à une admission en avarie commune sur la base des dispositions des Règles X et XI, et quand la cargaison ou une partie de celle-ci est acheminée à destination par d'autres moyens, les droits et obligations relatifs à l'avarie commune demeureront —sous réserve que les intérêts cargaison en soient autant que faire se peut avisés—aussi proches que possible de ce qu'ils auraient été si, en l'absence d'un tel acheminement, l'aventure s'était poursuivie sur le navire d'origine, et ce aussi longtemps que cela apparaîtra justifié en l'état du contrat et de la loi applicables au transport.

La part des admissions en avarie commune incombant à la cargaison, en application du 3ème paragraphe de la présente règle, ne pourra excéder la dépense qu'auraient supportée les propriétaires de la cargaison si celle-ci avait été acheminée à leurs frais.

Règle I—Jet de Cargaison

Aucun jet de cargaison ne sera admis en avarie commune à moins que cette cargaison n'ait été transportée conformément aux usages reconnus du commerce.

Règle II—Perte ou dommage causé par sacrifices pour le salut commun

Sera admis en avarie commune la perte ou le dommage causé aux propriétés engagées dans l'aventure maritime commune ou en conséquence d'un sacrifice fait pour le salut commun, et par l'eau qui pénètre dans la cale par les écoutilles ouvertes ou par toute autre ouverture pratiquée en vue d'opérer un jet pour le salut commun.

Règle III—Extinction d'incendie à bord

Sera admis en avarie commune le dommage causé au navire et à la cargaison, ou à l'un d'eux, par l'eau ou autrement, y compris le dommage causé en submergeant ou en sabordant un navire en feu, en vue d'éteindre un incendie à bord; toutefois, aucune bonification ne sera faite pour dommage causé par la fumée quelle qu'en soit la cause ou par la chaleur de l'incendie.

Règle IV—Coupement de débris

La perte ou le dommage éprouvé en coupant des débris ou des parties du navire qui ont été enlevés ou sont effectivement perdus par accident, ne sera pas bonifié en avarie commune.

Règle V—Echouement volontaire

Quand un navire est intentionnellement mis à la côte pour le salut commun, qui'il dût ou non y être drossé, les pertes ou dommages en résultant et subis par les propriétés engagées dans l'aventure maritime commune, seront admis en avarie commune.

Règle VI—Rémunération d'assistance

(a) Les dépenses encourues par les parties engagées dans l'aventure et ayant le caractère d'assistance, soit en vertu d'un contrat soit autrement, seront admises en avarie commune, pourvu que les opérations d'assistance aient été effectuées dans le but de préserver du péril les propriétés engagées dans l'aventure maritime commune.

Les dépenses admises en avarie commune comprendront toute rémunération d'assistance dans la fixation de laquelle l'habileté et les efforts des assistants pour prévenir ou limiter les dommages à l'environnement, tels qui'ils sont énoncés à l'article 13.1(b) de la Convention Internationale de 1989 sur l'assistance, ont été pris en compte.

(b) L'indemnité spéciale payable à l'assistant par l'armateur sous l'empire de l'article 14 de ladite Convention, dans les conditions indiquées par le paragraphe 4 de cet article, ou de toute autre disposition de portée semblable ne sera pas admise en avarie commune.

Règle VII—Dommage aux machines et aux chaudières

Le dommage causé à toute machine et chaudière d'un navire échoué dans une position périlleuse par les efforts faits pour le renflouer, sera admis en avarie commune, lorsqu'il sera établi qu'il procède de l'intention réelle de renflouer le navire pour le salut commun au risque d'un tel dommage; mais lorsqu'un navire est à flot, aucune perte ou avarie causée par le fonctionnement de l'appareil de propulsion et des chaudières ne sera, en aucune circonstance, admise en avarie commune.

Règle VIII—Dépenses pour alléger un navire échoué et dommage résultant de cette mesure

Lorsqu'un navire est échoué et que la cargaison, ainsi que le combustible et les approvisionnements du navire, ou l'un d'eux, sont déchargés dans des circonstances telles que cette mesure constitue un acte d'avarie commune, les dépenses supplémentaires d'allègement, de location des allèges, et, le cas échéant, celles de réembarquement ainsi que toute perte ou dommage aux propriétés engagées dans l'aventure maritime commune en résultant, seront admises en avarie commune.

Règle IX—Cargaison, objets du navire et approvisionnements utilisés comme combustibles

La cargaison, les objets et approvisionnements du navire, ou l'un d'eux, qu'il a été nécessaire d'utiliser comme combustibles pour le salut commun en cas de péril, seront admis en avarie commune, mais lorsque le coût des objets et approvisionnements du navire est ainsi admis, l'avarie commune sera créditée du coût estimatif du combustible qui autrement aurait été consommé pour la poursuite du voyage.

Règle X—Dépenses au port de refuge, etc.

(a) Quand un navire sera entré dans un port ou lieu de refuge ou qu'il sera retourné à son port ou lieu de chargement par suite d'accident, de sacrifice ou d'autres circonstances extraordinaires qui auront rendu cette mesure nécessaire pour le salut commun, les dépenses encourues pour entrer dans ce port ou lieu seront admises en avarie commune; et, quand il en sera reparti avec tout ou partie de sa cargaison primitive, les dépenses correspondantes pour quitter ce port ou lieu qui auront été la conséquence de cette entrée ou de ce retour seront de même admises en avarie commune. Quand un navire est dans un port ou lieu de refuge quelconque et qu'il est nécessairement déplacé vers un autre port ou lieu parce que les réparations ne peuvent être effectuées au premier port ou lieu, les dispositions de cette Règle s'appliqueront au deuxième port ou lieu, comme s'il était un port ou lieu de refuge, et le coût de déplacement, y compris les réparations provisoires et le remorquage, sera admis en avarie commune.

Les dispositions de la Règle XI s'appliqueront à la prolongation du voyage occasionnée par ce déplacement.

(b) Les frais pour manutentionner à bord ou pour décharger la cargaison, le combustible ou les approvisionnements, soit à un port, soit à un lieu de chargement, d'escale ou de refuge, seront admis en avarie commune si la manutention ou le déchargement était nécessaire pour le salut commun ou pour permettre de réparer les avaries au navire causées par sacrifice ou par accident si ces réparations étaient nécessaires pour permettre de continuer le voyage en sécurité, excepté si les avaries au navire sont découvertes dans un port ou lieu de chargement ou d'escale sans qu'aucun accident ou autre circonstance extraordinaire en rapport avec ces avaries ne se soit produit au cours du voyage.

Les frais pour manutentionner à bord ou pour décharger la cargaison, le combustible ou les approvisionnements ne seront pas admis en avarie commune s'ils ont été encourus à seule fin de remédier à un désarrimage survenu au cours du voyage, à moins qu'une telle mesure soit nécessaire pour le salut commun.

(c) Toutes les fois que les frais de manutention ou de déchargement de la cargaison, du combustible ou des approvisionnements seront admissibles en avarie commune, les frais de leur magasinage, y compris l'assurance si elle a été raisonnablement conclue, de leur rechargement et de leur arrimage seront également admis en avarie commune. Les dispositions de la Règle XI s'appliqueront à la période supplémentaire d'immobilisation occasionnée par ce rechargement ou ce réarrimage.

Mais si le navire est condamné ou ne continue pas son voyage primitif, les frais de magasinage ne seront admis en avarie commune que jusqu'à la date de condamnation du navire ou de l'abandon du voyage ou bien jusqu'à la date de l'achèvement du déchargement de la cargaison en cas de condamnation du navire ou d'abandon du voyage avant cette date.

Règle XI—Salaires et entretien de l'équipage et autres dépenses pour se rendre au port de refuge, et dans ce port, etc.

(a) Les salaires et frais d'entretien du capitaine, des officiers et de l'équipage raisonnablement encourus ainsi que le combustible et les approvisionnements consommés durant la prolongation du voyage occasionnée par l'entrée du navire dans un port de refuge, ou par son retour au port ou lieu de chargement, doivent être admis en avarie commune quand les dépenses pour entrer en ce port ou lieu sont admissibles en avarie commune par application de la Règle X(a).

(b) Quand un navire sera entré ou aura été retenu dans un port ou lieu par suite d'un accident, sacrifice ou autres circonstances extraordinaires qui ont rendu cela nécessaire pour le salut commun, ou pour permettre la réparation des avaries causées au navire par sacrifice ou accident quand la réparation est nécessaire à la poursuite du voyage en sécurité, les salaires et frais d'entretien des capitaine, officiers et équipage raisonnablement encourus pendant la période supplémentaire d'immobilisation en ce port ou lieu jusqu'à ce que le navire soit ou aurait dû être mis en état de poursuivre son voyage, seront admis en avarie commune.

Le combustible et les approvisionnements consommés pendant la période supplémentaire d'immobilisation seront admis en avarie commune à l'exception du combustible et des approvisionnements consommés en effectuant des réparations non admissibles en avarie commune.

Les frais de port encourus durant cette période supplémentaire d'immobilisation seront de même admis en avarie commune, á l'exception des frais qui ne sont encourus qu'à raison de réparations non admissibles en avarie commune.

Cependant, si des avaries au navire sont découvertes dans un port ou lieu de chargement ou d'escale sans qu'aucun accident ou autre circonstance extraordinaire en rapport avec ces avaries se soit produit au cours du voyage, les salaires et frais d'entretien des capitaine, officiers et équipage, le combustible et les approvisionnements consommés ainsi que les frais de port encourus pendant l'immobilisation supplémentaire pour les besoins de la réparation des avaries ainsi découvertes, ne seront pas admis en avarie commune même si la réparation est nécessaire à la poursuite du voyage en sécurité.

Quand le navire est condamné ou ne poursuit pas son voyage primitif, les salaires et frais d'entretien des capitaine, officiers et équipage et le combustible et les approvisionnements consommés et les frais de port ne seront admis en avarie commune que jusqu'à la date de la condamnation du navire ou de l'abandon du voyage ou jusqu'à la date d'achèvement du déchargement de la cargaison en cas de condamnation du navire ou d'abandon du voyage avant cette date.

(c) Pour l'application de la présente règle ainsi que des autres règles, les salaires comprennent les paiements faits aux capitaine, officiers et équipage ou à leur profit, que ces paiements soient imposés aux armateurs par la loi ou qu'ils résultent des conditions et clauses des contrats de travail.

(d) Le coût des mesures prises pour prévenir ou minimiser un dommage à l'environnement sera admis en avarie commune lorsqu'il aura été encouru dans l'une ou toutes les situations suivantes:

(i) lorsqu'il est engagé dans le cadre d'une opération conduite pour le salut commun qui, si elle avait été engageé par une partie extérieure à l'aventure maritime commune, lui aurait donné droit à une indemnité d'assistance;

(ii) lorsqu'il est une condition de l'entrée ou de la sortie d'un port ou d'un lieu quelconque dans les situations prévues à la Règle X (a);

(iii) lorsqu'il est une condition de séjour dans un port ou un lieu quelconque dans les situations prévues à la Règle XI (b), pourvu qu'en cas de fuite ou de rejet effectif de substances polluantes, le coût de toutes mesures supplémentaires prises pour prévenir ou minimiser la pollution ou le dommage à l'environnement ne soit pas admis en avarie commune;

(iv) lorsqu'il a un lien nécessaire avec le déchargement, le stockage ou le rechargement de la cargaison, chaque fois que le coût de ces opérations est admissible en avarie commune.

Règle XII—Dommage causé à la cargaison en la déchargeant, etc.

Le dommage ou la perte subis par la cargaison, le combustible ou les approvisionnements dans les opérations de manutention, déchargement, emmagasinage, rechargement et arrimage, seront admis en avarie commune lorsque le coût respectif de ces opérations sera admis en avarie commune et dans ce cas seulement.

Règle XIII—Déduction du coût des réparations

Les réparations à admettre en avarie commune ne seront pas sujettes à des déductions pour différence du "neuf au vieux" quand du vieux matériel sera, en totalité ou en partie, remplacé par du neuf, à moins que le navire ait plus de quinze ans; en pareil cas la déduction sera de un tiers.

Les déductions seront fixées d'après l'âge du navire depuis le 31 décembre de l'année d'achèvement de la construction jusqu'à la date de l'acte d'avarie commune, excepté pour les isolants, canots de sauvetage et similaires, appareils et équipements de communications et de navigation, machines et chaudières, pour lesquels les déductions seront fixées d'après l'âge des différentes parties auxquelles elles s'appliquent.

Les déductions seront effectuées seulement sur le coût du matériel nouveau ou de ses parties au moment où il sera usiné et prêt à être mis en place dans le navire.

Aucune déduction ne sera faite sur les approvisionnements, matières consommables, ancres et chaînes.

Les frais de cale sèche, de slip et de déplacement du navire seront admis en entier.

Les frais de nettoyage, de peinture ou d'enduit de la coque ne seront pas admis en avarie commune à moins que la coque ait été peinte ou enduite dans les douze mois qui ont précédé la date de l'acte d'avarie commune; en pareil cas ces frais seront admis pour moitié.

Règle XIV—Réparations provisoires

Lorsque des réparations provisoires sont effectuées à un navire, dans un port de chargement, d'escale ou de refuge, pour le salut commun ou pour des avaries causées par un sacrifice d'avarie commune, le coût de ces réparations sera bonifié en avarie commune.

Lorsque des réparations provisoires d'un dommage fortuit sont effectuées afin de permettre l'achèvement du voyage, le coût de ces réparations sera admis en avarie commune, sans égard à l'économie éventuellement réalisée par d'autres intérêts, mais seulement jusqu'à concurrence de l'économie sur les dépenses qui auraient été encourues et admises en avarie commune, si ces réparations n'avaient pas été effectuées en ce lieu.

Aucune déduction pour différence du "neuf au vieux" ne sera faite du coût des réparations provisoires admissibles en avarie commune.

Règle XV—Perte de fret

La perte de fret résultant d'une perte ou d'un dommage subi par la cargaison sera admise en avarie commune, tant si elle est causée par un acte d'avarie commune que si cette perte ou ce dommage est ainsi admis.

Devront être déduites du montant du fret brut perdu les dépenses que le propriétaire de ce fait aurait encourues pour le gagner, mais qu'il n'a pas exposées par suite du sacrifice.

Règle XVI—Valeur à admettre pour la cargaison perdue ou avariée par sacrifice

Le montant à admettre en avarie commune pour dommage ou perte de cargaison sacrifiée sera le montant de la perte éprouvée de ce fait en prenant pour base le prix au moment du déchargement vérifié d'après la facture commerciale remise au réceptionnaire ou, à défaut d'une telle facture, d'après la valeur embarquée. Le prix au moment du déchargement inclura le coût de l'assurance et le fret, sauf si ce fret n'est pas au risque de la cargaison.

Quand une marchandise ainsi avariée est vendue et que le montant du dommage n'a pas été autrement convenu, la perte à admettre en avarie commune sera la différence entre le produit net de la vente et la valeur nette à l'état sain, telle qu'elle est calculée dans le premier paragraphe de cette Règle.

Règle XVII—Valeurs contributives

La contribution à l'avarie commune sera établie sur les valeurs nettes réelles des propriétés à la fin du voyage sauf que la valeur de la cargaison sera le prix au moment du déchargement vérifié d'après la facture commerciale remise au réceptionnaire ou, à défaut d'une telle facture, d'après la valeur embarquée. La valeur de la cargaison comprendra le coût de l'assurance et le fret sauf si ce fret n'est pas au risque de la cargaison, et sous déduction des pertes ou avaries subies par la cargaison avant ou pendant le déchargement. La valeur du navire sera estimée sans tenir compte de la plus ou moins value résultant de l'affrètement coque nue ou à temps sous lequel il peut se trouver.

A ces valeurs sera ajouté le montant admis en avarie commune des propriétés sacrifiées, s'il n'y est pas déjà compris. Du fret et du prix de passage en risque seront déduits les frais et les gages de l'équipage qui n'auraient pas été encourus pour gagner le fret si le navire et la cargaison s'étaient totalement perdus au moment de l'acte d'avarie commune et qui n'ont pas été admis en avarie commune.

De la valeur des propriétés seront également déduits tous les frais supplémentaires y relatifs, postérieurs à l'événement qui donne ouverture à l'avarie commune, à l'exception des frais qui auront été admis en avarie commune ou qui incombent au navire en vertu d'une décision allouant l'indemnité spéciale prévue à l'article 14 de la Convention Internationale de 1989 sur l'assistance ou de toute autre disposition de portée semblable.

Dans les situations prévues au troisième paragraphe de la Règle G, la cargaison et les autres propriètès contribueront sur la base de leur valeur à leur destination d'origine à moin qu'elles n'aient été vendues ou qu'il n'en ait été autrement disposé avant l'arrivée à destination, et le navire contribuera sur sa valeur nette réelle à la fin du déchargement de la cargaison.

Quand une cargaison est vendue en cours de voyage, elle contribue sur le produit net de vente augmenté du montant admis en avarie commune.

Le courrier, les bagages des passagers, les effets personnels et les véhicles à moteur privés et accompagnés ne contribueront pas à l'avarie commune.

Règle XVIII—Avaries au navire

Le montant à admettre en avarie commune pour dommage ou perte subis par le navire, ses machines et/ou ses apparaux, du fait d'un acte d'avarie commune, sera le suivant:

(a) en cas de réparation ou de remplacement, le coût réel et raisonnable de la réparation ou du remplacement du dommage ou de la perte sous réserve des déductions à opérer en vertu de la Règle XIII;

(b) dans le cas contraire, la dépréciation raisonnable résultant d'un tel dommage ou d'une telle perte jusqu'à concurrence du coût estimatif des réparations.

Mais lorsqu'il y a perte totale ou que le coût des réparations du dommage dépasserait la valeur du navire une fois réparé, le montant à admettre en avarie commune sera la différence entre la valeur estimative du navire à l'état sain sous déduction du coût estimatif des réparations du dommage n'ayant pas le caractère d'avarie commune, et la valeur du navire en son état d'avarie, cette valeur pouvant être déterminée par le produit net de vente, le cas échéant.

Règle XIX—Marchandises non déclarées ou faussement déclarées

La perte ou le dommage causé aux marchandises chargées à l'insu de l'armateur ou de son agent, ou à celles qui ont fait l'objet d'une désignation volontairement fausse au moment de l'embarquement, ne sera pas admis en avarie commune, mais ces marchandises resteront tenues de contribuer si elle sont sauvées.

La perte ou le dommage causé aux marchandises qui ont été faussement déclarées à l'embarquement pour une valeur moindre que leur valeur réelle sera admis sur la base de la valeur déclarée, mais ces marchandises devront contribuer sur leur valeur réelle.

Règle XX—Avance de fonds

Une commission de deux pour cent sur les débours d'avarie commune autres que les salaires et frais d'entretien du capitaine, des officiers et de l'équipage et le combustible et les approvisionnements qui n'ont pas été remplacés durant le voyage, sera admise en avarie commune.

La perte financière subie par les propriétaires des marchandises vendues pour obtainer les fonds nécessaires en vue de faire face aux dépenses d'avarie commune sera admise en avarie commune.

Les frais d'assurance de l'argent avancé pour payer les dépenses d'avarie commune seront également admis en avarie commune.

Règle XXI—Intérêts sur les pertes admises en avarie commune

Un intérêt sera alloué sur les dépenses, sacrifices et bonifications classées en avarie commune, au taux de sept pour cent par an, jusqu'à l'expiration d'un délai de trois mois à compter de la date du dépôt du règlement d'avarie commune, en tenant dûment compte des paiements provisionnels effectués par ceux qui sont appelés à contribuer, ou prélevés sur le fonds des dépôts d'avarie commune.

Règle XXII—Traitement des dépôts en espèces

Lorsque des dépôts en espèces auront été encaissés en garantie de la contribution de la cargaison à l'avarie commune, aux frais de sauvetage ou frais spéciaux, ces dépôts devront être versés, sans aucun délai, à un compte joint spécial aux noms d'un représentant désigné pour l'armateur et d'un représentant désigné pour les déposants dans une banque agréée par eux deux. La somme ainsi déposée augmentée, s'il y a lieu, des intérêts, sera conservée à titre de garantie pour le paiement aux ayants droit en raison de l'avarie commune, des frais de sauvetage ou des frais spéciaux payables par la cargaison et en vue desquels les dépôts ont été effectués. Des paiements en acompte ou des remboursements de dépôts peuvent être faits avec l'autorisation écrite du dispacheur. Ces dépôts, paiements ou remboursements, seront effectués sans préjudice des obligations définitives des parties.

APPENDIX 4

RULES OF PRACTICE OF THE ASSOCIATION OF AVERAGE ADJUSTERS RELATING TO GENERAL AVERAGE AND THE YORK-ANTWERP RULES

EXTRACT FROM THE INTRODUCTION TO THE RULES OF PRACTICE

In the middle of the 19th century, when average adjusting as a separate profession was in its infancy, there was very little in the way of established law to guide the practising adjuster, and consequently many points of practice had to be decided in accordance with custom. Some of these customs were subsequently ratified by legal decision, but others were disapproved, and it became evident that unless steps were taken to establish a reasonable measure of uniformity among average adjusters, the profession would fall into disrepute.

It was to remedy this situation that the Association of Average Adjusters was founded in 1869, with the object, among others, of "the promotion of correct principles in the adjustment of Averages and uniformity of practice amongst average adjusters".

After the formation of the Association, one of its first tasks was to consider the areas of divergence in practice, and decide how the various so-called "customs" could be brought together into a uniform, if not universal, practice. This aim was largely achieved by the Association in the first fifteen years of its existence, by a two-fold approach:

(a) By the collection and refinement of the Customs of Lloyd's. This task was undertaken by a Special Committee, which reported to the Association in 1876. In the preamble to the Customs it was stated: "Nothing can be called a Custom of Lloyd's which is determined by a decision of the superior Courts; for whatever is thus sanctioned rests on a ground surer than custom. A Custom of Lloyd's then must relate to a point on which the law is doubtful, or not yet defined, but as to which, for practical convenience, it is necessary that there should be some uniform rule."

(b) By the adoption of Rules of Practice, relating to the adjustment of averages and the duties of adjusters in connection therewith. In the early days of the Association it was hotly debated whether these Rules of Practice should bind Members or not, and in the event it was decided that they would not be binding, although, naturally, they would carry considerable authority. Even now, if an average adjuster draws up a statement which is at variance with a Rule of Practice, he must place a note in his adjustment referring to the Rule of Practice and stating why he differs from it.

Since 1890, when the Customs of Lloyd's were reviewed and assimilated into the Rules of Practice, various new Rules and amendments to existing Rules have been adopted from time to time in order to regulate the practice of average adjusters in areas where the law is silent.

The Rules of Practice are divided into six sections according to the subjects dealt with. The Rules relating to General Average appear in two sections:

Section B
Rules which affect the adjustment of general average or the duties of adjusters in all cases, whatever may be the basis of adjustment.

Section F
Rules relating to the adjustment of general average under English law and practice.

The Rules contained in section F may be considered by some readers to be of little more than historical interest, in view of the fact that the vast majority of general averages are now adjusted in accordance with York-Antwerp Rules, but these Rules of Practice have been retained not only to deal with the minority of cases where the adjustment is prepared in accordance with English law and practice, but also to demonstrate the early steps taken in the movement towards uniformity.

SECTION B—GENERAL AVERAGE

Rules of General Application

Note: In this edition, the Rules relating to the adjustment of general average under English law and practice have been transferred to Section F.

B1 Basis of Adjustment

That in any adjustment of general average not made in accordance with British law it shall be prefaced on what principle or according to what law the adjustment has been made, and the reason for so adjusting the claim shall be set forth.

In all cases the adjuster shall give particulars in a prominent position in the average statement of the clause or clauses contained in the charter-party and/or bills of lading with reference to the adjustment of general average.

B2–B8 inclusive

Transferred to section F.

B9 Claims Arising Out of Deficiency of Fuel

That in adjusting general average arising out of deficiency of fuel, the facts on which the general average is based shall be set forth in the adjustment, including the material dates and distances, and particulars of fuel supplies and consumption.

B10–B23 inclusive

Transferred to section F.

B24 Contributory Value of Ship

That in any adjustment of general average there shall be set forth the certificate on which the contributory value of the ship is based or, if there be no such certificate, the information adopted in lieu thereof, and any amount made good shall be specified.

B25 Contributory Value of Freight

That in any adjustment of general average there shall be set forth the amount of the gross freight and the freight advanced, if any; also the charges and wages deducted and any amount made good.

The first paragraph of Rule B25, dealing with the basis of adjustment under English law and practice, has been transferred to Section F and re-numbered F22.

B26 Vessel in Ballast and under Charter: Contributing Interests

For the purpose of ascertaining the liability of Underwriters on British policies of insurance, the following provisions shall apply:—

When a vessel is proceeding in ballast to load under a voyage charter entered into by the shipowner before the general average act, the interests contributing to the general average shall be the vessel, such items of stores and equipment as belong to parties other than the owners of the vessel (e.g. bunkers, wireless installation and navigational instruments) and the freight earned under the voyage charter computed in the usual way after deduction of contingent expenses subsequent to the general average act. Failing a prior termination of the adventure, the place where the adventure shall be deemed to end and at which the values for contribution to general average shall be calculated is the final port of discharge of the cargo carried under the charter but in the event of the prior loss of the vessel and freight, or either of them, the general average shall attach to any surviving interest or interests including freight advanced at the loading port deducting therefrom contingent expenses subsequent to the general average act.

When a vessel is proceeding in ballast under a time charter alone or a time charter and a voyage charter entered into by the time charterer, the general average shall attach to the vessel and such items of stores and equipment as are indicated above. Failing a prior termination of the adventure, the adventure shall be deemed to end and the values for contribution to general average calculated at the first loading port upon the commencement of loading cargo.

When the charter to which the shipowner is a party provides for York-Antwerp Rules, the general average shall be adjusted in accordance with those Rules and British law and practice and without regard to the law and practice of any foreign port at which the adventure may terminate; and in the interpretation of Rule XI it shall be immaterial whether the extra period of detention takes place at a port of loading, call or refuge, provided that the detention is in consequence of accident, sacrifice or other extraordinary circumstance occurring whilst the vessel is in ballast.

In practice neither time charter hire, as such, nor time charterer's voyage freight shall contribute to general average.

The earliest Rule of Practice dealing with this subject was accepted in 1896, confirmed in 1897 and rescinded in 1926, when after reference to a Special Committee it was replaced by a new Rule, which was in its turn referred to a Special Committee in 1944 and rescinded in 1945–46. The text of the original Rule is printed in the report for 1897, pp. 34–35 and the subsequent Rule in the report for November 1926, p. 9.

B27 Ulterior Chartered Freight: Contribution to General Average

That when at the time of a general average act the vessel has on board cargo shipped under charter-party or bills of lading, and is also under a separate charter to load another cargo after the cargo then in course of carriage has been discharged, the ulterior chartered freight shall not contribute to the general average.

B28 Deductions from Freight at Charterer's Risk

That freight at the risk of the charterer shall be subject to no deduction for wages and charges, except in the case of charters in which the wages or charges are payable by the charterer, in which case such freight shall be governed by the same rule as freight at the risk of the shipowner.

B29 Forwarding Charges on Advanced Freight

That in case of wreck, the cargo being forwarded to its destination, the charterer, who has paid a lump sum on account of freight, which is not to be returned in the event of the vessel being lost, shall not be liable for any portion of the forwarding freight and charges, when the same are less than the balance of freight payable to the shipowner at the port of destination under the original charter-party.

B30 Sacrifice for the Common Safety: Direct Liability of Underwriters

That in case of general average sacrifice there is, under ordinary policies of insurance, a direct liability of an underwriter on ship for loss of or damage to ship's materials, and of an underwriter on goods or freight, for loss of or damage to goods or loss of freight so sacrificed as a general average loss; that such loss not being particular average is not taken into account in computing the memorandum percentages, and that the direct liability of an underwriter for such loss is consequently unaffected by the memorandum or any other warranty respecting particular average.

An earlier Rule of Practice dealing with this subject was accepted in 1874, confirmed in 1875 and rescinded in 1889. The text of this earlier Rule is printed in the report for 1875, p. 18.

B31 Sacrifice of Ship's Stores: Direct Liability of Underwriters

That underwriters insuring ship's stores, bunker coal or fuel, destroyed or used as part of a general average operation, shall only be liable for those articles as a direct claim on the policy when they formed part of the property at risk at the time of the peril giving rise to the general average act.

B32 Enforcement of General Average Lien by Shipowners

That in all cases where general average damage to ship is claimed direct from the underwriters on that interest, the average adjusters shall ascertain whether the shipowners have taken the necessary steps to enforce their lien for general average on the cargo, and shall insert in the average statement a note giving the result of their enquiries.

B33 Underwriter's Liability

If the ship or cargo be insured for more than its contributory value, the underwriter pays what is assessed on the contributory value. But where insured for less than the contributory value, the underwriter pays on the insured value; and when there has been a particular average for damage which forms a deduction from the contributory value of the ship that must be deducted from the insured value to find upon what the underwriter contributes.

This rule does not apply to foreign adjustments, when the basis of contribution is something other than the net value of the thing insured.

That in practice, in applying the above rule for the purpose of ascertaining the liability of underwriters for contribution to general average and salvage charges, deduction shall be made from the insured value of all losses and charges for which underwriters are liable and which have been deducted in arriving at the contributory value.

In adjusting the liability of underwriters on freight for general average contribution and salvage charges, effect shall be given to Section 73 of the Marine Insurance Act, 1906, by comparing the gross and not the net amount of freight at risk with the insured value in the case of a valued policy or the insurable value in the case of an unvalued policy.

B34 The Duty of Adjusters in Cases involving Refunds of General Average Deposits or Apportionment of Salvage, Collision Recoveries, or other Funds

That in cases of general average where deposits have been collected and it is likely that repayments will have to be made, measures be taken by the adjuster to ascertain the names of underwriters who have reimbursed their assured in respect of such deposits; that the names of any such underwriters be set forth in the adjustment as claimants of refund, if any, to which they are apparently entitled; and that on completion of the adjustment, notice be sent to all underwriters whose names are so set forth as to any refund of which they appear as claimants and as to the steps to be taken in order to obtain payment of the same.

That in cases where the names of any underwriters are not to be ascertained on completion of the adjustment, notice be sent to the Secretary of Lloyd's, to the Institute of London Underwriters, to the Liverpool Underwriters' Association, and to the Association of Underwriters of Glasgow, notifying such interests as have not been appropriated to underwriters.

And that in cases of apportionment of salvage or other funds for distribution, similar measures be taken by the adjuster to safeguard the interests of any underwriters who may be entitled to benefit under the apportionment.

B35 Memorandum to Statements showing Refunds in respect of General Average Deposits

That the following memorandum shall appear at the end of statements which show refunds to be due in respect of General Average Deposits, *viz:*—

> Memorandum—Refunds of general average deposits shown in this statement should only be paid on production of the original deposit receipts.

B36 Interest on Deposits

That, unless otherwise expressly provided, the interest accrued on deposits on account of salvage and/or general average and/or particular and/or other charges, or on the balance of such deposits after payments on account, if any, have been made, shall be credited to the depositor or those to whom his rights in respect of the deposits have been transferred.

B37 Apportionment of Interest on Amounts Made Good

That in practice (in the absence of express agreement between the parties concerned) interest allowed on amounts made good shall be apportioned between assured and underwriters, taking into account the sums paid by underwriters and the dates when such payments were made, notwithstanding that by the addition of interest the underwriter may receive a larger sum than he has paid.

SECTION C—YORK-ANTWERP RULES

C1 Salvage Services rendered under an Agreement

Expenses for salvage services rendered by or accepted under agreement shall in practice be treated as general average provided that such expenses were incurred for the common safety within the meaning of Rule "A" of the York-Antwerp Rules, 1924 or York-Antwerp Rules 1950.

An earlier Rule of Practice dealing with this subject was accepted in 1927, confirmed in 1928, and rescinded in 1942–43. The text of the earlier Rule is printed in the report for 1928, p. 32.

C2 Commission Allowed under York-Antwerp Rules

That the commission of 2 per cent allowed on general average disbursements under Rule XXI of York-Antwerp Rules 1924 and Rule XX of York-Antwerp Rules 1950 or 1974, shall be credited in full to the party who has authorised the expenditure and is liable for payment, except that where the funds for payment are provided in the first instance in whole or in part from the deposit funds, or by other parties to the adventure, or by underwriters, the commission on such advances shall be credited to the deposit funds or to the parties or underwriters providing the funds for payment.

C3 York-Antwerp Rules, 1924. Rules X(a) and XX

That, in practice, where a vessel is at any port or place in circumstances in which the wages and maintenance of crew during detention there for the purpose of repairs necessary for the safe prosecution of the voyage would be admissible in general average under Rule XI of the York-Antwerp Rules, 1924, and the vessel is necessarily removed thence to another port or place because such repairs cannot be effected at the first port or place, the provisions of Rule X(a) shall be applied to the second port or place as if it were a port or place of refuge within that Rule and the provisions of Rule XX shall be applied to the prolongation of the voyage occasioned by such removal.

C4 York-Antwerp Rules 1950 and 1974. Rule X(a)

That in practice, in applying the second paragraph of Rule X(a), a vessel shall be deemed to be at a port or place of refuge when she is at any port or place in circumstances in which the wages and maintenance of the Master, Officers and crew incurred during any extra period of detention there would be admissible in General Average under the provisions of Rule XI.

SECTION F—GENERAL AVERAGE ADJUSTMENT UNDER ENGLISH LAW AND PRACTICE

F1 Deckload Jettison

The jettison of a deckload carried according to the usage of trade and not in violation of the contracts of affreightment is general average.

There is an exception to this rule in the case of cargoes of cotton, tallow, acids and some other goods.

F2 Damage by Water used to Extinguish Fire

That damage done by water poured down a ship's hold to extinguish a fire be treated as general average.

F3 Extinguishing Fire on Shipboard

Damage done to a ship and cargo, or either of them, by water or otherwise, including damage by beaching or scuttling a burning ship, in extinguishing a fire on board the ship, shall be made good as general average; except that no compensation shall be made for damage by smoke or heat however caused.

The earliest Rule of Practice dealing with this subject entitled "Damage caused by water thrown upon burning goods" was accepted in 1874, confirmed in 1875, and rescinded in 1968–69:
It was then replaced by a Rule under the present title, which was in its turn rescinded in 1974–75. The text of the original Rule is printed in the report for 1875, p. 22 and the subsequent Rule in the report for 1968, pp. 18–19.

F4 Voluntary Stranding

When a ship is intentionally run on shore and the circumstances are such that if that course were not adopted she would inevitably drive on shore or on rocks, no loss or damage caused to the ship, cargo and freight or any of them by such intentional running on shore shall be made good as general average, but loss or damage incurred in refloating such a ship shall be allowed as general average.

In all other cases where a ship is intentionally run on shore for the common safety, the consequent loss or damage shall be allowed as general average.

The original Custom of Lloyd's under this heading, amended in 1876, was rescinded in 1968–69. The text of the Custom is printed, as confirmed as a Rule of Practice, in the report for 1891, p. 69.

F5 Expenses lightening a Ship when Ashore

When a ship is ashore in a position of peril and, in order to float her, cargo is put into lighters, and is then at once re-shipped, the whole cost of lightening, including lighter hire and re-shipping, is general average.

F6 Sails set to force a Ship off the Ground

Sails damaged by being set, or kept set, to force a ship off the ground or to drive her higher up the ground for the common safety, are general average.

F7 Stranded Vessels: Damage to Engines in getting off

That damage caused to machinery and boilers of a stranded vessel, in endeavouring to refloat for the common safety, when the interests are in peril, be allowed in general average.

F8 Resort to Port of Refuge for General Average Repairs: Treatment of the Charges incurred

That when a ship puts into a port of refuge in consequence of damage which is itself the subject of general average, and sails thence with her original cargo, or a part of it, the outward as well as the inward port charges shall be treated as general average; and when cargo is discharged for the purpose of repairing such damage, the warehouse rent and reloading of the same shall, as well as the discharge, be treated as general average. (See *Attwood* v. *Sellar.*)

F9 Resort to Port of Refuge on Account of Particular Average Repairs: Treatment of the Charges incurred

That when a ship puts into a port of refuge in consequence of damage which is itself the subject of particular average (or not of general average) and when the cargo has been discharged in consequence of such damage, the inward port charges and the cost of discharging the cargo shall be general average, the warehouse rent of cargo shall be a particular charge on cargo, and the cost of reloading and outward port charges shall be a particular charge on freight. (See *Svendsen* v. *Wallace.*)

F10 Treatment of Costs of Storage and Reloading at Port of Refuge

That when the cargo is discharged for the purpose of repairing, re-conditioning, or diminishing damage to ship or cargo which is itself the subject of general average, the cost of storage on it and of reloading it shall be treated as general average, equally with the cost of discharging it.

F11 Insurance on Cargo Discharged under Average

That in practice, where the cost of insurance has been reasonably incurred by the shipowner, or his agents, on cargo discharged under average, such cost shall be treated as part of the cost of storage.

F12 Expenses at a Port of Refuge

When a ship puts into a port of refuge on account of accident and not in consequence of damage which is itself the subject of general average, then on the assumption that the ship was seaworthy at the commencement of the voyage, the Custom of Lloyd's is as follows:

(a) All cost of towage, pilotage, harbour dues, and other extraordinary expenses incurred in order to bring the ship and cargo into a place of safety, are general average. Under the term "extraordinary expenses" are not included wages or victuals of crew, coals, or engine stores, or demurrage.

(b) The cost of discharging the cargo, whether for the common safety, or to repair the ship, together with the cost of conveying it to the warehouse, is general average.

The cost of discharging the cargo on account of damage to it resulting from its own *vice propre*, is chargeable to the owners of the cargo.

(c) The warehouse rent, or other expenses which take the place of warehouse rent, of the cargo when so discharged, is, except as under, a special charge on the cargo.

(d) The cost of reloading the cargo, and the outward port charges incurred through leaving the port of refuge, are, when the discharge of cargo falls in general average, a special charge on freight.

(e) The expenses referred to in clause (d) are charged to the party who runs the risk of freight—that is, wholly to the charterer—if the whole freight has been prepaid; and, if part only, then in the proportion which the part prepaid bears to the whole freight.

(f) When the cargo, instead of being sent ashore, is placed on board hulk or lighters during the ship's stay in port, the hulk-hire is divided between general average, cargo, and freight, in such proportions as may place the several contributing interests in nearly the same relative positions as if the cargo has been landed and stored.

F13 Treatment of Costs of Extraordinary Discharge

That no distinction be drawn in practice between discharging cargo for the common safety of ship and cargo, and discharging it for the purpose of effecting at an intermediate port or ports of refuge repairs necessary for the prosecution of the voyage.

F14 Towage from a Port of Refuge

That if a ship be in a port of refuge at which it is practicable to repair her, and if, in order to save expense, she be towed thence to some other port, then the extra cost of such towage shall be divided in proportion to the saving of expense thereby occasioned to the several parties to the adventure.

F15 Cargo Forwarded from a Port of Refuge

That if a ship be in a port of refuge at which it is practicable to repair her so as to enable her to carry on the whole cargo, but, in order to save expense, the cargo, or a portion of it, be transhipped by another vessel, or otherwise forwarded, then the cost of such transhipment (up to the amount of expense saved) shall be divided in proportion to the saving of expense thereby occasioned to the several parties to the adventure.

F16 Cargo Sold at a Port of Refuge

That if a ship be in a port of refuge at which it is practicable to repair her so as to enable her to carry on the whole cargo, or such portion of it as is fit to be carried on, but, in order to save expense, the cargo, or a portion of it, be, with the consent of the owners of such cargo, sold at the port of refuge, then the loss by sale including loss of freight on cargo so sold (up to the amount of expense saved) shall be divided in proportion to the saving of expense thereby occasioned to the several parties to the adventure; provided always that the amount so divided shall in no case exceed the cost of transhipment and/or forwarding referred to in the preceding rule of the Association.

F17 Interpretation of the Rule respecting Substituted Expenses

That for the purpose of avoiding any misrepresentation of the resolution relating to the apportionment of substituted expenses, it is declared that the saving of expense therein mentioned is limited to a saving or reduction of the actual outlay, including the crew's wages and provisions, if any, which would have been incurred at the port of refuge, if the vessel has been repaired there, and does not include supposed losses or expenses, such as interest, loss of market, demurrage, or assumed damage by discharging.

F18 Treatment of Damage to Cargo caused by Discharge, Storing, and Reloading

That damage necessarily done to cargo by discharging, storing, and reloading it, be treated as general average when, and only when the cost of those measures respectively is so treated.

A Custom of Lloyd's concerning cargo discharged at a port of refuge was rescinded in 1890–91, and an earlier Rule of Practice accepted in 1883 and confirmed in 1884 was rescinded in 1968–69. The text of the earlier Rule is printed in the report for 1884, p. 37.

F19 Deductions from Cost of Repairs in adjusting General Average

Repairs to be allowed in general average shall not be subject to deductions in respect of "new for old" where old materials or parts are replaced by new unless the ship is over fifteen years old in which case there shall be a deduction of one third. The deductions shall be regulated by the age of the ship from the 31st December of the year of completion of construction to the date of the general average act, except for insulation, life and similar boats, communications and navigational apparatus and equipment, machinery and boilers for which the deductions shall be regulated by the age of the particular parts to which they apply.

The deductions shall be made only from the cost of the new material or parts when finished and ready to be installed in the ship.

No deduction shall be made in respect of provisions, stores, anchors and chain cables.

Drydock and slipway dues and costs of shifting the ship shall be allowed in full.

The costs of cleaning, painting or coating of bottom shall not be allowed in general average unless the bottom has been painted or coated within the twelve months preceding the date of the general average act in which case one half of such costs shall be allowed.

F20 Freight Sacrificed: Amount to be made Good in General Average

That the loss of freight to be made good in general average shall be ascertained by deducting from the amount of gross freight lost the charges which the owner thereof would have incurred to earn such freight, but has, in consequence of the sacrifice, not incurred.

F21 Basis of Contribution to General Average

When property saved by a general average act is injured or destroyed by subsequent accident, the contributing value of that property to a general average which is less than the total contributing value, shall, when it does not reach the port of destination, be its actual net proceeds; when it does it shall be its actual net value at the port of destination on its delivery there; and in all cases any values allowed in general average shall be added to and form part of the contributing value as above.

The above rule shall not apply to adjustments made before the adventure has terminated.

F22 Contributory Value of Freight

That freight at the risk of the shipowner shall contribute to general average upon its gross amount, deducting such charges and crew's wages as would not have been incurred in earning the freight had the ship and cargo been totally lost at the date of the general average act and have not been allowed as general average.

APPENDIX 5

LLOYD'S STANDARD FORM OF SALVAGE AGREEMENT — LOF 1995

LOF 1995

LLOYD'S

NOTES

1. Insert name of person signing on behalf of Owners of property to be salved. The Master should sign wherever possible.

2. The Contractor's name should always be inserted in line 4 and whenever the Agreement is signed by the Master of the Salving vessel or other person on behalf of the Contractor the name of the Master or other person must also be inserted in line 4 before the words "for and on behalf of". The words "for and on behalf of" should be deleted where a Contractor signs personally.

3. Insert place if agreed in clause 1(a)(i) and currency if agreed in clause 1(e).

STANDARD FORM OF

SALVAGE AGREEMENT

(APPROVED AND PUBLISHED BY THE COUNCIL OF LLOYD'S)

NO CURE - NO PAY

On board the...

Dated....................................

+ See Note 1 above

IT IS HEREBY AGREED between Captain+..
for and on behalf of the Owners of the "..." her cargo freight bunkers stores and any other property thereon (hereinafter collectively called "the Owners") and...for and on behalf of ....

** See Note 2 above*

....(hereinafter called "the Contractor"*) that:-

1. (a) The Contractor shall use his best endeavours:-

(i) to salve the "..."and/or her cargo freight bunkers stores and any other property thereon and take them to #.. or to such other place as may hereafter be agreed either place to be deemed a place of safety or if no such place is named or agreed to a place of safety and

 # See Note 3 above

(ii) while performing the salvage services to prevent or minimize damage to the environment.

(b) Subject to the statutory provisions relating to special compensation the services shall be rendered and accepted as salvage services upon the principle of "no cure - no pay."

(c) The Contractor's remuneration shall be fixed by Arbitration in London in the manner hereinafter prescribed and any other difference arising out of this Agreement or the operations thereunder shall be referred to Arbitration in the same way.

(d) In the event of the services referred to in this Agreement or any part of such services having been already rendered at the date of this Agreement by the Contractor to the said vessel and/or her cargo freight bunkers stores and any other property thereon the provisions of this Agreement shall apply to such services.

(e) The security to be provided to the Council of Lloyd's (hereinafter called "the Council") the Salved Value(s) the Award and/or any Interim Award(s) and/or any Award on Appeal shall be in #.. currency.

 # See Note 3 above

(f) If clause 1(e) is not completed then the security to be provided and the Salved Value(s) the Award and/or Interim Award(s) and/or Award on Appeal shall be in Pounds Sterling.

(g) This Agreement and Arbitration thereunder shall except as otherwise expressly provided be governed by the law of England, including the English law of salvage.

15.1.08
3.12.24
13.10.26
12.4.50
10.6.53
20.12.67
23.2.72
21.5.80
5.9.90
1.1.95

PROVISIONS AS TO THE SERVICES

2. *Definitions*: In this Agreement any reference to "Convention" is a reference to the International Convention on Salvage 1989 as incorporated in the Merchant Shipping (Salvage and Pollution) Act 1994 (and any amendment thereto). The terms "Contractor" and "services"/"salvage services" in this Agreement shall have the same meanings as the terms "salvor(s)" and "salvage operation(s)" in the Convention.

3. *Owners Cooperation*: The Owners their Servants and Agents shall co-operate fully with the Contractor in and about the salvage including obtaining entry to the place named or the place of safety as defined in clause 1. The Contractor may make reasonable use of the vessel's machinery gear equipment anchors chains stores and other appurtenances during and for the purpose of the salvage services free of expense but shall not unnecessarily damage abandon or sacrifice the same or any property the subject of this Agreement.

4. *Vessel Owners Right to Terminate*: When there is no longer any reasonable prospect of a useful result leading to a salvage reward in accordance with Convention Article 13 the owners of the vessel shall be entitled to terminate the services of the Contractor by giving reasonable notice to the Contractor in writing.

PROVISIONS AS TO SECURITY

5. (a) The Contractor shall immediately after the termination of the services or sooner notify the Council and where practicable the Owners of the amount for which he demands salvage security (inclusive of costs expenses and interest) from each of the respective Owners.

(b) Where a claim is made or may be made for special compensation, the owners of the vessel shall on the demand of the Contractor whenever made provide security for the Contractor's claim for special compensation provided always that such demand is made within two years of the date of termination of the services.

(c) The amount of any such security shall be reasonable in the light of the knowledge available to the Contractor at the time when the demand is made. Unless otherwise agreed such security shall be provided (i) to the Council (ii) in a form approved by the Council and (iii) by persons firms or corporations either acceptable to the Contractor or resident in the United Kingdom and acceptable to the Council. The Council shall not be responsible for the sufficiency (whether in amount or otherwise) of any security which shall be provided nor the default or insolvency of any person firm or corporation providing the same.

(d) The owners of the vessel their Servants and Agents shall use their best endeavours to ensure that the cargo owners provide their proportion of salvage security before the cargo is released.

6. (a) Until security has been provided as aforesaid the Contractor shall have a maritime lien on the property salved for his remuneration.

(b) The property salved shall not without the consent in writing of the Contractor (which shall not be unreasonably withheld) be removed from the place to which it has been taken by the Contractor under clause 1(a). Where such consent is given by the Contractor on condition that the Contractor is provided with temporary security pending completion of the voyage the Contractor's maritime lien on the property salved shall remain in force to the extent necessary to enable the Contractor to compel the provision of security in accordance with clause 5(c).

(c) The Contractor shall not arrest or detain the property salved unless:-

- (i) security is not provided within 14 days (exclusive of Saturdays and Sundays or other days observed as general holidays at Lloyd's) after the date of the termination of the services or
- (ii) he has reason to believe that the removal of the property salved is contemplated contrary to clause 6(b) or
- (iii) any attempt is made to remove the property salved contrary to clause 6(b).

(d) The Arbitrator appointed under clause 7 or the Appeal Arbitrator(s) appointed under clause 13(d) shall have power in their absolute discretion to include in the amount awarded to the Contractor the whole or part of any expenses reasonably incurred by the Contractor in:-

- (i) ascertaining demanding and obtaining the amount of security reasonably required in accordance with clause 5.
- (ii) enforcing and/or protecting by insurance or otherwise or taking reasonable steps to enforce and/or protect his lien.

PROVISIONS AS TO ARBITRATION

7. (a) Whether security has been provided or not the Council shall appoint an Arbitrator upon receipt of a written request made by letter telex facsimile or in any other permanent form provided that any party requesting such appointment shall if required by the Council undertake to pay the reasonable fees and expenses of the Council and/or any Arbitrator or Appeal Arbitrator(s).

(b) Where an Arbitrator has been appointed and the parties do not proceed to arbitration the Council may recover any fees costs and/or expenses which are outstanding.

8. The Contractor's remuneration and/or special compensation shall be fixed by the Arbitrator appointed under clause 7. Such remuneration shall not be diminished by reason of the exception to the principle of "no cure - no pay" in the form of special compensation.

REPRESENTATION

9. Any party to this Agreement who wishes to be heard or to adduce evidence shall nominate a person in the United Kingdom to represent him failing which the Arbitrator or Appeal Arbitrator(s) may proceed as if such party had renounced his right to be heard or adduce evidence.

CONDUCT OF THE ARBITRATION

10. (a) The Arbitrator shall have power to:-

(i) admit such oral or documentary evidence or information as he may think fit
(ii) conduct the Arbitration in such manner in all respects as he may think fit subject to such procedural rules as the Council may approve
(iii) order the Contractor in his absolute discretion to pay the whole or part of the expense of providing excessive security or security which has been unreasonably demanded under Clause 5(b) and to deduct such sum from the remuneration and/or special compensation
(iv) make Interim Award(s) including payment(s) on account on such terms as may be fair and just
(v) make such orders as to costs fees and expenses including those of the Council charged under clauses 10(b) and 14(b) as may be fair and just.

(b) The Arbitrator and the Council may charge reasonable fees and expenses for their services whether the Arbitration proceeds to a hearing or not and all such fees and expenses shall be treated as part of the costs of the Arbitration.

(c) Any Award shall (subject to Appeal as provided in this Agreement) be final and binding on all the parties concerned whether they were represented at the Arbitration or not.

INTEREST & RATES OF EXCHANGE

11. *Interest*: Interest at rates per annum to be fixed by the Arbitrator shall (subject to Appeal as provided in this Agreement) be payable on any sum awarded taking into account any sums already paid:-

(i) from the date of termination of the services unless the Arbitrator shall in his absolute discretion otherwise decide until the date of publication by the Council of the Award and/or Interim Award(s) and
(ii) from the expiration of 21 days (exclusive of Saturdays and Sundays or other days observed as general holidays at Lloyd's) after the date of publication by the Council of the Award and/or Interim Award(s) until the date payment is received by the Contractor or the Council both dates inclusive.

For the purpose of sub-clause (ii) the expression "sum awarded" shall include the fees and expenses referred to in clause 10(b).

12. *Currency Correction*: In considering what sums of money have been expended by the Contractor in rendering the services and/or in fixing the amount of the Award and/or Interim Award(s) and/or Award on Appeal the Arbitrator or Appeal Arbitrator(s) shall to such an extent and in so far as it may be fair and just in all the circumstances give effect to the consequences of any change or changes in the relevant rates of exchange which may have occurred between the date of termination of the services and the date on which the Award and/or Interim Award(s) and/or Award on Appeal is made.

PROVISIONS AS TO APPEAL

13. (a) Notice of Appeal if any shall be given to the Council within 14 days (exclusive of Saturdays and Sundays or other days observed as general holidays at Lloyd's) after the date of the publication by the Council of the Award and/or Interim Award(s).

(b) Notice of Cross-Appeal if any shall be given to the Council within 14 days (exclusive of Saturdays and Sundays or other days observed as general holidays at Lloyd's) after notification by the Council to the parties of any Notice of Appeal. Such notification if sent by post shall be deemed received on the working day following the day of posting.

(c) Notice of Appeal or Cross-Appeal shall be given to the Council by letter telex facsimile or in any other permanent form.

(d) Upon receipt of Notice of Appeal the Council shall refer the Appeal to the hearing and determination of the Appeal Arbitrator(s) selected by it.

(e) If any Notice of Appeal or Cross-Appeal is withdrawn the Appeal hearing shall nevertheless proceed in respect of such Notice of Appeal or Cross-Appeal as may remain.

(f) Any Award on Appeal shall be final and binding on all the parties to that Appeal Arbitration whether they were represented either at the Arbitration or at the Appeal Arbitration or not.

CONDUCT OF THE APPEAL

14. (a) The Appeal Arbitrator(s) in addition to the powers of the Arbitrator under clauses 10(a) and 11 shall have power to:-

(i) admit the evidence which was before the Arbitrator together with the Arbitrator's notes and reasons for his Award and/or Interim Award(s) and any transcript of evidence and such additional evidence as he or they may think fit.

(ii) confirm increase or reduce the sum awarded by the Arbitrator and to make such order as to the payment of interest on such sum as he or they may think fit.

(iii) confirm revoke or vary any order and/or Declaratory Award made by the Arbitrator.

(iv) award interest on any fees and expenses charged under paragraph (b) of this clause from the expiration of 21 days (exclusive of Saturdays and Sundays or other days observed as general holidays at Lloyd's) after the date of publication by the Council of the Award on Appeal and/or Interim Award(s) on Appeal until the date payment is received by the Council both dates inclusive.

(b) The Appeal Arbitrator(s) and the Council may charge reasonable fees and expenses for their services in connection with the Appeal Arbitration whether it proceeds to a hearing or not and all such fees and expenses shall be treated as part of the costs of the Appeal Arbitration.

PROVISIONS AS TO PAYMENT

15. (a) In case of Arbitration if no Notice of Appeal be received by the Council in accordance with clause 13(a) the Council shall call upon the party or parties concerned to pay the amount awarded and in the event of non-payment shall subject to the Contractor first providing to the Council a satisfactory Undertaking to pay all the costs thereof realize or enforce the security and pay therefrom to the Contractor (whose receipt shall be a good discharge to it) the amount awarded to him together with interest if any. The Contractor shall reimburse the parties concerned to such extent as the Award is less than any sums paid on account or in respect of Interim Award(s).

(b) If Notice of Appeal be received by the Council in accordance with clause 13 it shall as soon as the Award on Appeal has been published by it call upon the party or parties concerned to pay the amount awarded and in the event of non-payment shall subject to the Contractor first providing to the Council a satisfactory Undertaking to pay all the costs thereof realize or enforce the security and pay therefrom to the Contractor (whose receipt shall be a good discharge to it) the amount awarded to him together with interest if any. The Contractor shall reimburse the parties concerned to such extent as the Award on Appeal is less than any sums paid on account or in respect of the Award or Interim Award(s).

(c) If any sum shall become payable to the Contractor as remuneration for his services and/or interest and/or costs as the result of an agreement made between the Contractor and the Owners or any of them the Council in the event of non-payment shall subject to the Contractor first providing to the Council a satisfactory Undertaking to pay all the costs thereof realize or enforce the security and pay therefrom to the Contractor (whose receipt shall be a good discharge to it) the said sum.

(d) If the Award and/or Interim Award(s) and/or Award on Appeal provides or provide that the costs of the Arbitration and/or of the Appeal Arbitration or any part of such costs shall be borne by the Contractor such costs may be deducted from the amount awarded or agreed before payment is made to the Contractor unless satisfactory security is provided by the Contractor for the payment of such costs.

(e) Without prejudice to the provisions of clause 5(c) the liability of the Council shall be limited in any event to the amount of security provided to it.

GENERAL PROVISIONS

16. *Scope of Authority*: The Master or other person signing this Agreement on behalf of the property to be salved enters into this Agreement as agent for the vessel her cargo freight bunkers stores and any other property thereon and the respective Owners thereof and binds each (but not the one for the other or himself personally) to the due performance thereof.

17. *Notices*: Any Award notice authority order or other document signed by the Chairman of Lloyd's or any person authorised by the Council for the purpose shall be deemed to have been duly made or given by the Council and shall have the same force and effect in all respects as if it had been signed by every member of the Council.

18. *Sub-Contractor(s)*: The Contractor may claim salvage and enforce any Award or agreement made between the Contractor and the Owners against security provided under clause 5 or otherwise if any on behalf of any Sub-Contractors his or their Servants or Agents including Masters and members of the crews of vessels employed by him or by any Sub-Contractors in the services provided that he first provides a reasonably satisfactory indemnity to the Owners against all claims by or liabilities to the said persons.

19. *Inducements prohibited*: No person signing this Agreement or any party on whose behalf it is signed shall at any time or in any manner whatsoever offer provide make give or promise to provide demand or take any form of inducement for entering into this Agreement.

For and on behalf of the Contractor	**For and on behalf of the Owners of property to be salved.**
....	....
(To be signed by the Contractor personally or by the Master of the salving vessel or other person whose name is inserted in line 4 of this Agreement)	(To be signed by the Master or other person whose name is inserted in line 1 of this Agreement)

INTERNATIONAL CONVENTION ON SALVAGE 1989

The following provisions of the Convention are set out below for information only.

Article 1

Definitions

(a) *Salvage operation* means any act or activity undertaken to assist a vessel or any other property in danger in navigable waters or in any other waters whatsoever

(b) *Vessel* means any ship or craft, or any structure capable of navigation

(c) *Property* means any property not permanently and intentionally attached to the shoreline and includes freight at risk

(d) *Damage to the environment* means substantial physical damage to human health or to marine life or resources in coastal or inland waters or areas adjacent thereto, caused by pollution, contamination, fire, explosion or similar major incidents

(e) *Payment* means any reward, remuneration or compensation due under this Convention

Article 6

Salvage Contracts

1. This Convention shall apply to any salvage operations save to the extent that a contract otherwise provides expressly or by implication

2. The master shall have the authority to conclude contracts for salvage operations on behalf of the owner of the vessel. The master or the owner of the vessel shall have the authority to conclude such contracts on behalf of the owner of the property on board the vessel

Article 8

Duties of the Salvor and of the Owner and Master

1. The salvor shall owe a duty to the owner of the vessel or other property in danger:

(a) to carry out the salvage operations with due care;
(b) in performing the duty specified in subparagraph (a), to exercise due care to prevent or minimize damage to the environment;
(c) whenever circumstances reasonably require, to seek assistance from other salvors; and
(d) to accept the intervention of other salvors when reasonably requested to do so by the owner or master of the vessel or other property in danger; provided however that the amount of his reward shall not be prejudiced should it be found that such a request was unreasonable

2. The owner and master of the vessel or the owner of other property in danger shall owe a duty to the salvor:
(a) to co-operate fully with him during the course of the salvage operations;
(b) in so doing, to exercise due care to prevent or minimize damage to the environment; and
(c) when the vessel or other property has been brought to a place of safety, to accept redelivery when reasonably requested by the salvor to do so

Article 13

Criteria for fixing the reward

1. The reward shall be fixed with a view to encouraging salvage operations, taking into account the following criteria without regard to the order in which they are presented below:

(a) the salved value of the vessel and other property;
(b) the skill and efforts of the salvors in preventing or minimizing damage to the environment;
(c) the measure of success obtained by the salvor;
(d) the nature and degree of the danger;
(e) the skill and efforts of the salvors in salving the vessel, other property and life;
(f) the time used and expenses and losses incurred by the salvors;
(g) the risk of liability and other risks run by the salvors or their equipment;
(h) the promptness of the services rendered;
(i) the availability and use of vessels or other equipment intended for salvage operations;
(j) the state of readiness and efficiency of the salvor's equipment and the value thereof

2. Payment of a reward fixed according to paragraph 1 shall be made by all of the vessel and other property interests in proportion to their respective salved values

3. The rewards, exclusive of any interest and recoverable legal costs that may be payable thereon, shall not exceed the salved value of the vessel and other property

Article 14

Special Compensation

1. If the salvor has carried out salvage operations in respect of a vessel which by itself or its cargo threatened damage to the environment and has failed to earn a reward under Article 13 at least equivalent to the special compensation assessable in accordance with this Article, he shall be entitled to special compensation from the owner of that vessel equivalent to his expenses as herein defined

2. If, in the circumstances set out in paragraph 1, the salvor by his salvage operations has prevented or minimized damage to the environment, the special compensation payable by the owner to the salvor under paragraph 1 may be increased up to a maximum of 30% of the expenses incurred by the salvor. However, the Tribunal, if it deems it fair and just to do so and bearing in mind the relevant criteria set out in Article 13, paragraph 1, may increase such special compensation further, but in no event shall the total increase be more than 100% of the expenses incurred by the salvor

3. Salvor's expenses for the purpose of paragraphs 1 and 2 means the out-of-pocket expenses reasonably incurred by the salvor in the salvage operation and a fair rate for equipment and personnel actually and reasonably used in the salvage operation, taking into consideration the criteria set out in Article 13, paragraph 1(h), (i) and (j)

4. The total special compensation under this Article shall be paid only if and to the extent that such compensation is greater than any reward recoverable by the salvor under Article 13

5. If the salvor has been negligent and has thereby failed to prevent or minimize damage to the environment, he may be deprived of the whole or part of any special compensation due under this Article

6. Nothing in this Article shall affect any right of recourse on the part of the owner of the vessel

LLOYD'S

STANDARD FORM OF

SALVAGE AGREEMENT

PROCEDURAL RULES

---

made by the Council of Lloyd's

(pursuant to clause 10(a)(ii) of LOF 1995)

1. The Arbitrator appointed by Council under clause 7 of LOF 1995 shall within six weeks of his appointment or so soon thereafter as can reasonably be arranged hold a preliminary meeting unless a consent order shall have been agreed previously between the parties and approved by him.

2. With a view to ensuring that the arbitration proceeds as speedily and economically as possible, the Arbitrator shall at such preliminary meeting give all such directions as may be fair and just having particular but no exclusive regard to:-

    (a) fixing dates for :-

    (i) Proof of values
    (ii) discovery
    (iii) expert evidence
    (iv) application(s) for interim awards
    (v) the Arbitrator to monitor progress in the interlocutory stages of the arbitration
    (vi) the hearing of the arbitration.

    (b) (i) the interests of unrepresented parties and/or security
    (ii) the form of the hearing in cases where shortened and/or simplified procedure may be appropriate
    (iii) the reading of documentary evidence before the date appointed for the hearing of the arbitration
    (iv) skeleton arguments or pleadings but only in special and appropriate circumstances

3. In case of non-compliance and/or late compliance with any such order the Arbitrator shall fix such terms as may be fair and just.

4. Nothing in the foregoing shall prevent any party from making application(s) for other preliminary meetings or restrict or curtail the existing powers of the Arbitrator.

5. **Appeals**
In any case in which a party giving notice of appeal intends to contend that the Arbitrator's findings on the salved value of all or any of the salved property were erroneous or that the Arbitrator has erred in any finding as to the person whose property was at risk, a statement of such grounds of appeal shall be given in or accompanying the notice of appeal.

5.9.90
17.5.94
1.1.95

APPENDIX 6

RULE XIII—DIRECTIVE TO MARKING SURVEYORS

It has become apparent that considerable differences of practice exist between marking surveyors, and the following is therefore circulated with a view to the removal of any inconsistencies. It constitutes a considerable alteration of any existing practice and it is emphasised that it applies only to cases in which Rule XIII of the York-Antwerp Rules 1950 applies. No alteration of practice should be made in connection with cases marked according to the York-Antwerp Rules 1890 and 1924.

In applying Rule XIII of the York-Antwerp Rules 1950, deductions new for old, in accordance therewith, shall be made only when, but in all cases where, old material is replaced by new. The deductions shall be confined to the cost of the new material, the cost of the manufacture of the new article from the new material and the cost of such final preparation of the new material or the new article as may be necessary for fitting or otherwise. All other costs, including the actual fitting costs, shall be allowed in full together with the cost of preparing any old material for the fitting of the new article and the cost of removal of the old article.

Costs of transport of new material or new parts shall be allowed in full except such local transporting costs as occur upon the repairers' or manufacturers' premises or in the drydock or yard. These shall be treated as part of the cost of manufacture or as part of the cost of preparation for fitting.

The following are examples showing the application of the above:—

(a) Renewal of shell plate

In Full

All access work such as removal and replacement of keel blocks, close and spar ceiling, and air and sounding pipes. Burning out rivets or old welding, removing old plate, riveting or welding new plate in place and caulking.

Subject to Deduction

Material for new plate, making template for new plate, shaping and punching holes and supplying rivets and welding rods.

(b) Renewal of bedplate

In Full

Removal of engine room skylight, gratings, ladders, pipes. Stripping down all running parts, disconnecting and removal of cylinders, columns, crankshaft and bearings and their subsequent replacements. Removing holding down bolts, lifting out old bedplate. Placing new bedplate in position, lining up, fitting chocks and bolting down.

Subject to Deduction

Material for new bedplate, manufacture of new bedplate. Preparation of new bedplate for fitting.

(c) Renewal of hold insulation

In Full

All access work such as removal and replacement of brine grids or batteries, main brine circuits, cargo battens, hatch beam, hatch covers and plug hatches. Stripping out the old insulation and fitting new insulation.

Subject to Deduction

Material for, manufacture of and preparation for fitting of new insulation. Also painting or varnishing new material.

(d) Renewal of tail shaft

In Full

Drawing old tail shaft, all access work, removing coupling bolts, removal of propeller, drawing out gland, removing packing, etc., bedding the propeller on to the new shaft and key. Fitting shaft in place, fitting propeller, rubber ring and repacking the stern gland.

Subject to Deduction

Material for the new shaft and liner, manufacture of new shaft and liner, preparation of new shaft for fitting including reaming out coupling bolt holes, and supply of new bolts, rubber ring and packing.

(e) Renewal of crankshaft

In Full

Removal of engine room skylights, gratings, ladders, pipes. Stripping down all running parts, disconnecting and removal of cylinders, columns, crankshaft and bearings. Placing new crankshaft in position and refitting all parts removed for access.

Subject to Deduction

Material for new crankshaft, manufacture of new crankshaft and preparation of new crankshaft for fitting, including reaming out coupling bolt holes, supplying new bolts, supplying new or remetalling bearings and machining. Scraping new or remetalled bearings to bed down new crankshaft therein.

Note: If bearings are not renewed or remetalled the cost of bedding down the new crankshaft to be allowed in full.

(f) Remetalling of bottom end

In Full

All removals for access, dismantling bearing. Removal of old bearing ashore and running out old metal. Fitting the remetalled bearing and refitting all parts removed for access.

Subject to Deduction

Preparation of old bearing for remetalling and remetalling and machining ready for fitting.

ADDENDUM

Deductions from costs of scraping and painting bottom

The deductions applying to scraping and painting bottom were not dealt with under the directive. They are specially provided for in Rule XIII, Clause A—up to one year old—reading:

> "All repairs to be allowed in full, except scaling and cleaning and painting or coating of bottom, from which one-third is to be deducted."

These words contemplate that the deduction should apply to the labour costs as well as to the cost of the paint, since the cost of scaling and cleaning in particular do not include any element other than labour.

Deductions from cost of painting (other than painting bottom)

Where it is the paint work which is damaged, e.g. as in the case of hold paintwork, the deduction is to apply to both the cost of the paint and the cost of labour applying it, since the labour element cannot be divorced from the benefit provided by the new paint.

But in the case of new paint being required to cover a new part fitted to the ship, e.g. as in the case of a new plate, the cost of the paint and the cost of labour applying it are *not* subject to deduction, since this painting would have been required even if the damaged part had been repaired and replaced, e.g. by removing, fairing and refitting a plate.

APPENDIX 7

RULE XXII—GENERAL AVERAGE DEPOSITS

RESOLUTION OF THE XIIITH GENERAL ASSEMBLY OF THE AIDE

Resolved: That this General Assembly, having received and approved the report of the Working Group on General Average Deposits, recommends as follows:

1. Assessment of the percentage of the general average deposit

It is in the interest of the shipowner to consult the average adjuster regarding the percentage of the general average deposit to be furnished by the concerned in cargo, and average adjusters should so advise their clients at the earliest opportunity in every case of general average when deposits may properly be demanded.

2. The lodging of general average deposits in separate accounts, as envisaged in Rule XXII of the York-Antwerp Rules

In all cases where it is appropriate to do so, the average adjuster should recommend that general average deposits should be lodged in a special account in the joint names of a representative nominated on behalf of the shipowner and a representative nominated on behalf of the depositors, in a bank to be approved by both, as envisaged in Rule XXII of the York-Antwerp Rules. Where the general average deposits are lodged in a country where the operation of a joint account is not permitted, or is discouraged by the law, the average adjuster is at liberty to make other arrangements, provided that in so doing the rights of the parties are preserved as far as possible.

3. The question of transfer from the country in which the deposits are initially lodged to the country in which the adjustment is to be drawn up or in which the liquidation of the general average is to take place

(a) To the extent that such activity is not contrary to any local law or currency regulations, the average adjuster should use his best endeavours to care for the general average deposits from the time that they are lodged until such time as the general average is liquidated and the excess of the general average deposits are refunded.

(b) Whenever it may be necessary to do so in order to enable the trustees properly to control the general average deposit funds, the amounts which have been collected should be transferred, if possible, to one single country in which:

(i) There are no restrictions on the free transfer of funds out of that country, or permission to transfer the funds can be obtained without difficulty, and

(ii) The deposit funds can be placed in an interest bearing bank account in a currency suitable to the needs of the particular case.

The country in which the funds are held need not necessarily be the country in which the adjustment is being drawn up.

(c) The question if, how and when to transfer the deposit funds may be decided by the average adjuster according to his own good judgment.

4. Interest

The average adjuster should recommend to the joint nominees that the general average deposit funds should be placed in an interest-earning account whenever that is the most reasonable and practicable course.

5. Transfer of general average deposit funds to another currency

(a) When the currency of adjustment is stipulated by a clause in the bill of lading or contract of carriage, or has otherwise been agreed by the parties to the general average adjustment, the average adjuster may consider it appropriate in some cases to recommend to the joint nominees that the general average deposit funds should be transferred into the currency of adjustment.

(b) In any other case, the average adjuster should, in the exercise of his role set out in recommendation no. 3(a), have regard to the relative stability of the currency in which the general average deposit funds were originally lodged and any advantage which might be gained by re-investing the funds in any available stronger currency.

19 September 1985.

INDEX